D1578388

AN IDIOT ABROAD

&

THE FURTHER ADVENTURES OF AN IDIOT ABROAD

Karl Pilkington is the bestselling author of seven books: *The World of Karl Pilkington*; *Happyslapped by a Jellyfish*; *Karlology*; *An Idiot Abroad*; *The Further Adventures of An Idiot Abroad*; *The Moaning of Life* and *More Moaning*. He was part of the Guinness World Record-breaking podcast *The Ricky Gervais Show*, which was downloaded over 300 million times and became an animation for HBO in the USA. He also starred in three series of Sky 1's global hit *An Idiot Abroad* and two series of *The Moaning of Life*.

Also by Karl Pilkington

AN IDIOT ABROAD

&

THE FURTHER ADVENTURES OF

AN IDIOT ABROAD

KARL PILKINGTON

Illustrations by Dominic Trevett

CANONGATE

This edition published in 2017 by Canongate Books

An Idiot Abroad first published in Great Britain in 2010 by
Canongate Books Ltd, 14 High Street, Edinburgh EH1 1TE

Further Adventures of An Idiot Abroad first published in Great Britain in 2012 by
Canongate Books Ltd, 14 High Street, Edinburgh EH1 1TE

canongate.co.uk

1

British Library Cataloguing-in-Publication Data
A catalogue record for this book is available on
request from the British Library

ISBN 978 1 78689 238 6

Typeset by Cluny Sheeler, Edinburgh

Printed and bound in Great Britain by Clays Ltd, St Ives plc.

MIX
Paper from
responsible sources
FSC
www.fsc.org   FSC® C018072

AN IDIOT ABROAD

The Travel Diaries of Karl Pilkington

WITH RICKY GERVAIS

AND STEPHEN MERCHANT

INTRODUCTION

'HE IS – I DON'T KNOW THE POLITICALLY-
CORRECT TERM – A MORON. A COMPLETELY
ROUND, EMPTY-HEADED, PART-CHIMP MANC.'

RICKY GERVAIS

'HE'D'VE BEEN HAPPIER IN MEDIEVAL TIMES
IN A VILLAGE WHERE YOU DIDN'T TRAVEL
BEYOND THE LOCAL COMMUNITY.'

STEPHEN MERCHANT

STEPHEN: He's a real, genuine freak that we have often thought we would like to introduce to the world, like to Victorian show-men, like P.T. Barnum and his fat friend who are just saying, 'Look, you must come and observe this wonder of the world!'

RICKY: I mean, he is – I don't know the politically correct term – a moron. A completely round, empty-headed, part-chimp Manc.

STEPHEN: In many regards we've often described him – and it's appropriate – as being like some kind of real-life Homer Simpson.

RICKY: Yes.

STEPHEN: Homer is arrogant and yet an idiot. Small-minded, petty, but at his core a good person.

RICKY: And lovable. Absolutely lovable. He's got child rights because he says the most awful things so naively and sweetly. Things like, 'Chinese people don't age well . . .' I go, 'What?' He goes, 'They don't age well.' He says, 'You'll never see a thirty-five-year-old one.' I go, 'What do you mean?' He went, 'Well, they're good-looking when they're young but then they age overnight. They're like a pear.' I mean, racism, you know . . .

STEPHEN: It's not racist. It's just ignorant.

RICKY: It's just ignorance, he thinks that. I went, 'Well, some of the oldest people in the world are Chinese.' He went, 'Are they though?' He thinks they might be lying. He thinks these old Chinese boys might be thirty-five by lying about they're age 'cos they don't age well. I mean, he's an idiot. I mean, his theories, his outlook on life. He really would never go away if it wasn't for his girlfriend.

STEPHEN: He'd've been happier in medieval times in a village where you didn't travel beyond the local community. That would've been fine for him.

RICKY: Yeah, making up his own theories about the moon.

STEPHEN: Terrified because he doesn't know where it goes during the day.

RICKY: Yeah, he's quite remarkable. So I think we should broaden his outlook. And they say travel broadens the mind. So I think it'd be amazing to send him round the world . . .

STEPHEN: Well, yeah. I mean, he's travelled, but it's only been to places like Majorca. Somewhere safe. A little two-week package holiday.

RICKY: If it wasn't for his girlfriend, he wouldn't do anything. His job at home is washing-up. He looks forward to that because it's something he's done. Often I call him and he says, 'I'm washing up' like it's a big event. One day he'd started a diary and he did the washing-up and took his girlfriend's shoes to the cobblers. Now I hadn't heard the word 'cobblers' in ages . . .

STEPHEN: I didn't realise cobblers still existed. I thought they were only in fairytales.

RICKY: Yes, exactly. And she makes him go on holiday. When she books a holiday he goes, 'Oh, I gotta go or I'd just stay at home alone', and when he does that he forgets to eat. Once, right, someone at the radio station where he used to work sent us an email that Karl had sent by mistake, right? It was an email from his girlfriend. She was out that night and so, in detail, she was telling him where the quiche was in the fridge, cut up into pieces, and she'd even put 'EAT' on it.

STEPHEN: Didn't he try and put fish fingers in a toaster or something?

RICKY: Yeah, he did that once. No, sausages.

STEPHEN: Sausages.

RICKY: Yeah, she came home, going, 'What are you doing?' He'd forgotten to drink so he had kidney stones. I mean, he is . . .'

STEPHEN: He's a typical little Englander and he doesn't like going out of his comfort zone. That's key. You know, he's got everything around him that he's happy with and he's comfortable with. Even when he goes on holiday, you know, he's the sort of person who packs some teabags. He's not comfortable going beyond things he doesn't understand. And he thinks he's not interested. What excites us in the idea of forcing him to get out there. We'd like to see him go out into the world, experience other cultures, other peoples, and see if, in any way, we can change his outlook on the world.

RICKY: Yeah. Can I just say that I've got to admit that Stephen's motives are a lot purer than mine. He wants Karl to enjoy it . . .

STEPHEN: I've travelled. I've been to many exotic places. I genuinely think travel broadens the mind. I've become a richer person for it . . .

RICKY: I want him to hate it. I want him to hate every minute of it for my own amusement. That's it. I think we've gotta send him economy. I think we've gotta put him up in shacks and awful hotels. I think we've got to expose him to some of the most mind-blowing degradation that we can. And that'll be funny. Nothing is funnier than Karl in a corner being poked by a stick. I am that stick and now I have the might of Sky behind me. This is one of the funniest, most expensive practical jokes I've ever done. And it's gonna be great.

STEPHEN: I'm hoping as well that he'll be poked by some real sticks.

RICKY: I know. What country do they poke you with sticks?

STEPHEN: There's gotta be a country where they poke you with sticks . . .

RICKY: There's bound to be. There's bound to be one of those weird little countries where, if you see a man with a round head, you're allowed to poke him with a stick. One of those unrepealed laws. Just find me that country!

CHAPTER ONE
THE PYRAMIDS

'ASCENDING THE PYRAMID, I COULD NOT BUT THINK OF WATERLOO BRIDGE IN MY DEAR NATIVE LONDON – A BUILDING AS VAST AND AS MAGNIFICENT, AS BEAUTIFUL AS USELESS AND AS LONELY.'

WILLIAM MAKEPEACE THACKERAY

'I REALLY CAN'T BELIEVE WHAT A STATE THE PYRAMIDS ARE IN. I THOUGHT THEY HAD FLAT RENDERED SIDES, BUT WHEN YOU GET UP CLOSE, YOU SEE HOW THEY ARE JUST GIANT BOULDERS BALANCED ON TOP OF EACH OTHER LIKE A MASSIVE GAME OF JENGA THAT HAS GOT OUT OF HAND.'

KARL PILKINGTON

FRIDAY 17TH OCTOBER

My Seven Wonders experience started today with a trip to get my injections. I've never had to have an injection to go on holiday before. I don't tend to go to extreme places normally. I like my holidays to be the same as being at home but in a different area. The time we were in the Cotswolds and could only get whole milk instead of semi-skimmed was almost enough to make me turn around and go back home, so this is going to be a challenge for me.

I was booked into a clinic off Tottenham Court Road in London, which seems a bit odd, as this area is mainly known for its electrical shops. It would be like going to Chinatown for a curry. They told me I had to have six injections – Tetanus, Typhoid, Yellow Fever, Rabies, Hepatitis A and B. I asked if I could have the injections in my arse, as I have just moved house and need to be able to use my arms when they deliver my new washing machine. (I'm guessing this isn't a problem Michael Palin has ever had to worry about.) The nurse said she had never been asked to put injections into an arse cheek and said I was worrying too much and that my arm should be fine.

She gave me the jabs and said I was covered for every worst-case scenario, including being bitten by a dirty chimp. I told her this is why we have over-population problems. Why are idiots who annoy dirty chimps being protected?

△△△

SATURDAY 18TH OCTOBER

Good job I didn't have the injections in my arse, as I had to sit on it all day waiting for the washer/dryer to be delivered. They gave me a window of 8 a.m. to 6 p.m. That window has a name. It's called Saturday.

I was up at 7.50 a.m. It turned up at 5.40 p.m.

My arm ached after fitting the machine into the kitchen.

△△△

MONDAY 23ᴿᴰ NOVEMBER

I did some filming today with Ricky and Steve. They told me the places I would be visiting: Egypt, Brazil, India, Mexico, China, Jordan and Peru. I have to confess, these are all places I've never really fancied visiting. If it wasn't for the Wonders I doubt most people would go to these destinations. Me and Suzanne mainly go to the Cotswolds, Devon, Spain or Italy. I'm not a proper traveller. I don't like to be challenged or have too much of a change and prefer a week away just to relax rather than broaden my mind. I'm not very adventurous. Maybe I'd see the Wonders if time travel was possible but then I also had a really nice time in Majorca back in 2007 in a villa with four bedrooms and its own swimming pool which was only £300 for the week, so I'd probably just end up using the time machine to go back to that holiday as I know I enjoyed it, plus I wouldn't have to pay again as I paid for it back then.

Steve told me that some of the areas we would be visiting are quite dangerous. Krish, the producer, said I shouldn't worry, as we will have a man with a gun protecting us at some of the locations. Being attacked by a dirty chimp with rabies doesn't seem such a worry anymore.

WEDNESDAY 25TH NOVEMBER

I had to go and get my medical done to make sure I was fit enough for the challenge of travelling around the Seven Wonders of the World. It was a really posh clinic on Harley Street. I knew it was a classy place, as the waiting room had all the same style chairs, which is rare. Most doctors I have been to have loads of different styles that have been bought at various times. It always reminds me of Christmases at home when we'd borrow chairs from various neighbours so we could seat everyone for dinner.

They say you can tell the quality of a doctor's by the magazine selection. The place on Harley Street had loads. They had every magazine you could wish for and some that you wouldn't. One of which was *Boyz*, a gay magazine. I was the only one in the waiting room so thought I would have a flick through it to see what gays like to read about. There wasn't much reading to be done, as it was just picture after picture of half-naked men (mainly the lower half) dressed as mechanics, farmers and plumbers with their tackle out. I've never understood what gay blokes get from looking at these pictures, as they have knobs of their own to look at. Other than the pictures there was the odd bit of text that was always a pun on the knob and bollocks. The main one I remember was Suckcocko. The puzzle was exactly the same as a normal Sudoku, just with the knob twist to its name.

I had my medical. The doctor said I was in good shape for my age. It's the first time someone had ever brought my age into my health. It made me feel quite old.

△△△

WEDNESDAY 9TH DECEMBER

I was picked up at 4.30 a.m. and taken to the airport for our flight to Cairo. Six hours later we were on the road to our hotel. I hadn't been told anything about who or what I'd be meeting, eating or seeing. Apparently that's the way each trip is going to work, which I know will annoy me, as I don't really like surprises. Not big ones anyway. Just having a pack of Revels holds enough of a surprise for me.

The first thing that hit me about Egypt was the traffic. It was mental. There was a song in the 1980s by a girl group called The Bangles who sang 'Walk like an Egyptian' yet no one seems to be walking anywhere here – everyone is driving. They make every three-lane road into a six-lane road, and cram so many people into their cars it's ridiculous. Passengers are squashed up against the windows like those Garfield cats that people used to stick on their car windows in the 1980s. The horns are in constant use, but this might be because there are so many people crammed into the car someone's arse is accidentally pressing against the horn.

It was a long journey to the hotel. As we drove, all the nice hotels seemed to disappear until we finally pulled up at a place called The Windsor. It is one of the oldest hotels in Cairo and it is situated in one of the roughest areas. It even has a security scanner at the entrance, as if to prove how dodgy the area is. As I walked through, my belt set off the bleeper. It was enough to startle me, but it didn't seem to wake the security man.

As well as being one of the oldest hotels, it had the staff to match. You wouldn't get people of this age working in hotels in England. An old fella brought my case from the coach. We were parked right outside the entrance, but it took the old fella the same amount of time it took me to fill out all the forms and collect my key. It reminded me of the time I was moving flats and I found a company that did removals and was cheaper than everyone else. They charged £10 an hour. I realised what an error I had made when the man turned up. He must have been close to 70 years old. It took him 30 minutes to climb the stairs to our third-floor flat. He had a sweat on just bringing us the empty boxes. It cost a fortune in the end.

Another man took me to my room. I was on the second floor, just where the cleaners congregated. I couldn't believe it. Not the fact that it's where they congregated, but the fact that the hotel had cleaners. It was also clearly a bit of a storage area, as there was a piano outside my door and five TV sets stacked on top of the wardrobe in my room. I was given the full tour of the room: 'Telephone there. Bathroom here.' He said one or two other things, but I could not hear properly due to the creaking of the floorboards and the noise of the traffic outside. There were two beds separated by a fluorescent tube light on the wall that, once you switched it on, showed up all the damp stains on the walls in their full glory.

I wandered downstairs to meet up with the crew and bumped into the owner outside. I don't know if he was waiting to meet me to check if everything was okay or if he was about to have his piano lessons. He was in his late sixties and looked smart but tired. He was keen to tell me that Michael Palin had stayed here once. If these are the sorts of places Palin stayed in, no wonder he went round the world in 80 days. He was obviously keen to get home as soon as poss.

The owner then introduced me to his dad, who was in his nineties, at least. I wish I hadn't met him, as it would have made asking for a better room a lot easier.

At 4 p.m. we ordered food. Most of us asked for chicken kebabs, apart from Jan, our cameraman, who is more of a hardened traveller than the rest of us. When we were talking about the worst places we had visited on the coach ride into Cairo and I had said a week in Lanzarote was pretty grim, Jan announced he had done three months in Antarctica. Finally, at 5.30 p.m. our food was brought to the table. It actually left the kitchen at about 5.22, but all the staff were quite old and shuffled slowly from the kitchen to our table.

Went to bed. Nodded off counting the car horns outside.

△△△

THURSDAY 10TH DECEMBER

I met Ahmed this morning. He's a local lad who is an expert on the Pyramids and Egyptian history in general. I was worried that I wouldn't be able to understand him, but his English was better than mine. He may as well have talked Egyptian to me, as the English words he used went right over my head. One of the words he used was 'tintinnabulation', which he told me means a ringing or tinkling sound.

He took me to a mosque. Praying and religion are a big deal in Egypt. Ahmed prays five times a day. I would never keep to it if I lived here. I struggle having my five fruits a day. Religion has never been a big part of my life. I wasn't christened. My mam told me not to tell many people about not being christened, as she said I would be a prime target for witches. To this day I don't know what she meant by that.

Ahmed told me about how he believes that after death you go to a place that is perfect in every way. I said I'm quite happy with my life as it is now. In Ahmed's perfect world he listed not having to use the loo. I told him going to the toilet is one of my favourite parts of my day. It's proper 'me time' where

I get to clear my head and think about things with no other disturbances, but after seeing the toilets in Egypt I can understand why he thinks this way. They are just holes in the ground with a hose for cleaning up.

We then went off to old Cairo to see the market.

The markets are made of up tiny, rough roads, crammed with motorbikes and vans. The stalls themselves sell mostly clothing, cotton and wool. 'How can I take your money?' was a popular shout from most of the store owners as I browsed at the wide selection of tat on offer.

I wanted to buy a gown for Ricky, as he likes to slob out when he's at home. Most days he has his pyjamas on by 5 p.m. I found one pretty quickly, but it took 45 minutes to get the price I wanted. I wish they just had price tags on the products to save the hassle of haggling. If you nipped out for bread and milk you could be gone for hours. The only good thing about this way of buying products is that you would never have that awkward situation when you're a penny or two short and have to ask a shopkeeper to let you off.

We passed a man with crates full of living rabbits and pigeons. They were being sold as food. I've never eaten rabbit but I've never had one as a pet either. I like the way you could get one as a pet though and eat it if you found it too much trouble to look after. I think we'd eat guinea pigs too if they weren't so expensive.

The new market was also full of tourist tat. Headscarves, ashtrays, toy camels, plastic pyramids. Even though I had no intention of buying anything when I set out for the market this morning, by the time I left I had purchased a plastic cat and an eagle for me mam. I'm hoping she will find it handy, as she used to have two birds. But one died, so she replaced the dead one with a pebble with one of the dead bird's feathers glued on it so Kes, the other bird, still feels like he has company. I figured that the eagle from the market would make a good replacement.

I stopped to have a cup of tea, but it wasn't very relaxing, as I was constantly hassled by people trying to sell me wallets, glasses, lighters, fags, necklaces, rings and watches.

I witnessed the call to prayer for the first time today. It's something that can't go unnoticed. It's the only time the car horns are drowned out, by the singing of prayers from different parts of the city.

Everything comes to a halt. The only time I experienced something like this was when I worked at a printer's when I was eighteen. All the printers and packers and guillotine workers all stopped at 11 a.m. to listen to 'Our Tune' with Simon Bates on Radio 1.

During the call to prayer each area of the city tries to be louder than the other. Everyone seems to get involved, and they may as well, as there is no escaping it. It makes you think about religion even though you weren't thinking about it, in the same way I'd suddenly fancy an ice-cream when the ice-cream man's chime would sound. The only time I was aware of religion growing up was when Songs of Praise came on the telly on a Sunday evening. This was always my cue to go and have my bath for the week ahead.

△△△

FRIDAY 11ᵀᴴ DECEMBER

Ricky called last night. He was moaning 'cos I hadn't been in touch. He said he had left loads of messages asking me to call him, but I can't access them, as I've been locked out of my phone after entering the wrong security code more than four times. I told him I could still get texts, but that they cost me around 70p to receive them.

RICKY: What about email? You got email on your phone?

KARL: Yeah, but I don't really wanna answer them 'cos they're like 70 pence at a time or something. I got an email from Oxfam, saying if I wanted to buy some goat again. That's cost me a quid.

RICKY: Even if you don't answer it or retrieve it?

KARL: If it gets to my phone, I'm charged for it. That is it. So don't start sending me pictures of your head and that.

RICKY: You're an idiot then, because now I'm gonna send you a message or an email every couple of minutes. Why do you tell me these things?

KARL: Dunno.

Ahmed took me to the Cairo Museum today. I hated it. It was exactly what I thought it would be like. I've never enjoyed museums. I had also seen a lot of this stuff at the Millennium Dome when there was a King Tut exhibition on. I didn't want to go to that either, but Suzanne, my girlfriend, had arranged for us to see her brother there. It was like the Cairo Museum. Box after box of some old ornament painted gold. Even the corpse of King Tut was in a box. Most people were more impressed by the fact that Jilly Goolden, the wine critic, was having a tour.

Ahmed told me they were expanding the museum so it could fit more tourists inside, but I think this will just encourage the museum people to put even more old boxes on display. It's interesting to see that people had so much clutter even thousands of years ago. The only way to get rid of it all was to bury it, and then some archaeologist went and dug it all up. Humans have always been hoarders of tat. I think that's why lofts were invented; it's somewhere to stick all the crap we collect in our lives rather than bury it.

Ahmed explained how many of these items were made for the kings to take into their next lives. This would annoy me if I lived back then and people kept saying, 'Hey, King Karl, I've got you a lovely gift.'

'Have you? Let's have a look.'

'No, it's for when you're dead.'

'Well, I'd rather see it now, if I'm honest.'

'No, it's all wrapped for when you're dead.'

'Will you stop going on about me being dead!'

Surely I should choose what I'm going to be surrounded with in my next life? At least then I'd have time to have a chariot boot sale to get rid of my least favourite things.

I left the museum, as I couldn't take anymore. It was too busy for me, with people pushing and shoving. There were even some people there with babies in prams screaming their heads off. It's not a great place to take a baby, is it?

I noticed there was a KFC outside, so I had one, as I needed something that reminded me of home. I went to place my order, but the girl behind the counter pointed to a note on the counter. The note informed customers that it was a deaf KFC. I was confused. Did this mean they only served deaf people? The girl behind the counter pointed out the menu. There were instructions on how to place an order, which basically involved pointing to the items you wanted, which is the way I normally order my food when I'm abroad anyway. It was quick and easy and quite a good idea, as I was worried that no one would speak English and I wouldn't be able to order a Zinger Meal. It turned out that not speaking meant life was a lot easier.

It was nice to be in a fast food restaurant that didn't have dance music blasting out of the speakers and staff yelling at each other like they are working on the floor of the Stock Exchange. Service was fast and friendly, due to the fact the staff weren't stood around gabbing by the milkshake counter as they normally do in most fast food chains. I saw a man using a videophone to chat to someone using sign language. I've never thought about videophones being used for the deaf. We used to watch a lot of TV with subtitles when I was younger, not 'cos anyone in our family was deaf but 'cos my dad worked nights so we all had to be quiet.

Suzanne called today. She was annoyed, as the boiler was playing up at home and she had asked me to sort it before I left. I always have problems with boilers.

Ricky sent me a text that just read: '70p.'

△△△

SATURDAY 12 TH DECEMBER

I wore the jellabiya that I bought for Ricky last night. I wanted something comfy to relax in so opened it and tried it on. I ended up sleeping in it too. That's the good thing with the local dress – it's so light and comfy. If you lived and worked here you could wear them as pyjamas and then just get up at five to nine, roll out of bed and go to work in them. I think this is the reason you see doctors wearing those light blue pyjamas.

KARL'S FACTS

THERE ARE ACTUALLY 118 PYRAMIDS IN EGYPT. NOT JUST THE THREE EVERYONE TALKS ABOUT.

THE 'GREAT PYRAMID' IS BUILT FROM ABOUT 2.3 MILLION STONE BLOCKS, WEIGHING AN AVERAGE OF 2.5 TO 15 TONNES EACH. IT'S ESTIMATED THAT THE WORKERS WOULD HAVE HAD TO SET A BLOCK EVERY TWO AND A HALF MINUTES.

THE GREAT PYRAMIDS NOW STAND A FULL THREE MILES SOUTH OF THE SPOT WHERE THEY WERE ORIGINALLY BUILT OWING TO THE AMOUNT THAT THE EARTH'S SURFACE HAS SHIFTED IN THE LAST 4,500 YEARS.

EVEN THE BUILDERS HAD TOMBS.
WHEN AN AMERICAN WOMAN WAS
THROWN FROM HER HORSE IN GIZA,
THE STUMBLING BLOCK TURNED OUT
TO BE THE TIP OF AN ENORMOUS
BUILDERS' NECROPOLIS, CONTAINING
OVER 600 TOMBS.

CONTRARY TO POPULAR BELIEF, NOT
A SINGLE MUMMY HAS BEEN FOUND
INSIDE THE PYRAMIDS. MUMMIES
HAVE MOSTLY BEEN FOUND IN THE
VALLEY OF THE KINGS.

DEBUNKING ANOTHER POPULAR MYTH, THERE
ARE NO HIEROGLYPHICS, OR ANY FORM OF
WRITING, IN THE GREAT PYRAMID.

Same thing – wear them in bed, and if you're on call and get woken in the night, you can go straight to work.

The only problem with wearing a jellabiya is there is no waistline, so it's impossible to know if you're putting on weight.

Steve called last night. I told him the museum visit was a waste of time. He was annoyed with me but said he had arranged for me to go on a Nile cruise. I can't say I was looking forward to it. I don't like the idea of being trapped in a space with a lot of other people and having no way of leaving. I told Steve it sounded too much like organised fun, but I had no other plans, so I went along with it.

I met the manager. A smart man in his late fifties or early sixties with jet-black dyed hair and mascara, he gave me a quick tour of the massive boat, which was set over three floors. He introduced me to his captains and cooks and then finally to a quiet man whose job it was to dive into the Nile to collect any items that are dropped by the guests. The manager explained how he has dived to collect cameras, watches and jewellery for careless guests. As the manager spoke about other items he has rescued, he stood there all in black with his polo-neck jumper tucked in his trousers like a baddie in one of the Bourne Identity films. I asked if I could throw something in the Nile for him to collect later. The manager agreed. I was quite excited about it and went to eat.

The food was good. I had soup to start then turkey and veg, followed by some chocolate cake.

The entertainment I had to sit through consisted of a man who whizzed round on the same spot for fifteen minutes, an Egyptian comedian who had an annoying voice, and a belly dancer. I have never been into this sort of entertainment. I've never been to a strip club or lap-dancing place, so I didn't know what was the best thing to do. Is it more polite to look at the woman's babajangers and arse, as she dances around shaking everything, or is that pervy? But if I just kept my head down and showed more interest in the turkey on my plate, would that be an insult to her? In the end I did a bit of both.

Once the dancing was over I went to find the manager and his diving friend. I asked if he was sure it was okay for me to throw something in. He said yes, it was, no problem. I asked the manager to check with the diver that he was happy, but the manager just said that if he asks the diver to do something, he does it. I said I wanted to throw my Egyptian mobile phone in the river, but the manager was not happy for me to do that. We ended up agreeing that we would throw in a salt-and-pepper pot. But before we threw it in, he wanted to wrap it in bright pink gaffa tape so it was more visible in the dark, muddy waters of the Nile.

I started to doubt the man's ability to retrieve the salt-and-pepper pot and asked again if the diver was happy to do this for us. The manager spoke on his behalf again and said, 'Of course.'

I was just about to chuck the salt-and-pepper pot when the manager asked me to wait, as the boat needs to stop nearer to the edge where the current of the river is not as strong and the water isn't so deep. It all started to sound like a made-up job. The baddie from *The Bourne Identity* then got off the boat and pointed to where he wanted me to throw it. So, hang on, the diver can only retrieve items if passengers drop them overboard close to the edge where the current is not strong and if they happen to have wrapped them in pink gaffa tape and have let the diver know before dropping them?

An argument then broke out between the manager and the diver. I asked what was wrong. The manager said the diver didn't want to do it. I said it wasn't a problem. I said I wouldn't have asked if he hadn't brought it up. It all put a bit of a dampener on the night. I just think the manager wanted to impress us so much he was willing to throw a member of staff overboard for us.

I said I enjoyed the turkey and left.

Strange night.

△◁△

SUNDAY 13TH DECEMBER

I went into Cairo today and started to feel a rumble in the belly. I was told there was a toilet in the market. It turned out to be one of those public toilets you have to pay to use, but I didn't mind, as I felt like I was going to get my money's worth the way my belly was feeling.

Trouble was, I didn't have any money on me to give to the old man at the entrance so I just walked past him. I opened the first cubicle to find a traditional Egyptian toilet. I then looked in cubicles two and three with no joy. I was close to using the urinal when cubicle four saved the day. It had a westernised toilet. I rushed in, shut the door and went to sit down when I noticed it wasn't a complete westernised toilet. There was no bloody paper, just a tap with a hose attached. I contemplated giving it a go, but I really can't see how you can clean yourself properly using just a hose. It's the equivalent of trying to wash your car with just a hose. You can't. You'd end up just spray-ing off the mud flaps. You need a sponge. I turned to leave but couldn't, as there was no bloody handle on the door. I was locked in. I banged on the door but no one came. The man on the front door couldn't hear me banging, probably due to the call to prayer. I'm glad I didn't pay to use the place. It stank, had no toilet paper and no handle. I tried to call Krish or Christian but I had no phone signal. I couldn't even sit down, as there was no toilet seat.

I was there for about ten minutes before someone opened the door to use the toilet. 'No handle,' I said. He was English and told me you have to pay to use the toilet and in return you get the handle. I've never heard anything like it.

'Why doesn't he just sell toilet paper 'cos there's none in there,' I said.

The English guy whipped out a roll from his bag and said he never leaves the hotel without it. 'I keep it in my bum bag.'

Never has the name 'bum bag' been so appropriate. In he went. I thought about waiting for him to finish and asking if I could borrow a few sheets but I didn't fancy hanging around. Where's an Andrex puppy when you need one?

I rejoined Krish and Christian, who hadn't even noticed I'd been gone for 30 minutes. They had been busy sorting out where we were going to eat.

'What sort of place do you fancy going to?' asked Krish.

I wasn't fussed. 'Just somewhere with toilets,' I said.

I was taken to a fancy place run by a man called George.

George, the owner, told me he would give me a proper traditional taste of Egypt, which worried me. What I'd seen of Egyptian food so far consisted of brown/beige mush that you dip bread into. I'm not a fan of this type of food. Hummus and couscous doesn't seem like a proper meal to me.

I used the toilets. They were nice and clean, and had handles and everything. Fancy.

We had to wait for 40-odd minutes before the dishes came to the table. George sat with me whilst I ate. It all looked okay. I just had a mouthful of each and asked questions later. It turned out I'd tried an ox's brain, tongue and eye, and its knob and bollocks. Why would anyone want to eat this? Why would you take a big animal like an ox and eat either end of the beast but not the nice meaty bit in-between?

I suppose I came to Egypt to experience new things, and this was a first for me. I would normally be eating beef and veg on a Tuesday.

My stomach was a lot quieter than it was this morning. I think eating all that odd food had sent it into shock, so before I went to bed I had some Jaffa Cakes I'd brought with me to try and give my stomach something it was used to.

△△△

MONDAY 14TH DECEMEBER

I met a local man today. His name was Mahmoud. He's 22 years old and makes his living from giving camel rides close to the Pyramids. He invited me round to his house. His front door was open to anyone – even his camel. This seems a bit odd, when I'm not even allowed to keep a cat in my flat due to the rules in my lease.

On my arrival I used the toilet, as I don't think the knob and bollock I had eaten yesterday agreed with me. The toilet seemed to be in use. By a chicken. Mahmoud chased it out. I was going to explain to him that a supermarket I worked at got a warning from Health and Safety for storing Pot Noodles in the staff toilet, but he was struggling to understand my accent as it was. I asked if there was somewhere to wash my hands. He pointed to the sink in the kitchen that was occupied by another chicken, a dead plucked one this time, surrounded by floating carrots and potatoes. He didn't seem to mind that I rinsed my hands over his dinner.

Mahmoud's wife was sat on the kitchen floor cutting potatoes. He explained how he could have four wives but he has just the one at the moment. I asked if he would go for a totally different kind of woman for wife number two. That's how I would do it. I said Snow White had seven midgets and she had every characteristic covered. I wondered if that's how he would choose his wives. He said he's after a stronger one. He said it like he was talking about buying a new car.

That made things a bit awkward, so we left the house to take a camel ride to see the Pyramids.

I've never been on a camel before. They are not very comfy animals to ride. They have a lump in them for a start. Plus I was nervous, as the last time I rode an animal it was a horse at a fête when I was younger and it bolted after a woman put her fag out on its arse. I slid underneath and got kicked in the head.

Mahmoud led us along some pretty busy roads, which didn't make us very popular, as we held the traffic up. We eventually got to the desert but couldn't see much due to the sandstorm. My face was being battered by tiny grains of sand. The way Egyptians like to make money out of everything I'm surprised the tourist board hasn't advertised it as 'A day out in a sandstorm. The ultimate exfoliating experience.'

The plan is to get a closer look tomorrow.

⌂⌂⌂

TUESDAY 15TH DECEMBER

I went to the Pyramids site again, this time by van. It was heaving today. We were there early, but we still weren't the first. Coachloads of people were entering. The first thing you see is the Great Sphinx. I'm not a fan of this sort of thing

– a lion's body with a human head. A few men were selling models of it. The problem is, the nose is missing from the Sphinx, which means all the models they were selling also had the nose broken off, which just makes it look like a damaged ornament.

I really can't believe what a state the Pyramids are in. I thought they had flat rendered sides, but when you get up close, you see how they are just giant boulders balanced on top of each other, like a massive game of Jenga that has got out of hand. I was told how it was only one of the Pyramids that was a Wonder of the World, even though there are three of them, which is odd, as they all look the same. It's the Great Pyramid that's the official Wonder. I'd be annoyed if I was the builder who built one of the other two if my workmate was getting all the praise for building the 'Great One'. It wouldn't surprise me if it was one of the other builders who knocked the nose off the Sphinx in anger after hearing that news.

I'm sorry to say they didn't look as impressive as they do in the photos I've seen of them. They always look like they are sat in the middle of a desert with nothing around them, but in reality you can see a lot of blocks of flats in the background and the Pizza Hut at the entrance and there is a lot of rubble around them too.

I'm coming back tomorrow to get a tour with a guide.

△△△

WEDNESDAY 16TH DECEMBER

We went to see the Pyramids again today. I was meant to meet up with Dr Hawass, who is the main man who looks after the Pyramids site, but he cancelled last-minute, as he was ill, so

I got a tour from a man called Aladin. He knows everything there is to know about the Pyramids.

He loves them, which I find odd 'cos it's not like he's a project manager who comes every day and sees the development of them – they've looked like this for years and they'll not change or be done up.

Aladin began by raving about how the Pyramids were built. I don't enjoy tours like this. They are more like a history lesson. Too many dates were being mentioned. I watched other people who were on tours and their faces also looked disappointed and uncertain – as if they weren't sure what they were meant to do now they'd seen the Pyramids. It's the same sort of feeling you get when you visit someone in hospital and you've had the small talk and given them their grapes and you want to leave, but feel like it's too early to go. That's how I felt.

△△△

THURSDAY 17 TH DECEMBER

I was told by Krish that I'm going to meet a couple today who actually have a use for the Pyramids and that we'll be going inside one finally. It's probably the first time I've been excited since I've been in Egypt.

I went to meet them at their apartment. They were called Andrew and Seija. They run something called Galactic Light and go into the Pyramids quite often, as they explained, 'to connect with the powers of the Cosmos, the Unity or the Christ Grid around the planet, and Atlantis. As the great Pyramid is the focal point of the whole Grid system, it is connected to all sacred monuments around the Globe, as well as to the centre of our Galaxy and the centre of the planet Earth. It is an amazing, magnificent monument transcending space and time.'

That lost me a bit. I just wanted to see what one looked like inside after being disappointed by its lack of kerb appeal.

They had a nice apartment though, with a great view of the Pyramids from the toilet. They taught me how to relax and went through some mantras that we would be doing once we were inside the Pyramid.

All was going quite well, and I was starting to feel quite calm, until the call to prayer began. There was a speaker right outside their living-room window that blasted out the prayer for a good 20 minutes.

This really was the main thing that put me off living in Egypt. I asked Andrew if they were aware of the speakers when they bought the place. I bet the estate agent got them in and out way before any call to prayer took place. After I had learnt a few chants, we had burgers and chips and headed for the Pyramids. It was the end of the day, but we had permission to be there after all the other tourists had left. It was quite eerie. There were no coaches or camels or people selling tat, and it was dark.

We entered the Pyramids and made our way up some steep steps that Andrew and Seija said were around 150 metres tall. We then had to squeeze through a small gap on our knees to get into a place called the King's Chamber. I'm not that good with guessing sizes but I'd say you could get 50 people in there at a push.

The walls were a pinkish granite that looked impressive, but the stone coffin at the end of the room looked a bit of a mess. The stone looked like it had been cut roughly. It was as if by this point in the construction (23 years in) everyone had had enough and rushed to complete it. It's like when you have an extension done on your house and you end up with a snag list of jobs like cracked plaster or loose plug sockets that take longer to get done than the extension itself.

The lid was missing from the stone coffin and so was the mummy. Andrew and Seija lit some candles, which wasn't that clever, as it was roasting in there already, with no ventilation, and there were no fire escapes, but I didn't say anything, as I didn't want to ruin the mood. They started the mantra. Seija then led me towards the stone coffin and made me get in it. I didn't know this was the plan, but as they led me, they chanted the mantra all the way so I couldn't stop to ask what was happening. It was one of the weirdest experiences of my life. I lay there, as still as I could, in a 4,000-year-old coffin while two strangers chanted over me. I was in there for about five minutes in all, and then Seija and Andrew pulled me out so that Seija could have a go.

Before we left, Seija asked if I had felt any cosmic powers. I wanted to say yes, but I hadn't, so I decided to be honest with her. She seemed disappointed by this news.

As weird as it all was, it was an amazing final experience, and it did make my trip to Egypt and the Pyramids all worthwhile. How many people can say they've lain in a candle-lit coffin in the middle of the King's Chamber in one of the Great Pyramids?

It was also the only time I had been in Egypt when I couldn't hear the call to prayer or beeping of car horns or even, as Ahmed would say, any sort of tintinnabulation.

CHAPTER TWO
CHRIST THE REDEEMER

'FEAR NO ANTICLIMAX: CLIMBING THE STATUE IS A STUNNING EXPERIENCE BY DAY, AND NOTHING SHORT OF MIRACULOUS AT NIGHT.'

THE ROUGH GUIDE TO BRAZIL

'I'M PRETTY SURE IF IT WAS PLONKED ON A ROUNDABOUT IN STRETFORD, NEXT TO THE ARNDALE CENTRE, IT WOULDN'T GET A LOOK-IN.'

KARL PILKINGTON

TUESDAY 9ᵀᴴ FEBRUARY

The heat as we left the airport this afternoon was mental. I never normally sweat on my head but today I was dripping. Even my ears were sweating. Ricky and Stephen told me that all this travelling was going to bring me new experiences, but sweaty ears were not on my list.

As we drove in the sunshine past the golden sands of Ipanema beach I was doing a bit to camera about how much I thought I was going to enjoy my time in Rio. Then I got to my destination, Hostel Piratas de Ipanema, and my heart sank.

'The rules of the hostel are to clean the kitchen after you've used it,' said Fredericko, the owner, before I'd even put my bags down.

'You'd best go through the rules again with the bloke who used it last then,' I said.

The place was well minging. Half-empty coffee cups, crushed lager cans, unwashed cutlery and half-eaten yoghurts whose friendly bacteria had no doubt been battered by the unfriendly bacteria in this place.

Fredericko was a 46-year-old hippy who was popular with the kids who were hanging around. He had a constant grin on his face, smoked self-rolled fags, and wore bleached jeans which had been cut down into shorts. Shame he couldn't have used some of the bleach in the kitchen rather than on his pants.

He led me on a long, winding walk to where I would be sleeping. We set off down a dark corridor with just one electric fan that was missing its safety guard and was plugged into the wall with bare wires which buzzed dangerously. It reminded me of a previous trip to Alcatraz. Young people in surf shorts and bikinis wandered by. We continued up some dodgy stairs and across a balcony that wobbled until we finally reached my dormitory. It was a dark room with 20 or so beds in it and looked like something out of the film Annie. More young people came and went. I am too old to be here, I thought to myself. The last time I felt like this was when I finally got round to having swimming lessons at the age of 14. Most of the other kids were a lot younger than me – seven or eight. They thought I was the swimming instructor.

Fredericko stopped at a bunk bed near the window. 'This is the best bed in the hostel,' he told me proudly. I couldn't work out why, until I met a lad from Hull who explained that if you needed to empty your bladder in the night you could use the window instead of having to walk to the toilets. Not exactly en suite, but I suppose I shouldn't moan.

The mattress was badly stained. Mine looked worse than the others due to the fact that I had daylight showing up stains that you couldn't see on the others. Someone's underpants hung on the end of the bedpost. I was going to move them then I thought they might attract the flies away from me so I left them.

I asked Christian, the show's director, how much it cost to stay here. He said £4 a night. And then Christian said goodbye and left with the rest of the crew to check in to their rented house on Rua Saint Roman.

I decided to try to get an early night. I nodded off to the sound of a kid who looked about nine years old strumming away on a guitar on another bunk bed.

WEDNESDAY 10TH FEBRUARY

I was woken by Christian pointing a camera in my face. It must have been about 7 a.m. I had slept quite well. All the beds now had people in them. Bare legs dangled from the bunks and the odd bollock was hanging out, waiting for any bed bug that was ready for a bit of breakfast in bed. I went to have a wash. The toilets were in worse condition than the kitchen.

We went for breakfast in the back of a supermarket where you pay for your food by its weight. I like this idea. They should put a twist on it and charge people by their body weight. If you're heavy you get charged slightly more, thus helping you to cut down on your food intake. I had some toast and a bit of papaya. This was the first time I'd ever eaten papaya. It was okay, but if someone told me I'd never eat papaya ever again, I wouldn't be bothered. I feel like this about most fruit. There is too much fruit in the world, and I don't like buying a lot of it, as it goes off so quickly. Maybe that's why we're told to eat five portions a day, just to get through the stuff before it turns mouldy. First things first, I went to see if I could find a cheap hotel 'cos I didn't want to stay another night in Fredericko's hostel. But everywhere was booked up, due to it being carnival season, or at least that's what they told me. It could have been because I looked such an unwashed scruff in my shorts and slept-in T-shirt, and they just didn't want me in their hotel. Madonna and Beyoncé were in town. If Madonna got a glimpse of me in such a state she would probably take pity and adopt me to go with the rest of her collection.

Finally, Christian and Krish said I could stay with the rest of the crew at their house on Rua Saint Roman. That cheered me up. Christian then told me I was off to meet a local man who would show me around Rio de Janeiro. His name was Celso. He was 47 years old and walked with a stick. This was quite good, as he shuffled along at a slow pace which was perfect in this heat. Within seconds of meeting him he gave me a gift. It was a condom on a string. I opened it to see a series of diagrams of two blokes putting a condom on each other. There was no need for so many drawings of men's knobs. You only need one to demonstrate how to pop it on. I asked Celso if he was gay, but he didn't answer.

Instead he took me to a health spa where he wanted to get his body waxed. Celso invited me into the small cubicle to watch. He told me a lot of men have this done in Rio to get rid of unwanted body hair, so they look better and tan better on the beach. He told me I was too hairy and should have it done too. I said no. Celso told me he has his body done every four months. I read the price list. To have hair removed from the anus would cost approximately eight English pounds. I don't know why anyone would need this doing. Who needs to get such a thorough, all-over body tan? Celso told me how he had his testicles done once and how much it hurt. Maybe this is why he walks with a stick.

After watching for a bit I decided to just get my lower back done. This is my only body hair that does seem rather long. The fact that I have to tuck it into my underpants made me realise that it was probably time to get rid of it.

It hurt – a lot more than I imagined it would. I said, 'No more . . . that's enough,' and went to get up, when Celso told me that the lady had only removed half of it.

With the waxing complete, Celso decided to celebrate by buying some new swimming trunks. He said he wanted to buy me a pair too. I said I didn't want them as I wouldn't wear them. He bought them for me anyway.

The place the crew is staying at is okay. Nothing fancy. It is quite a rough area and police are guarding the street due to a drug raid that happened a few weeks ago, so it feels pretty safe. I have a mattress with no bed and no light in the bathroom, but it's fine compared to Fredericko's hostel.

We have a cook who made some nice chicken and beans for tea.

THURSDAY 11TH FEBRUARY

Celso took me to the beach today. He asked me if I had brought my new swimming trunks. I hadn't. I did try them on last night, but the truth was I didn't like them. I didn't know how to break the news to him.

We had a long walk along the beach whilst chatting about various things – from life in Brazil to how kids these days get away with doing whatever they want. I asked about his leg problem. It was something to do with diabetes. We must have been walking for 50 minutes or so, when he suddenly announced his legs were starting to ache and he wanted to sit down. As I turned to look for a deck chair and umbrella, Celso told me how much he liked this part of the beach. It's known as the gay beach. I said, why don't we walk another five minutes or so to another part of the beach, but he insisted on staying. Everyone seemed to know him. I asked him again if he was gay. He didn't give me a straight answer.

I was feeling pretty uncomfortable and a little bit annoyed that Celso had brought me to this bit of the beach, so I decided to sit in silence as he wriggled about in the deck chair loosening his shirt. A camp friend of his then came over to say hello. He was the gayest man I had ever met in my life. Every word out of his mouth was gayed up. Imagine if Kenneth Williams had a gayer brother – that was this man. He told me I should loosen up and strip off some of my clothing. I refused. Even if I had wanted to, I wouldn't now. Celso took this as his cue to remove his shorts and show off his new purchase. I wanted to leave. Celso's gay friend said I had great legs and that gay men would love me here in Brazil. He said I had 'great novelty value' but then told me I wasn't his type, as he was into black men. I had nothing to say in reply. He wouldn't give up though. He commented on my hairy legs and said I would be classed as 'a bear' in the gay community. Again, I had little to say.

I remember Ricky telling me once that if a lion could speak English we wouldn't be able to understand anything it said because the lion would have lived such a different life to us. I never understood what he meant until today.

Celso had a massage by a local man called Nelson Mandela. Celso looked like he was loving it.

I asked Celso's friend if Celso was gay. He said it was up to Celso to tell me. I turned to Celso, who now had his legs wrapped round his neck and his head wedged between Nelson Mandela's thighs, but decided that I would ask him some other time.

I left him to it and went back to the apartment.

We had chicken and beans again for tea.

FRIDAY 12TH FEBRUARY

We were up early today. 5 a.m. We were going to Christ the Redeemer. Forget body waxing and sunbathing on gay-only beaches, this is the whole reason I am here.

We set off in a van we had hired while we stayed in Rio. It came with a driver who said his name was Bin Laden. He was a miserable fella. He didn't like anyone touching the air conditioning or having too many bags on board.

We got to the Big Jesus just as the sun was coming up. Christ the Redeemer isn't as big as I'd thought it would be, but being there on our own so early in the day felt quite special. It's so high up you can look down through the clouds over the whole of Rio. God knows how they got him up here. The bloke who delivered my washer/dryer from Comet moaned about getting up to my flat on the third floor. I suppose that's why it could be a Wonder of the World.

I think the other reason that makes Christ the Redeemer one of the Wonders is the setting. I'm pretty sure if it was plonked on a roundabout in Stretford, next to the Arndale Centre, it wouldn't get a look-in.

As the sun came up so did the flying ants. Hundreds of the bloody things. Big ones too. There is no need for ants to have the ability to fly. They are useless when it comes to walking. I've watched them. They tend to cover the same piece of ground time and time again and they are even worse at flying.

We went back down to meet a woman called Dolores who loves the Big Jesus. I had a coconut on the way, which was another first for me. A drink and food all in one. It didn't look like the normal coconuts you win at fairgrounds. There was no hair on it. I don't know if that's how they grow here or if it's that Brazilians hate hair on anything and they've waxed them.

Dolores turned up in a beach buggy and took me back up to the Jesus, pointing out various landmarks as we drove, including the house where Ronnie Biggs used to live.

It was busy at Christ the Redeemer now. It wasn't half as relaxing as it had been earlier this morning. There were hundreds of tourists crammed around the bottom shouting and pushing about. Groups of 20 people being led by a guide who was trying to shout above the other guides who were leading bigger groups. Even the flying ants had sodded off because it had become so crowded. Dolores gave me some facts. It stands at 130 feet and has a chapel in the base. I told her that I like the setting but wasn't really blown away by the statue. As I was saying this, a couple from England passed by. I asked them what they thought. They weren't fans either and said they preferred the statue in Lisbon. Dolores was not happy with this comment and said they didn't know what they were talking about.

She told me that to get a really amazing view I should take a helicopter ride around the statue.

Chicken and beans was served for tea again tonight.

SATURDAY 13 TH FEBRUARY

I was woken at 5.10 this morning by Christian. He said we needed to leave by 5.30 for our helicopter ride. I was really struggling. I didn't have much sleep last night. I was woken around 3 a.m. by something outside. I could hear movement in the long weeds. I got up and could see a shadow moving in the crack of the front door. I thought it might have been someone trying to break in. I couldn't ignore it so I decided to just open it and see who it was. It was a chicken. At three in the morning! What is a chicken doing awake at this hour? I don't know if having a chicken walk across your path is some sort of bad omen in Brazil. I took it as bad news anyway, as it looks like we'll be having chicken for tea again.

I grabbed a banana for breakfast and joined Bin Laden and the crew in the van. Forty minutes later I was getting on board a helicopter. I've never been on one before. I was pretty nervous, as these things don't glide if the engines fail. I sat in the back and was given headphones to wear, and off we went. There

EGYPT

EGYPT

IT TURNED OUT I WAS THE ONLY ON BOOKED ON THE OFFICIAL WINDSOR HOTEL TOUR OF CAIRO.

TRYING RICKY'S JELLABIYA ON FOR SIZE.

I WAS TOLD IT WOULD STOP ME HEAD GETTING BURNT.

EGYPT

THE CAMEL ISN'T THE ONLY THING THAT LOOKS LIKE IT'S GOT THE HUMP.

EGYPTIAN LUNCH AT PIZZA HUT. 7-INCH CHICKEN SUPREME THAT COMES WITH A SIDE ORDER OF COUSCOUS. I LEFT THE COUSCOUS.

30 MINUTES LATER I WAS DOING WHEELIES ON IT.

BRAZIL

ME AND CELSO.

TURN THE PHOTO UPSIDE DOWN
AND IT LOOKS THE SAME.

TRYING TO AVOID THE NUDISTS.

WEIRD INNIT?

BRAZIL

was no safety briefing, none of the usual info you get given before take-off. There was nothing to hold on to either. Even in the back of a Ford Fiesta there is a handle on the ceiling to hold on to, but there was nothing here.

We skimmed about 20 feet above the sea along Ipanema and Copacabana beach, which worried me as it meant that even if I survived a crash I would then have to try and swim in the roughest waves I've ever seen. But once I'd got used to the sensation I started to enjoy it. It's one of the best ways to get around. We went round Christ the Redeemer four times, and it looked amazing. Dolores was right. I was getting a great view. I looked down at all the tourists crammed round the bottom like ants (mind you, they could have been ants, knowing what it's like down there). It definitely looked more impressive from this angle. It looked taller than 130 feet. I felt I had to say how good Jesus looked. Let's face it, while I'm whizzing round his head in a helicopter at high speed, he's the last person I want to slag off. The only thing that didn't look in proportion was his chin. He looked like Jimmy Hill. I put the dodgy chin down to the fact that the sculptor may have rushed it due to all the flying ants, but once back on ground and we could all hear each other clearly enough to hold a proper conversation, Christian told me he hasn't got a big chin, it was meant to be a beard. I really enjoyed my ride in the helicopter. Probably the best part of the trip so far. Back at the house and my happy mood disappeared when Steve called and told me that Celso had invited me round to his place so I could find out more about Brazilian life. I said I thought it was a waste of time. I'd spent quite a lot of time with Celso over the last few days and I hadn't learnt that much from him. I still didn't even know if he was gay or not. Steve told me to stop whingeing and to go.

STEPHEN: Hello, mate. What's going on? How's it going at the hostel?

KARL: Oh, I left that in the end. It did my head in.

STEPHEN: You left it?

KARL: Yeah, it was ridiculous. I mean I'm not that fussy and that, but it was minging. There were underpants hanging on the end of my bed and they weren't even mine.

STEPHEN: Well, how long did you last in there?

KARL: Just did a night.

STEPHEN: Lightweight.

KARL: It's not lightweight, honestly. It wasn't even safe. I shouldn't have been there. I mean, I had injections before I came that protect me from being bitten by a dirty chimp, but I'm a bit worried that stopping there I wasn't protected. So a night was enough.

STEPHEN: Well, I've got a bit of good news for you.

KARL: Go on.

STEPHEN: Pack up your stuff because I don't know what place you're staying in now but I'm sure it's nothing compared to where we're going to send you . . . You've already met Celso, your local guide. Lovely fella. You got on with him, and that's a treat. He has personally invited you to stay with him in his place.

KARL: But what's . . . what's the point of this, seriously? Steve, do you know him? Have you even spoken to him?

STEPHEN: But he's already your mate. You don't just turn down hospitality like that, not when you're in another country.

KARL: I wouldn't go that far.

STEPHEN: If someone gives you a bed for the night, you take it, my friend.

KARL: Listen, if he's a mate, why hasn't he told me if he's gay or not? Why's it such a big issue?

STEPHEN: But what's that got to do with anything? That's got nothing to do with it, mate! He's just offering you a bed.

KARL: Yeah, but that's what worries me.

STEPHEN: He's giving you a bed for the night, alright? You've already been whingeing about how you're not happy where you're staying. He's offered a bed for the night – nothing wrong with that.

KARL: But, honestly, he's a right queen. It will be like staying with Aunty Nora. I bet he's got ornaments all over the place. I bet everything's got a valance on it. I bet everything's sort of frilly everywhere. I mean, it would be nice for an hour . . .

STEPHEN: If your Aunty Nora invited me to sleep with her, I'd be round there in a flash.

KARL: Well, what am I doing with him? Is it a night in? Can we just have a game of cards or . . .?

STEPHEN: It's just a game of cards. You haven't got to go out partying.

KARL: Honestly?

STEPHEN: Yes.

KARL: Has he got wi-fi?

STEPHEN: I don't know if he's got wi-fi. But that's a question you ask him. That's the first question through the door. 'Thanks, mate, have you got wi-fi?' Karl, treat it like a B&B. You know you don't have to be sensitive.

KARL: Ain't that a gay term? I've heard that B&B is a gay term for bum and bollocks. Honestly, I heard someone talking on the train, and he said, 'Oh, I'm having a bit of B&B tonight – a bit of bum and bollocks.'

STEPHEN: [laughing] Let us know how it goes . . .

KARL: Yeah, alright. I'll talk to you later.

STEPHEN: All the best, mate.

KARL: See ya.

We got the Metro. It was chaos. People were pushing and shoving to get on the train worse than they do in London. It took an hour to get there. When we got off I was surprised to see the sort of area Celso lived in. He came across as a man who would have quite a fancy lifestyle. In reality, his place was a flat in a five-storey block. Old people sat outside playing dominoes. Kids played football and two toothless women stood chatting at a cola stand. It wasn't really grim, in fact it reminded me a bit of the estate I grew up on, except the old and young people seem to mix here.

'Hiiiiiiii', shouted a camp voice. It was Celso, topless and waving a hanky between the security bars of his front window. We made our way up the stairs, avoiding a snappy dog whose owner sat behind a locked gate staring at us.

I knocked on Celso's door. It was covered in posters for various carnival events and an advert for condoms. I wondered if these were put up for visitors to read to pass the time it took for Celso to shuffle his way to his front door. Eventually, he opened the door wearing just his silk boxer shorts and flip-flops. He had been spraying his plants and was moaning how hot it was. He seemed quieter and less confident today.

It was a tiny flat. About the size of one I used to live in, except it was cluttered, which made it feel even smaller. There was so much in the room my eyes didn't know what to focus on.

He offered me a glass of nut juice. Of all the things to get juice out of, I can't think of anything less juicy. I was still getting my head round the fact that carrot juice existed, now nut juice.

I told Celso that I found it odd that I'd only known him for a few days and yet I was welcomed into his flat. Celso explained that it is a Brazilian tradition that if you are invited to stay over it is rude to refuse. I could tell by his face that he was serious – more serious than the way he looked whilst trying on the trunks in the swimwear shop. He said I must stay in his bed. I'm normally quite good at nipping situations like this in the bud, but he kept going on about Brazilian tradition and how he would be upset if I didn't stay. So, in the end, I agreed.

I was left with Krish in the lounge while Christian went with Celso into his bedroom to interview him. I browsed through his CDs. Dinah Washington, Dionne Warwick and Bette Midler. A lot different from the rap music that was blasting from the cars outside.

Forty-five minutes later Celso came into the living room wearing a dress, wig and make-up. I told him he reminded me of my Aunty Nora. Other than the eye make-up being a bit over the top, he looked quite good. He said I should now call him Lorna Washington. He was a drag queen. He had to go off to do a birthday party and a wedding. I asked him if this meant he was gay. He said something along the lines of 'What do you think honey?' Still not a straight answer.

Celso then told me to make myself feel at home. He told me to help myself to more nut juice. He left me his phone number, and showed me how the TV remote worked and gave me a selection of DVDs to watch, including *My Fair Lady*. It reminded me of times when my mam would go out when I was younger and give me money to get some toffees from the off-licence and tell me not to answer the door to anyone.

His cab came. I watched through the bars on his window as Lorna Washington went to work under the watchful gaze of his neighbours.

It was warm in his flat. A fan hung from the ceiling but made little difference. I sat wondering if it was part of Brazilian tradition to invite someone to stay but then fuck off out for the evening. Seems a bit odd to me. I couldn't get the DVD to work so watched a little bit of TV. I then went to the toilet where I disturbed four massive cockroaches. I can't stand those things. They move too quickly for my liking. There was also so much clutter that it made it easy for them to hide. I felt itchy. I then noticed a few bites on my legs. I think I found a new species on me that evening.

It's hard to explain the amount of clutter there was, but put it this way, it was difficult to see a space to put anything down on any surface due to stuff. I don't know why Celso kept some of the items, as I couldn't work out what some of the things were. Christian actually lost his phone in there and couldn't find it. Finally I snapped. I decided I couldn't stay any longer. I don't like being in tight spaces. The more I looked around, the more I got worked up. Plus the cockroaches didn't help. I found a dead one in the kitchen. The fact that I've heard cockroaches are one of the toughest creatures on planet earth – they can survive a nuclear attack and live for a week without a head – yet this one couldn't survive in Celso's place made me realise it wasn't healthy for me to stay there.

It was 1.30 a.m. I thought it would be rude to just leave, so I called Celso and told him it was too hot and noisy to stay. He didn't sound that disappointed.

I was back in my own bed at 2.45 a.m.

SUNDAY 14ᵀᴴ FEBRUARY

I woke up this morning feeling guilty about leaving Celso's place. But then it occurred to me that maybe Celso had only invited me round 'cos he wanted me there for security whilst he was out working. Krish and Christian agreed that it was best that we'd left, so I didn't feel too bad.

We went to a block party today. It was the worst party I have ever been to. Aimlessly walking about as people blew whistles and made noise with air horns. I would normally avoid things like this. I remember not enjoying the Queen's Jubilee street party when I was a kid. Scruffy Sandra ate loads of the trifle me mam had made and didn't bring anything to the party. This block party was worse. There was no trifle whatsoever. People just stood around looking a bit bewildered. It was like wandering amongst the staff of an office block who are stood on the street 'cos a fire alarm has gone off. At least the noise from a fire alarm is necessary. The noise these lot were making was just noise pollution. There was a bloke walking around dressed as a pink poodle in some pants that left his arse exposed. Maybe this isn't a block party and this is an office block on fire and he's singed his arse. He got annoyed when strangers pinched it.

I saw Celso's gay friend. He was with another man. I'm not sure if it was his boyfriend as he wasn't black.

I told Krish that I'd had enough. We went back home.

I didn't really enjoy today. I had some Toblerone to cheer me up.

I said it would be nice to go to a quiet beach to get away from all the noise. Krish said he knew where a nice quiet beach was but we'd have to get up early to get there. I agreed.

We ate chicken and beans again. Christian said he would speak to our fixer about getting the cook to do something different for tomorrow.

MONDAY 15TH FEBRUARY

Got up at 5.20 this morning to go to the quiet beach. Even Ipanema and Copacabana beach would be quiet at this time of the day. Krish said it would take an hour to drive to our destination. Bin Laden seemed miserable. I don't think he likes an early start.

Unsurprisingly we were the first on the beach, apart from a man who was serving drinks under a canopy. We found a nice patch and got comfortable. I was sat enjoying the view when I was disturbed by a banging noise. I turned and saw the man under the canopy smashing ice. I also noticed he had his knob out.

I told Krish, and he didn't seem that surprised. It was a bloody nudist beach. I've never understood why people like to do this, least of all at 7.30 a.m. It wasn't that hot yet, as the sun hadn't come up properly. He still had his T-shirt on, so why couldn't he keep his shorts on? I watched, as he kept bending down to pick up more ice. It's like he was trying to wind me up. Every time he bent down his arse and balls swung in my direction. He looked like the back end of a bulldog.

More fellas turned up, chatting with their arms folded and their knobs and bollocks out. There were a few women too. Two large ladies in their late forties sat behind me. I had no idea if they were completely nude because their breasts hung that low they covered the more private areas.

A man came over and gave me a leaflet listing the rules of the beach. It had lots of useful instructions, including advice on what men should do if they had a moment of excitement. The leaflet suggested sitting down as soon as possible or entering the sea and staying there until the excitement goes away. With the women I had on view, I don't think there was any chance of any of that.

Abricó Nude Beach
Welcome to Rio de Janeiro's First Nude Beach

Resolution 64/94 Secretary of Environment Rio de Janeiro
Decision of the Tribune of Justice Rio de Janeiro 9th September 2003
City law number 4059 of may, 18th, 2005

Code of Ethics*
Naturism is a way of life in harmony with nature and characterized by the practice of nudism in a group setting with the intention of encouraging self-respect, respect for others and respect for the environment.
International Nudism Federation – INF

The following are prohibited:
1) Practicing sexual or obscene acts;
2) Acting in a disrespectful or aggressive manner toward anyone, at any time, for any reason;
3) Aggressively or passively make fellow nudists and other beach goers feel uncomfortable;
4) Playing sports outside of designate areas;
5) Satisfying biological needs in public areas;
6) Leaving trash behind when leaving the beach;
7) Using, carrying or selling any substance whatsoever which can be construed by law to be an illicit drug or other illegal object or substance;
8) Film, record or video nudists (by any means, at any distance) without the express permission of all those in focus.

* This code of ethics is the same for any other municipal beach in Rio de Janeiro with the exception of number 8). All rules will be enforced by the appropriate civil authorities, members of the Abricó Naturists Association – ANA and is applicable for all nudists and non-nudists while at this beach.

OBS:
Nude means uncovered genitals. Topless is not considered nude.

In this area everybody should be nude. Policemen, security professionals, life guards, fishermen with fishing equipment going to fish on the rocks and divers who will not stay on the beach may enter and stay dressed inside the second area while passing through or on duty. Teenagers from 13 y.o. should respect all rules.

On all other days, clothing is optional on Abricó Nude Beach until further notice. All are welcome to Abricó Nude Beach. Please follow the rules. If you see anyone breaking any of these rules, please notify any association member, the police or the lifeguards.

Abricó Nude Beach is restricted to the sand, water and rocks directly adjacent to its beach area, which starts at the signs at its entrance.

Tips

Avoid aggressive or unfriendly behavior and expressions, as well as, loud screaming, loud conversations, jam sessions and loud music. People who look for out-of-the-way nude beaches like Abricó are normally interested in enjoying quiet seclusion and communion with nature.

Avoid staring at others for whatever reason. Respect others and respect their spatial requirements.

If male beach goers should become excited and reach an erection, remain discreet about it and **avoid** exhibitionist behaviors. Remain seated or go to the water until this condition passes. Penis erection is natural but provoking or exhibiting oneself in this state is not appropriate at this beach.

Always apply sun block especially where you usually wear clothes, including the genital areas. Be discrete but do not feel embarrassed about this. Avoid handling genital parts.

Remember, on a nude beach you attract more attention and criticism if you keep your clothes on. So, take off your clothes as soon as you arrive and blend in.

Cigarette butts and straws are trash and should be taken to the orange trashcans provided on the beach or back home.

Members of the Abricó Naturists Association – ANA are always present on the beach on Saturdays, Sundays and holidays. Look for us and come say hello!

President: Pedro Ribeiro
Tel: (21) 2542 9807 / (21)9441-5652
E-mail: anabrico@anabrico.com
Site: www.anabrico.com
Newsletter Website: www.jornalolhonu.com
Brazilian Nudist Federation Website: www.fbrn.com.br
Abricó call in the beach: (21) 8639 0368

PREFEITURA
MEIO AMBIENTE

"NUDITY IS A NATURAL HUMAN STATE: NUDE IS SIMPLY NATURAL!"

Half an hour later, the man who gave me the leaflet came back and asked me to get nude or leave. I said, 'I'll leave, thank you very much.'

I couldn't go far though. Krish and Christian and Jan (cameraman) and Freddie (soundman) had to get more pictures for the telly programme.

They were told they would have to be naked if they wished to carry on filming. So they got naked. It was the first time I felt like I got my own back on them for all the stuff they've been putting me through.

Back at the house Krish told us we were going to a favela tomorrow. They normally liked to keep everything a secret up until it happened, but Krish said he had to tell me about this, as the favelas are the roughest parts of town where drugs and guns rule and he would have to give us a Health and Safety briefing. What's going on? I didn't come to Brazil for danger. Krish was suddenly acting all serious, which was hard to handle when earlier today I'd seen him walk about a beach with his knob out.

A different cook was cooking tonight. She made spicy beef with beans.

TUESDAY 16TH FEBRUARY

I got up 30 minutes earlier than I needed to today as I wanted a ham toasty for breakfast and the toasty machine takes 20 minutes to warm up. I thought about how this could be my last ever meal as we were going to a favela today. In that context I suppose I shouldn't complain about having to wait for the toaster to warm up.

Over breakfast there was a lot of talk about the film *City of God*. Apparently, the favela we were going to was similar to the one that was in the film. Everyone but me had seen the movie. I seemed to remember hearing about it, but was put off 'cos I heard it had subtitles and I don't like films with subtitles. I may as well read the book.

Krish explained that we would have to sit on the back of a motorbike, as the favelas are not really suitable for vans. It's the first time Bin Laden looked happy the whole time I've been here. Easy day for him. So I got on the back of a big bike that was being ridden by a bloke called Johnny who was a local from the favela. We darted round corners and went down alleyways. As we whizzed through the streets I saw guns on every corner.

Big ones too. The crew followed behind. At certain points we were told not to film, as the gang leaders did not want to be captured on film. We had to point the cameras down to the ground so they could see we were not secretly filming.

Finally the bikes pulled up, and I was introduced to a man called Henrique. He had no weapons. He was not a gang leader. He was going to teach me a Brazilian dance called the samba.

Henrique took me to a derelict building where for two hours he taught me various moves. I showed him a few of my own moves, which he described as 'crap'. Bit harsh, I thought. The first 30 minutes seemed like fun, and I wasn't taking it too seriously, until Henrique told me I would be dancing in the Rio Carnival. Even though I'm not that well travelled I had heard of this and started to feel worried. I trained harder now. Henrique told me 4,000 people would be watching, and it was a big deal for the team I would be dancing with. They had been training all year and were hoping to impress the judges enough to go up a league in the main competition. But the harder I

KARL'S FACTS

BIG JESUS WAS BUILT IN 1931.
CONSTRUCTION STARTED IN 1922
AND IT TOOK NINE YEARS TO
COMPLETE.

IT IS MADE OF REINFORCED CONCRETE
AND SOAPSTONE. IT TAKES ABOUT 220
STEPS TO SEE THE STATUE UP CLOSE.
THE STATUE STANDS 38 METRES TALL
AND WEIGHS 635 TONNES.

THE SCULPTOR RESPONSIBLE
FOR CHRIST THE REDEEMER,
PAUL LANDOWSKI, WON A
GOLD MEDAL FOR SCULPTURE
AT THE 1928 OLYMPIC GAMES.

FAVELA

tried, the more frustrated I became. There was too much to remember. In the end Henrique suggested we stop for food.

We went to a local café. The food was really, really tasty, but then I guess if your customers are coming in with grenades, machine guns and rocket launchers you wouldn't want to serve them mush.

After eating we trained some more and Henrique gave me a costume I would have to wear. It was a ridiculous thing, an Andy Pandy-style outfit with blue feathers. It made me look gormless, but Henrique told me that was the least of my worries. He told me to remember to smile. This isn't something I do a lot. I do smile, but not as much as some people. Even when I'm happy inside, my face does not always show it.

We trained for another hour or so, then stopped, as Henrique was tired due to the fact he'd been dancing at the carnival for the last three days. I was knackered after three hours. There is nothing I can do about my fitness though. There's not time, so I'll just make sure I try to get an early night and eat well.

Beef and beans again tonight. I just had beef, as I am now sick of beans.

Before I went to bed I practised my dancing in my room and then did some smiling in the bathroom mirror. It didn't look very natural to me, but then I couldn't see myself very clearly due to the fact that we had no electricity in the toilet.

WEDNESDAY 17TH FEBRUARY

Carnival day. I felt more worried about having to dance in front of a large crowd today than I did this time yesterday when I was heading into the druggy, gun-ridden favela.

We were at the carnival site for 1 p.m., but when I arrived, I was told I wouldn't be dancing until 8.45. I was already dressed in my big, feathered Andy Pandy outfit and had no other clothes with me, so I just sat in the van with Bin Laden while everyone else went to set up the camera equipment. It was a long afternoon. Bin Laden and I didn't speak due to our language barrier. Mind you, he's such a miserable sod, it wouldn't surprise me if he had good English but just didn't want to chat to me.

I fell asleep for an hour or so until Krish and Christian woke me and said Henrique was in the parade close by. We tracked him down, and he gave me a few more moves that were easier to remember than the stuff he taught me yesterday. He then said if I forgot my moves to just use lots of energy and remember to smile a lot.

We had a Bob's Burger – Brazil's equivalent of McDonald's – and after that everything is a bit of a blur. I don't remember much about what happened from then until the start of the parade. Henrique told me where to stand and repeated his tips about 'giving off energy'. He kept reminding me to smile. Fireworks exploded, and so did my stomach. I don't know if it was my nerves or the Bob's Burger I'd eaten earlier, so I quickly used a toilet, as I didn't like the idea of getting halfway down the parade and doing a Paula Radcliffe in front of 4,000 spectators and half as many judges.

I found a toilet and was charged two reals (about 60p) to use it. It was grim. I sat on the dirty toilet and saw myself in the mirror hanging on the back of the door. There I was wearing the Andy Pandy outfit and a stupid gormless hat. How did it come to this?

I didn't have time to worry though, as the owner of the loo was banging on the door. I hate being rushed on the toilet. She banged again. I got outside where the woman was pointing at the price on the door and repeating 'Two moments . . . two moments'. Sixty pence only buys two minutes of usage. Maybe I should have had the beans last night. The way them things go through you, I could have saved myself 30p.

I made my way through the crowds to the start of the parade. It was busy now. Henrique put me with an oldies' group. There was a woman wearing glasses who looked like Jim Bowen off Bullseye. It didn't really help me being put with the old ones though, as it just added to the pressure. I suddenly thought, if I can't keep up with this lot, that'll really knock my confidence.

And then the drums sounded and we were off. I was in the zone and gave it my best shot.

Fifty-five minutes later I crossed the finishing line. I haven't felt that knackered for years. I had a huge blister on my foot, and felt really dizzy and weak but glad it was all over.

Henrique looked pleased with me, which was good. I asked him if the class would be going up a league, but he said he wouldn't know for a few days.

THURSDAY 18 TH FEBRUARY

We went home today.

I left for the airport at 1.30 p.m. and flew home via Lisbon, as there was no direct flight. I tried to look out of the plane window to see if I could see the statue that the English couple I'd met said was better than Christ the Redeemer, but it was too cloudy. I was back at home in London for 12 p.m.

I preferred Christ the Redeemer to the Pyramids. 1–0 to Brazil. Christian just told me that Henrique's dance team missed out on promotion by 0.2 points.

CHAPTER THREE
THE TAJ MAHAL

'THE GATEWAY THROUGH WHICH ALL DREAMS MUST PASS.'

RUDYARD KIPLING

'IT'S WEIRD HOW IT IS CLASSED AS ONE OF THE MODERN WONDERS OF THE WORLD. YOU WOULDN'T THINK SO BY THE SURROUNDINGS. IF IT WAS ON ONE OF THEM PROPERTY PROGRAMMES, THE POTENTIAL BUYERS WOULD SAY, "IF YOU COULD PICK IT UP AND PUT IT SOMEWHERE NICER WE'D BUY IT." IT REALLY SHOULDN'T HAVE BEEN BUILT HERE.'

KARL PILKINGTON

THURSDAY 25 TH FEBRUARY

When I was getting ready for my trip to India today, Luke the producer gave me a pack of 28 adult nappies. Not the usual going-away gift, is it? I hadn't planned on needing these in my life – well, not at least until I was well into my eighties – but I packed two of them just in case.

Everyone I talk to about India has mentioned 'Delhi Belly'. It's assumed that if you visit India you will get ill. I think it's the only place in the world that has this reputation. It must be a great place to open a restaurant. There's no comeback if a customer gets the shits from eating your food – except, well, 'Welcome to India'. It's as if it is on the menu: starter, main course, pudding, coffee and then the shits.

Luke said we might have some days where we are far from a loo, so if I'm not feeling well the adult nappy might come in handy. I don't like the idea. I worry that if I get used to the fact that I can empty my bowels anywhere I like then they might get lazy and start emptying themselves when I get back home and I'm no longer wearing a nappy.

I was given some friendly bacteria sachets to take too. They are supposed to make my stomach stronger, but I imagine the bad bacteria in India will batter this stuff in no time. In the end I packed more drugs to bung me up than clothes to wear.

FRIDAY 26TH FEBRUARY

I had a first-class seat on the flight to New Delhi. I think they call it 'New' Delhi to give the impression things have changed – a bit like them washing powder ads that say 'New and Improved'.

The flight was delayed for five hours. Reclining in the first-class lounge, it's the only time I've ever been happy to hear about a delay. But I suppose it's only delaying the inevitable. I imagine it's like having a power cut when you're due to go on the electric chair.

SATURDAY 27TH FEBRUARY

It took seven hours to get to Gandhi International Airport. I'm not sure how Gandhi would feel about having an airport named after him. It's not that special, is it? I don't know much about Gandhi other than he helped the poor, much like Bob Geldof and Lenny Henry did in the 1980s. I wonder, if Gandhi was around now, if his reputation would be as good, or if some tabloid would have found some dirt on him. Luke told me he took care of a group of poor people called 'the untouchables' – or Dalits. These people were considered the lowest of the low – shit shovellers, really. I wonder if the place was tidier back then when there were more shit shovellers? There is rubbish everywhere. I suppose when people just ate fruit and meat then everything either was eaten by animals or wasted away, but since we now have plastic bottles and crisp packets and polystyrene there are piles of it everywhere. I haven't noticed any bins anywhere yet.

We drove into Delhi in a van with a local driver. The sounds were the same as Egypt, and the road safety was similar too. Car horns beeped constantly. I'm not sure what the point of a horn is when everyone is using them at the same time. It's impossible to know if the horn is aimed at you. Large families stuffed themselves into tiny cars. Groups of four wobbled around on single mopeds wearing no helmets. The buses were crammed too. In a country with a population of over one billion, I wondered what the chances were of getting a seat on a bus in rush hour. In one of the buses we overtook I was sure even the driver was standing.

Nothing here seems finished. Roads are dug up, pavements half laid. I saw a wall that was still being built already being painted.

I passed a market where skinned chickens lay out on make-shift tables covered in flies. Not so much served as chicken 'n' chips but chicken with shits. I know I'm going to get ill – it's just a matter of how quickly.

Every time we stopped at a junction, someone would tap on the window of the van for money. I didn't have any. I gave one man whose legs were all twisted my bottle of Coke. Our driver went mad at me and told me not to give them any-thing.

It was interesting sat in the van looking out on all the mad-ness, but I knew that at some point the van would pull up and I would have to step out into this crazy place.

Eventually we did pull up, and Luke told me to wait at a busy junction for a local lad called Ashek who would be picking me up on a rickshaw. It was like Piccadilly Circus – completely mental. It was a spot where three roads went into one. There were all sorts of modes of transport. I saw a man on an ele-phant. I don't understand why anyone would want one of these to get around on. There was only one man sat on the top. I wondered if local people got annoyed with people who ride elephants. Is it the same as people in London getting annoyed with owners of those big 4x4 gas-guzzlers that block up the city? Like a 4x4, these elephants must take quite a bit of fuel to feed and yet they only carry one bloke.

There were donkeys, horses, goats and pigs. A zebra crossing in India is, literally, a zebra crossing. There was a man on a pushbike carrying the biggest load I have ever seen on a bicycle. It totally covered the bike, and underneath it the owner was desperately struggling to pedal. And to make matters worse he had a man sat on top of the load. Ridiculous. If this man got on a plane, God knows what he would class as hand luggage. He wasn't alone though. Another pushbike passed us carrying a pile of flattened cardboard that must have been 15 feet high. They were like human ants – unbelievably strong. It made me feel bad about moaning about the weight of my old Sunday paper round, when all the extra supplements used to weigh my bag down.

There were hundreds of rickshaws in this area, which didn't help, as each one stopped to see if I needed a lift, and I wasn't sure if any of them were Ashek. After 40 minutes Ashek finally turned up. He said he was sorry for being late but that he hadn't been well. He looked pretty tired for a young fella. His English wasn't great, but it was better than my Indian.

Ashek drove me around, and I took in even more depressing sights. People on every street corner seemed to have an arm or a foot or a leg missing. He took me to meet his boss, who owned all the rickshaws. He said he wanted to train me to ride one. I've always been good on bikes so I was happy to give it a go. He said he would train me at a place called the dust bowl. It was a large, open area with a little bit of grass but mainly bald, dusty ground. The grass to hardened soil ratio was probably the same as the hair to skin ratio on my head. Kids played cricket and football. Families sat around chatting while some poorer people lay around and sniffed glue.

I gave the cycling a go on the rickshaw and I thought I was quite good, but the boss said he would have to fail me because

I rode too fast and didn't smile enough. Smiling has never come naturally to me, plus India isn't a place you want to smile, mainly 'cos it's best to keep your mouth shut so the flies can't get in.

Ashek invited me to his home, where he also works in the evening selling chicken kebabs. We made our way down tiny, narrow streets lined with rotting meat, guts, blood and chicken carcasses. The deeper we went, the more the fly population increased. When I was a kid, we had a fly in our house that hung around so often it became part of the family. My mam named it Harry the House Fly. She even put its name down on the form when I was doing a sponsored walk. I used to think it was happy living in our house, but I suppose India is the ultimate place for a fly. These dirty lanes were like an All You Can Eat drive-through for bluebottles.

Everywhere we walked we got plenty of attention due to the camera and sound men. The locals love to get on camera. I walked down the street feeling like the Pied Piper. At one point I must have had about 30 to 40 people surrounding me. I'd seen footage of Gandhi surrounded like this and always thought it was because he was very popular, but now I wonder if it was just because he had a camera crew with him.

We got to Ashek's place. It was tiny. I used to live in a really, really small place that was so small everything was en suite. I could have a bath, wash up and watch telly all at the same time, but this place was ridiculously small. It was one room with a shutter for an entrance and no windows. Basically, it was a small garage. At a guess I'd say it was 20 feet by 6 feet, and half of that was taken up with Ashek's kebab equipment. The living area was just a space of 6 feet by 5 feet at the back. You couldn't get more minimalist. No ornaments, no telly, no seating – just a blanket to sit on.

Why is a lad who's working all day on the rickshaw and all night selling kebabs living in this? I suppose Ashek worked all the time as there was no point having time off. He had nowhere to relax.

He told me that I'd be staying with him tonight. I looked around the room and asked where would be best for me to sleep. I was feeling tired, and then it started to get very confusing:

'We don't live here,' Ashek said.

'You don't live here?'

'Yeah.'

'You do live here?'

'No, no.'

'I don't understand. What do you mean? Do you live here?'

'Yeah, I live but because today are made for you . . . okay?'

'No.'

'Okay, let me explain. We don't live here.'

'You do live here, or you don't live here?'

'I live here, yeah.'

'Right, fine.'

'But now, tonight, we do not live here.'

'Who does live here?'

'Yeah.'

'WHO?'

'Both you and me, because this is too hot for you.'

'Because it's too hot for me?'

'Yeah, yeah.'

'So we're not staying here tonight?'

'No, no, no, no. You get insulted here.'

'I wouldn't be insulted if this is where you sleep. I don't mind sleeping here. Where are we staying?'

'My friend.'

'Where does your friend live?'

'He lives near to us.'

'It's gonna be the same as this, isn't it? They all look the same.'

'No, no.'

'But now I'm putting your friend out. I don't even know who your friend is and I'm taking advantage . . .'

'You are not such a thing as that.'

'I don't mind staying here.'

'Nah, they don't mind. Only you and me here, okay?'

'I tell you what, how about this: I leave you to have a nice night's sleep? You've been working hard all day. Why don't you stay at your friend's house, and we'll stay here?'

'No, no.'

'Why? I want you to have a good night's sleep. You were shattered before. I thought you were gonna collapse on me. You turned up late, you annoyed me at the beginning, I'll be honest. I was thinking, who is this bloke? He's let me down. My first day in India, where is he? You turn up, you're a nice fella. You were ill, so I can't have a go at you. You show me how to ride a bike, you show me your business, you welcome me into your house. I want you to have a bit of goodness in your life for a change. You've been working all night, you've been sweating selling chicken, after being on the bike all day. I want you to have a good night's sleep. So go to your friend's, have a good night's sleep and let me be here, honestly. I'll be fine with that.'

'No.'

'What's this place like? Explain it to me. Is it nice?'

'This place?'

'The place we're going to. Do I get an explanation of what it's like, or do you want it to be a surprise?'

'No, no, no.'

'We've got a bed?'

'Yeah.'

'Definitely got a bed?'

'Yeah, yeah, yeah.'

'Are you familiar with the Goldilocks story? These three bears, they're never happy. They've either got a bed that's too big or a bed that's too small, and I'm wondering whether I'm better off here, than in a place I haven't seen.'

'But the other is better for you.'

'It's better for me?'

'Yeah, definitely.'

'And what is that based on? What makes you think I will be happier in this other place? Will there be a telly?'

'Yeah.'

'Toilet?'

'Yeah.'

'Let's go then.'

We got to his friend's house. He was an older man. I'd say he was in his sixties. He was pleased to put us up for the night. The place was okay. Basic but clean. Ashek wasn't lying – there was a toilet but it wasn't the usual type. It was the same style as in Egypt, so he gave me a demo on how to use it. I know it doesn't sound like a great night in, but after the day I'd had it felt quite normal, although there was nothing English to watch on the telly.

I tried to have some of my friendly bacteria powder before I went to sleep, but as soon as it hit the back of my throat I sicked it back up. It was like the Indian bacteria had already taken over control of the entrance to my throat and was letting none of this friendly stuff in.

I'm definitely going to get ill.

SUNDAY 28TH FEBURARY

I was up early and had tea and biscuits. That makes it sound quite civilised, but Ashek's mate kept burping. I don't think it's rude to do that here. I'd have joined in but I've never been able to burp. When he wasn't burping he was coughing up phlegm. Once he started doing it, his wife joined in. I wondered if it was like yawning – once someone does it, everyone joins in. Since I've been in India I've heard more burps than mobile ringtones. I think they believe in the saying 'Better out than in'.

As we were about to leave, Ashek gave me a gown to wear. He said, cryptically, that the place I would be going to today would require me to wear this.

I was being kept in the dark again. It's the not-knowing part of these trips that's wearing me out the most.

I switched on my phone and received a text message from Steve:

Hi Karl, India's not all poverty and urban chaos, mate, time to get your arse up north, out of Delhi, to a place called Haridwar for some exposure to the spiritual side of India. Kumbh Mela is the biggest religious festival on the planet, only 20 million pilgrims expected. Just one hurdle – to get over there it's an eight-hour overnight bus ride.

I was annoyed as I really don't like crowds and I'm not into spiritual stuff.

I asked Luke how I was supposed to get there. He said I should grab a rickshaw and ask to go to the bus station. So I did. It was a motorised one. We passed plenty of cows, but in

India they're not in fields – they just roam down streets and sit in the middle of roads causing traffic jams. I saw four cows in the middle of the dual carriageway. I asked the driver if seeing four cows sat down in the middle of a dual carriageway meant it was going to rain. He didn't understand.

I got dropped off near the main bus depot. As soon as I got off the rickshaw I was hit by more madness. A young lad covered in blood was cutting the heads off live chickens and throwing the headless bodies into a bin that rocked from side to side as the chicken's legs kicked for the last time. Other people seemed to be covered in blood too, or at least that's what I thought until I was dragged by a local man into his garden where there were lots of people covered in red, green and yellow paint, dancing to the sound of a drum. Before I had a chance to ask what was going on, someone poured a bucket of water over my head and then pelted me with some kind of multi-coloured powder. I looked like a Dulux colour chart.

Apparently this is an annual festival called Holi Day. I don't know what the powder was but it was burning my throat and nose. My trainers were wrecked too. I wish Luke had warned me 'cos I've only had this pair since Christmas and normally my trainers last me a full year. People were dancing to the beat while others ran around with more handfuls of the colourful powder. I'm sure I was being picked on more than others because I had a camera crew following me. As I've already said, people love to get on camera here. It wouldn't surprise me if the lad cutting heads off chickens wasn't even a butcher. It might just have been a way to get my attention and try and get on TV.

I finally got to the bus station. It was grim. It was a dark, concrete structure that let in no daylight. The buses were little better. I've seen stock cars in better condition than these battered old buses that were parked all over the place with no indication of where they were going. I met a man who worked there. I told him where I wanted to go. Well, I wanted to go home if truth be told, but I told him I had to get to Haridwar. He led me towards a long queue but didn't stop at the back – he walked me right to the front. I don't know what he was thinking. It's not as if I didn't already stand out in the crowd. I had a camera crew following me, and for anyone who didn't notice that, I was also covered in multi-coloured paint from the Holi Festival. Even the blind would have heard me pushing my way to the front from the squelching of my trainers.

Then it all kicked off. A gang of men rushed forward to complain about my queue jumping. I couldn't blame them. I'd be angry if I was them. I said I was happy to go to the back of a queue. I was in no rush to get to a religious festival where there were due to be 20 million people anyway. It was all pretty awkward, and the bus was running late, but in truth this was no surprise. Delhi probably got its name from the word 'delay'.

This was another new low for my trip to India. As I waited, a man shuffled around my feet. I thought he was a shoe-shine man, but it was just a man with no legs dragging himself around begging. It's such a depressing place. Luke explained that the local people deal with all this disability by believing that these people were bad in their last life, so God has punished them by sending them back to live their next life with less limbs.

I eventually got my ticket and made it onto the crowded bus, where the aisle was crammed with bags. I struggled with my rucksack. As luck would have it, the man who had been the most angry in the bus queue was on the same bus. He was still red from anger. I was still red from the Holi festival.

KARL'S FACTS

THE TAJ MAHAL TOOK 20,000 WORKERS 22 YEARS TO BUILD.

MORE THAN 1,000 ELEPHANTS WERE USED TO TRANSPORT THE CONSTRUCTION MATERIALS.

THE TAJ IS PINKISH IN THE MORNING, MILKY WHITE IN THE EVENING AND GOLDEN IN THE MOONLIGHT. LOCALS BELIEVE THAT THIS WAS SUPPOSED TO DEPICT THE CHANGING MOODS OF WOMEN.

MONDAY 1ˢᵗ MARCH

We're into March already. I always forget February is a short month. I wish the days were shorter while I was here in India, never mind the months.

We got to Haridwar in one piece, which was a surprise. The roads in India are in a right state. I thought they were speed bumps at first and then realised they were just bumps and holes.

As we got close to the festival site, there were tents as far as the eye could see. It looked similar to Glastonbury except instead of kids wearing low-slung jeans and parkas, it was full of old men with beards wearing robes and beads.

Luke told me I was staying at Lahore Hotel. I didn't have very high hopes for it, so it was a nice surprise to find that it wasn't too bad. I was put up in a smart tent overlooking the Ganges. It had electricity and a bathroom with a shower and a normal toilet. This couldn't have been better timed, as I was on my last legs and I was starting to get stomach cramps.

I had a shower and washed off all the paint from the Holi Day festival. It was like a scene from *Psycho* as the water ran red in the shower. And then I worked my way through six cotton buds getting the paint out of my ears.

Once I was cleaned up I went to look at the Ganges. This was the first time since being in India that I'd had a little bit of calmness. Luke told me the Ganges is the holiest river in the world. I said India has the holiest roads in the world, I'll give them that.

Later we ate some curry and went to bed.

TUESDAY 2 ND MARCH

The old saying 'A change is as good as a rest' came to mind this morning. India couldn't be more of a change, yet I don't feel rested. I'm also scared to relax too much as my bowels are not in good working order. I popped a nappy into my little bag today. I didn't tell Luke because I knew that he would want to film me packing it for the TV show.

The other reason I'm finding it hard to relax is that there always seems to be something going on – something to take in. I think I've blinked less since I've been here as I don't want to miss anything, so my eyes have been open longer than normal. Maybe that's why my eyes are tired. Plus I didn't sleep well last night due to the noise outside. I woke up around 2 a.m. to some bloke on a microphone ranting on about something. Everything he said was followed by a massive cheer. It sounded like there must have been thousands of people listening to him. It was impossible to sleep. I wish I hadn't cleaned all the paint from the Holi Festival out of my ears as it had muffled things a bit.

Every day from 7 a.m. to 8 a.m. and again from 6 p.m. to 7 p.m. a chanted mantra gets played on speakers that are attached to lampposts. First, a man sings a version of the mantra, and then the same song is sung again by a woman. You can't escape it. It's like the time Bryan Adams was number one with '(Everything I Do) I Do It For You' and every radio station you clicked on was playing it. I'm going to be sick to death of hearing it by the end of the week. That's if Delhi Belly doesn't get me first.

Luke mentioned that a lot of people go to the Kumbh Mela festival to 'find themselves'. That's a saying I've never under-stood. If I did want to find myself, I don't think I'd find me at a festival with 20 million other people. I hate crowds. The other thing I worry about is what happens if I do 'find myself' and then I go home and I am all different, and Suzanne's going 'What's happened to you?' and then she doesn't like the new me that I have found. So I have just created a new problem. And then I will start to hate myself because I am not the person I thought I was. That's opening a whole can of worms. I know who I am. Bloody hell, I'm getting enough bills for Karl Pilkington so I hope I am him, 'cos if I'm not, I have no idea who I'm paying for.

I'm also worried about going to a religious festival because I'm just not that interested in it. I've never needed religion in my life. I'm not bothered that some people are into it – it's their choice – but I'm not, so what am I doing here? Even if I did get into it, I wouldn't stick at it. I don't tend to stick at anything as I get bored quite quickly. That's the reason my dad never let me keep the tortoise I found. He said they live too long and I'd lose interest. I never had gobstoppers as a kid for the same reason.

Luke gave me a newspaper to look at while we ate. It had news of Cheryl Cole's relationship problems. Weird that Cheryl Cole's love life makes it into the papers here, given all the problems there are in India. I also read about how the locals collect cow dung and clad their houses with it as a form of insulation, and then chip it off and use it to light fires with. I don't know if it's possible for houses to have 'kerb appeal' here with that going on. And I saw an advert for an Elephant Man who was due to be at the festival. He has a facial deformity but he's treated like a god as he looks a bit like the Indian god Ganesha, who has the head of an elephant and the body of a woman. I've seen quite a few ornaments of this god around India. There's also another god that has about five heads. If I see one of them as an ornament I might get it for me mam as me dad is always being heavy-handed and breaking ornaments, and the head is the first thing that breaks. At least with this one he could drop it a few times before me mam has to bin it.

There was another article about a man at the festival who has held his right arm in the air for 12 years. All the muscle has wasted away, and his nails are really long. It seems like a waste of an arm when so many people in India are missing limbs.

Then Steve called. I think he was trying to cheer me up:

STEPHEN: Alright, mate. How you getting on?

KARL: Well, I've had better holidays . . .

STEPHEN: It's not a holiday! I have to keep reminding you it is not a holiday, my friend. You are making a travel programme for the television. We haven't just sent you around the world for a holiday.

KARL: No, I know, but there should be a little bit of that. When you see people travelling around, they're normally happier than I have been here. That's all I'm saying. I have had a lot of low moments, more than I have ever had, actually.

STEPHEN: What have been your low moments this time?

KARL: Well, what do you want to know? I've been covered in a load of paint. I've seen disabled people everywhere. I've had the shits. So which one do you want to go with first?

STEPHEN: Why were you covered in paint? Did some paint fall on you? I don't understand . . . Did you walk under a ladder and some bloke drop paint on you?

KARL: It's what they do here. I don't know if they have a job-lot of powdered paint around and it's just their way of getting rid of it. There are certain things in life they just have to get shot of . . . Like 'eat 5 fruits a day' . . . It's 'cos there's loads of fruit in the world, they come up with these things.

STEPHEN: Right, I see. But this sounds like fun. People invited you into their lives. Why wouldn't that be interesting?

KARL: Because it's awkward i'n't it? I met a bloke called Ashek. Lovely bloke, really hard worker, but then it's depressing 'cos he invites me round and you know he's living . . . You know that flat I had, in town?

STEPHEN: Yeah, that was a tiny little place.

KARL: Right, it was smaller than that.

STEPHEN: Blimey. Why didn't you buy him a mirror? 'Cos mirrors are always supposed to open up space, aren't they?

KARL: Because he would have had the reflection of his own kebab shop so it would have been like he could never escape from work.

STEPHEN: Yes, but, Karl, I have said to you before, the reason why people travel is to broaden their minds. The one thing about you is that you're not good at empathy. You find it very hard to put yourself in other people's shoes. This is important. This is an eye-opener, a discovery for you. You get to see the world for what it is. Not everyone has got it cushy, not everyone has got it easy. When you're back in London you'll be thinking about him and realising that life's not so difficult.

KARL: No, right, listen. You're preaching and all that, but you're not here. You don't know where I am. You don't know where I've been. You also sent me a text message saying get down to this festival – have you seen what's there?

STEPHEN: Well, I am jealous of you, my friend. The Kumbh Mela festival is the largest spiritual festival in the world. It only happens where you are every twelve years. Millions of people walk across India to be there.

KARL: Yeah, but that's because the buses are hopeless.

STEPHEN: Karl, you are fascinated by people. You are fascinated by differences. You've always admitted that. There's people there doing extraordinary spiritual feats of endurance – blokes putting their hand in the air for years, people who lie on beds of nails. They're fascinating. Surely you want to get inside their minds? Surely you want to understand what makes them tick? We're not trying to convert you, we're trying to get you out there to explore and to meet people. This is an extraordinary opportunity.

KARL: What if I tell you this though, the bloke you're talking about, right, with the hand in the air, right. I saw some pictures of him today in the paper, and in one picture it was his left hand, and in another picture it was his right. How's that happened? What's going on there?

STEPHEN: Go and find him and ask him. You don't know what the rules are. They may be allowed to switch hands every ten minutes. I don't know. Maybe in one of them he was just putting his hand up to ask a question at a local meeting, and in the other one he was doing his spiritual thing. We don't know, but these are things you can ask . . . (Phone cuts off) Hello?

STEPHEN: Hello.

KARL: Right, what happened then, that's India for you. That's someone who's just sort of left the cable hanging out. Nothing's finished here, that's the other thing that annoys me. You go on about finding yourself and asking what is life really about, but they should forget all that and get the drainage done and get the roads re-tarmaced. There are other things in life that need sorting out. I'm not interested in all this spiritual stuff. Yes, I like the odd ghost story. Yes, I like the odd person who looks a bit weird, it sort of interests my eyes for a few seconds, but it doesn't mean that I want to be in the middle of twenty million people to see it.

STEPHEN: You've got to be out of your comfort zone. That is the very nature of what you are doing.

KARL: I've been out of me comfort zone since I've been here.

STEPHEN: Life is different from all the other tiny little worlds that you think it's all about. It is a fascinating, giant world out there. You've got to experiment and see these things. You don't have to be right in the middle. You can hang around on the outskirts and meet some interesting people. You're not going to get crushed. You know you are not a tiny little animal that needs to be nurtured – you're a fully-grown man who can look after himself. You're going to be fine.

KARL: You see, if you had said, how about going up into space and having a look down on it, I'd be happy with that. That would be an amazing sight. I'd be on me own. I wouldn't be crushed. I could still say I had seen it. In fact, I'd do the lot up there. Let's get all the wonders done in one go instead of all this piss-arsing about staying in places that I'm not happy in, having the shits, eating curry left, right and centre. There is only so much of it you can take. I don't want to moan . . .

STEPHEN: You don't want to moan, you don't want to moan!

KARL: But I don't understand why you think I have got to 'find myself'. Where's that come from? You've never said that to me since I've known you.

STEPHEN: I'm not saying that. I'm not saying that you have to 'find yourself'. You could try and find yourself and have a look for me while you're there. It's up to you, I don't mind. I am saying, just go and experience it. You don't have to have a religious epiphany, you don't have to find spirituality or god, you don't have to become Hindu – just go.

KARL: But that's like going to a brothel and going, 'don't mind me, I'm just going to stand over here and watch.' Either you get involved or you shouldn't be there, and that's how I feel. I shouldn't be there. I've got no aim in life to suddenly find myself or . . . Or this spirituality stuff you keep on harping on about. It's not me, and what happens if you change me and you change me a lot, and then we don't get on? What then? You've lost a mate.

STEPHEN: We're not getting on right now so what's the problem? Maybe you will be a calmer and nicer bloke by the end of it. Maybe you will be someone who is not whingeing all the time! Bloody hell, mate, you've been to Egypt now. You've been to Rio . . . I thought you would start to see how things are different around the world.

KARL: Yeah.

STEPHEN: It's a beautiful, weird and extraordinary place.

WEDNESDAY 3 RD MARCH

I was told that when I go to the Kumbh Mela festival I'm not to wear any leather otherwise I won't be allowed in. It's the cow thing again. I still don't know who came up with the cow rule.

I saw lots of babas at the festival today. These are people who walk about with next to nothing on and have ash all over their bodies. I was blessed by quite a few of them. The interpreter told me I had to give each one of them 100 rupees (£1) if I took a blessing. It could be an expensive place to be if you had a cold and kept sneezing.

I did some yoga with a baba. He laughed because I couldn't stretch as well as he could. It was hardly surprising really as he was stark bollock naked apart from a pair of shades, while I was wearing combat pants with the pockets stuffed full of toffees I'd taken from the first-class lounge at the airport. The guide said if I gave him some more money he would show me more. I don't know what more there was to see from this fella. The way he was bending upside down in my face I could have checked his prostate gland. Instead I asked if he knew the one-armed baba or the Elephant Man. He pointed me in the right direction and I wandered off.

As I walked, another baba who looked like Bill Oddie tried to get me to smoke some drugs, but I turned him down. The interpreter said I might have disrespected him by doing this. I asked Bill Oddie if he knew the one-armed baba. He said he did. It felt a bit like a big council estate where everyone knows each other, but only by their nickname. On the estate I grew up on there was Scruffy Sandra, Jimmy the Hat, John the Screw, Fred the Veg, Shorts Man, Miss Piggy and Tattoo Stan (he was my uncle).

We found Elephant Man. To be honest, I couldn't tell if he was happy as his face didn't have any sort of expression. He also had what looked like little tumours all over his body. It sounds strange to say it, but he didn't look that weird to me. I don't know why, maybe it's 'cos I've seen a lot of extraordinary things while I've been in India. The other thing was, he wasn't wearing much. I think he probably would've looked weirder if he had been wearing a pair of jeans and a shirt and tie. I don't know if that makes sense, but it does to me.

I asked how old he was as it was impossible to tell. I've always thought about that when I've watched the Elephant Man film. He could've got on a bus and taken the OAP seat, or bought fags underage. The baba said he was around 45/46. He said he was happy with his condition. He was looked at as a god and was proud to be part of this clan. And he said he wouldn't have an operation to sort it out.

I think the man he was sat with felt left out and wanted some attention. I say this 'cos he suddenly got up and wrapped his knob and bollocks around his walking stick and then jumped up and down. It looked unbelievably painful. I asked what he was playing at. Our interpreter said something about how sex is not important to him and he lets people know this by wrecking his knob and bollocks. I asked if he had to have the walking stick because he was pulling that trick day-in day-out, but the interpreter didn't want to ask.

It was definitely one of the strangest moments of my life – sat in India with a man with the head of an elephant while his mate twisted his tackle around a stick. There you go, Steve. I've broadened my mind.

I eventually met the one-armed man I had seen in the paper. He was surrounded by lots of hangers-on. It seemed like he was the main baba to be with. I sat down and gave him 200 rupees, and he blessed me and gave me some ash to eat. I know it sounds odd, but after having curry three times a day, eating ash was a refreshing change. I asked why he'd decided to do this endurance thing with his arm. The translator told me it's not a new thing – there are some babas that do it with one leg up, both hands up, both legs up. They never stand on their feet. Apparently doing it is a way to get closer to connecting with the gods and to focus on what life is about.

I asked a few questions the translator didn't want to ask the baba. I asked if the baba was right-handed before he did this. I wanted to know how much he gave up for his beliefs. I then asked if he could remember the last thing he did with his arm before he gave it up. Again the translator didn't want to ask. I told him I thought it was a good question as it must have been quite a significant moment in his life. Eventually the translator asked and then told me that the baba didn't want to answer. In fact, he said that we should leave. I really hope I didn't upset him.

I thought about the one-armed man on the way back to the tent. We all dedicate our lives to something. I've been with Suzanne for 17 years. That's dedication. I don't know if the one-armed man is married – I should have asked that. And how would he help around the house? Other than the ironing, most chores would be impossible. Suzanne wouldn't be happy if I said, 'You'll have to change the sheets on your own from now on as I'm gonna stick me arm in the air for the rest of my life.' It's just a great excuse to be lazy, really. I noticed in every picture that the baba's sat down. It's not like he's running about having to make his other arm do extra work to pull his weight. He's just sat there doing nothing.

Bit daft, really.

THURSDAY 4 TH MARCH

I met a guru in an ashram today. He was an old, friendly fella. He was called Swami Ji. We talked to each other about our beliefs. He told me how our hearts should control our actions, but too many people let their brains rule their lives. I said that I'm like that. The only time my heart tells me anything is when it gets heartburn, and it's telling me I've had too much pie. Pastry does that to me.

I think he liked me. We had a good laugh together, and even though we had totally different lives we agreed on a lot of the rules by which we lived. We meditated, and I had a go on his rubber dinghy, and then I swam in the Ganges. I wasn't planning on getting in, but I liked the way he listened to my point of view after I had listened to his, so I felt that I should do something for him. Maybe that was my heart talking.

India is finally starting to feel quite normal.

I'm staying in his ashram tonight and have to be up early as we are making our way over to Agra to finally see the Taj – that, after all, is the whole reason for being here. But I don't know if my memories of India will be of a building. They'll be of the weirdness of the place.

I checked my phone before I went to bed. Ricky had left a message for me:

> RICKY: Alright, mate, how's it going? Just having a cup of tea. Just catching up on Sky Plus, just got back from New York – flew overnight, first class, ba, don't get better than that. Slept all the way after a few glasses of champagne. Those flat beds are amazing, aren't they? Yeah, speak to you later. Bye. Must get on with it.

I hate to think how much it cost me to listen to that.

FRIDAY 5 TH MARCH

I was woken early and had breakfast with the guru. We had some spicy Rice Krispies and a spicy biscuit with some really sweet, milky tea. Not the way I normally like it, but I drank it anyway as I didn't want to offend him. I suppose that is my heart telling me how to act instead of my head again. My arse may get involved later though.

And so we set off to see the Taj. I was expecting it to be a full day of travelling, until we pulled over and Luke asked me to come and meet a Hare Krishna. He gave me a tour of his cow sanctuary. These cows were spoilt rotten. It's all to do with the Hare Krishna god being a fan of cows. I helped wash one, and then they sang a song to it and blessed it. It didn't look very happy. It looked embarrassed, if anything.

They then got me to help make some dung cakes. These are the same cowpats I had seen in the newspaper that the locals use to clad their homes with, and then chip off to help fires burn for longer. They told me to get both hands into the big fresh pile of dung and to make a pancake by slamming it on the ground and then patting it flat. Odd how they made a point of saying how the dung was 'fresh', as if that makes it more acceptable to stick your hands in. It's the first time I've heard the word 'fresh' used while in India.

I made two dung cakes, and they got me to sign my name in them.

Before I left, they took me to the gift shop. I was the only one in there, which was no great surprise given that all the products were made from cow poo and piss. Hardly Bodyshop, is it? In this day and age, when every product has to list all its contents on the label, a shop like this is never going to be big business. They packaged them up well, but as the saying goes, 'You can't polish a turd'. And believe me, this place has tried.

They were selling face creams, soaps, cures for baldness and obesity, soap and a special urine 'antiseptic aftershave for men'. The man rubbed some of the baldness cure cream onto my head. It was definitely a hairdressing 'first'. Back home I ask my barber to do a number two, but normally it stands for the shaver guard size – not literally a number two.

As I write this, I'm back in the van on the way to Agra. It seems like a more mental place than Delhi. I think the choice of names in India really sums the place up. I've already said Delhi sounds like 'delay', and now I think about it, India sounds like 'In Dire' and Agra like 'Aggro'. It can't be a coincidence.

I will have to stop writing now as the roads are bad and I feel sick. It's difficult to know if it is car sickness or the smell of cow shit on my head that's causing it.

SATURDAY 6 TH MARCH

I really didn't sleep well at all last night. I felt really ill. Woke up in the night being sick, and I also had a dodgy belly. The toilet is too far from the sink which is not what you need in India as both are often required at the same time when it's coming out of both ends. I've spent more time sat on the loo in this hotel room than anywhere else. To me, it's a loo with an en suite bedroom.

To be honest, I wasn't really in the mood to see the Taj Mahal, what with the Delhi Belly and everything, but we had to go as we only had permission to film in there for today.

Luke told me it is a mausoleum that took 22 years to build. The Mughal Emperor Shahjahan had it built for his wife, who died giving birth to their fourteenth son. It was supposed to stand as the perfect symbol of love.

It seems to me like it was something the man had always wanted to build but his wife didn't let him, so when she died he used it as an excuse to build his dream. My uncle always wanted a plasma telly, but his wife didn't want him wasting money on one. Soon as she died he got one.

We went to get a closer look. It's weird how it is classed as one of the modern Wonders of the World. You wouldn't think so by the surroundings. If it was on one of them property programmes, the potential buyers would say, 'If you could pick it up and put it somewhere nicer, we'd buy it.' It really shouldn't have been built here.

There were hundreds of people outside: half of them selling postcards, plates, key rings and snow domes; the others were tourists.

As soon as we got in we were greeted by another queue. This time it was to get on the Princess Diana bench. This is where Diana had her photo taken when she was having her problems with Charlie. Everyone said this is why she looked so miserable, but to be honest I think it was nothing to do with him. I just think she was sick of being in India. It does have that effect on you. If you're having a low moment in your life, India isn't a great place to come to try and get over it. I'd have suggested Center Parcs to her over this place.

There was a woman sat on the bench who was trying to re-enact the famous Diana shot. A man with a camera directed her. 'You look too happy. Look sadder.'

I was shown around by a guide called Remish. He was better than most guides. We chatted as we walked, which made a change from just being talked at for an hour. He told me how the building was perfectly symmetrical. Again this seemed an odd idea for a structure that was built to show true love. I wondered if the man had some sort of OCD.

Remish showed me some optical illusions. When I moved backwards and then forwards while looking at the Taj from an archway, it gave the illusion that it was moving with me. There was also a marble effect that messed with your eyes and gave the impression the marble was cut at angles when it was actually flat. All of which was very clever, but I didn't really understand why the Mughal emperor would put optical illusions onto his wife's tomb. It would be like having a Sudoku carved into your loved one's gravestone.

The more I saw, the more impressed I became with the workmanship. Maybe I liked it for the wrong reasons, but it really was amazing.

We decided to lose the crowds and catch a view of the Taj from a boat on the Humana River. It was much quieter on this side of the building. In fact, it was probably the most relaxed I'd been since arriving in India. No car horns, no begging, no shouting, no mantras. It was almost perfect. I say 'almost', as I noticed a plume of smoke coming from the edge of the river just next to the Taj. I asked Remish what it was, and he told me it was where they were burning dead bodies.

Like I've said, you're never far away from something mad when you're in India.

INDIA

INDIA

TRYING TO BLEND IN.

A COW CELEBRATING HOLI DAY.

ME RIDING ASHEK AROUND ON HIS RICKSHAW.

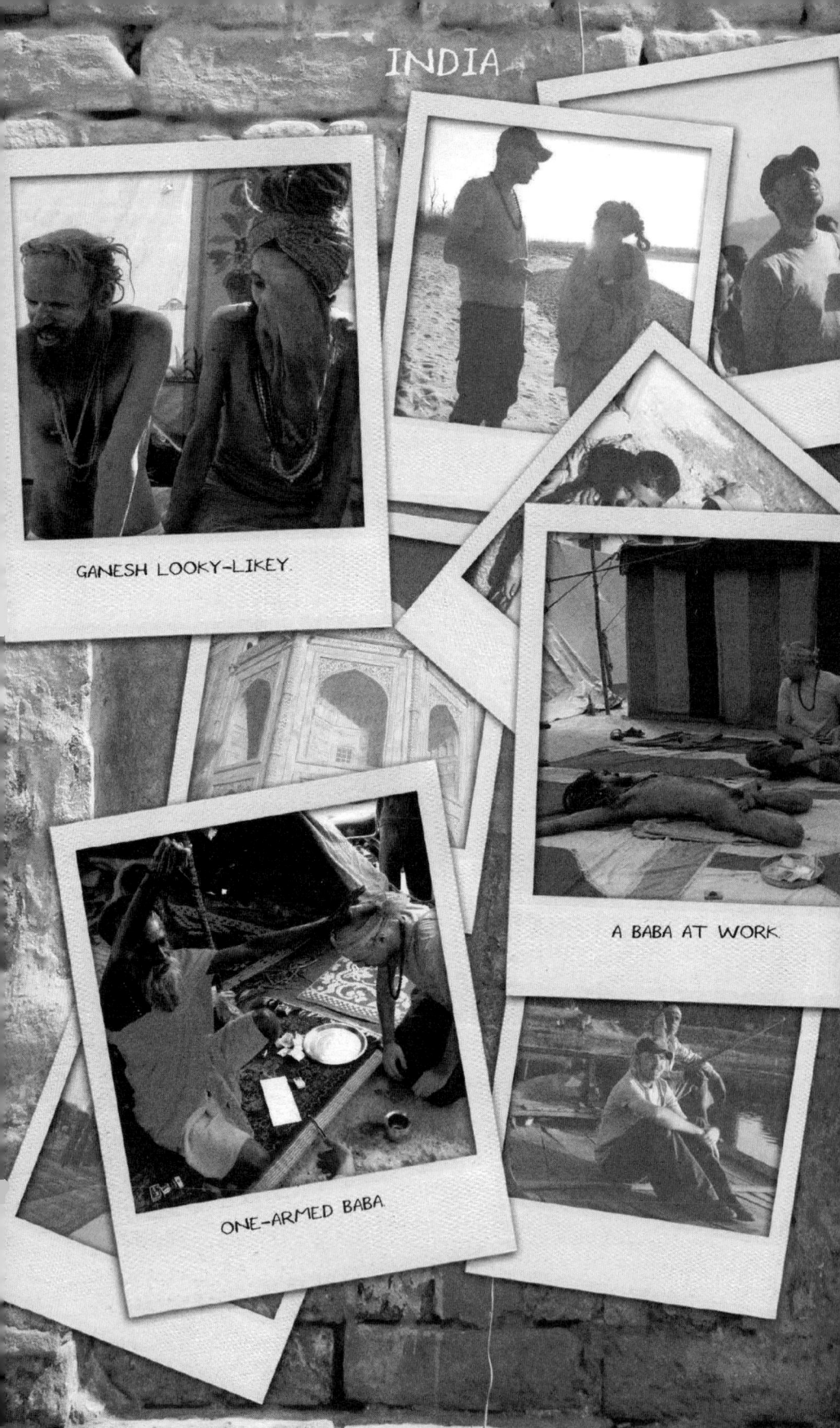

INDIA

GANESH LOOKY-LIKEY.

A BABA AT WORK.

ONE-ARMED BABA.

SAINT DEATH. A FEW YEARS OLDER THAN THE POPE.

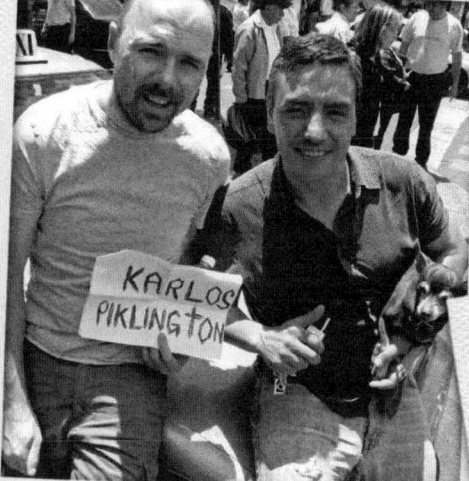

KARLOS PIKLINGTON

ME AND EDGAR THE CAB DRIVER.

THIS IS JACK HE LOOKS FRIENDLY BUT HE'S A KILLER.

THE PROFESSIONAL'S NAME IS SHOCKER. IM SHOCKING.

I DON'T BELIEVE IN FIGHTING TILL THE END.

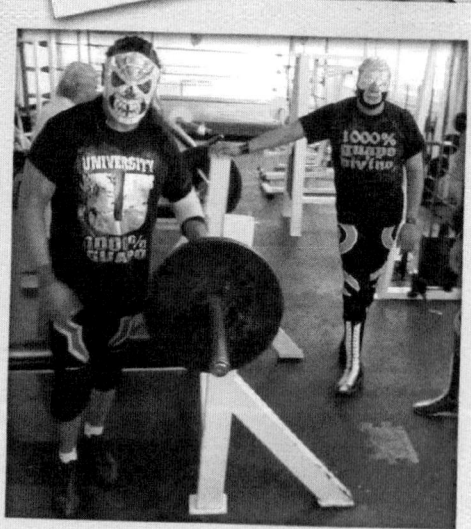

HARDLY L.A. FITNESS IS IT?

WE'RE PLAYING TWISTER HERE. IM WINNING.

CHAPTER FOUR
CHICHEN ITZA

'THE MOST FAMOUS, SPECTACULAR AND CONSEQUENTLY MOST FREQUENTLY VISITED OF MEXICO'S MAYAN SITES.'

1,000 PLACES TO SEE BEFORE YOU DIE

'IT'S AN ODD ONE, THE CHICHEN ITZA. IT WAS BUILT BY THE ORIGINAL MAYANS AS A PLACE FOR SACRIFICE AND RIPPING OUT PEOPLE'S HEARTS AND CUTTING HEADS OFF. NOT EXACTLY ALTON TOWERS, IS IT?'

KARL PILKINGTON

THURSDAY 1ST APRIL

I'm quite lucky really. It's only just hit me that not many people get to go and see the things I'm seeing and get paid for the privilege. I looked at a world map in a bookshop the other day to see where I've already been. It wasn't that long ago when I was telling Ricky that he was daft for having a world map in his house. I remember saying, 'Why do you need that? It's not the sort of map you'd ever need in your glove compartment in the car, is it?' Mind you, they do maps of the universe now. At what point do you take that with you when you leave the house? It's not as if astronauts would even buy it as I've heard the universe is forever expanding so the book's out of date before the ink's even dried.

I got my stuff together today. Jamie the producer came and chatted while I packed. I told him I had no idea about Mexico. The only thing I could think of was Chiquito, that Mexican restaurant you normally find in those shopping centres off motorways. They have wraps and spicy dips, which I quite like, but liking the food doesn't mean you'll like the country. I like curry, but India was the worst place I'd ever been to.

Jamie told me that Mexico is quite a lawless place. I don't know if that's a bad thing. If I lived in a place where there were no laws I don't know if I'd do anything too differently. I think most people who do illegal stuff are doing it 'cos they know it's wrong. They do it for the buzz. I nicked stuff as a kid, but it was stuff I didn't really need. I nicked from my local newsagent – things like rulers and pens, and a protractor. I didn't even know how to use it, but I knew I shouldn't have been taking it. If they'd been free, I wouldn't have been interested.

Now Jamie has told me this lawless stuff, I'm guessing Mexico will be like the game Grand Theft Auto I used to play on my

PlayStation. You could just drive around running people over or shooting and blowing things up, but you soon get bored with it. I think you need to feel like you have a purpose in life.

The only other thing I'm aware of in Mexico is cactus. Odd things, they are. I'd never buy one. They're for people who can't look after nice plants. They're not that nice to look at. The only place I ever see them is in doctors' and dentists' waiting rooms. My auntie has a few but she's put them in her porch as some sort of security round her windows. She uses them as natural barbed wire.

FRIDAY 2 ND APRIL

Good Friday. Our flight today was with a Mexican airline and I'm not a fan of flying with foreign airlines as all the announcements were in Mexican before English, which worried me. In an emergency everyone would be well out of the aircraft before I even knew what was happening. I suppose this is a good reason to learn a language.

It was a long flight, about 12 hours. I'm not very good at sitting in a chair for any length of time – it's one of the reasons I could never go on Mastermind. I suffer with Restless Legs Syndrome. My legs aren't happy unless they are walking somewhere or moving about. People who don't have it can't understand it. I sometimes go to bed and leave my legs hanging out the side with my feet on the ground as this takes away the odd sensation. I'm the only person I know who has to go to bed before my legs do.

What didn't help was the plane having a big screen at the front that kept informing us of how long there was to go before landing. I don't like knowing stuff like that. I had to turn the word count off my laptop when I was writing my other books as it does my head in knowing I have to write 40,000 or so words. There's a saying that goes 'Why use 100 words when you can say it in 10?' I'll tell you why – I have a word count to meet.

I was picked up at the airport by a bloke called Edgar. He couldn't pick me up right outside the airport as he was not an official taxi driver. He called me to say he was on the other side of the dual carriageway. I had to cross the busy roads while getting directions off him on the phone and dragging my suitcase. It was like playing Frogger. He was holding a sign that said 'Karlos Piklington'. I couldn't be bothered correcting him. People in England always get it wrong – Pillington, Pilockton, Pillickington and Dilkington – so I could hardly have a go at him.

Edgar's cab was quite battered. He had a dog but not a dog that I would have expected a man like Edgar to have. It was a Chihuahua called Jack. It was hyperactive. If it wasn't jumping all over me and trying to have it away with my arm, it was coughing up hairballs. The problem with Chihuahuas is they have bulbous eyes so it looked like it was choking even when it wasn't. Edgar explained that it had been given to his mam as a gift, but she gave it to Edgar to look after. We were given me mam's mam's dog when she died. It was a poodlestyle thing that had been spoilt rotten. It never really settled with us as we didn't have time to spoil it. It ended up looking a bit of a mess after crawling under our car and getting covered in oil. It also got hit by a car and ended up running sideways like a crab. It used to howl whenever the *Coronation Street* theme tune was coming from the telly as it must have reminded it of me mam's mam, who was a big fan. Me dad had it put down one Christmas. *Coronation Street* had been on almost continually over the festive period and the howling was doing his head in.

Edgar chatted a lot, like most cabbies, except his opening gambit wasn't about football or politics. He just wanted to know if my girlfriend had a nice arse. I told him there was plenty of it. He laughed. Talk of Suzanne's arse broke the ice, which was good. I might have to bring it up again with other people I meet if the conversion becomes a struggle.

Edgar then put his stereo on and said he would play me some traditional Mexican music. It sounded quite upbeat and reminded me of the music my mam used to have blaring out of the caravan in Wales from our 8-track player. I asked what the song was about, and he told me it was about drug dealers in Mexico. He explained the lyrics – something about a car that is found in the middle of the road with the doors open and the passengers have had their heads cut off and blood is oozing out of the car. I don't know how the story ends as his dog was coughing up hairballs again and I couldn't really hear what Edgar was saying.

After a few miles Edgar pulled his car over and told me he wanted to show me Santa Muerte. In English this translates as 'Saint Death'. It was a glass box about the size of the small kiosks you get outside Tube stations selling chocolate, crisps and fags. There were no crisps in this box, but there were fags along with a skeleton dressed in robes surrounded by booze. The poorer people and criminals of Mexico who are not very religious but not quite atheists either worship Saint Death. I've never thought about it before but I suppose bad people might need someone to pray to, too. As we looked at the skeleton, a car with tinted windows pulled over for a few seconds. The men in it bowed their heads before skidding off again.

We drove on to an Easter festival that Edgar said it would be worthwhile my having a look at. Easter seems to be a big deal in Mexico. I saw people acting out some Bible story on stage watched by hundreds of people. I heard choking, but it wasn't

Edgar's dog this time. It was coming from a man who was being hanged. The thing is, Mexico loves violence so much it could just be something to keep the crowd interested before the Jesus bit happens. Kids aged two and three were sat on their dads' shoulders so they could see the hanging being acted out.

I wandered off around the market where I found a woman selling dead crickets. Ricky used to buy them to give to his pet salamander, but it was locals who were knocking these ones back. I'm not sure how long a bag of crickets should last – I don't know what the recommended daily allowance is – but one old man who I'd expect to see sucking on Werther's Originals couldn't get enough of them. They were quite cheap so maybe it's the low cost that attracts people to them. Or should that be locust? Oh, never mind.

They were stacked high on a metal tray with half a lime placed on the side as a garnish. Flies circled. Maybe they were a pudding for anyone who was after a second course.

I'm not very good with strange food. I don't like the stuff that chef Heston Blumenthal knocks up, like bacon-and-egg ice cream. I don't want to be challenged when eating, I just want to get rid of hunger.

Jamie the producer kept asking me to try a cricket. He said he wasn't going to let me leave without eating one. So I did. It didn't taste bad but it wasn't great either. I'd heard street food was a big thing here in Mexico but I didn't think it meant the creatures that lived on the street.

I carried on watching the Easter parade. I'm not a big fan of Easter, though I did have a chocolate egg before I left that was a gift from Suzanne's mam. She knows I'm a fan of chocolate more than a fan of religion, but I am a fan of chocolate. I think that's how most people are with Easter. It's a religious event that's been created to get fat, greedy people interested. I don't know why we celebrate with an egg. Bit odd that it's all about Jesus being crucified and giving up his life, and then years later we give him respect for what he did by eating a chocolate egg . . . with a small bag of Smarties inside. Are Kinder Eggs sold all year round for really religious people who never forget?

I stood on a busy corner and waited for something to happen. Twenty minutes later a crowd came walking up the street. In the middle was a man who was dressed like – and looked like – Jesus, carrying a massive cross while being lightly whipped. Jamie told me that every year there is a long list of people who want to play Jesus. It is a real privilege to get the part. I never wanted to play him in the school nativity play, which is just as well as I was never offered it. I got to be a shepherd and say the line 'We've travelled from afar' and then I played the drum during the song 'Little Donkey', even though I wasn't supposed to, as the drum was actually there for 'We Three Kings', but I couldn't help myself. Still, it was more than me mate Carl Grimshaw got to do; his job was to hit a triangle as the star appeared in the sky. This is the problem with overcrowded inner-city schools – there aren't enough parts for everyone in the nativity story. I'm surprised Mrs Mathews didn't change the carol to 'We Six Kings' just to get more kids involved.

I was walking alongside Jesus when he started to struggle carrying the big oak cross up the steep hill. I could imagine that this is how it really was all them years ago, if you took away the taco and candyfloss stalls. Jesus dropped the cross. I thought it was all part of the act until I saw the equivalent of a St John's Ambulance man getting out a tube of Savlon to rub on Jesus's leg, which ruined the illusion a bit. And all this was happening as a man dressed as a guard played the recorder, an instrument I thought was only played by four-year-olds. All in all it was really doing my head in.

They eventually got to a field where the crosses were erected, and Jesus and two other fellas were sacrificed. Not for real – though Jamie did say they used to put real nails through their hands and feet but stopped in the late 1980s, maybe thanks to the invention of Unibond No More Nails.

Before we left, one of the other blokes who was on a cross (not sure who he was playing the part of as I don't know the story well enough) was taken down and put into an ambulance. Not exactly a happy family day out, this one. A chocolate egg would lighten the mood a bit.

We got to the hotel quite late and I fell straight into bed.

Woke up in the night to use the toilet (don't think the cricket I ate agreed with me) to find that it wouldn't flush. The ballcock had lodged the water inlet so the cistern wasn't filling. I fixed it. It's not exactly the sort of problem Michael Palin has to deal with, is it? I noticed a sign stating that toilet paper should be put in the bin and NOT DOWN THE TOILET. I think we should do this at home. We would get fewer criminals nicking people's identities if they had to rummage through bin bags full of used toilet tissue.

SATURDAY 3ᴿᴰ APRIL

I woke up this morning to find that Ricky had sent me a text.

> Call me. Need to go over the rules of Mexican wrestling with you.

I called him.

RICKY: Did you get my text?

KARL: I got something about wrestling.

RICKY: Yeah, did you pack any shorts or swimming trunks or anything? Maybe a leotard?

KARL: No, I didn't pack anything like that. No.

RICKY: That was a long shot, wasn't it? But, listen, you'll be all right. I've arranged for you to do a bit of wrestling.

KARL: Wrestling?

RICKY: Yeah.

KARL: What does that have to do with the Seven Wonders? I'm here to see a wonder.

RICKY: Yeah, well, the general public will count it as a wonder, seeing you in a Boston crab being flung around. It's an honour. It's huge in Mexico. Wrestlers are like superstars. They're heroes, and they've got outfits and nicknames. What I would like to see maybe is you in a flesh-coloured body stocking and like a Spiderman mask, but it's completely orange. If you get a stretchy one, it'll fit your perfectly spherical head. Or maybe just stick you in a hollowed-out pumpkin or something and then you can be the Satsuma Kid or the Tangerine Dream, or we can just get that bloke who calls you out to go, 'And here's Karl Pilkington. He's got a head like a fucking orange.' Sound all right?

KARL: Is it like old-fashioned wrestling where not much happens and you sort of just push each other around?

RICKY: Yeah. I'm sure once they teach you a few moves and how to land without breaking anything important, it'll be fine. Oh, and explain to them the safest thing for you is to land on your head. Tell them that you're not like other men, and that as long as they aim for the little, round, really hard, hollow bit on the top that you probably won't sustain any major injuries. Imagine if some fella, right, picked you up and threw you across the ring, and you got up and started quoting Oscar Wilde. Picture that. If they literally knocked some sense into you. Just go and enjoy it.

KARL: Well, I've had enough practice. I mean, you've had me in a headlock now and again.

RICKY: And they probably won't be as heavy as me.

KARL: But they are wrestlers. There's no more surprises here is there? It's not naked sumo or anything?

RICKY: No, that's when you go to Japan.

KARL: All right.

RICKY: Enjoy yourself.

I haven't seen wrestling since the 1980s. I used to watch it with me dad on Saturday afternoons – Big Daddy and Giant Haystacks and the rest. It was a good thing to watch as a kid as it was never that violent. It was just two sweaty, old, overweight men pushing and shoving each other until one of them wanted to stop to get something to eat. There doesn't seem to be any sport for fat people since they stopped it.

By about 1983 people were embarrassed to say that they watched it. That's probably why some wrestlers started wearing masks; they were embarrassed to be involved with it.

Mexican wrestling was different. Ricky was right. They do dress like superheroes.

I met Sandy, the woman who ran the wrestling arena. She took me through some photos of the wrestlers she looked after. She had all shapes and sizes. Something for everyone. El Porky, a little, chubby fella who looked like Russell Grant; midgets; big women; and sexy women.

I texted Suzanne to let her know I was about to do some wrestling. She just said to be careful but then went on to ask how to set the DVD player up as it wasn't plugged into the telly. It's not the greatest encouragement, is it? It's not the sort of message Rocky got from Adrian before a big fight. I didn't bother replying.

Sandy took me to meet the wrestler I'd be training with. His name was Shocker. He was built like a brick shithouse. He looked bigger because he did that thing all people with muscles do of tucking his T-shirt into his jeans. I asked Sandy if I could get one of the midget fighters but she said none of them was around today.

I explained to Shocker that he would have to be careful with me as I did my back in when I was a kid by trying to kick my height and landing on my arse, my wrist is also weak from a crash I had, and I've got a trapped nerve in my leg. He didn't really seem to be listening, which was a worry. He gave me an outfit to wear. I looked a mess. I decided to name myself Shocking.

I did some weights and about 45 minutes in the ring with Shocker and two other fellas. I felt so sick. I'd eaten some marshmallows earlier – not the greatest pre-fitness food – so that combined with being thrown around was not a good idea.

Shocker was a year older than me, but I felt a lot older. I had to stop as I felt exhausted and really dizzy. I was trying to get out of the ring when one of the other two wrestlers grabbed me and sat on me whilst wrapping my legs around my neck. I felt helpless, like a deer that was slowly being eaten by an anaconda. The only memory I have was how the wrestler's balls that were thrust into my face left a saltiness on my lips. At first I assumed it was from the tacos, and then I realised I'd not eaten any today.

I stayed in and watched Shocker fight tonight. He was with two other wrestlers, the Blue Panther and El Porky. They won. The crowd seemed to love El Porky. It must annoy Shocker when he trains so hard and eats so well to then have to fight with a bloke whose main exercise is to the fridge and back.

Off to bed now 'cos I'm knackered. The Mexican altitude makes everything tougher and more tiring. I reckon I could have beaten Shocker if I was on my own turf.

SUNDAY 4TH APRIL

I had about four hours sleep then was woken by police sirens. They have a selection of sirens to choose from. One goes waaa

. . . waaa, then there's woo woo and wooooooooooo and daaa daaa. The copper seemed to decide to go through the choice of sirens at four in the morning outside my room. He was like one of them people on the Tube in London who decides to use their commute to see what other ringtones they've got on their mobile.

I had breakfast downstairs while having to listen to a loud American woman who kept asking why the French bloke who ran the hotel sounded French rather than Mexican. I could see she was annoying him, but he just smiled. She was doing my head in. Where is a noisy police siren when you want one?

Then Steve called.

KARL: Alright, mate. How's it going?

STEPHEN: Not too bad. How about you?

KARL: It's all right, you know. I'm not having a bad time here. Yeah, I'm actually liking this one. Which is an odd thing to say 'cos I was wrestling yesterday.

STEPHEN: You were wrestling?

KARL: Yeah. Ricky set something up. I went to a wrestling place 'cos it's big over here. They love their wrestling.

STEPHEN: How did you get on?

KARL: It depends. If it's edited badly it will come across that I'm weak, but I got a few good moves in there. And there was three against one so, you know, it was hard work.

STEPHEN: Well, I know you like crowds, and there is a big, very authentic Mexican Easter Sunday celebration happening today. The government is trying to ban it. You know bureaucrats, off the wall. But there's a local fella, Carlos. He's taking part and he wants to get you involved.

KARL: What do you mean 'get involved'? What do you mean about the banning bit?

STEPHEN: I don't know the ins and outs of it. You'll have to speak to Carlos. All I know is that they're trying to close it down. Maybe you could use your showbiz time to try and save it. Maybe there is something about the event that makes them worried. I'm not sure. That is for you to investigate, my friend.

KARL: But I've been here for a couple of days and I've seen that they're not really bothered about the health and safety of anything. So if they're actually worried about the health and safety of something it must be pretty mental.

STEPHEN: Well, you're meeting Carlos at some place called the Rambo Chicken so maybe that's got something to do with it.

KARL: The Rambo Chicken? There's a chicken named Rambo?

STEPHEN: I don't know the ins and outs of it. I haven't been there. I'm envious of you, as always.

KARL: I'm meeting him at a chicken called . . . is that what . . . is the Wonder called Chicken Eats Ya? Is that what that's named after? Is that what this is all about? A tough chicken?

STEPHEN: It could just be an incredibly violent chicken. I don't know, my friend. I am just a messenger from Carlos.

KARL: All right then. I'll go and see him.

STEPHEN: Cheers, mate. And it's nice to see you finally embracing this.

KARL: No, honestly, I am. I haven't been moaning that much at all on this one. I think you will be proud of me.

STEPHEN: Good, mate. I'm already proud of you.

Carlos was a decent enough lad. He took me round the food market. I saw loads of chicken heads laid out on a tray. It looked like the kids' game Guess Who? I eat chicken – big fan of it – so I should be happy to eat its head, but these ones didn't look happy. At least when you see a fish head they don't have an upset expression on their face, but the chickens looked proper dead with their eyes rolled into their heads and beaks open. Carlos said Mexicans just boil them and they're ready to eat. I wonder if someone has got chicken heads mixed up with chicken eggs.

Before we left the market I tried donkey meat. This was the worst meat I have ever had. It's dark, chewy, fatty, smelly meat. I've heard the dodo died out due to it not tasting nice, in which case I think the donkey will be next.

Carlos then took me to his neighbourhood. People were out on the streets. Small papier-mâché bulls were being painted. Carlos told me that local people attach fireworks to these model cows, stick them on their heads and then run into a crowd. Mexico is like MTV's *Jackass*. As we were walking down the street I saw the man who was making the fireworks. I'm not sure if he saw me as he only had one eye. At home he'd be retired now after an accident at work like that. Here in Mexico they say, 'Carry on working. You have another one.' He was working out of two carrier bags. One contained paper that he was using to make the tube, the other bag was full of gunpowder.

We carried on to Carlos's home, where I met his parents. While we were having a drink there was a massive explosion. It reminded me about what Steve had said about the event being banned. Carlos said it has already been banned in many areas of Mexico due to deaths. Jamie the producer came in from outside acting all weird. I asked him what was going on, but he wouldn't say. He then asked if I wanted to get involved and run down the street with a bull on my head while fireworks went off. I said the cyclops firework-maker had put me off going any-where near this event. I asked Carlos if he would be doing it. It turned out that Carlos normally stays in on this day as it can be quite dangerous on the streets. His mam and dad went on to say how they normally go away for the weekend but stayed this time as they knew I was coming.

Outside, I saw a crowd of about 300 people and a papier-mâché cow covered in fireworks. People were throwing buckets of liquid over themselves. I thought it might have been petrol just to add a bit more danger to the whole thing, but Carlos told me it was water so they can't catch fire. The fuses were lit, and the crowd ran. I hid behind a wall until the fireworks stopped then I told Jamie the producer that I wasn't hanging around. But as I walked down the road I heard people shouting. I turned to see I was being chased by what seemed like the whole neigh-bourhood. I legged it. Carlos caught up with me, and we ran into a house that belonged to his cousin. He said we should go up to the roof where we would be safe.

What the hell has this got to do with Easter?

We stayed on the roof for a good two hours, dodging fireworks. Finally, there seemed to be a quiet spell – I suppose the one-eyed firework-maker couldn't keep up with the demand – so we ventured out to a local place for something to eat. It was my kind of place – mainly old people. There was a live band playing nice, happy-sounding music. It was all in Mexican but it sounded good. But then who knows, it could have been about someone having their head cut off like the stuff Edgar told me. I sat and watched old people dancing while munching through some biscuits that were on the table until an old woman came over and dragged me up. I thought she might have lost her husband recently so I felt I had a duty to give her a dance, but then I saw her five minutes later with another bald-headed fella. I think she was just old and her eyesight had gone a bit and she thought I was him. I really don't know how people get to be old in this mental town.

MONDAY 5TH APRIL

I caught sight of a few local newspapers today. They all had gruesome pictures on the cover. There was a big photo of a car accident with dead bodies and a picture of an old man who had shot himself in the head. Back home a headline like 'Shocking Images Inside' normally end up being just of Charlotte Church on a beach with a spot on her arse. I suppose if you're seeing bloody images like this every day they're bound to become less shocking and make you more immune to violence.

The papers were also carrying an image of the Chichen Itza with Elton John's face next to it. He's just played a gig there.

That's where we were heading too.

We flew to Cancun today to get closer to Chichen Itza. On the way to the hotel we stopped off at a graveyard. I often have a walk round graveyards when Suzanne and me go away for the weekend. We like looking at how long the people lived for. This graveyard looked a lot different to any I'd seen before. It was really colourful. The graves were painted in blues, pinks, yellows and reds. They looked more like the beach huts you get in Kent. And the whole family seems to get buried together – some of these graves were bigger than the flat I used to live in. I like this. Why does a graveyard have to be so morbid? Andreas, who has been with us during filming, told me that they have a thing in Mexico called the 'Day of the Dead'. It's a massive celebration of death where everyone has a day off to remember friends or family, and in Mexico with all this violence I'm guessing there is a lot of remembering to do. I like the Day of the Dead idea. We have a day dedicated to eating pancakes so why not have a day for the dead? I don't know why we don't like talking about death in Britain. I wanted to do a TV pro-gramme on death, but everyone I met to talk about it said they don't think people want to hear about it. It's about time we did something to make people less worried about it.

I suppose that Grim Reaper image we use to depict death doesn't help. He's a morbid-looking fella, isn't he? Just 'cos he's the bringer of bad news, why does he have to look so fed up? My postman brings me nothing but bad news in the form of bills, but I can't shut him up. Perhaps the Grim Reaper has just been in the job for too long. Getting rid of the hoodie would be a good start.

I like the hotel, it's quite fancy. The towels in the bathroom are laid out to look like a family of swans. I wonder if they do other animals for different days. I'll keep an eye on it.

KARL'S FACTS

CHICHEN ITZA TRANSLATES AS
'AT THE MOUTH OF THE WELL
OF THE ITZA'.

THE BUILDINGS OF CHICHEN ITZA
ARE CONNECTED BY A NETWORK
OF PAVED ROADS CALLED SACBEOB.
ARCHAEOLOGISTS HAVE FOUND
ALMOST 100 SACBEOB CRISS-CROSSING
THE SITE.

THE MAYANS OFFERED UP HUMAN
SACRIFICES TO THE GODS. IN SOME
MAYAN RITUALS PEOPLE WERE KILLED
BY HAVING THEIR ARMS AND LEGS
HELD WHILE A PRIEST CUT THE
PERSON'S CHEST OPEN AND TORE
OUT HIS HEART AS AN OFFERING.

TUESDAY 6TH APRIL

I met a man called Eugene today who took me to meet some charros. Charros are Mexican cowboys who do horse shows. I wasn't looking forward to it. I never played at being a cowboy even when I was younger. I was given a cowboy outfit when I was about five, but that was only because the shop had run out of Batman costumes. I didn't even wear jeans until I was about 17 'cos I didn't think they were comfy. And for me a horse is too much hassle anyway. They take over your life and cost a fortune. A girl who lived next door but one to us had a horse but couldn't afford to look after it properly. She didn't even have a stable for it, so they just kept it in their house. I saw it in their lounge one day when I was going door-to-door selling plants to make some money.

The other reason I never got into horses was 'cos my dad didn't rate John Wayne as an actor so I didn't get to see many westerns on the TV. Oh, and then there's that time I came off a horse at a local fête and was dragged along being kicked in the head. That's probably the main reason why I'm not a fan.

Eugene took me to a market before going to the ranch. He bought me lunch, rabbit in a spicy sauce. He had the rabbit's head. He said it was the best part as you get the brain. I didn't bother fighting him for it.

When we got to the ranch, I met the main men, who were brothers. They wore the proper cowboy kit and showed me some of their skills, from lassoing to doing a skid on a horse. They were really good. The first shock of the day was not from horses though, but from a swarm of bees that flew over us. It looked like a black cloud. It took my breath away. I quite like a bee on its own, but en masse they're quite frightening. Eugene said he hoped they weren't African bees as they could kill us.

He said if one African bee stings you, they leave a smell that makes the other bees attack. He said even if you jumped in water they would wait for you to emerge and then get you. I'd never heard of this. I'm going to look it up on the internet once I'm back home.

Once the swarm had gone, I was given a horse called Espanner. It was so well trained it almost second-guessed what I wanted it to do. Eugene gave me a small whip to speed the horse up, but whenever it got a glimpse of the whip it bolted. I wanted to give the whip back to Eugene but every time I tried the horse saw it and bolted. This is what I don't like about horses. They're too big and they have a mind of their own.

After an hour or so of trotting and learning a few tricks Eugene said the charros would like to celebrate all my progress by drinking some tequila. I've never been a fan of the stuff but I said okay as I didn't want to be rude. The charros turned up with a huge bottle of the stuff and poured me a big one – with a worm in it! I've seen booze with insects and creatures in it before but I've always avoided it. I've seen scorpions and snakes shoved into bottles but I just thought it was a way of ripping off the customer, as they're getting less tequila due to all the space taken up by having a huge lizard in there. They do it in Thai restaurants in London. You ask for a drink, and it comes in a glass with loads of seaweed and pebbles in it like a scene from *Finding Nemo*.

Eugene said I was lucky to get the worm and that I should try it as it is very tasty. I said I'd eat half if he had half. Before I'd finished saying that he had eaten his half. Now I was left with half a worm, which in a way is worse than a full one. As I put it close to my mouth I gagged and with my hand shaking so much I ended up dropping the worm.

'I'm not bothered about it being on the floor. That isn't a problem. It's just a bit of soil. I can eat that,' I said.

Eugene said, 'We can wash it.'

Great. 'Do you chew or do you just swallow?' I asked.

Eugene said, 'Of course you chew. And you try to figure out the flavour and everything.'

I said, 'I don't know what a worm should taste like. I don't know if it's off. Do you know what I mean? There's no reference point. I swear it's still moving. It's just pissed up. Look at me hand shaking. I can't hold it still.'

Eugene said, 'You can't imagine how expensive a couple of hundred grammes of this is at a restaurant. In the most expensive area of Mexico City for this kind of worm they are, like, I don't know, £50 at least.'

'For worms?'

'For worms. And they are very good.'

'And that's a romantic night out, is it?'

'It might be. They are known to be an aphrodisiac.'

I decided. 'Right, here we go. Just do it. It's like me neck knows what's happening. It's going "no, I'm not letting it in". Did you see that then? I was almost sick. Something came up. A couple of crickets from the other day probably. Come to say hello, it's a mate of his. Why can't I do this? Errr. I can't do it. I can't. Have I got to chew it? It's still in there . . .'

I finally swallowed.

'Oh, there you go.'

Eugene then tried to get me to ride a bull.

I refused.

He asked again.

I asked to see the bull first.

I saw the bull.

I refused.

I don't know why, with all these horses about, anyone would need to ride a bull around here. One of the brothers started to do a hand signal at me. Eugene said it was a signal that suggested I was scared. I told him I had worked that out myself. It wasn't difficult. He was basically mimicking an arsehole opening and shutting.

I said he could make all the hand signals he wanted.

The charro then went and got his son, who looked about two or three years old, and sat him on the bull. I doubt this kid could even ride a bike, yet here they were sticking it on a bull with no helmet or kneepads just to try and make me look like a chicken. I told them they could stick their younger baby on it if they wanted as I wouldn't be getting on it.

I headed back to the van as I wasn't going to be pressurised into riding a bloody bull. Everyone was shouting me back, but I took no notice and kept walking. Then I heard buzzing. I looked up to see about 300 bees crawling and flying all over the place. I legged it.

Nowhere is bloody safe here.

WEDNESDAY 7TH APRIL

Woke with a sore arse after all the horse-riding and also from the spicy rabbit I ate yesterday.

I just noticed the cleaner has made a swan again out of the bath towel, but it seems she didn't have time to do them properly today. The baby swan just looks like a flannel. And I've left all my soap and shampoo in the other hotel, which is well annoying as it was all new for this trip. I had to use the free stuff, which isn't very good for me as I've got sensitive skin.

We didn't do much today. Just sat on the balcony and had a walk around the local shops. I didn't buy anything. Suzanne expected a gift when I got back from Egypt, Brazil and India, but I never saw anything she'd like. And now, I figure, I don't really need to get her anything as she has probably stopped expecting stuff.

As I write this I have just discovered a basket of chocolate in the hotel room. I decide to try a Mexican Milky Bar. I wish I hadn't. The chocolate seems off to me. It's like the heat has melted it and then someone has frozen it again. I'm not prepared to pay for that so I've wrapped it up again, put it back in the basket and covered it with a bag of M&Ms.

THURSDAY 8TH APRIL

I met some Mayan people today. They are the ones who built the Wonder years ago. They lived in the middle of nowhere in huts made of straw and bamboo shoots.

One of them was a guy called Luis who didn't live in the village anymore but had family who did. As I arrived, his uncle was about to set off to get some honey. We decided to go with him. I just thought we'd be nipping to a local shop until I saw a big pole with an axe strapped to the end. We would be getting the honey from a wasps' nest.

Everything they eat has to be caught or killed as there was no local shop. Luis showed me a few plants they get food from and a tree that supplied a type of gum that could be used to clean your teeth with.

As I walked with Luis and his uncle, a local man who was leaning on his wall next to his hut watched us. He had the happiest face I'd seen in years. There was a younger lad playing with a piece of rubber who looked like he didn't know what day it was. But when you live in a place like this I don't think days of the week matter.

I asked Jamie about it. 'It can't be good for you, this, can it? This sort of remoteness. He hasn't even been to Mexico City. Brain numbing, innit?'

Jamie said, 'What do you think you'd do if you lived here?'

'I don't know. I wouldn't hang around here. I think I'd have to keep walking. You're all right up until about the age of six, because you've got a slide and swing, but after that it's a lot of hanging around. It's like waiting for a bus that's never coming. And I don't know how I would react to that. Hanging around just waiting all day. Cleaning your teeth with that stuff.'

'If you were the chief of this village what changes would you make?'

I said I'd bring in a shop.

'What kind of shop?'

'Just a hardware shop to make life easier. Sell toothpaste. That's a start, innit? I don't know. Maybe bring some more people in. That would be good.'

'How would you get them in?'

'Maybe have an open day sort of thing. Get people here. Chat about stuff. But the thing is, if you're doing nothing all day what do you chat about? It's like them old people you see sat at restaurant tables that are with each other all day. Nothing to talk about other than what flavour ice cream they're going to have for pudding. You need to stimulate your mind, don't you? I don't know how you can do that here. Yeah, you can plant stuff, but you have to wait ages for something to happen.'

Jamie asked me what kind of stuff I'd bring in.

'Like a film, to show them what else goes on.'

'Which film?'

'Just stuff, *Die Hard*? You know, Bruce Willis. Action stuff.'

'Which *Die Hard* would you show first?'

'Probably 2. Is that the one with the plane?'

Jamie said it was.

The smiling man was still looking on. So Jamie asked me if I wanted to go and chat to him.

'I don't know. What would he have to tell me? Interesting though, i'n't he? Look at him. Don't you think he's got a good face? Luis, what would they talk about? I was just thinking if I lived here, part of like living somewhere is talking to your neighbours. A bit of gossip.'

Luis said, 'Oh, they talk about what has happened in the day. What they found in the cornfield, in the jungle.'

'Doesn't that get a bit samey? "Oh, I found another chicken." "Yeah, I know. We found one yesterday and the day before." Do you know what I mean? Are there any surprises?'

Luis said, 'Sometimes they find gold in this area. We're part of the ancient city, and if you're out walking you can find a bowl with some simple coins in it. Gold.'

'Gold?'

'Yes, because when they had money the ancient people put it in a bowl underground for safekeeping. And they are lucky. If you find something from the ancient times this is good for you. And some relics, for example. Relics, little things inside the vegetation. Well, those things are new for them, and they feel more happy.'

'Is he on a lunch break? What's he doing? 'Cos he hasn't done much in the last ten minutes.'

Luis spoke to the man in Mayan. He answered.

Luis said, 'He says he is just watching us. Watching us. Because this is new for them.'

'What? Having us here?'

'Yeah. Watching people from different places is new for them.'

We walked towards the wasps' nest. I heard it before I saw it. It sounded like there were thousands of wasps in it, but Luis said there would only be a few hundred. I was still worried. I said I'd like to get the wasps' nest for his uncle so I stood on an old wall made of rocks and stretched as high as I could to hack away at the branch that held the nest. It was about the size of a basketball. Just as I got close to unhooking the nest, the wall beneath me collapsed, and I went arse over tit while trying to keep hold of the 20-foot stick with the axe on the end. Luis's uncle took over. He climbed the tree and got really close before dropping the nest. He told me not to worry as wasps always fly upwards. He sounded certain, but I don't like taking things for granted. It would only take 10 or 20 mental wasps to decide they were sick of people ripping their nests down and I'd be done for. I told him about the film *My Girl* with Macaulay Culkin, who dies from bee stings after messing with a nest, but neither of them had seen it. Maybe that would be a better film to start with, rather than *Die Hard 2*.

Luis's uncle picked up the nest and, as they predicted, all the wasps had left. He gave me some of the wasp honey to eat. It was tasty. We then took the nest back to their hut where the family totally stripped it. There was Luis's uncle, two big women, a grandma and about five kids all in the one hut. They made me eat some wasp larva in a tortilla wrap. What am I doing? I didn't want to eat insects before I came to Mexico, now I'm eating them before they are even bloody born.

In return I gave them a packet of Monster Munch and a chunky Kit-Kat. They seemed to enjoy them. I think they got the better end of the deal.

Later Luis said he wanted to take me for a swim in a cenote.

This is a massive hole, about 150 feet deep and full of natural water. I'm not a fan of swimming but thought at least if I went I wouldn't have to hang around being forced to eat cockroach sorbet or whatever else they'd found under a rock.

I enjoyed today.

FRIDAY 9TH APRIL

I was up early this morning to see the Wonder. Jamie wanted me to see it without having tourists everywhere. Problem was I still couldn't see it, as we got there so early it was still pitch black.

We wandered around in the dark for 30 minutes trying to find the Chichen Itza and eventually found it once the sun came up. I may as well have had a lie-in. I didn't have a guide today as Jamie and Barney decided I'd get all the information I needed by listening to an audio guide on some headphones.

It's an odd one, the Chichen Itza. It was a place built by the original Mayan people and was known for sacrifices (Elton John sang a song called 'Sacrifice' – maybe that's why he played here) and ripping out people's hearts and cutting heads off. Not exactly Alton Towers, is it? So it's an odd thing to make into a tourist attraction. May as well start doing tours around Fred West's house if this is what people want.

Considering that the Mayans live in huts made from bamboo and straw these days it seems a bit over the top that they built such a big, strong structure as a place to cut off heads.

The Chichen Itza is just a pyramid with four sides, with stairs on each side leading to some kind of bungalow on the top. Thinking about it, all those stairs defeat the idea of the bungalow on the top.

I tried to imagine what it would be like on the day of sacrifice. I suppose years ago it would have attracted big crowds 'cos there was nothing else to do. The audio guide didn't talk much about how the head-cutting was done, but I imagined crowds gathered at the bottom and the head being cut off at the top and rolling down one of the sets of stairs. It must've been a bit of a gamble for a spectator picking a staircase and waiting. It would have been better if they had gone for a Helter Skelter-type design so no matter where you stood, everyone would see a rolling head.

The crowds of tourists started to enter around 8 a.m. I noticed tour guides getting groups of people to clap in front of the pyramid. It creates an odd echo, which I put down as coincidence, but the guide said the pyramid was designed to make this sound as it's like the cry of the quetzal, a sacred Mayan bird.

Unfortunately the clapping didn't stop from that point on. No wonder Elton John played here. It's probably the only place he can perform that 'Circle of Life' song that was in the *Lion King* film and get applause.

I wandered away from the tourists and found another cenote like the one I swam in yesterday. The audio guide said this would have been the Mayans' main source of water. Some say these holes were made by meteorites that hit Earth millions of years ago. Apparently the cenote was another place they sacrificed people.

I was looking into it when I noticed I was surrounded by lizards. Big ones. I gave one of them a bit of one of my Hobnobs. It seemed to love it. It ended up eating two to itself.

I realized then that I had swapped lives with a lizard on this latest trip. Here it was eating my Hobnobs and there I'd been eating crickets, worms and wasp eggs. It's odd to think the

Mayans have probably never tried a Hobnob, yet this lizard had.

Back at the hotel, I found that the cleaner had left my Milky Bar out on the dressing table. I felt like a kid who'd been caught nicking again. Great, I thought, she found that but she didn't make me a proper flannel swan.

I told Jamie they might get charged about £2 for some chocolate. He said Sky should be able to cover the cost.

SATURDAY 10TH APRIL

We went home today. We had to fly into Dallas to get a connecting flight. While I was killing time in the airport, I decided to get some perfume for Suzanne from Duty Free. I soon wished I hadn't bothered. It was a right pain in the arse. Due to security, I had to put the small perfume box into another box that was about four times bigger and then check in the box, as I was not allowed to take any liquid onto the plane. I almost missed my connecting flight. The other annoying thing about that bloody box was that Suzanne looked disappointed when she opened it – I think she thought it was a bigger and better present judging by the outer box.

Checked online. African bees can kill a man.

CHAPTER FIVE
THE GREAT WALL

'THERE IN THE MIST. ENORMOUS, MAJESTIC, SILENT AND TERRIBLE, STOOD THE GREAT WALL OF CHINA. FEARLESSLY IT WENT ON ITS ENDLESS JOURNEY. LEAGUE UPON LEAGUE TO THE FARTHERMOST REGIONS OF ASIA IN UTTER SOLITUDE, MYSTERIOUS LIKE THE GREAT EMPIRE IT GUARDED.'

W. SOMERSET MAUGHAM

'IT WAS KNACKERED. SO KNACKERED THAT IT WASN'T REALLY A WALL. I REMEMBER HEARING THAT YOU'RE SUPPOSED TO BE ABLE TO SEE THE GREAT WALL OF CHINA FROM THE MOON, BUT THAT HAS GOT TO BE BOLLOCKS 'COS EVEN AS I STOOD RIGHT NEXT TO THIS BIT, I HAD PROBLEMS SEEING IT.'

KARL PILKINGTON

SATURDAY 17 TH APRIL

The odd thing with China is, they like to go out of their way to do things differently. Even something simple like reading a book they mess with. They read books from top to bottom and then back to the top again. It looks like they're agreeing with everything they're reading. Their food looks different too. I used to walk through Chinatown on the way to work and the food I'd often see hanging in the restaurant windows was bright red chickens. I don't know if they did something odd to the chickens, or if they had just been sat in the window for so long that they had got a tan.

I like to have Chinese food maybe once a month but the idea of having it every day for a week doesn't excite me that much. China is also the country that seems to eat anything that moves. When I was growing up, there were always rumours of the Chinese eating dogs. When Small Terrance took over the local chippy and sold Chinese as well as fish and chips, people on the estate started to blame him for their missing pets.

Ricky and Steve think I should eat anything the locals eat, but I don't see the point of this in the long run. If the locals eat toads, and I try it and find that I really like it, I won't be able to find any butchers that sell toad back in London, so what's the point of getting a taste for it in the first place?

I also associate crazy inventions and technology with China. I have a book that is full of odd Chinese inventions. I remember seeing a hat with a toilet-roll holder on the top, and a picture of small mops on cats' feet so when they wander around the kitchen waiting to be fed they can clean the floor at the same time.

The Great Wall of China is the reason I'm visiting the country. I can't say I'm looking forward to seeing it. I always have a problem liking things that I'm told I should like. This has been the problem with most of the Wonders I have seen so far. The fact that this one is called the 'Great' Wall of China annoys me. I'll decide if it's great or not. It might end up being the 'All Right Wall of China' to me.

I'm expecting the Chinese to be really polite. I don't know why. I don't know if I read it somewhere, or I was told, or I've just come to that conclusion based on the fact that all the Chinese people I have met in my life so far have been polite. Which makes me wonder even more about the Wall being 'Great'. Even if it was rubbish, I have a feeling the Chinese would be too polite to say so. I suppose I'll find out, soon enough.

SATURDAY 24TH / SUNDAY 25TH APRIL

It was a really long flight. Out of the plane window I saw the sun, then the moon, and then the sun again. But I am glad to have seen the sun so much, because it doesn't look like I will be seeing much of it while I'm here, due to all the pollution. When we landed the sky was a murky, foggy grey. It was really cold as well. I had to get me coat out. I thought China was full of sweatshops but I don't know how in these temperatures.

We left the airport and got dropped off in town. Krish the producer said I should try and find my hotel by asking local people for directions. Great. I asked about 15 people, and not one of them spoke English. I showed the name of the place where I was staying on a piece of paper to an old man, and he grabbed my arm and walked with me. I thought he knew where the hotel was, but he just took me to a small seat, sat me down and then pummelled my back. He was a massager. He must have been about 80 years old but he was still pretty heavy-handed. I've never been touched by such an old man. But then again, was he really old? I've always thought that the Chinese don't age very well, that they look healthy and good-looking until about the age of 35, and then they just look old. I told Ricky once I thought that they maybe aged overnight like a pear, but he didn't understand what I was going on about.

This bloke who was massaging my back might only have been about 38. You decide.

Normally, a massage would be given with the sound of pan-pipes or a CD of whale noises, but in Beijing all I could hear was throats being cleared and spitting. It mustn't be rude to spit here, as everyone seems to do it. Finally, I found a young girl who translated what was on my piece of paper to a rickshaw driver.

The hotel I'm staying in seems nice enough, although my room is pretty small. I have a kettle and teabags, and next to that I have two goldfish in a bowl. I'm not sure if they're for company or for a snack. There is also a budgie hanging outside the window. I think I'll be happy here. I ate a packet of my Monster Munch that I had brought with me, and then we wandered off to an old local market. The smell was similar to Chinatown in Manchester and London – that sort of sweet and sour smell. The first thing I saw was a man on a street corner crouching next to a few washing-up bowls full of large catfish and eels. As I was looking at the fish, he pulled out three carrier bags. One was full of toads. At first I thought they were dead, as there wasn't much movement, but then one of the 80 or so toads tried to escape. The man grabbed it when it jumped and cut its head off. He then continued his way through the rest of them. It was a complete toad massacre, all because one had tried to get away. One by one, he took the head off, stripped the skin off the body, put the meat into one bag and the skin in the other. The toads went from hopping in carrier bag number one to being dead and stripped in bags two and three in a matter of seconds. I didn't find it easy to watch, but he was impressively fast and seemed to know what he was doing. The scissors cut through the toad's neck in one easy cut. They were just a basic pair of scissors similar to the ones I've got at home, the sort you use to cut string and wrapping paper, Sellotape . . . and toads' heads. He was an expert at toad stripping. He seemed pleased to show us his skill. He could probably do it blindfolded, like those soldiers you see putting together a machine gun.

As we watched, a few policemen turned up, and Krish thought we had better move on, as we were not supposed to be filming around there. They like to protect how China is perceived, and there was a chance that they could take the tape from the camera off us. We went to a newer part of the market. The stalls and layout looked more similar to the markets I see at home, until I got a closer look. They were selling insects. Rows and rows of bugs on sticks. They had big black scorpions, snakes, worms and locusts all laid out like they were queuing to get on Noah's Ark. People had told me about street food in China, but I didn't think it meant making food out of stuff that normally crawls the street. Most of the bugs had been dipped in some sort of oil to make them look more tempting to the eye while the lizard looked like someone had just found it crushed under a breezeblock and stuck a stick up its arse. Seeing all this makes me wonder if the old woman in the nursery rhyme who swallowed a cat to catch the bird to catch the spider was Chinese. That sounds like a normal diet round here.

Our van driver stopped off to eat some duck foetus eggs. They looked rank. I said before I came here that the Chinese eat anything that moves; I've now found out that they'll eat stuff before it's even had a chance to move. Why they can't just wait for it to be born and eat it as a duck I don't know. They might as well eat duck sperm to save even more time. I've heard that they also eat 100-year-old eggs but I don't know how anything gets to be that old here without someone eating it. We went back to the hotel. I ate one of my five Twix bars and another packet of Monster Munch. I should've brought more.

MONDAY 26TH APRIL

I didn't sleep very well because the buzzer for the front door of the hotel is next to my room. It sounds like a car alarm. Roadworks also started really early, which seemed to irritate the budgie, so then it tweeted for half an hour. I don't know how it isn't dead. It's freezing out there. I checked my phone. My mam had emailed to ask if I was okay and wanted to know if I would be seeing the Terracotta Army, as she had seen it on the telly and it looked good. Talking about the Terracotta Army reminded her that me dad had painted her gnomes, so she'd attached a photo to her email. Suzanne had also texted to say good night. The time difference is going to make it tough to have a chat with anyone at home. Seven hours' time difference.

Just as I nodded off, Krish woke me up to tell me that Steve had left a message on my phone. I hadn't been listening to voicemail, as it's too expensive, but Krish said I needed to hear it to find out what plans I had for today.

STEPHEN: Hello, Karl, mate. It's Stephen here. Listen, I've got a little treat arranged for you today. I know that you're fascinated by the strange, the weird, the esoteric, and obviously

> one of the big parts of Chinese culture is fortune-telling. So we've arranged for you to go and see a fortune-teller, to get some predictions about your future, my friend. Enjoy.

I wasn't happy about this. I don't want to know what the rest of my life is going to be like. Even if what he says is nonsense I think it will play on my mind and stop me getting on with my life. The best thing about life is the surprises, and we're getting fewer and fewer surprises these days. Even the simple thing of waking up in the morning and opening the curtains to see what the weather is like is a nice surprise, but now *Countryfile* with John Craven has taken that away with its five-day forecast. In truth, the only thing that would have been handy about knowing my future is that we wouldn't have booked into this hotel, as we'd have known about the bloody roadworks outside. In the morning I got up and had a hard-boiled egg and some odd bread, and then headed over to the fortune-teller.

The place didn't look very mystical. It was on a dual carriage-way with a 'wash while you wait' car wash on one side and a block of flats on the other. It turned out that the fortune-teller didn't speak a word of English, so we had to use a translator. After asking the date and time of my birth he got straight on with the fortune-telling.

The translator said, 'The south side of your house is quite low. Is that right?'

'Err, low, yeah, I'm on the ground floor. It's low. Yeah, I'll give him that.'

Mr Sow, the fortune-teller talked in Chinese.

The translator said, 'You will have to pay attention to your health because you have some kind of heart problem.'

'Oh, here we go . . . What sort of heart problem?'

The translator said, 'Something to do with your heart, blood vessels, so you really need to take care of that.'

'It's weird, because my dad had a problem with his heart, and they say it runs in the family.'

The translator said, 'You be very careful if you do have a problem. It's probably something to do with your heart.'

'Is it going to kill me then? Is this what he's telling you? That the problem with the heart is going to finish me off?'

'Ninety per cent.'

'Ninety per cent!'

'But maybe we can change it.'

'All right, that sounds better.'

The translator said, 'Do a lot of good things. Try to raise the goodness in your life.'

'Wha–? I've got to look at the good things in my life? Do a lot of good things, like helping people? I do loads of that. I do loads of good. Tell him I do Tools for Africa – four quid a month, Help the Aged – I think they get a fiver, deaf kids, and the latest one was Red Cross, so that's four charities each costing on average five quid a month so that's 20 quid a month I'm giving to charity.'

The translator talked in Chinese to Mr Sow, then said, 'Well done. Otherwise you would be even worse. You would be more ill than you are now.'

After he told me this news he asked me to write down three sins. After quite a bit of thinking, I went with the following:

SIN 1 I AM SORRY ABOUT NICKING MARS BARS FROM THE NEWSAGENT'S THAT I DELIVERED PAPERS FOR. I HELPED MYSELF TO ONE EVERY DAY, SEVEN DAYS A WEEK,

FOR OVER TWO YEARS (MAYBE THIS IS WHY I'M GONNA HAVE A HEART ATTACK).

SIN 2 I AM SORRY FOR OPENING THE POST THAT WAS ADDRESSED TO BRUCE (THE MAN WHO USED TO OWN OUR FLAT) INSTEAD OF FORWARDING IT ON.

SIN 3 I AM SORRY FOR PUTTING PUTTY IN CARL GRIMSHAW'S HAIR WHEN I WAS A KID. IT ALL GOT TANGLED UP, AND HE HAD TO HAVE HIS HEAD SHAVED. HIS MAM WENT MAD AT ME BECAUSE HE HAD A FUNNY-SHAPED HEAD AND THIS MADE IT STAND OUT EVEN MORE.

Mr Sow then told me he would burn one of the sins and I must take the other two and dispose of one on a mountain and the other in the sea. He and his workers then did a small ceremony for me, which involved standing with a joss stick in the freezing cold while people danced around me setting fire to paper. All this standing about in the cold can't be good for a man with a heart problem. Later, we went to a local place for something to eat. I played it safe and had some noodles but ate another Twix when I got back to my room.

TUESDAY 27TH APRIL

I woke up at 4.30 a.m. I still have jet lag. I looked out of the window to see that even the budgie was asleep . . . or dead.

To kill some time I picked up a book in my room with quotes from a man called Mao Tse-Tung. He was a Chinese states-man. He once said: 'We think too small, like the frog at the bot-tom of the well. He thinks the sky is only as big as the top of the well. If he surfaced, he would have an entirely different view.'

It made me think about how I was a bit like that frog before I started to travel the world for this programme. Having said that, I'm not sure it's even worth the frog coming out of its well to see more of the sky anyway, as it's pretty grim here with all the pollution, plus the fact that it ain't safe for a frog in China 'cos someone would come along and grab it, cut its head off and eat it. So, all in all, it wasn't good advice from Mao Tse-Tung. I had a hard-boiled egg for breakfast again. The crew were filming on the street today, getting pictures of traffic and local people. As they worked, I realised I needed the loo. I popped into one that was close by and was greeted by two blokes squatting on their haunches. The cubicles didn't have doors on them.

One of the men gave me a wink. At first I thought he may have just been straining then I noticed it was one of the chefs from where we ate last night. The other fella was busy natter-ing on his mobile, probably taking an order for a takeaway. I nipped out and told Krish about my dilemma. I have always struggled with these hole-in-the-ground toilets. It's not so much the hole in the ground, more the fact that there is no door. It's odd to think they built the Great Wall of China but can't be bothered to get a bit of MDF, stick some hinges on it and make a door. There were no sinks or toilet paper either. I wonder if I can find one of them toilet-roll hats I saw in my invention book. I went to an indoor market while they carried on filming. The place was filled with replica goods being sold at low prices: clothing, DVDs, mobile phones, watches and shoes. I bought a mobile-phone holder, a coat and a DVD to watch, as there are no English-speaking channels on the telly. I was going to get something to eat but even this place, which is specifically aimed at tourists, still offered up odd food. Blood cake was everywhere. Big blocks of the stuff. A block of blood should not have the word 'cake' after it. It doesn't kid me into wanting some. They may as well say 'Shite Gâteau'. I drove back in the bus with everyone else. The driver broke wind twice. He didn't seem embarrassed about it. When I got back the others told me the coat looked nice enough but probably isn't very waterproof.

I had some more noodles at the place on the corner and was told by Krish that I would be seeing the Wall tomorrow.

I watched the DVD I bought before I went to bed. It was a pirate copy so the quality was really poor, but the film wasn't very good anyway – it had been recorded with a camcorder in a cinema. I saw a bloke get up and leave the cinema about 35 minutes in, so even he thought it wasn't very good.

They're probably right about that coat not being waterproof.

WEDNESDAY 28TH APRIL

I was up early again so I managed to talk to Suzanne before she went to bed. I told her that I was off to see the Wall. I told her that I can't be doing with the Wonder part of these trips, but she said it should be the icing on the cake. But the thing with me is, I don't really enjoy the icing on a cake. I often pull off the icing and leave it. The icing is just there to get your attention, but I wouldn't say it's the best bit. And that's how I feel about the Wonders – they're the reason I'm going everywhere, but they're never my favourite bit. I've never liked wedding cake due to the amount of icing, but then imagine a wedding cake without it; just a dark, stodgy, horrible dry sponge. The icing covers up the mess, and that's how I feel about most of the Wonders. They use them to get people to visit a place that you probably wouldn't think about visiting. Maybe blood cake would look better with icing though.

We had the usual hard-boiled egg for breakfast and made our way over to the tour buses. Ricky and Steve had arranged for me to get a lift on a tour bus so I could learn a few things about the Wall before seeing it.

There must have been about 50 coaches parked up ready to head over to the Great Wall. After asking around I found the right bus. It was a full bus. About 50 people. About 50 Chinese people. The tour guide got on. He was also Chinese. He turned on the microphone and started his tour in Chinese. Brilliant.

I didn't have a clue what was being said so I just tried to enjoy the trip. The passengers all looked really old, but maybe I'm just right about them not ageing well. The average age seemed to be about 70. I don't understand why so many old Chinese people have not seen the Wall at some point in their life already, which makes me think it can't be very good. If they're late in their life and haven't bothered to make the journey to see it before now, what does that tell you?

In a way it's just as well I can't understand the Chinese tour guide as I wouldn't have been able to hear him anyway due to the amount of coughing and clearing of throats on the bus. Coughing and clearing of throats must have the same effect as yawning as everyone was doing it. I was sat next to an old woman who looked like butter wouldn't melt in her mouth . . . mainly due to the fact that she'd cough it up with the rest of her phlegm before it had a chance to melt. Every minute she'd clear her throat and then spit into a carrier bag she had with her. I couldn't wait to get to the Wall. With all this spit flying around I suppose I'll find out if this coat I have bought is waterproof or not. Eventually we pulled up in a huge car park next to some market stalls selling novelty Chinese hats, woolly hats, scarves, fridge magnets and plates. I bought a woolly hat as it was freezing and then joined the massive queue to get in.

Once I was through the entrance I could see the Wall for miles, like a long snake making its way across the mountains. It was pretty impressive. I wanted to stop for a few minutes to take it all in, but the guide shouted at me to move along. I told Krish that we may as well go it alone now, as we were not going to gain anything by staying with a guide who only spoke Chinese. He agreed.

We managed to find a bit of the Wall that wasn't too busy. I looked at it. It looked quite new. I was trying to understand what all the fuss was about, but it wasn't easy when I knew nothing about the Wall. Krish gave me a guide to China that had a chapter on the Great Wall. It said it was heavily restored in both the 1950s and 1980s. Surely it can't count as a Wonder if it's not original? If when I went to see the Taj Mahal in India I got there to find a new house built there with a double garage and a gravel driveway, they couldn't still sell it as the Taj Mahal, so why is the Wall getting away with it? Bloody hell, is everything fake in China? The coat I bought, the DVD and now the Wall.

I said I'd had enough and wanted to leave. I had another message on my phone.

STEPHEN: Hello, mate, Steve Merchant here. How you doin'? I heard that you went to see the Great Wall of China today, or 'the Wall' as it's known in China. I'm sure you enjoyed it.

MEXICO

WHY THE LONG FACE?

SUZANNE WARNED ME ABOUT BROKEBACK MOUNTAIN.

ONE TOO MANY TEQUILAS.

THE FORTUNE TELLER, OR MISFORTUNE TELLER IN MY CASE.

MY SINS ARE ABOUT TO GO UP IN SM

I BOUGHT THESE THEN WISHED I HAD
WITH ALL THE POLLUTION IN BEIJIN
YOU CAN'T ACTUALLY SEE THE SUN.

CHINA

CHINA

JORDAN

HOLIDAYS FROM HELL

ANDY McNOB

THE NACHMEN

Obviously, it's amazing. I know you like a bit of DIY so I imagine you'd love to see how a nice wall has been made, and Ricky and I want you to see more of it. In fact, we were having a chat and we'd like you to see all of the Great Wall. Literally all of it. We want you to travel the entire length of the wall. So, enjoy it! See ya!

I didn't want to see any more of the Wall, but Krish said it would be worthwhile as I'd get to see other parts of China along the way.

We're staying at a different place tonight. It's a house in the middle of nowhere. It looked quite new at first but on closer inspection it was falling apart. The front door wouldn't close, and it is really cold, and my room smells damp. There's a few teabags but no milk.

THURSDAY 29ᵀᴴ APRIL

I saw an old, original part of the Wall today high up in the mountains. It was knackered. So knackered that it wasn't really a wall. I remember hearing that you're supposed to be able to see the Great Wall of China from the moon, but that has got to be bollocks 'cos even as I stood right next to this bit, I had problems seeing it.

I don't know what would make me happy. I didn't like the brand new Wall, and this old bit isn't impressing me either. I'm harder to please than Goldilocks. Still, the journey wasn't a complete waste of time, as I got rid of one of my sins on the mountaintop.

We drove on to a small village where we decided to get out and take a wander. I passed a house with a man doing some D.I.Y. I couldn't work out what he was making, but I guessed that it wouldn't be a toilet door. I asked Krish if I had time to nip in and get a closer look. It turned out the man was making a coffin. Huge thing, it was. I asked who it was for. He said it was for the woman who lives in the house. At that point the woman came to the door. She told me that it is normal practice to have a coffin made for you at your house. She was 69. After what the fortune-teller told me maybe I should get this fella's number.

I'm not sure I like the idea of having the coffin made in my own front garden. Every day when you leave the house, there it is. It's probably the only time I wouldn't want a handyman to complete the job in the estimated time. Plus, the flat I live in has not got the space to have something like that just sat there, and if I popped it outside I would have to get a parking permit for it.

As the man worked away on the coffin, the woman looked on, inspecting it as if she was having her porch painted. She said, 'Once this is done, I'll feel much happier. Because I'll know it has been done. And I will know what sort of coffin I'll be in when I die. I will be much happier.'

She told me that her husband died 20 years ago at the age of 50 and his coffin wasn't ready. They don't normally plan to have the coffin made until they are around 70, so he ended up being buried in the one that was prepared for her mam.

We left them to it and carried on walking. I saw another coffin outside another house. This one was finished and painted black, and it was pushed up against the wall ready for whoever needs it. If we did this, my mam would have filled hers with clutter in no time. Wherever there's a space, she fills it with something. Saying that, it wouldn't be so bad if they got rid of the lid and used it as a big windowbox or something, and popped some flowers in until it was needed.

While I'd been checking out the coffins Krish had arranged for me to have some lunch at a local's house. In return I chopped some wood for their fire. There was a woman and her husband with a small kid. The gran also lived with them. The kid wore some pants with the arse cut out. These are popular here, as kids are potty-trained before they learn how to remove pants. Something else I learned about young kids in China was that parents like their children to have flat heads at the back. I never got the full story. I must look online when I get home.

As I was chopping the wood, I turned to see the woman of the house throwing something around in the air and then bashing it on the floor. It was a toad. Ten minutes later it was cooked in a bowl with some pork and salad. I took some pork and salad, and commented on how nice it was, but the gran kept pointing to the bowl of toad. I said I was okay with the pork, at which point she basically wrestled with me and forced a piece into my mouth. That isn't normal, is it? Hardly the sort of thing you see on *Come Dine with Me*. I yelled at her, which I suppose is a bit rude, but I didn't like being force-fed toad. I told her that the baby needs help being fed, not me. I grabbed some and forced it in her face. She didn't seem too happy about it either. I wouldn't be surprised if no one eats toad in China, and it's just something Ricky and Steve sorted out to wind me up.

I left the village and saw more of the Wall that afternoon. As I got higher up, my phone picked up a message. It was from Steve.

STEPHEN: Hello, mate, it's Stephen here. Hope you're doing well. Just want to leave you a quick message. We've sorted

> something out for you – one of the great elements of Chinese culture and popular of course in the UK in the 1970s. We've arranged for you to see some kung fu. Yeah, enjoy it! See ya.

Great.

FRIDAY 30ᵀᴴ APRIL

Saw more of the bloody Wall today on the way to the kung fu school. I don't have much more to say about it. Krish tried to sell it to me by saying it's impressive because it's so long, but so is the M6, and that's older than a lot of this Wall.

We got to the Shaolin School where they teach kung fu. It's not something I've ever been into – kung fu, or any martial art for that matter. I've always thought it just made fights longer than they need to be. Any kung fu film where you see a fight can go on for ages. I bet most of the time people who have a fight in China forget what the argument was about by the time they've finished fighting. There can only be one winner so why not just get it done sooner? To me it's like people who have it away all night. I had some neighbours like that once; they'd be at it all night. Why? Get the job done and get to sleep.

When we arrived at the Shaolin School there were kids everywhere doing kung fu. All in sync and all wearing the same uniform. It was nothing like PE lessons at my school. Most of that lesson used to be spent in Lost Property trying to find shorts that fitted me. No one remembered their own kit. It was more like Trinny and Susannah than a PE lesson.

KARL'S FACTS

ACCORDING TO LEGEND, A HELPFUL DRAGON TRACED OUT THE COURSE OF THE GREAT WALL FOR THE WORKFORCE. THE BUILDERS SUBSEQUENTLY FOLLOWED THE TRACKS OF THE DRAGON.

THE CHINESE INVENTED THE WHEELBARROW AND USED IT EXTENSIVELY IN BUILDING THE GREAT WALL.

DURING ITS CONSTRUCTION, THE GREAT WALL WAS CALLED 'THE LONGEST CEMETERY ON EARTH' BECAUSE MORE THAN ONE MILLION PEOPLE DIED BUILDING IT.

THE LENGTH OF ALL CHINESE DEFENCE WALLS BUILT OVER THE LAST 2,000 YEARS IS APPROXIMATELY 31,070 MILES. EARTH'S CIRCUMFERENCE IS 24,854 MILES.

A man called Leo introduced himself and said he would give me a guide around the place. He was a teacher and kung fu expert who explained why the art is such a big deal in China and how training methods can produce extraordinary skills and abilities.

First he took me up into the hills, where there were four students who demonstrated some of their skills. One smashed a wooden pole over another's back, another broke a metal bar on his head, and one bent a sharp spear using the ground and his neck. I didn't see the point of some of these tricks. I told Leo the only one I thought that might come in handy was smashing the metal bar, as I'm always banging my head, but he told me the spear to the throat was useful too, as the throat is one of the most sensitive parts of the body and this activity makes it stronger. At that moment Leo went and poked me in my throat with two fingers. I didn't even see it coming. It took my breath away for a moment. He was fast. I wouldn't be surprised if he'd checked my prostate gland at the same time.

The youngest of the students was a ten-year-old lad with a runny nose who did a forward roll and bounced off his head. This kid didn't smile much. I don't think he liked being at this school. Leo said the lad practised landing on his head every day and it would help strengthen his neck. At the moment it just looks like it's helping clear the snot out of his nose.

Leo kept telling me that a healthy body makes a healthy mind. I told him this is not always the case. 'Look at Stephen Hawking', I said. I don't think he knew who he was though. Before Leo left he said he wanted to give me some training tomorrow morning and would meet me at 4 a.m. I told him it was a daft time to get up. I said I would meet him at 5.30 a.m. He was adamant that we meet at 4 a.m., so in the end I had to agree. I'm staying in another hotel tonight. It isn't very nice. There are spit stains all over the carpet. I tried to get an early night but couldn't due to a kid outside who went up and down the corridor on a tricycle, so I got up and ate my last Twix.

SATURDAY 1ST MAY

I was woken at 4.05 this morning by violent banging on my door. It was Leo. He told me I was late, handed me my outfit and stormed off.

He had relaxed a bit by the time I got in the van, but not as much as the driver, who broke wind twice during a 15-minute journey. It's amazing how acceptable spitting and farting seem to be. I don't know what you would have to do to be classed as rude in this country.

Leo worked me hard. I had a run, did some serious leg stretches, then he had me doing a toad hop up some stairs and throwing needles into a tree. He put his hand through some bricks (maybe that's why the Great Wall is such a mess?). I also tried to attack him when he seemed off guard. Each time he had me on the floor. I liked Leo and I have bruises to remember him by. I was aching a lot, so Krish said that the Chinese are into massage stuff and I should take advantage of having one as it would do me good after the workout I'd been having.

On the way to the massage we stopped off at a little café. It was a bit rank, but there was nothing else around and we were hungry, as we'd been up since 4 a.m. Loads of plates were brought to the table. I tucked in. Then Emma the translator walked in and told me I'd been eating dog. If the camera had been rolling I'd have thought I had been set up, but it wasn't, and everyone else looked at their plate to see if they had eaten it too. They hadn't. Just me. Just my luck. It didn't taste that good. I just thought it was cheap beef. Even food that I have at home tastes different here, so I didn't really question what it was.

Oh, well. Isn't there a saying that goes 'You can't keep an old dog down'? Guess I'll find out in the next few hours. Over at the massage place, I entered a really warm room that seemed to have way too much furniture in it for its size. I was greeted by a woman who asked me to remove my trousers and gave me some shorts. She rubbed my legs and feet, which was lovely. And then she set fire to them. Mental.

She dipped some rags into some type of oil and then placed them on my legs and set fire to them. I've no idea what good it does. I should be able to relax when having a massage but instead I was yelling me head off while looking for a fire extinguisher. She didn't stop though. You'd have thought that, even though she couldn't understand English, me yelling my head off would indicate that I wasn't happy. Like I've said, the Chinese mess with everything for the worse.

I was pissed off with Krish for putting me through that and then got even more wound up when I picked up a message from Ricky.

RICKY: Oh, come on, mate, always be in contact. You never answer your phone. I've called a few times now. You're not on holiday. You've still got other business to attend to. You know the rules – give us a call, always be in contact, always be available for work. This is bad, son.

How can he still be so annoying when he's so far away? I called him when I got to the next hotel.

KARL: How's it going?

RICKY: Why haven't you called? Did you get my message?

KARL: Yeah, I got your message, but I've been in the middle of nowhere, haven't I, looking at the Wall.

RICKY: Not really in the middle of nowhere. There's a billion people in the place you're in, so I don't think you could ever be in the middle of nowhere.

KARL: Well, when you see it you'll see how lonely I've been. I've been in the middle of nowhere looking at a wall. It's really weird here.

RICKY: Why?

KARL: Just . . . Everything. Everything that happens here, it's just weird. It feels weird. The atmosphere's weird. Eating toad was weird.

RICKY: You didn't eat toad?

KARL: I had a little bit of toad.

RICKY: I thought that was a myth. I didn't realise they really did eat toad there. I thought you just made that up.

KARL: A woman forced me to have a bit of toad. I was worried about getting a taste for it. That won't be happening. What else have I been up to? Toilets. Do you know how when I go into a public toilet I nip in with a coin and open the door? Well, you couldn't do that here, 'cos there's no doors on the toilets.

I was walking down the road the other day, and they were filming some stuff on this street, traffic and stuff. I say, 'I'm just nipping in here.' Walked in, was greeted by two fellas squatting.

RICKY: What did they say?

KARL: Well, to them it's normal, so they just sort of gave me the nod. I wandered in, and straight away . . . When you open the door you don't turn a corner or anything, you walk in, and they were just sat there. They were chefs from the place on the corner, so that's reassuring.

RICKY: Oh, no. Unbelievable.

KARL: Honest to God, one of them was on the phone taking an order. I've never seen anything like it. I don't think I could ever get used to that. You need to have your own space when you're doing that. And they're just there, one's on the phone, the other one's just sort of looking around.

RICKY: That's unbelievable. Are you impressed with the Wall?

KARL: It's nicely done, but then again it should look all right – the bit I saw they did up in the eighties.

RICKY: The oldest bits are hundreds of years old. What did they do, just wallpaper and plaster over it? What d'you mean they did it up?

KARL: They did it up and made it nice, and it's just like any wall that you'd see anywhere. There's nothing special about it. It's the China Wall because it's in China. It's not great. I don't know why they use the word 'great' in it.

RICKY: Were there loads of people on bicycles?

KARL: Not that many. But then the few I've spoken to have had old relations who've been, like, knocked over . . . One fella lost a leg, from being on a bike. So I think they must have cut down on the nine million bicycles. I saw one get crushed by a van, so there's definitely not nine million. It's at least one less.

RICKY: I don't think you should get all your information about China from Katie Melua songs either. I don't know if that one's official.

KARL: Well, I knew nothing about this place before I came here. People have been saying 'Oh, well, what did you think? What did you expect?' I knew nothing. I was thinking about the Philip Bailey song 'Chinese Wall'. He certainly didn't say it was built in the 1980s. I think that song's older than the Wall . . . Honestly, I've had enough. I want to come home now.

RICKY: I don't know what people watching Sky are gonna do with the information on Chinese people having a shit with no door while taking an order for food. But, you know, it's the truth.

KARL: It is the truth.

RICKY: All I'm taking from this is, the next time I order a takeaway I'm gonna ask the fella 'What are you doing now?' I'm never gonna order a Number Two, I tell you that.

KARL: Or a King Poo Chicken.

SUNDAY 2ND MAY

Such a gloomy day today. We went to see the end of the Wall. It runs straight into the sea. There weren't many tourists about. It reminded me of an old seaside town in Britain. There was a man selling hot dogs, a woman selling postcards and a man hiring out little, battery-powered go-karts. I counted 24 people, and that's including the hot-dog seller. You'd expect more at a Wonder of the World, wouldn't you? I didn't mind though. It was the best thing about this part of the Wall.

I had a go on a battery-powered go-kart and left. On the way back, we passed a truck on the motorway full of dogs. It must have had about 100 dogs in it, all of which I presumed will be eaten.

I've never really understood the problem with eating dog. After all, it's just a meat and should just be like eating pig, cow, sheep or chicken, but people look at it differently. There are times when I think having another meat would be handy, as there are seven days in a week but only four main meats, which means that by midweek I have to start eating things I've already eaten. Why don't we like the idea of eating dog?

We followed the truck to see where it was going. We ended up at a dog farm. It looked like any other farm. I wandered in where there was a big Alsatian wandering about. 'Free Range' dogs, I thought, until I met the bloke who ran the place who said it was his pet dog. I then saw the dogs that are there to buy as food. They were mainly St Bernards. He said these big dogs can easily feed a big family. St Bernards are the ones you normally see as rescue dogs with a drum of brandy round their neck. The Chinese probably look at this as a meal with a free drink. The man who ran the dog farm then got out a brochure with the different dogs that people eat.

I decided to have a word with him through our translator. 'It's weird, because you've got a dog yourself. It's odd to see big dogs trapped in small spaces. Yet your dog runs free. I didn't think you'd be a dog lover, really.'

The translator said, 'My pet is different from all those dogs, because he's specially for guarding the gate.'

'Right. Yeah. And how's business? Is it busy? Lot of people want to eat dog here?'

The translator replied, 'A lot of different people come to buy the dogs. Big ones and small ones, because I have all kinds of dogs.'

'What's your dog's name?'

'Fluffy.'

'You wouldn't sell this one then?'

'I've trained him already, so I wouldn't sell.'

'So what happens now? If I wanted to buy one of these dogs, would I buy it and take it away, or do you kill them and prepare them for somebody to sell as food?'

The translator said, 'We only do the farming here. We don't kill the dogs. So, if somebody wanted to buy one, they would take it away and kill it.'

I asked him if it was one of his favourite meats.

'China has a long history of dog eating.'

'Do you enjoy it? I had it and I thought it was like beef. I couldn't tell the difference.'

'Dog meat tastes very different from beef. We have a minority of North Koreans. They love eating dog.'

I asked him if it was a poor man's food.

'You eat it no matter if you're poor or rich. But my pet, my Fluffy, I would never eat him. If he died, I could never eat him.'

'See that's the bit I don't understand really. Surely, when it's your own dog, you know where it's been and how it's lived. So, I think that would make it easier for me to eat it than eating a dog that I know nothing about. And what about cat? Do people eat cat here?'

'Cats – normally we use them as pets and I can never remember anybody eating cats.'

'I don't understand that really. To me it's just the same. If you're eating dog I don't see the problem with eating a cat. If anything it's easier 'cos they're not as friendly, cats . . . they sort of come and go as they please.'

The translator explained. 'Because cats are quite small, and there's not much meat on them, but in Guangdong Province people do eat cats as well.'

Of course they do.

MONDAY 3RD MAY

When I got home I checked online about the thing I heard about babies having square heads. Apparently, sometimes a book is tied round the back of the baby's head to help flatten it. Parents do this because a flat head is a sign of beauty. I also read that it stops babies rolling about when they're in a cot.

Bizarre.

CHAPTER SIX
PETRA

'ONE OF THE MOST PRECIOUS CULTURAL PROPERTIES OF MAN'S HERITAGE.'

UNESCO

'AS IMPRESSIVE AS THE ENTRANCE WAS, IT WAS STILL A CAVE YES, IT HAS GOOD "KERB APPEAL". BUT ONCE I STUCK MY HEAD INSIDE THERE REALLY WAS NOTHING TO IT. IF YOU ADD THAT TO THE FACT THAT IT WAS OUT OF THE WAY AND YOU HAD TO CLIMB OVER 800 STEPS TO GET TO IT, IT'S FAIR TO SAY THAT IF IT WAS ON *LOCATION, LOCATION, LOCATION* IT WOULDN'T BE ON MY SHORTLIST.'

KARL PILKINGTON

SATURDAY 22ND MAY

I was told this morning by Luke and Ben, the director and producer, that we would be travelling right through Israel, on through Palestine and finally into Jordan. I wasn't happy about this. When I told me Dad I was going there he said that he wasn't going to tell me mam 'cos she would only worry. Every time I hear about Israel on the news it's normally something bad. It's never a light-hearted news story. It's never a story about a man who's grown the world's biggest melon, is it? Its problems are normally related to religion, and seeing as I'm not into religion in the slightest, I don't understand the situation in Israel and it's too complicated to learn overnight, I'd rather leave it. It's the same reason I've never bothered learning chess. The problem I have with all this religion stuff is that I can't relate to it. I think most people got into 'cos it gave them something to do on a Sunday, but since all the shops are now open it isn't required as much.

Steve said I may as well visit the place, as there is so much history in Israel it would be a shame not to stop off and see some of it while I'm in that neck of the woods. I suppose he thought I must have some interest in history as it was him and Ricky who called up my school 20 years after I had left and asked for my exam results, which I had never collected. They found that all I had achieved was a grade E in GCSE history.

One of my wisdom teeth is playing up. My dentist said it is known to happen with some people when they're stressed. My teeth seem to know I'm stressed before I do. Maybe that's why they're called wisdom teeth.

We got to Israel really late. The only place that was open was a 24-hour breakfast cafe. I've never agreed with these places as they just encourage people to get up late. Breakfast should be a treat for those of us who have to get up early. I had some pancakes and eggs.

I finally got to bed at 3 a.m. It would have been slightly earlier, but Luke told me that Ricky had requested that I have a shave before we start filming.

SUNDAY 23RD MAY

I was woken up at 7 a.m. by Luke and Ben.

I asked them what I was doing today that is so important that I had to have a shave. Luke told me it's got nothing to do with any of today's activities, it's just 'cos Ricky said my head looks rounder on the telly once it's shaved.

Luke changed the subject and said he had to give me a safety briefing. It wasn't the best time, considering my brain wasn't properly awake. It reminded of the time a policeman came round to our house when I was a kid and got me out of bed at 3.30 a.m. It was about a car that had been stolen and for some reason I was linked to it. I swear the policeman came round at this time because he knew I was too sleepy to make up any lies. My brain wasn't awake then, and it wasn't awake when Luke kicked off the safety briefing:

'Right, there's a high level of risk to your personal safety in Israel and the occupied Palestinian territories. The prolonged, on-going conflict is punctuated by occasional ceasefires. When no long-term resolution has been reached, regular military incursions including rocket fire and airstrikes take place, and the fall-out is indiscriminate. The situation remains unstable and extremely unpredictable, so, just on a general level, you got to be wary of that when you go out the door . . .'

That's not the sort of stuff I'm good at taking in when I'm wide awake, so it was never going to go in at 7 a.m. I've never understood how people can listen to Radio 4 in the morning, due to the level of concentration needed.

Anyway, I didn't have much option so I had a shower and got in the van. Luke didn't tell me where we were going. After a little while I noticed that the van had driven into some sort of training camp. I hopped out and met a man named Ronan. We were having friendly chit chat about my time in Israel when a car screeched up, and two or three men – it might have even been four – jumped out and pushed me to the ground. They threw a bag over my head and tied my arms behind my back. I was then dragged off and dumped in the back of a car, where they sat on my back and tightened up the plastic ties on my wrists. I could feel the ties cutting into my skin. As the car drove off, my head started banging against the wheel arch while a man yelled at me in some language I didn't understand. At which point my wisdom tooth starting aching again.

I've always thought I was good at dealing with bad situations. A tramp in Manchester once tried to nick my trainers off me in Piccadilly Gardens. I acted like I was mad and he gave up. But in the back of this car in the middle of Israel I couldn't even do that, because of the language barrier. I was helpless.

Finally, I was dragged from the vehicle and taken inside somewhere and shoved into a seat where someone continued to yell at me – this time in English.

'Who is your manager? What is their phone number?'

I told them it was Richard Yee, at the TV company back in London. I didn't know his phone number though. Who knows phone numbers these days? There is no need to remember numbers now they're all programmed into your phone. I don't even know my own home number off by heart as I never really call it. Having said that, I don't even use it when I'm at home. It's got to the point that I don't even answer it when it rings, as it's normally a woman who thinks it's her doctor's number. There's about five messages on the answer machine from her telling me her throat is still sore and the rash hasn't gone away. Maybe that's how Dr Shipman started.

After about what felt like 20 minutes (but was apparently only five) the bag was removed from my head. Luke and Ben were in the room with Jan the cameraman and Freddie the soundman. In my panic I'd completely forgotten we were making a telly programme.

The terrorist man told me that I have a lot to learn. I should always carry a document explaining who I am and what I am filming, along with the phone number of my manager. I had nothing on me. I didn't even take a note of which hotel I was staying in.

He then gave me a phone and asked me what I would do with it if I were in trouble. I told him I'd call my girlfriend as I don't know anybody else's number off by heart. He asked me to tell him what I would say to her.

'I wouldn't want to panic her straight away so I'd say, "How is everything?" and then say, "Right, listen . . . a bit of a problem . . . I was taken away." She's probably sat there going, "What do you mean?" And I'll go, "Shhh, quiet. I'm on low battery . . ."'

'Where are you? Where are you?' The terrorist was pretending to be Suzanne now, which was a bit weird.

'Shhh, don't shout, because they can hear me. I'm in a bush.'

'In a bush? Why? Where? What country?'

'Well, you know where I am . . .'

'Where?'

'You see, you never listen to me, you see! You keep going on about your haircuts.'

'Where are you, where are you?'

'I'm in Israel.'

'Where are you?'

'Stop talking!'

'I'm coming. I'm coming over.' I tried a different tack.

'Can you call Richard?'

'Richard?'

'Yes, Richard!'

'Richard, right. What's his phone number?' The terrorist had me again.

'You're right. I'm useless.'

I was shaking for a good half hour afterwards. Normally if I get the shakes like this it's 'cos I need a Mars Bar or a Twix for a sugar hit – I think I might even have a touch of diabetes. But today it was 'cos of the stress. Even though my brain knew it was all just a test, the rest of my body didn't.

The main man at the security camp told me I needed to have contact information for people back in London with me at all times, and that I needed a code word that could be used to warn the team back in London that there was a real situation.

I told Luke to tell London that I'll use the words 'Congress Tart' as my emergency code. Congress Tarts were my favourite cakes when I lived in Manchester, but I can never find them in London. For some reason the name is still rattling around me head so it may as well be used for something. I hope Luke tells London 'cos I'm starting to take this seriously now.

Once I got back in the van I noticed I had a voicemail message from Steve.

STEPHEN: Alright, Karl. It's Steve, mate. I don't want to worry you, but I've been talking to some of the health and safety people, and obviously you are in quite a volatile region. We're a bit worried because you are with a TV camera crew, you might be seen as a journalist and you could perhaps attract some unwanted attention. At the far extreme there's the danger that you could be kidnapped and taken hostage, and you could be used as a bargaining chip. That could be a bit of a downer for the show. So you should have some extreme scenario training, as a precaution. They'll teach you a few things so if you are in any trouble you'll know how to deal with the situation. And the other thing is that it will give you a flavour of what a lot of Israeli men over 18 have to do every year. You know you have to do military training in Israel? They do three years, you'll be doing half a day or something. No need to panic, but I would take it very, very seriously indeed. Alright? Bye.

It would have been nice to get that message a little earlier.

We travelled on to Jerusalem in the afternoon. There were young soldiers everywhere carrying guns – big guns. It looked like a scene from Bugsy Malone. There were people in all sorts of religious clothing. I went down one alley and was faced with a mob of monks coming at me so turned to go the other way when I was faced with a pack of nuns. I nipped down another alley where there were more soldiers marching towards me. It was like playing Pac-Man.

I saw a famous wall called the Wailing Wall. I'd never heard of it before today. It's a really old wall that Jewish people love. They use it to pray at. There was a big section of it for men and a smaller section for women. Not sure why they can't share a wall. They'd had to build another wall to divide the wall.

There seem to be lots of walls here. It's a good place for a bricklayer to live. We're not a fan of walls back home. I'd say we have fewer walls than ever. Open-plan offices and open-plan homes seem to be all the rage. No wonder Banksy, the graffiti artist, tends to do more stuff abroad these days.

I watched people pray for a bit. Some read from bibles, some kissed the wall and some pushed handwritten notes into the cracks. I met a Jewish fella called Dov. He told me that people write down their sins or wishes and place them into the wall for God to see. Every little crevice had a note shoved in it. It looked like a local postman had had enough of his round and had just dumped everything in his bag. I'm sure there was even junk mail in some of the cracks, from insurance companies and pizza delivery shops.

I had a bagel and left.

Steve called me this evening.

STEPHEN: Alright?

KARL: I don't know what you were thinking sending me to Israel. I suppose you think it's a lovely place that's got no dangers . . .

STEPHEN: What dangers have you encountered?

KARL: They don't have handbags here, it's guns, everybody's got a gun.

STEPHEN: Well, yeah, obviously it's a very volatile region. I mean, you know that is a problem . . .

KARL: I had a bag over my head today.

STEPHEN: Why did you have a bag over your head?

KARL: Because I've had the training that you sorted me out with.

STEPHEN: Oh yeah, yeah, the training, yeah, of course . . .

KARL: You just forgot about that, did you? You forgot that you sorted out a fella to stick a bag over my head and a gun up my arse.

STEPHEN: But you come from Manchester. That's everyday up there, isn't it?

KARL: No, no, no, different league this, Steve.

STEPHEN: So they dragged you into the van with the bag on your head. What happened next?

KARL: They did some 360s in a car park and then dragged me off to a hut somewhere, and then started yelling at me again asking who my manager was. There was about 30 seconds where I actually thought, 'This is real.'

STEPHEN: Surely that's made you more aware of the environment you're in? And again, it's broadened your mind, hasn't it? I mean, when the sack was over your head, what sort of thoughts were racing through your mind? Were you thinking about Suzanne? Were you thinking about me and Ricky?

KARL: I was in total shock. I don't think you realise how bad it was. Nothing was going on in my head.

STEPHEN: Well, they say that when you're confronted with the last moments of your life the rest of your life flashes before your eyes. What was flashing before your eyes, Karl?

KARL: Well, not much, 'cos I had a bag on my head so I couldn't see anything.

STEPHEN: It doesn't literally flash before your eyes. It's not everyone from your life doing a little dance in front of you, 'Oh, there's Aunty Mord. I haven't seen her since 1973.' That's not what they mean, they mean in your mind. Anyway, listen, talking about experiencing the extremes of life I'm very excited for you to meet someone tomorrow who believes that he is Jesus Christ. You're in a very spiritual environment.

KARL: So when you set that up, what were you thinking? Why is this good for me?

STEPHEN: OK, there is a psychological condition known as the Jerusalem Syndrome in which people who travel to that most spiritual of places are often so overwhelmed with the sense of spirituality that they start to believe that they have a spiritual power, or that they are somehow connected to the religion to which they subscribe. It might be very interesting to try to understand how that can impact on someone. You're living at the extremes of life here, Karl. This is exciting, man. Today you thought you were kidnapped and you were going to be done for, tomorrow you're meeting someone who's pushing at the very parameters of consciousness. They've always talked about the Second Coming . . . How do we know that this isn't the big man himself?

KARL: Have you got any questions for Jesus?

STEPHEN: Have I got any questions for Jesus?

KARL: Yeah. What would you ask him if you were in my shoes? I don't want to annoy him.

STEPHEN: Well, I don't know if you could annoy him. I imagine that even if it annoyed him he'd forgive you.

KARL: That's true.

STEPHEN: There's not much that would annoy the big JC, I would have thought.

KARL: What does the 'H' stand for? People always say Jesus H. Christ – what's his middle name?

STEPHEN: I'm not sure that's part of the official mythology, to be honest. I think that might have been introduced later. I mean, you can ask him that. By all means ask him – he might have a good answer. I've also heard the phrase 'Christ on a bike': you might want to ask him if he's got a bike.

KARL: Alright then.

STEPHEN: Well, good luck, mate. I hope you have an informative time tomorrow.

KARL: Yeah, I think it could be alright, quite interesting – but he's not mental?

STEPHEN: If you believe that you are Jesus Christ, you're not going to be a dangerous man, are you? You're going to be a peaceful person.

KARL: But are you saying that this syndrome means that he can't switch overnight? He couldn't be someone else tomorrow, could he? It's a syndrome where you're definitely Jesus all the time – tomorrow he's not going to turn up and say 'I'm Joe Pasquale today'?

STEPHEN: No, he's not going to wake up and go 'Hello, I'm Simon Cowell'. I don't think that's a problem.

KARL: I'm just checking.

〜〜 ‖ 〜〜

MONDAY 24TH MAY

I wondered if I'd have any nightmares after being attacked yesterday, but I had a good night's sleep.

At breakfast, Luke told me we would be meeting Jesus in the market today. It sounded daft, but I suppose he's got to shop just like anyone else.

When we got to the market I asked various people if Jesus was around and got some pretty mixed reactions. Some people pointed me to where he normally hangs out, others said I was wasting my time and that he was a crazy man. I passed quite a few men with long hair and beards, but I suppose when you live in a place near where Jesus lived, you might copy his style in the same way a lot of kids tried to look like Noel and Liam Gallagher in Manchester when I was growing up.

I kept asking around until finally a young lad told me he was also waiting for him. I asked him if he had an appointment with him and he told me he meets Jesus every day. I was just asking what I should call Jesus when a motorbike swerved up onto the footpath, driven by a man in robes with long hair and a beard. The motorbike had blankets covering it. The young lad I was stood with told me this was Jesus and that he tries to make the bike look like a donkey.

Jesus parked, got off his bike and rolled out a mat and sat on it. A crowd of around 40 or so people started gathering and before long an argument broke out between Jesus and a woman. From what I could make out it was something to do with a holocaust. I pushed my way to the front of the crowd and told him that Steve had sent me.

'Hi, I'm Karl. How you doing? I'm here to see you. Can I sit down?'

'You're a very brave man,' said Jesus.

'Why am I brave?' I asked.

'Brave because you sit here and you can see the crowd – they don't like prophets.'

'Why not?'

'Why? Because I'm telling them bad things, of course, and they hate me because of it. They don't like me, period.'

'Can't you give them some better news than "there's a holo-caust coming"?'

'Yeah, but I've said that there's a way to prevent it – by changing their hearts.'

'And they don't like it?'

'No, they don't like it.'

At that point he started shouting something in various l anguages that seemed to offend quite a few people. I tried to yell louder than everyone else to keep the conversation going.

'Do you have any days where you just think, "I can't deal with having to do this"?'

'Huh?' I'd lost him.

I tried again, even louder this time.

'People yelling at you all day? I think if I was you, I'd sort of be like "Oh, I can't be bothered with this". Do you know what I mean?'

'I don't have any other option.'

The shouting carried on in Hebrew. Jesus sat and took it whilst lighting a Marlboro cigarette.

A tourist called out to him, 'Messiah, Messiah, I have health problem, let me touch your vest and cure me.'

'Leave me alone, you crazy French guy.' Jesus shouted back.

'May I touch your vest, Messiah?'

'Don't touch my nothing!'

I left, as I felt I was never going to get a proper one-to-one with Jesus. Maybe if the real Jesus were still around this is what it would be like for him – people either abusing him or hassling him. Even though modern life is better than biblical times, people need help more than ever. I recently noticed a helpline on a bottle of HP brown sauce. I called it to see if anyone was there. There was, so I hung up as I didn't actually need any help.

I was standing in the shade, out of the sun, when a lad came over who had been watching us film. He asked me to go with him. He led me to the car park where he had a camper van with a massive speaker on the roof. Rave music blared from it. Him and four of his mates danced. They asked me to join them. So I did, for a couple of songs. I then said I had to get back to the hotel and they offered me a lift.

As we drove, one explained to me that they are known as the Nachmen. They believe in spreading happiness through the power of dance. I was polite and said 'very good' as I just wanted to get back to the hotel. They then pulled up at some traffic lights that were on red and jumped out and started dancing again. The drivers around us looked puzzled, but smiled.

The Nachmen told me they cheer up hundreds of people stuck in traffic jams every day. I said that it's probably them who are causing the traffic jams. At this point the lights went to green. The drivers around us suddenly didn't look so happy. They were beeping their horns, asking us to get a move on. Five hundred yards down the road at the next set of lights the same thing happened again. All the Nachmen hopped out and danced on the main road and on top of the van like the kids from Fame.

'I get my kids to join in with me. They love it, it makes them so happy,' one of them explained to me.

'But aren't they late for school every day when you're forever saying, "Get out! The lights are red!" "But Dad . . . I'm missing English!"?'

'No, no. It is good for them', the Nachman assured me.

They pulled up on a roundabout quite close to where the hotel was for a long dance. Two of the guys were on the roof, and the music was louder than ever. So loud that we didn't notice the police siren until the police car had pulled up next to us. The police got out and told us we couldn't film next to the main road because it was a distraction to the other drivers. The fact there was a van with several people dancing on the roof with music blaring apparently wasn't an issue.

I left them to it.

TUESDAY 25 TH MAY

We went to another big wall today. It was massive and went on and on as far as the eye could see, separating Israel from Palestine. It's a horrible looking wall. Big slabs of concrete with barbed wire on the top. I had to go through a check point and show my passport.

When I got to the other side I met a local Palestinian man called Kais, who took me to Bethlehem. He took me into a church to show me the spot where Jesus was supposed to have been born.

Kais had brought some flutes with him because the story goes that the shepherds came to Jesus's birth carrying flutes. But we were told by the man in charge that we couldn't play them, which was a blessing in disguise to be honest, as they are the most irritating-sounding instruments.

We had to wait our turn to see the special spot, while other visitors went in and cried. Some people placed beads and crosses on the spot, and one guy placed his mobile phone on it as if he was hoping it would charge the battery. I really can't see how they know this is the exact spot. My mam doesn't even remember the hospital bed number at Wythenshawe hospital where I was born and she was there, so I doubt this was right. It wasn't what I'd imagined either – I thought I was going to see a little hut with straw and a cradle, but it looked like a fireplace.

With me not being religious I didn't get anything from the moment. Although when I get a Christmas card with a little image of the nativity scene on it at least I can say I've been there.

On the way back to the wall I saw some graffiti done by Banksy. I knew he'd love it here.

KARL'S FACTS

PETRA WAS FOUNDED BY A NOMADIC ARAB TRIBE KNOWN AS THE NABATAEANS. IT WAS THE CAPITAL OF THE NABATAEAN KINGDOM FROM THE 4TH CENTURY BC. AND WAS THEN CAPTURED BY THE ROMANS IN THE 2ND CENTURY AD.

THE CITY WAS REDISCOVERED IN 1812.

PETRA WAS USED AS THE LOCATION FOR INDIANA JONES AND THE LAST CRUSADE IN 1989.

PETRA MEANS 'ROCK' IN GREEK.

WEDNESDAY 26TH MAY

We're finally headed into Jordan today. It was a long old trip. We drove through nothingness for hours and then we eventually reached the Dead Sea. I'd seen pictures of it in the guidebook. There is so much salt in it there was a photo of a man floating on his back while reading the paper. I asked Luke if we could stop off so I could have a go. He said okay. I think he still felt bad about the prank hostage incident.

I read a sign that said the Dead Sea was the lowest point in the world. It didn't feel any different and the sun didn't look that much further away, though Ben, Luke's assistant, said something about not having to wear suntan lotion as the UV rays don't reach this far. But now I think about it, Ben's job is to make sure we don't go over budget, so it wouldn't surprise me if this was his way of making sure we didn't buy suntan lotion for everyone.

The Dead Sea was very muddy looking and it wasn't very sealike. It was more like a lake. I was up for getting in it, though, as I have a little bit of eczema on my leg and the mud and salt are supposed to be good for the skin. Hippos roll about in mud all the time and you never see them with eczema so there must be some truth in it.

I waded in, but it was hard to stand up as the dark green mud sucked you down. Straight away the salty water started to sting all the cuts on my wrists and knees that I got from being kidnapped. I didn't realise I had so many cuts. It's like when you only find out you have a paper cut when you eat a bag of salt-and-vinegar crisps.

I was the youngest person in there by a mile. Everyone else looked to be in their seventies. Maybe this is why they call it the Dead Sea – all the visitors are close to death. Having said that, it could just be that they're here on holiday and other than float about in the sea there isn't much to do. So maybe they're young but really wrinkly from being in the sea all day.

I lay back and floated. It was really good. Well, that was until Luke pointed out that I had something in my belly button. At first I thought it was a fag end until I flicked it out and got a closer look. It was phlegm. I glanced around and saw that a lot of people seemed to be blowing their noses and coughing up phlegm, especially when they had accidentally got a mouthful of saltwater. I started to wonder if the dark green mud was mud or snot.

Ricky called as I was floating:

RICKY: What's going on?

KARL: I'm just in the Dead Sea.

RICKY: Floating around?

KARL: Yeah, just floating around with someone's gob.

RICKY: What?

KARL: I've just had a bit of gob on me.

RICKY: Urgh.

KARL: There are old people in here just, y'know, clearing their throats and that. I just had some in my belly button.

RICKY: Oh, that is disgusting!

KARL: Maybe that's why I'm floating around. Ninety per cent catarrh or whatever it is.

RICKY: I was going to say taste it, to see how salty it is – but don't. What have you been doing?

KARL: Pretty stressful here.

RICKY: Why? You seem to be okay, floating around like you're on holiday.

KARL: No, this is the first day I've done something relaxing.

RICKY: Hmmm. It's like you're in a spa or something, but with phlegm. New phlegm treatment: 'Do you want the aromatherapy or the old people's gob treatment?' 'I'll have the aromatherapy please.' Now, did you enjoy that camel ride in Egypt?

KARL: You know I didn't.

RICKY: Was it uncomfortable?

KARL: Yeah, it's the worst animal you can sit on, innit? It's got a lump in it.

RICKY: Yeah, well, I think you're going to need to give it another go because, y'know, you've gotta get used to it, haven't you?

KARL: Well, I don't mind having another quick go.

RICKY: Yeah, you say a 'quick go', but I think the Wonder of Petra is about two days away on a camel.

KARL: Two days?

RICKY: Yeah. So, I mean, relax in that lovely, salty, gob-ridden water because you are going to have a sore arse in a couple of days' time. So I'd soak it if I was you.

KARL: What? We're going the whole way on a camel?

RICKY: Well, you might as well. Silly to change, innit?

KARL: But what's the point?

RICKY: Camel, direct, no change. Much better than, y'know, 'Oh, let's get a train, let's get a bus, let's get a coach, let's get a helicopter.' No, let's just get one camel all the way.

KARL: Well, this call is costing me money even though you called me, so there's no point arguing.

RICKY: Karl. Get out of the Dead Sea, put some clothes on and do some fucking work. You're not on holiday.

KARL: I've been doing work for four days. This is good for the programme. I'm explaining to people how there's loads of salt in it, you float about and it's good for your skin.

RICKY: It's not good for your skin if you're covered in old people's vomit and sick and gob and phlegm and snot. I've never seen that on any Alan Whicker or Michael Palin show.

KARL: Exactly. This is the truth.

RICKY: Well, can't you talk about the Wonders?

KARL: Well, if you would've fucking sent me there! You sent me to Israel! Let's get to the Wonder, I agree with you. Jesus! Oh yeah, I met him yesterday. I met Jesus yesterday.

RICKY: Did you?

KARL: Yeah. Couldn't get a word in edgeways. I couldn't get through to him.

RICKY: You'll see him just walk past you in a minute. At least Jesus would only get old people's gob on the bottom of his feet.

KARL: See you later.

I had to go through another checkpoint on the way into Jordan. They opened my suitcase and I immediately felt guilty even though I had nothing to be guilty about. They went into my toilet bag and pulled out loads of ear buds. I don't think they had seen them before 'cos they looked confused as they passed them around.

We got to the hotel at 8 p.m., but the staff couldn't find the key for my room. They took me to another room but the door only opened a quarter of the way before jamming, so I couldn't get my case in. They eventually gave up and took me to a posh room. They opened the door and asked me if the suite would be okay. I said it would, but the knickers and bra on the bed are not my type. The room was already being used.

They eventually got me a room at 9.15 p.m. It overlooks the entertainment area, where a fat man was singing 'My Way'. He's still singing now as I type this at 10.30 p.m.

I just looked in the mirror and noticed that I've burnt my back in the sun, so Ben was talking through his arse about the UV rays.

THURSDAY 27 TH MAY

I was up early today. Luke asked me to meet him at the front of the hotel with my luggage, as we would be making our way over to the Ancient Wonder of Petra.

Luke introduced me to a man called Mr Mohammed. Mr Mohammed asked me to get in one of two pick-up trucks parked outside. They were really old and battered and each one had a camel strapped in the back. He put my case right next to a camel's arse. Mr Mohammed said we would be crossing the desert on the camels, but we would need to drive to the edge of the desert first. I asked Mr Mohammed about what Ricky had said – that it would take 48 hours to cross the desert. He said it would, and I couldn't help looking back at the camels, who looked old and seemed to be moaning already.

Mr Mohammed got in one van and I got in another, which was being driven by a young lad. Then the driver's dad climbed in and squeezed down next to me. The camels had more room than I did! The dad was an old-looking fella with a big moustache, and he wore a gown with a suit jacket on top. His name was Saba. He didn't speak much English. I tried to explain a bit about my life. I told him I was from London and had a girlfriend called Suzanne, who I had been with for 16 years.

Within two minutes of leaving the hotel car park the van I was in broke down. Maybe that's why they have a camel in the boot – it's an emergency mode of transport. The young lad whipped the bonnet open and sorted it like it was something that happened quite often.

It took about an hour to get to the desert. When we arrived, Mr Mohammed gave me some clothes to wear that made me look like a proper desert adventurer. Before getting on the camel I popped some sun cream on my face. Mr Mohammed asked what it was. I told him it was suntan lotion; he then told me that proper Bedouin people rub their face with sand to stop getting burned. This was to be the first of many things I was told by Mr Mohammed that sounded like a load of bollocks. A lot of what he said as we crossed the desert didn't seem right to me. For example, he told me that the area we would be staying in that night had a shop and I would be able to buy a Twix. Really?

I tried different topics of conversation with him, but he didn't understand me. In the end, he started to sing so I left him to that while I just looked around. There was nothing going on. There was literally no one else around. All I saw in about five hours were two beetles.

I was expecting us to do an hour or two in the desert, and then be told by Luke that that is all we need for the programme. Six or seven hours later I realised that that wasn't going to be the case. At about the eight-hour point the camel that Mr Mohammed was on started to moan quite loudly, and kept sitting down, and then, eventually, it just gave up altogether.

The vans had to be called and the camels were loaded into the back once again. Saba, the man with a big moustache I sat next to on the way to the desert, was not happy. It turned out the camels belonged to him and he was annoyed that we had been out on them all day. I said I thought these animals were meant to be the ships of the desert. If so, we'd ended up with the Titanic.

I had to share a lift with Saba. I couldn't tell if he was ignoring me because he was annoyed or just because he didn't speak much English.

It turned out that I would be staying with him tonight at his tent, along with his family of 14 kids, in the middle of nowhere. I wasn't too bothered as I was so knackered that I could've slept anywhere. I asked Mohammed what time everyone would be going to bed, but he said they would be staying up later tonight as they have a guest to entertain. I said they shouldn't worry on my account and that we should all go to bed, but he explained that Saba was preparing food.

As Saba made dinner the rest of the family sat around smoking something that made their eyes big. I thought it was drugs but it was just strong tobacco. Mr Mohammed said that as the guest I should have some, but I refused. He said that this was rude and would annoy Saba. I tried to explain that I don't smoke and am not planning on starting now. It felt to me like we were bonding.

We sat down for food. They brought a massive plate that had some animal head in the middle with rice and milky type sauce poured over it. They call it mansaf. I ate some as I didn't want to be rude, but I wasn't really liking it. I like my meat quite well cooked and this wasn't. Mr Mohammed then said that Saba had insisted that the guest gets the best bit – the best bit being the eye. Two things worried me: firstly, I didn't want to eat an eye, and secondly, what sort of animal only has one eye?

Mr Mohammed said I'd offend Saba if I didn't eat it, but as far as I was concerned we had already fallen out over me not smoking the tobacco so what was the point? I gave the eye to a cat that was wandering around the tent.

Before I nodded off that night I told Mr Mohammed that we shouldn't hang about in the morning as I don't think Saba likes me very much. Mr Mohammed then explained that Saba wasn't happy that a man of my age was dating a 16-year-old girl. It turned out he'd misunderstood me in the car when I said I had been with Suzanne for 16 years.

FRIDAY 28 TH MAY

I didn't sleep too well last night. I was aware of the insects that came out of the sand and crawled all over me. In the morning I got up and tried to use the toilet. I still couldn't do the crouching toilet. I don't know why. I've been to quite a few countries now and yet I still haven't mastered it. We had tea for breakfast with some bread, and then left.

Mr Mohammed wanted to carry on by camel now that they had rested, but I persuaded him to go by car. I say 'persuaded'; he tried to get me on a camel, but I refused and sat in a pick-up truck until he agreed to drive.

Finally, we got to the Ancient Wonder. Almost there now. The trip is almost done . . . or so I thought.

I'd barely had a chance to take it in when Ricky called. He told me I'd be staying in a cave tonight. I asked him why and he just said, 'It would be funny', and then the line went dead.

So I called Steve.

STEPHEN: Hello, mate.

KARL: Hiya. I've just spoken to Ricky. He called up as I was at the Wonder, and he said, 'You like staying in caves and all that, so you're staying in a cave tonight.' What's all that about?

STEPHEN: Well, I remember before you went you said you would rather live in a hole and look at a palace, than live in a palace and look at a hole. You said it was more about the view for you.

KARL: Yeah, but I didn't . . .

STEPHEN: So we thought, well, if that's what Karl wants, and he's been complaining, let's give him exactly what he wants.

KARL: But I didn't literally mean that that's what I would like.

STEPHEN: Well, you know, I thought you would've learnt by now, after all your travels, that you should never try and second guess anything. You never know what you're going to learn.

KARL: It's just never been a wish, it's never been something that I've thought about because it's going backwards. How is that moving me on, when I'm actually going backwards? I mean, when was it that people lived in caves? I don't know anyone who was knocking around back then. There is no one in me family that can say 'me great-great-great-great-gran used to live in one'.

STEPHEN: You could learn a lot about yourself, you know, stripping away all of the creature comforts that you're used to. You know, back to basics. It's exciting.

KARL: I like nature. I've been playing with beetles while I've been here. There's been all sorts of stuff knocking around, but . . .

STEPHEN: There could be loads of bugs and creepy crawlies in a cave, if that's what you're into. If you're into beetles and bugs, then . . .

KARL: Yeah, I like looking at them, but I don't want to sleep with them. There's a big difference. Honestly, if you could see me now you'd go, 'What are you doing?' I'm stood here in all this get-up because the fella who's been showing me around dressed me up like this 'cos he said it's better in the heat. He took me across the desert yesterday for eight hours when it was meant to be for two days, but the camel packed up, so in the end he said, 'Oh, we'll get in the van then.' It's like, well, if we've got a van what are doing using the fucking camels? I don't even know if he knows what he's going on about because as soon as we get to a place where there's history and I have lots of questions he says, 'Oh, I've got to leave you now.' Of all the trips that I've done I don't know what I'm taking away from this one. I really feel like it's just been sort of an extreme holiday living in a tent with kids. I didn't get on with him in the end because I didn't take a fag off him.

STEPHEN: Oh dear, you've been insulting local people by not engaging with their customs again.

KARL: Yeah, but I said 'No thank you'. I was dead polite.

STEPHEN: Well, think about how he's going to feel if you turn down his cave.

KARL: Well, I don't know. I'd have thought cavemen wouldn't get upset that easily.

STEPHEN: I don't know if he's a caveman. That was a more general term. Just because you live in a cave, you're not a caveman.

KARL: Well, what is it then? Where's the line then? You're a man, you live in a cave. Ok, I'm going to do it because I've got nowhere else, but I honestly thought this was it.

STEPHEN: Good attitude.

KARL: Alright. I'll let you know how it goes then.

I met Ibrahim in a cafe. He had quite a caveman-type face and hair style. The only thing that ruined the look was the fact he seemed to have that 'wet look' gel in his hair that Michael Jackson used to use. Either that or his cave is really, really damp. He was a nice fella, though. He gave me a tour of the caves. There were loads of them. It was like The Flint-stones.

A lot of them are now empty after the government moved everyone out in the 1980s, to protect the archaeological site. I could really imagine what it was like to live there back in the day. I can picture myself coming out of a little hole in the morning, armed with just a club, thinking, 'What am I going to do today?' I would probably spend my time inventing things 'cos it would have been a lot easier to do that back then. It's really difficult to come up with ideas now. I designed a see-through toaster, the idea being that you don't have to keep popping the toast up to see if it's cooked to your liking. Then I looked online and found that someone had already done it. I also came up with the idea of luminous tissue paper after not being able to find the tissues in the dark one night when I had a cold. I looked that up online, too, and it already existed.

The only thing that would get on my nerves if I lived here is this sort of 'open door policy'. Not having a door doesn't help. Anyone you know could walk past and see that you're in and keep nipping in. That's one thing that might mess up the invention thing. You might be thinking of something really good and people are constantly popping in going, 'Oh, alright Albert, how's it going?' 'I had an idea for something just then and it's gone now. Go away!'

Ibrahim took me to the cave where he was born and the one he lived in when he was younger. It was nice big cave with a living room and his bedroom just off that. He then took me across the path to where they moved to when he got a little bit older and needed a bigger place. He was showing me around like he was on some property programme: 'Here's the living space; this area was where we cooked.' It all seemed quite normal until he pointed out the tomb in the lounge. The presenter would have told him to keep that bit of information to himself if he was selling it.

We eventually got to the cave he now lived in. It was simple but nice. I was imagining a dark damp place with sharp rock everywhere, but it was all nice and smooth. In fact, the walls in my bedroom when I was a kid were sharper 'cos my dad went through a phase of Artexing everything. It was trendy in the 1980s to have prickly walls. I used to wake up every morning with scratches on my arse.

Had some chicken that Ibrahim cooked on a fire. It was some of the tastiest chicken I had ever had.

I think being a caveman would have suited me down to the ground. I think my brain would have suited that time more as it can't keep up with stuff these days.

I think I was born too late.

I fell asleep watching geckos run across the ceiling. Suppose that was one good thing with Artex – the sharpness kept the geckos out.

SATURDAY 29TH MAY

I slept really well in the cave and only woke up once, when a cat wandered in. This is another problem when you haven't got a front door. The night in the cave was my favourite experience since being here. Ibrahim made me feel really at home. I felt like I could do what I wanted. Suzanne always says I'm rubbish at making people feel relaxed 'cos I 'm always saying 'take your shoes off', or 'put your cup on a mat'. But when you live in a cave you don't worry about things like this.

We're going home tomorrow so I used the last day to have a walk around and see more of the Petra site. Ibrahim told me I should make the effort to go and see the monastery. It was one hell of a climb, over 800 steps. It looked very similar to the site that I had seen on my arrival, but bigger. It had a fancy, carved-out front, but it was all a bit damaged and chipped. People say that that's because it's so old, but I wonder if it ever looked perfect. You only get one go at chipping at rock so if the fellas who did it made a few mistakes it could have looked like this from day one.

And as impressive as the entrance was, it was still a cave. Yes, it has good 'kerb appeal', but once I stuck my head inside there really was nothing to it. If you add that to the fact that it was out of the way and you had to climb over 800 steps to get to it, it's fair to say that if it was on *Location, Location, Location* it wouldn't be on my shortlist. It wasn't as cosy as Ibrahim's place where we stayed last night, either.

I noticed there was a cave across from it so made my way over and sat in it. And it was there that I finally proved my point to Ricky and Steve. It was much better to look out of a hole at a palace, than live in the palace looking at a hole. I think the same rule applies with humans. I think I'd rather be an uglyish looking person than a beautiful one, as how often do you have to look at yourself? If you're quite ugly and you're sat facing someone who is pretty at work, who's got the better deal?

SUNDAY 30TH MAY

We flew home today. I checked in with Richard at the TV company and asked if he'd been told what the emergency code word was. He had no idea what I was talking about.

JORDAN

JORDAN

JORDAN

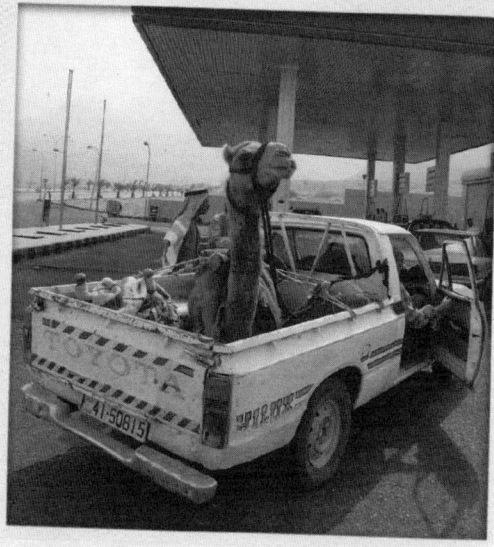

LOOK WHAT SABA GOT FREE WITH HIS NECTAR POINTS.

MR MOHAMMED.

BIN THERE.

JORDAN

PERU

PERU

WILDER WAITS FOR MY VERDICT ON THE COOKED WORM.

MY PRESENTATION TO THE DRAGONS DEN.

SAY IT WITH FLOWERS.

PERU

MY OPPONENT IN THE WORLD
STARING COMPETITION.

IF THEY HAD SUDOKUS HERE, THIS
SORT OF THING WOULDNT HAPPEN.

THE SLOTH MOVED AS FAST AS
IT DOES IN THIS PHOTO.

SEVEN-NIL TO ME.

PERU

CHAPTER SEVEN
MACHU PICCHU

'IN THE VARIETY OF ITS CHARMS AND THE POWER OF ITS SPELL I KNOW OF NO PLACE IN THE WORLD WHICH CAN COMPARE WITH IT.'

HIRAM BINGHAM
(DISCOVERER OF MACHU PICCHU)

'MAGNIFICENT. I AM SPEECHLESS.'

KARL PILKINGTON

ECUADOR

COLOMBIA

Iquitos

Amaz[...]

Santa
Rosa

breakfast

Rio Javari

Spent 2 nights
here

Watch out!

B R A Z I [L]

SOUTH

PACIFIC

Lima

OCEAN

Machu
Picchu

Ollantaytambo

Cusco

[B]OLIVIA

MONDAY 14ᵀᴴ JUNE

It took ages to get to where we were going. The first flight went from Heathrow to Madrid. It was full of Spanish people – angry Spanish people due to it being delayed. The Spanish are already quite animated as it is, but even more so when they are annoyed. A man sat next to me was flapping his arms about so much the pilot could have turned the engines off and we'd have stayed in the air.

We had a burger and chips in Madrid airport and then got a night flight from Madrid to Lima. I'm not a fan of night flights. I worry the pilot isn't at the top of his game. I'd prefer it if the cockpit wasn't closed 'cos at least you could keep an eye on him and make sure his eyelids weren't drooping. I could go and have a chat with him like you can on a bus. I don't think it helps that all the controls are so close either. Surely it would be better to give him more space and maybe put some of the controls a bit further away so he has to get up now and again to wake him up a bit.

Once in Lima we had to get another flight to a place called Iquitos. We were staying at a hotel there for the night. I was given a room on the top floor. It was really, really hot due to the fact that the roof was made out of tin. There were also some big windows that helped to increase the heat and the aircon unit was so old it seemed to give off more heat than cool the place down. I ended up sleeping on the floor, as heat rises and it was the coolest place I could find.

TUESDAY 15 ᵀᴴ JUNE

I was woken up at 3.45 this morning and taken to an army base to catch another plane. Turns out it was one of them small planes that takes off and lands on water.

In fact, it was the smallest plane I have ever been on. It sat about ten people. It was also the first plane I've ever been told to leave due to an emergency. Freddie the soundman complained about heat coming off the engines when they started them. I didn't really notice after my hotel room experience last night. But Freddie was right to be worried. One of the engines was on fire so we had to wait while about six men opened it up and put it right.

Then we all got back on again. It stank of petrol fumes, which started to give me a headache. I was sat behind the pilot, who was called George. I asked him if everything was okay. He did that hand signal which means 'so-so'. It wasn't the signal I wanted to see. Pilots in the film *Top Gun* always gave each other big smiles with a positive thumbs-up. George looked like his head was somewhere else. If this plane goes down so will mine.

Everyone was fairly quiet on the flight. I just watched as George flicked switches, pulled levers and ate home-made sandwiches from clingfilm. Now and again he would go to pull a lever only for his co-pilot to grab his hand before he had the chance to pull it. A man sat behind him doing some kind of paperwork. Maybe it was coordinates for the flight. Maybe it was just a Sudoku. Maybe it's best not to see what the pilot is up to during a flight.

We flew over miles and miles of trees. I was looking out the window for any sort of activity when the plane took a dive and landed in a river. Turns out it was the Amazon. Richard the director told me I would be staying in the jungle to get a real taste of Peru. At least it'll make a change from petrol.

We unloaded our kit and got on a long thin boat. We had two of them between us. We were in the middle of nowhere. The plane left us. I had no phone signal. Richard the director could see I didn't look too happy. He told me I should be excited because I was standing next to the Amazon. I was just worried about what Ricky and Steve had arranged for me while I was there.

I had a wee in the Amazon. Until Richard told me I should be careful because there are some tiny fish that can swim up from the water through my urine and into my knob! Is that how amazing the Amazon is? The fish in there would really rather live in my knob than the river.

Richard then played me a message on his phone that Steve had recorded telling me that if I was going to experience the jungle then I would need my jungle bag which had been packed with all the survival kit I would need to get me through. I looked in my jungle bag. The first thing I found was a small torch and a whistle which didn't look of a high standard – more like the type of thing you'd get in a Christmas cracker. Next was a first aid kit. By the look of things it had already been used. The aspirin, Imodium and plasters had already been taken with just the wrappers left behind. There was also a pair of cycling shorts and a box of flavoured condoms; not sure what they are for. I know I needed protection from mosquitoes and rabies and typhoid, but condoms? I wondered if Steve had made a mistake and given me his gym bag instead of the jungle bag, until I found a pair of leech protectors. These were like big socks that I would have to wear over my trousers to stop the leeches sucking my blood. But things like this will just make the leech evolve to have stronger jaws and teeth, in the way that the giraffe grew a long neck to reach food that was high up. We are our own worst enemy when it comes to stuff like this.

There was also a book that contained loads of horrible pictures of people who had been bitten and eaten away by some jungle creatures. There were no details of what the creatures looked like or what to do if you got bitten so I presume he had put it in just to worry me. It did. I remember seeing a programme on the telly going on about something called a botfly which lays an egg under your skin and then it grows to the size of a cola bottle sweet and you can see it wriggling about under your skin. Why do they have to do that? All the space in the world and they're laying eggs under humans' skin. A while back I heard bears have to stick leaves up their arse to stop ants crawling up there and biting them! I know the world is getting overpopulated but it isn't that crowded that things have to live up an arse. No wonder Paddington Bear left Peru for London. When you've got bears wanting to leave the country it makes me wonder what I'm doing here.

Richard introduced me to a man named Matt who was on the other boat with all the camera equipment. He was our paramedic, apparently. This just worried me even more. Sometimes I think it's good not to know where I'm going or what I'll be doing, but having small nuggets of information like 'that's our own paramedic' makes my mind go into overdrive and I start to worry even more. It's like my mind likes to worry me. It never thinks of the good things, it just likes to stress me out.

We eventually pulled up. Wilder, who was travelling with us and knows the jungle like the back of his hand, said this is where we would stay as it would be dark soon and we still needed to clear an area to set up our tents and start a fire.

I was knackered, hot and dizzy, and when I got off the boat I fell straight into the clay-type mud on the banks of the river. Any energy I did have was now being sapped by the mud that was trying to suck me in. I really wanted to go home, more than I've ever wanted to on any other trips, but I had no option. We made our way through the jungle. As Wilder chopped away at the trees with a machete to make a path, he kept telling me to be careful where I was walking and to look out for snakes. He then stopped suddenly in front of a tree. It had big spikes sticking from its bark. He warned me not to touch it. What the hell am I doing here, I wondered, in a place where you can't even trust the trees?

Just as I was about to say I couldn't walk any further, Wilder announced that we had got to our base. I sat while the tents were set up. Wilder told me to make sure nothing had crawled onto or into my bags before putting them in the tent. I tried, but it was hard to tell, and then I made my bed. I say 'bed'; I had a tent mat from Halfords (a place not known for jungle survival gear) and a bag of socks for a pillow.

I went to bed at 7.30 p.m. Lots of insects were already crawling and flying around my small one-man tent. I don't ever remember going to bed as early as this in my whole life but I just wanted the day to end.

WEDNESDAY 16 TH JUNE

I think I had about 30 minutes' sleep last night. It was really hot in the tent and I couldn't open the zip as more creatures and mosquitoes would have got in. The only time I let any fresh air in was when I had to empty my plastic water bottle which I had peed into three times throughout the night – some of which ended up on my Halfords mat as I couldn't see when it was getting full and I was just going by the sound. Suzanne had packed me some hand wipes. This made me laugh as I was sweating like an ape, was kneeling in my own piss and was covered in mud from when I fell over earlier – and I had baby wipes.

I remember being terrified in the night by a noise that sounded like a gorilla yelling. I don't know if there are gorillas round here but it must have been a big animal to make such a deafening noise. My tent was at the end of the row, and I was sure I was going to attract the gorilla with all the piss I had poured out near the entrance to my tent. I lay there listening to my heart pounding in my head. It was amazing that I could hear my heart as the sounds in the jungle at night were so loud. I'm not surprised there are a lot of nocturnal animals and creatures in the jungle, they have no choice but to be awake at night due to all the bloody noise.

I heard the gorilla growl again. It seemed closer this time. I looked at the time and it was only 2.22 a.m. It was one of the longest nights of my life.

Three hours later I got up. Just getting dressed took so much more effort than normal due to lack of space. I put on the clothes I'd worn yesterday as I didn't know how long I'd be in the jungle for, and if I couldn't wash there was no point putting fresh stuff on.

I left my tent and Matt the paramedic shouted me over. He had found a scorpion under his rucksack. Wilder came over and picked it up with his machete and a stick. It looked pretty evil. It looked like Batman's car. Flat, black and evil. Wilder went and chucked it into the woods. I thought he would have picked a camping area that was safe from these types of creatures, but obviously not.

Wilder then offered me some breakfast of worms he had caught. I said no, thanks. Half a cooked rat was his next offer. I had my boil-in-the-bag beans and sausage.

I got my small camera out and went looking for insects and creatures on my own. I watched hundreds of ants climbing up and down a tree. I saw a black snake but didn't turn on the camera fast enough so missed it. Things that don't look like insects sometimes are insects so a lot of the time I found myself filming something thinking it was a stick insect for it to turn out to be just a stick.

Richard the director was talking to the cameraman and soundman so I thought that this was a good time to get out my toilet that I had taken with me. I say 'toilet'; it was a camping chair that I had cut a hole into where I could place a bin bag. I went to my tent to get it to discover it wasn't there. I went mad at Richard telling him that it wasn't funny and wanted to know who had taken it. He said he didn't know what I was talking about. I asked Wilder and he acted the same way. I then went and looked in every tent but couldn't find it. I asked Wilder again and said if the others had told him to hide it he must tell me where as I had gone to a lot of trouble buying, altering and carrying it to the jungle. He took me into the woods where a path had already been cut and the chair set up. I thought he had done it especially for me until I noticed a small M&S bag next to the chair. Someone had already used it. I thought it may have been a joke and that the bag just contained soil so picked it up to check. I hadn't even undone the knot fully when the stench hit me. Someone had used it. No one would tell me who, but it smelt English to me.

I got another bag and told everyone to leave so I could try out my invention for myself. When I sat down in it the hole ripped and I fell right through. I'd brought this over 6,000 miles and it couldn't handle one sitting. I was fed up.

Wilder then took me on a boat down the Amazon. I think he could sense I needed to get away from the base. I had a go at piloting the boat, which was good. I got covered in mud again when I got off for a pee, and saw more giant ants and some pink dolphins. He had mentioned that there were dolphins in the water when we were on our way to our base yesterday, but I didn't believe him. In the end we saw about five or six. Richard the director and Freddie the soundman were particularly excited about seeing them. Dolphins tend to do this to people. I get sick of hearing people say they are really intelligent. People don't say they are intelligent for a fish, they just say they are intelligent as if they could wire a plug and do well on *University Challenge*. It annoys me 'cos I constantly get called a div and an idiot by Ricky and Steve and others, and yet dolphins are being called intelligent. They can't all be bright. Out of this group of six there must be two or three stupid ones.

When we got back to camp Richard told me that he had an electronic device that he has to hit a button on each day that sends a message to London giving them our location so they know that we are okay. It would be nice to be able to speak to Suzanne as she is good at calming me down when I'm fed up. In the last 16 years I haven't gone more than a day without talking to her at some point.

I went to my tent and passed Richard on the way. I noticed he had left the satellite phone that was for real emergencies near the entrance and he wasn't there, so I tried calling Suzanne but it didn't work. Not sure if I was doing it wrong or if it just didn't work. I wanted to tell Richard that it didn't work but then he'd know that I'd tried to use it so I couldn't.

I asked Matt the paramedic if I could try his hammock tonight as my tent was too small. He gave me a spare one that he had. It took me about 30 minutes to put up. It was nice having a little job to do to take my mind off things. It was one that you get inside and zip up. It slowly swung from left to right. Quite calming in a way. It was probably the closest feeling you can get to being back in the womb. That was until a mosquito started whizzing round my head. It must have got in when I did. I had a quick nap in the hammock but decided I couldn't sleep in one all night so gave up on it.

Later I sat in the gloom round a fire and had boil-in-the-bag casserole while trying to shoo away a spider that looked dangerous.

Went to bed around 8.45 p.m. There was quite a big spider in my tent but it was busy catching smaller flies and insects that will probably bite me when I'm asleep, so I decided to leave it be.

I woke up around 10 p.m. to the sound of something heavy landing on top of my tent. No idea what it was. I then had an urge to go to the loo. I couldn't go into the woods as it's just too dark to see what might be crawling around me. So I ended up doing it in my tent into a carrier bag.

This was a new low point.

THURSDAY 17 TH JUNE

When I woke up I looked for the spider that had been in my tent. It had gone, which seemed strange. There is a fact that says most people will accidentally eat ten spiders in their lifetime while sleeping. I've probably had my lifetime allowance since I've been here.

I looked for more insects this morning with my small camera. I filmed some ants. I decided to focus on one ant to see what it was doing. It walked along and then attacked another ant, then that ant started to fight back so another ant came along to stop it, and the one that started it all then sneaked off, and then more ants got involved in the fight. Within seconds there was a full-on riot going on, and yet the one who started it was now nowhere to be seen. Nature is amazing, but it goes to show, you get thugs in all walks of life.

I'm starting to get sick of eating boil-in-the-bag food. Someone back at the London office didn't know that Spotted Dick was a pudding so we're having to eat them as a main course.

I took some Ginger Crunch biscuits with me into the jungle as a treat. Suzanne had bought me some Happy Faces biscuits, which are my very favourite, but you don't get many in a packet, plus I didn't think it would be wise to have a biscuit with a smiling face looking all smug when there was a chance of feeling quite low in the jungle. I'd made my way through half the packet of Ginger Crunches when Wilder called me over with a sense of urgency. He had caught a boa constrictor close to my tent. It was about six feet long. It took Wilder about 15 minutes to catch it using his hands and a stick. These are the snakes that have mouths that expand, which means that they can eat things that are bigger than them. I've never understood this. I saw one on YouTube that ate a hippo. It just lay there, bored, probably feeling a bit sick, not being able to move, with this hippo inside it for weeks while it digested it. It looked like a hippo in a snake-skin sleeping bag. I tried to give this one that Wilder had caught some Ginger Crunches but it didn't seem keen. Wilder managed to take it away from our base.

Later I stripped down to my underpants and let Dr Dolittle (aka Matt the paramedic) look at my bites to see if anything looked bad. He didn't seem too concerned about anything. But then again he never does. I'm sure he's just treating this like a bit of a holiday.

FRIDAY 18ᵀᴴ JUNE

Richard played a message to me this morning that Steve had recorded before we left the UK. He said I'd be going to see a tribe today further down the river. He said they were once cannibals. I think this was meant to scare me, but it didn't. I don't think it's that weird that people used to eat people. I asked Richard if there was any possibility that they would eat me. He didn't know. I think I'd be okay about eating a person but I think I'd like to know about them before I tucked into them, a bit like the way we like to know if the chicken we eat is free range or not.

Maybe it's what they do once one of the tribe dies. Someone dies, and they go 'Right, Molly was a lovely woman. Stick her in the oven', and then while she's baking – don't know how long that would take – everyone could be chatting about her. 'Molly was such a lovely woman, wasn't she? You know she had her faults, like everyone else' . . . chatting away about her. Get her out the oven. Still talk about her, 'She had a good arse, did Molly', 'Yes, she did, let's have a bite'. To me that is more respectful than just sticking them in the ground. You're saying you love them that much, you're prepared to eat them. You can't do more than that.

We loaded up the boats and set off in search of the tribe. After a little while the river suddenly got thinner and I felt like I was being watched. I then noticed we were being watched by men with orange-painted faces, straw skirts and spears. I waved. They didn't wave back. Maybe they didn't notice, so I waved again. They still didn't wave back.

I got off the boat and fell into more mud. The tribesmen still didn't give off any emotion. I climbed up from the river and noticed the whole village seemed to be lined up. I wasn't sure if this was to make me feel welcome or to worry me that there were more of them than us. I didn't know where to look when I was introduced to the women as they didn't bother with wearing anything on their top half. I thought I'd just keep my head down and look at the floor as I walked by, but even though I did this I could still see the breasts of the older women.

They took me to a spot where I could put up my tent. All the kids sat and watched. The older people all seemed to get on with their jobs, apart from one woman who looked a bit mad and was wandering around on her own swinging an axe. It's funny how no matter where you live there's always a local nutter.

Just as I got the tent up, the clouds opened and it chucked it down. I got my soap out and had a shower in it. I could see the tribespeople watching me through the doorways of their straw huts. I might have been playing a dangerous game, thinking about it; if they were cannibals, taking my clothes off and washing my body is like prepping some meat before cooking it. It was nice to feel clean though.

They lit a fire as it grew dark. If I was going to get eaten, now was the time.

I put my diary away, as I thought I should keep my eyes on the locals.

SATURDAY 19TH JUNE

I woke up this morning to find myself still in my tent, not in a pot. I slept okay, other than being woken early by a spraying sensation from a dog peeing on my tent. I thought it was waterproof. Turns out it wasn't.

I had a wander about round the village. A kid had a toad on a bit of rope as a pet; another kid showed me his baby sloth. He kept putting it on the floor, and it would try and crawl away, but what chance has one of the slowest-moving creatures on earth got of getting away?

I then saw the locals annoying a frog. They had suspended it by four sticks and some string and were rubbing its glands with another stick. This made the frog sweat. They then collected all the sweat before releasing the frog to use again at a later date. Then a local man called Eric had the sweat put into a cut on his skin. He sat and waited. Then he was sick. The tribespeople believe the frog sweat makes you throw up all your weaknesses and gets you pumped up ready for the hunt. They use frog sweat like we use Lucozade.

The local women then took my shirt off and painted me and dressed me in their dress. They covered me in red spots to make me look like a panther. With all my mossy bites I didn't need much make-up.

They took me to the woods and taught me how to use a bow and arrow. I had about 15 goes but didn't manage to hit the target.

We went back to the camp. It felt like the blokes had lost a bit of respect for me since seeing my skills with an arrow. This was confirmed when they all went to hunt but left me behind. Not that I was too bothered, as I don't like the idea of killing stuff.

I got quite bored as there was nothing to do. The women were all sat around chatting. I wonder if this is why sloths evolved to move slowly. There's no point in moving fast when living somewhere like this as nothing needs to be done in a rush.

I ended up playing Connect 4 on my own. I played this when I was a kid. I pick which colour I think will win then place all the discs in with my eyes closed. Once all the pieces are in I open my eyes to see if I picked the winning colour. The kid who had the sloth came over, and I tried to teach him how to play but he didn't seem to get it. He just liked putting the pieces in the holes.

Once he'd wandered off I went and cleaned my clothes in the Amazon as they stank. Some of the younger people from the tribe were down there fishing and cleaning pots and pans. As I was washing my clothes I remembered reading about a tribe that only used the numbers one, two and three. Apparently they had no real need for the number four onwards. Maybe this was why the kid didn't understand the game Connect 4.

When I got back to the tent the men were back from the hunt and were setting up a fire again. It looked unsafe to me. All the wood was leaning to one side. Kids were playing around the side where the wood was leaning and everybody was wearing straw skirts. It was a disaster waiting to happen. Just when I thought it couldn't get any more dangerous a man came walking up with a small crocodile on his back. He popped it on the floor next to the kids, who were next to the fire, which was next to the people in flammable clothing. All we were missing was the local mad woman with her axe.

The men then danced around the fire as a woman chopped up the crocodile. They offered me some. I said I was okay, thanks, as I'd had some Spotted Dick for tea.

I went to bed at 9.30ish once the fire had died down and there was no chance of it spreading to my tent.

SUNDAY 20TH JUNE

We left the tribe this morning and made our way down the river for about four hours to a place called Angamos where we would be staying the night at a hostel. We got to the hostel and decided we would be better off staying in our tents as the rooms were rotten. The mattress had more stuff living in it than the jungle we had just left. We ended up just taking one room (Room 5) to put all the equipment into. The plan was that we could all use the toilet and sink in that room.

We had some food in a locals' place. Richard said it was a café, but I think it was just a normal house where the owner was making some money from us. I thought this for two reasons: 1) we were the only ones there; and 2) our table was next to the bedroom.

Got back and went to use the loo in Room 5 and was shocked at the state of it. Christian the producer was not well and had made a mess of it and the walls surrounding it. Even the cockroaches were running out the door. For the first time in my life I was aware that my face did a disgusted look. I decided I'd rather do it on the street than sit in there.

I couldn't believe I'd just about done a week in Peru. It had been perhaps the longest week of my life. If a doctor ever tells me I only have a month left to live I will return and do this trip again as it'll feel like I have lived a lot longer.

KARL'S FACTS

MACHU PICCHU TRANSLATES AS 'OLD MOUNTAIN'.

THE INCAS DIDN'T USE ANY KIND OF MORTAR TO STICK THEIR STONES TOGETHER. INSTEAD THEY CUT THE STONES WITH SUCH PRECISION THAT THEY FIT TOGETHER SO TIGHTLY THAT YOU COULDN'T EVEN PUT A THIN KNIFE BLADE BETWEEN THEM.

MACHU PICCHU STANDS
2,4 30 METRES ABOVE
SEA-LEVEL.

WHEN MACHU PICCHU WAS 'REDISCOVERED' IN 1911
A GROUP OF QUECHUANS WERE FOUND LIVING ON
THE SITE. A BUNCH OF FEMALE MUMMIES WERE
ALSO DISCOVERED.

THE SECRET OF THE INCAS, STARRING CHARLTON
HESTON, WAS SHOT ON LOCATION AT MACHU
PICCHU IN 1954. THIS WAS THE FIRST TIME
THAT A MAJOR HOLLYWOOD STUDIO HAD FILMED
ON LOCATION.

MONDAY 21ST JUNE

I had to get on another small plane again today. Wilder was flying with us. He is terrified of flying as he's already been in two plane crashes. He had to take some Valium to prepare himself for the flight. The news that they were using our flight as a training exercise for a young pilot to learn how to fly while carrying a heavy load due to all our kit didn't help to calm him either. To be fair, this made me nervous too.

We ended up in a nice hotel in a place called Cusco, which is a bit closer to the wonder of Machu Picchu. Cusco is so high up there is 30 per cent less oxygen here. I had to take altitude tablets otherwise I could have died. Just walking a few steps was really tiring. I'd like to see the sloth from the tribe live here. It would never move. It would be like an ornament with a heartbeat.

We booked into a hotel. There were oxygen tanks in the room but you had to pay to use them. I normally avoid taking anything from hotel minibars due to the mark-up on the price but they really have you with the oxygen tanks. I had to break the seal and have a go to make sure I knew how to use it, in case I woke up out of breath in the night. I know Machu Picchu is supposed to take my breath away, but not like this.

I was aware of my heart working harder and I was getting a slight headache behind the eyes, which is another symptom of altitude sickness. I also have a bad stomach. Not sure if it's due to the altitude or just that my body has relaxed since leaving the jungle and tribe. Hopefully it will clear up before I have to do the trek up to Machu Picchu.

Called Suzanne after not speaking to her for five days. She said she had missed talking to me but it has reassured her that if I was dead she could cope without me. I'm glad she's got something out of my travels. £1.50 a minute for that little bit of information.

I called Ricky too.

KARL: How's it going?

RICKY: All right. You out of the jungle?

KARL: Yeah, just about, left yesterday. In Cusco now, there's 30 per cent less oxygen.

RICKY: Because of the altitude?

KARL: Yeah. In me room there's a bottle of oxygen, just in case I go a bit dizzy and that.

RICKY: Have you felt sick or dizzy?

KARL: Yeah. I've felt dizzy, got the shakes, got a little headache behind me eyes, I've got pins and needles in me feet and me brain works slower because less oxygen is getting to it.

RICKY: Jesus, I think your brain working slower is a problem. Thanks for pointing out your headache is behind your eyes. I think you'll find that is where your brain is and that's where most headaches are.

KARL: Not always. I sometimes get them just below my ears.

RICKY: Surely that's a neckache. You wouldn't say I've got a headache in my gums, would you? You'd say I've got toothache.

KARL: It takes it out of you, this. The plane going out to the jungle set on fire, that was a good start. I had to jump out quick because smoke was coming out of the engine. That's just what you need, that's a nice little panic on the heart, just when you are going into high altitude, more pressure on it.

RICKY: Where was the pain in your heart? Just behind your ribcage or in your chest?

KARL: I'm just aware of it sort of throbbing at the moment. I can hear it in my ears more. I'm more aware that I'm alive.

RICKY: Oh well, that's a breakthrough.

KARL: Well, it's not good though, is it? You're meant to have a slow heartbeat like a tortoise, that's why they live for ever. But just stood here now talking to you I'm breathing more. I'm normally a really quiet breather but I'm aware of my breathing. I'm aware of my heart.

RICKY: One step at a time. You've described where your head is, you know where your heart is, soon you won't have to concentrate on breathing. A lot of people do that involuntarily, so once you get that underway and you know you're aware you're alive that's good. So, all in all, this has all been worthwhile.

KARL: Yeah, but I tell you what, you couldn't handle it. I would love to see Steve here. I would love to see him dealing with this.

RICKY: Steve cannot afford to lose any blood to insects. He's got to be anaemic anyway. He is the palest person: I've said it before, he's like one of those small fish. If you took his shirt off, I think you would see his heart. So you would definitely be aware of his heartbeat.

KARL: The thing with Steve is, I think he has altitude sickness all the time, with his height.

RICKY: [laughs]

KARL: So anything else been going on at home? Because I've had no phone contact while I was in the jungle I don't know what's going on.

RICKY: What do you want to know?

KARL: I don't know. Has anyone died? I don't know . . . Just something.

RICKY: I had a meeting with everyone, and they weren't sure about the title *Karl Pilkington's Seven Wonders*. I came up with an idea that they really liked which they're pushing through. I wanted to run it by you: *An Idiot Abroad.*

KARL: Well, no, we didn't say anything about that. We said it's *Karl Pilkington's Seven Wonders.*

RICKY: Yeah, but they were saying, who's Karl Pilkington?

KARL: Yeah, but who's the Idiot Abroad?

RICKY: You're the Idiot Abroad. They loved it, they absolutely loved it.

KARL: Well, they would because you said it. You know what they're like. They all sit there going, 'Yeah, Ricky, that's great. Yeah. Yeah, we'll do that.' We're not having *An Idiot Abroad*. It's *Karl Pilkington's Seven Wonders*. I've been through a load of shit here. You're sat there giving them bloody shit titles. We're not having *An Idiot Abroad*, we're not having it. It's the one thing that I said I'm happy with. I don't want people thinking I'm a div. It's *Karl Pilkington's Seven Wonders*. I'm back in a couple of days. We'll have another little meeting about that. Was there all croissants there and free coffee? All sat about on their arses, 'Yes, Ricky, any other ideas? Another coffee?' I'm sick of that lot. You've got my heart going more now.

RICKY: [laughs] I'll see you later.

KARL: All right, see ya later.

TUESDAY 22ND JUNE

Richard bought me some walking shoes today ready for our walk up to Machu Picchu. I said all shoes are for walking in.

I met a man who gives spiritual advice to anyone who is about to climb the Wonder. He was a local man who lived in the hills. His name was also Richard. I met him in the middle of a field in the middle of nowhere. He sat me down and did a little ceremony. He opened up a small parcel full of bits and pieces. There was all sorts of tat in it. String, chunks of plastic, seeds, powders, paperclip . . . at one point I'm sure I saw a used ear plug. He was mixing them all together like some sort of mad witch. He then rubbed the package all over my body (well, up to my shoulders as he couldn't reach above them). He then got a guinea pig from a box and rubbed my body with it. He said all the badness from my body was being transferred into the guinea pig. God help it. He then took the package of tat and said he would bury it in the hills. Sweet Jesus, if he's doing that every day that hill is a right landfill.

WEDNESDAY 23ᴿᴰ JUNE

Up at 4 a.m. today to start our walk on the Inca trail up to Machu Picchu.

My stomach is still bad so just had two hard-boiled eggs for breakfast. We had to get a train from where we were staying to the bottom of Machu Picchu. When we got to the station we were told that Michael the cameraman could not get on the train as the ticket that had been booked was in another cameraman's name. Richard suggested we leave him to sort it out so that we would not lose time. Freddie the soundman stepped in to do the camera and Christian, Richard's assistant, took on the job of sound. It was like some kind of work experience day. The way I felt, I fancied letting the train driver do my job.

Freddie started using loads of sayings he had probably picked up from working with other cameramen; words like 'focus' and 'white balance'. I don't think he really knew what he was doing though. Richard must have thought the same. He said we should wait for Michael even though we had no idea what time he would get to us as there was no phone signal. He eventually turned up an hour and a half later.

After a quick toilet stop we set off. We had four or five porters with us. These are men who help carry heavy loads. They can carry as much as a donkey. Even though they were carrying a lot of gear they were still hard to keep up with.

I'd only been going for 30 minutes and felt shattered. No wonder there is 30 per cent less oxygen here. I think it's due to all the tourists climbing this hill to the Wonder. More exercise means more breathing. If they sorted out a lift or some escalators to the top I think there would be a lot more oxygen to go round.

I had to let everybody else go ahead as my stomach was rumbling again. I had to crouch behind a bush. Never mind the Inca trail, I've left a Pilkington trail.

We passed old buildings made of rock that were constructed without the use of cement. I don't know if that was always the plan or if the man who was supposed to deliver the cement refused to carry it all this way. The buildings looked like bungalows to me, which seems odd when the whole idea of living in a bungalow is less stairs, yet they've been built on a hill.

I caught up with the porters, who had stopped to eat. They were tucking into some squashed guinea pig packed with green pesto. I think that's what it was; maybe it was the guinea pig that was used to soak up all my badness yesterday. There were a couple of porters who were not eating but were sat playing a flute. Why on earth, after walking for hours and hours in a place where there is 30 per cent less oxygen, would you start playing a wind instrument?

Richard asked me if I was excited about getting closer to Machu Picchu. I said I wasn't. How could I be? I was still ill, hot and exhausted. The views were amazing, we were on top of the world, but why people would live up here just doesn't make sense. My mam and dad have retired to Snowdon in Wales but they're sick of it being a 15-minute drive to the local Spar supermarket. Living high up just isn't practical.

We had been walking for about eight or nine hours. We got to a point called the Sun Gate that looked down onto Machu Picchu. It looked like more of the same that I'd seen earlier. Bungalows made from rocks with the roofs missing. I wonder if these were ever finished.

I don't think they corroded away, I just think they couldn't get people to live in them so didn't bother completing the project.

I was really tired and was concerned that by the time we got to the Wonder it would be totally dark. I told Richard I thought it was pointless going any further. He said I had to go for the programme. I think he was worried the Sky bosses would be angry if we went back home with no footage.

I called Steve to try and get him on my side.

KARL: Hello. How's it going?

STEPHEN: All right, mate. Where do I find you?

KARL: I'm kind of at the Wonder.

STEPHEN: Kind of at the Wonder? Or at the Wonder?

KARL: I'm at the Wonder, but, er, listen, it's a long story, but you know I've been in the jungle.

STEPHEN: You've been in the jungle, yeah. Did that go all right?

KARL: Er, yeah. It seems ages ago. I did that. I've done the tribe thing. I did all that. I've been really ill. And then I get to this thing thinking that I'm just gonna be seeing Machu Picchu, right, but then I found out I had to walk up a massive hill. I got up at four o'clock this morning. There was a problem with the train. I've only just got here. So, I've been walking about eight hours. Now I'm at a point where I can see the Wonder, the cameraman can see the Wonder. The sun is going down. If we try and walk there it is going to get dark and we're not gonna see anything. But Richard, who is in charge, is worrying, saying 'Sky want to see the Wonder'. I think we can see it from here. Have you got a problem if we just see it from here? Have a look from here and go?

STEPHEN: Well, how far away are you from it?

KARL: What, in walking time or with me eyes? With me eyes I can see it.

STEPHEN: No, I mean how far away is it? Can you see it, like, with all its detail?

KARL: Yeah.

STEPHEN: I'm not sure I'm happy about this, Karl. Let me just tell you my concerns, mate. I want to see the Wonders of the World in HD. I feel responsible, you know. I've got you this gig with Ricky on Sky. It's a major thing. They are putting all their money behind this. This is make-or-break for them. *24* has finished now. They've got nothing on Sky, mate. Do you know what I mean? You having a hazy shot through some hazy light of the Wonder I am worried about. Can you not just bed down for a few hours? Get a bit of kip? Set off tomorrow early and make it to the Wonder?

KARL: No, I'm not doing any more of that. Honestly, you cannot see what I can see. I am telling you now, if we go over there the viewers of Sky will be seeing old rock in darkness. It will be very clear dark. It will be the clearest dark they've ever seen. But I have been walking for eight hours and the view from here is magnificent. And I'm not just saying that because . . .

STEPHEN: Are you just saying that? Are you being honest with me?

KARL: I think it looks magnificent.

STEPHEN: Karl, I have never heard you use the word 'magnificent' in my life so I am suspicious.

KARL: The sun is sort of bouncing off a mountain and going through the rock. And you can see the green. From here it looks good. What I am worried about is if we get up close and it doesn't look good. It's like a person's face. From a distance you go, 'They look all right', but up close you go, 'Bloody hell'. So, I reckon, this is the last episode so let's just finish on a beautiful long-distance shot. Honestly, I think this works. This is the way to end it. Just a nice shot with the sun going down. It works a treat. I'm telling you. I am speechless.

STEPHEN: Tell me what you can see of the Wonder right now. What is your genuine reaction? Forget that you've got to worry about what's going to be on the telly. What's your reaction right now?

KARL: Well, if I am being honest, I am pissed off, aren't I? I've been up since 4 o'clock. I've had two hard-boiled eggs and the shits. So it's not the greatest way to see it. But I'm just thinking about the viewer here. I am not being selfish. And I reckon for the TV programme, and that's what this is about, this is what Sky want, the Seven Wonders of the World . . .

STEPHEN: Karl, what would Michael Palin do in this situation?

KARL: He'd probably do a voice-over. He probably wouldn't be here now at this stage. There is no way he would walk up that hill. You would see a close-up of it and he would be going, 'Machu Picchu, home of the Inca. Hundreds of years ago they lived here . . .' and so on. I can do that back in London. If the cameraman takes a load of pictures of it now, when I get back to London I will write something up. And I will sell it to the viewer.

STEPHEN: Karl, you know what, you have grown as a human being these past few weeks. I feel like perhaps at the beginning I could have bullied you into going over there. Now I feel like you are going to do whatever you want to do, mate. You're a different person. I'm not sure I know the real you anymore. So, if you feel like you don't want to go over there, if you feel the viewers of Sky are not going to be deprived, then I trust you.

KARL: Mmm.

STEPHEN: 'Cos I know you're not gonna let them down, you're not gonna let me and Ricky down, and you're certainly not going to lie.

KARL: No.

STEPHEN: I trust you.

KARL: It will be good. Steve, have a good one and don't bother telling Ricky or anything. I will speak to him when I get back.

STEPHEN: Alright.

KARL: See you.

The Final Questionnaire

By Ricky Gervais and Stephen Merchant

1. TRAVEL BROADENS THE MIND, OR SO THE PHRASE GOES. BEARING IN MIND THAT YOU ALREADY HAVE A PERFECTLY ROUND HEAD, HOW MUCH BROADER DOES IT FEEL NOW YOU'VE VISITED ALL THESE AMAZING COUNTRIES?

It doesn't feel that different. I've just put some new memories in there which means I probably had to lose a few of the older ones from when I was a kid, which is annoying as they were happier memories than the new ones from this trip.

2. WAS THERE ANYTHING YOU SAW THAT YOU WISH YOU HADN'T?

The naked bodies on the nudist beach in Brazil. What I don't get is that Brazilians hardly wear anything anyway. I can almost understand nudism in the UK because most people have to dress up for work – wearing shirts and suits etc – so maybe it's nice to feel free from clothing. But in Brazil they nip to the shops in a g-string and flip-flops anyway, so why the need to go stark bollock naked?

3. IN RETROSPECT, WHAT ONE THING WOULD YOU TAKE TO EACH PLACE TO MAKE LIFE EASIER?

A chemical toilet.

4. WHO WOULD WIN IN A FIGHT BETWEEN THE STUDENTS AT THE SHAOLIN KUNG FU SCHOOL IN CHINA AND EL PORKY, SHOCKER AND THEIR FRIENDS AT THE WRESTLING ARENA IN MEXICO?

Shaolin Kung Fu School without a doubt. Leo the head man put me on the floor just using his little finger! My little fingers don't do anything, they're just observers to what my other fingers are doing.

5. OX'S BOLLOCKS, BLOOD CAKE, ASH, CRICKETS, DONKEY, WORM, SPICY RABBIT, TOAD, MONSTER MUNCH . . . YOU'VE EATEN SOME PRETTY TASTY THINGS ON YOUR TRAVELS. WHICH WAS YOUR FAVOURITE?

I took Monster Munch crisps as a treat in case the local food wasn't nice, but in the end I ate so many bags of Monster Munch that I am now sick of them, so all this travel hasn't really broadened my mind, all it has done is take something away that I enjoyed before I started my journey. So I'm worse off.

6. IF WE COULD MOVE ONE OF THE SEVEN WONDERS OF THE WORLD TO THE END OF YOUR ROAD AND REBUILD IT, PIECE BY PIECE, WHICH WOULD YOU CHOOSE?

None of them, as it's hard enough getting a parking space as it is without having loads of tourists clogging me street up.

7. IF MICHAEL PALIN WAS HEADING OFF TO VISIT THE SEVEN WONDERS OF THE WORLD, WHAT PIECE OF ADVICE WOULD YOU GIVE HIM?

I'd just tell him not to go on any trips to places that Ricky and Steve have suggested. I'd tell him not to bother with the 'Wonders' and tell him to just sit back and watch rather than go chasing specific experiences. India was a mad place. It's like when you use a Dyson vacuum cleaner on a floor that looked quite clean, but then you realize there was all sorts of dust and mud on it. India is like that – it seems normal, but when you look closer loads of odd stuff is going on.

8. WHAT DO YOU THINK OF BRITAIN NOW?

The UK seems very wasteful, but I thought that before I travelled the world. We replace instead of repair. We buy two for one when we only need one in the first place, and we have too many health and safety rules. I dropped some food on the floor recently and was told that there is a three-second rule – if it's been on the floor for longer than three seconds you shouldn't eat it. And yet half the stuff they eat in China has been crawling about on the floor for weeks or months before they swallow it, and it ain't done them any harm.

9. DO YOU WHINGE LESS NOW YOU HAVE SEEN TRUE HARDSHIP?

I don't whinge, I moan. There's a difference. I like moaning. I think it's more natural to moan, being 'happy' is a man-made condition. I think we kid ourselves into thinking we're happy. A moan is good for the brain, it makes it work harder.

10. WHAT'S THE FIRST THING YOU DID WHEN YOU GOT HOME FROM EACH TRIP?

I opened me post. When I say post, I mean bills. That's all the postman brings me these days. To be honest, I'm happy when there's a postal strike. Suzanne would then make me something nice for tea. Sausage, beans and potato cakes normally, though like the Monster Munch I'm getting sick of sausage, beans and potato cakes now.

11. WHY WERE YOU SO OBSESSED BY WRITING ABOUT GOING TO THE TOILET?

Going to the loo is one of my favourite pastimes. It's 'me time', or at least normally it's 'me time' but in China it wasn't as it's an open-door policy, actually not even open-door 'cos there isn't a floor. It's just a room with a few toilets in it with everyone crouching. It's odd how it's something we all do in the world, but we look at it in different way. In Britain we try to make it a pleasant thing by having comfy toilet-seat covers or toilet-roll covers. In China it's a group activity and they have no seats or toilet rolls to cover.

12. ARE THERE ANY CUSTOMS YOU CAME ACROSS ON YOUR TRAVELS THAT YOU WOULD LIKE TO INTRODUCE TO THE UK?

Yes, I'd like people to automatically take their shoes off when they enter your house so I don't have to have that awkward moment of telling them to take them off 'cos I've just vacced up.

13. IF YOUR NEW FRIENDS MAHMOUD, CARLOS, ASHEK, LEO AND WILDER WERE COMING TO THE UK FOR A WEEK, WHICH BRITISH 'WONDER' WOULD YOU TAKE THEM TO SEE?

I think I'd take them to 'Ripley's Believe It or Not' museum in Piccadilly Circus. No matter what language you speak, everyone is interested in seeing the man whose face was on backwards, and the horse-faced woman.

14. WHERE ARE YOU AND SUZANNE GOING ON YOUR HOLIDAYS NEXT YEAR?

Suzanne wants to go on a safari, and seeing as I had an injection at the start of all this to protect me from a dirty chimp, I may as well make use of it.

THE FURTHER
ADVENTURES OF
AN IDIOT
ABROAD

Introduction

I was hoping to write this book as a diary like the last one, but the day I tried to start it I woke up in my hotel room in Thailand with my eyes burning and my head completely numb. It was my own fault. I'd assumed the sachet on my bed in the hotel room was some kind of menthol stuff to put on the pillow to help me breathe more easily as I slept, but I later found out it was medical gel to ease aching leg muscles. It was at this point that I decided I wasn't in the right frame of mind to start a diary.

Looking back, it was no bad thing. I very rarely enjoy any of my trips at the time as my head is all over the place. I'm not always feeling my best, what with the flying and the throwing up and the stupid stuff that Ricky and Steve make me do. So the idea of writing the book once I was safe and sound and a bit happier back at home made sense. I've realised that coming back home is the best thing about going away in the first place.

This second set of trips was set up after a meeting with Ricky and Steve in their office. They came up with the idea of getting me to pick seven things that I would put on my Bucket List.

We'd actually had a similar conversation a few years ago as part of the podcasts. At the time, Ricky asked me what I want to do before I die and I said I wanted to kick a duck up the arse. It's just something I always have the urge to do when I see them sitting at the edge of a pond.

For the first series of *An Idiot Abroad* Ricky and Steve sent me round the world to see the Seven Wonders, hoping it would broaden my mind. This time it seemed like they were trying to flatten it.

'Come on. You can pick anything. Make your dreams come true! What about sky diving?' said Steve. 'That's a classic Bucket List experience.'

'Not for me it isn't. No. I'm not sky diving.'

'Bungee jumping?'

'Not a chance. Forget the whole idea.'

I've never been one for danger. I've done some daft things in my time like putting sausages in the toaster, and climbing out of the bathroom window to go and do my paper round when me mam hid the front door keys from me, 'cos she didn't want me going out delivering papers one bad winter. But they didn't really strike me as dangerous at the time, and they all served a purpose.

'Okay,' said Ricky. 'How about we make a big list and you can choose what you want to do from that?'

In the end it felt like I was going to be in control, so I agreed.

This book tells the stories of the things I chose to do, plus the extra things that Ricky and Steve threw in along the way. That was the plan anyway, but when I sat down to write the book I realised that between the first series and the second series, the latest Christmas Special with Warwick Davis, and all the other random stuff I've done in my life, I've actually ticked off more than 60% of the Bucket List. I reckon that's got to be some sort of record. So in the end I've decided to write about all of them and also throw in an opinion or two on the remaining things on the list. Most of these are things that have never appealed, like:

#67 Join the Mile High Club ✗ 'oh yes!

This is when people have it away in the toilets on a plane. I guess this explains why there are always queues whenever I need the loo on a flight. I wish they'd use the system they use at the supermarket meat counter where they give you a ticket with a number on which the pilot could then read out when it's your turn to use the toilet. This has got to be safer than people stood queuing in the aisles.

I'm guessing here but I bet people only do the mile high club thing on the outward journey as after two weeks of being away with someone you're normally sick of them and would rather watch the inflight movie. Also it's the return journey when the toilets get blocked due to everyone having dodgy guts after eating foreign food. On my flight back from India there's no way anyone could have had a romantic moment in there after the state I left it in.

So that's the book. Sitting down to write it has been a nice way to sum up three years of travelling.

What follows is the original list of the 100 things I could choose from. As you can see, kicking a duck up the arse wasn't on it.

100 Things to do before you die

1. Fly a fighter jet
2. Climb Sydney Harbour Bridge
3. Spend a night on your own private desert island
4. Drive a Formula 1 car
5. Ride the Rocky Mountaineer train in Canada
6. Fly in a helicopter over the Grand Canyon
7. See elephants in the wild
8. Explore Antarctica
9. Climb Mount Everest
10. Travel into space
11. Ride a camel to the Pyramids
12. Travel the Trans-Siberian Railway
13. Catch sunset over Ayers Rock
14. Go wing-walking on a bi-plane
15. Climb Mount Kilimanjaro
16. Come face to face with mountain gorillas in their natural habitat
17. Gamble in Las Vegas
18. See orang-utans in Borneo
19. Spot a polar bear on the ice
20. Swim with dolphins
21. Get into the Guinness Book of World Records
22. Watch a sumo match
23. Drink a beer at Oktoberfest
24. Participate in La Tomatina festival in Spain

25. Cross a country on a bike
26. Master a musical instrument
27. Spend a night in a haunted house
28. Meet someone with your own name
29. Ride the world's biggest rollercoasters
30. Scuba dive at the Great Barrier Reef
31. Complete a bungee jump
32. Paraglide from a mountain
33. Go ice-climbing
34. Skydive from a plane
35. Experience base jumping
36. Meet the Dalai Lama
37. Research your family tree
38. Go up in a hot air balloon
39. Try a jet pack
40. See a space shuttle launch
41. Meet your idol
42. Cycle a leg of the Tour de France
43. See the northern lights
44. See the glaciers before they melt
45. Learn a martial art
46. Get a complete makeover
47. Learn another language
48. Drive a Cadillac along Route 66
49. Leave a job you hate
50. Become a vegetarian for a week

100 Things to do before you die

51. Stand at the North or South Pole
52. Visit every USA state
53. Be part of a flash mob
54. Visit the Seven Wonders of the World
55. Explore the Galapagos Islands
56. Spend the night in an igloo
57. Spend 24 hours in a jungle
58. Stand on the international date line
59. Learn to fly a plane
60. Go storm-chasing in Tornado Alley
61. Get a tattoo and/or a piercing
62. Invent something
63. Ride something bigger than a horse
64. Build your own house
65. Skinny dip at midnight
66. Run a marathon
67. Join the Mile High Club
68. Be an extra in a film
69. Protest at a demonstration
70. Run with the bulls in Pamplona
71. Canoe up the Nile
72. Continue your gene pool
73. Write a novel
74. Visit Angel Falls in Venezuela
75. Trek the Inca Trail on Machu Picchu
76. Climb Mount Fuji

77. Sleep under the stars
78. Ride a gondola in Venice
79. Have lunch with the Queen of England
80. Walk the Great Wall of China
81. Do some charity work
82. Experience a full moon party
83. See Mount Rushmore, USA
84. Go on an African safari
85. See the statues on Easter Island
86. Touch an iceberg
87. Shake hands with the Pope
88. Climb an active volcano
89. Go to the Burning Man Festival in California
90. Partake in a Japanese tea ceremony
91. Float in the Dead Sea
92. Jump from a cliff into the sea
93. Swim the English Channel
94. Take part in a fire-walking ceremony
95. Drive or 'mush' a dog sled
96. Spend the Fourth of July in the USA
97. Go whale-watching
98. Live with the Masai people
99. See the wildebeest migration in the Masai Mara
100. Hunt with a tribe

CHAPTER ONE

#3 Spend a night on your own private desert island ✓

VANUATU

Happiest place in the world

arseboarding

defender of the flag → Karl

Nambas: leaf pants

Prince Philip

land dive

NEW ZEALAND

Auckland

bald wookie noise

Wilson?

Queenstown

TASMAN SEA

PACIFIC OCEAN

RICKY: We've sort of compiled a Top 100, which we've taken from loads of lists, and these seem to be the most popular 100 things to do before you die. So, anything you fancy there?

STEPHEN: What sort of things have you heard of in a typical bucket list?

KARL: Daft stuff like sky diving and bungee jumping.

RICKY: Why is that daft though?

KARL: It's not worth doing. There are certain things I wouldn't risk my life for.

RICKY: Well, crossing the road is dangerous.

KARL: Yeah, but I'm good at that. I'm more in control there. I don't like the idea of relying on other people.

STEPHEN: So, why do you think people do it then?

KARL: Because they're idiots. They're normally people that have, sort of, gelled permed hair. Australian types.

RICKY: You're not jealous of their hair, are you?

KARL: No, I just think they're the sort of people who haven't got enough problems.

STEPHEN: I think you'll probably find that jumping out of a plane is on here, as is bungee jumping, but obviously there are 100 options.

RICKY: Spend a night on your own on a desert island.

STEPHEN: You hate people for a start, so you're not going to have to associate with anyone.

RICKY: It will be sunny, there will be no people there, you just walk around naked . . .

KARL: No, I wouldn't do that.

RICKY: Why? There's no one there.

KARL: No, I still wouldn't do it. Robinson Crusoe didn't walk around with his knob out, did he? You think no one's about and then a cruise full of tourists comes round and I'm stood there with my knob and bollocks hanging out. And there's all the sand, it's not good to be nude in the sand.

(Ricky laughs)

KARL: Can I take stuff or what?

STEPHEN: What sort of stuff you wanna take? Bucket and spade?

KARL: Yeah, I'd take a bucket and spade. Something to do, innit.

(Ricky and Stephen laugh)

KARL: You can go a bit mad though, can't you?

RICKY: Not in a day. What if you were there and who came walking down the beach but me?

KARL: Yeah, that would be a nightmare.

STEPHEN: If you choose this one, we'd send you to the Vanuatu islands. They're in the South Pacific, it's a beautiful place, glorious weather, so it's not like we're sending you to the Isle of Sheppey. Alright . . . Interested?

KARL: No restrictions on what I can take?

RICKY: What are you thinking of taking?

KARL: Just enough to keep me entertained for the night.

RICKY: What's that though?

KARL: Bag of Revels.

RICKY: DVD player?

KARL: There's no power, is there?

RICKY: Well, you could have batteries. What film would you watch?

KARL: *Castaway*

STEPHEN: What book would you take?

KARL: Probably a crossword book or a wordsearch.

RICKY: I love that. He's on a desert island, the happiest place on earth, and he's watching *Castaway* and doing a crossword. That's amazing. Okay, so spend a night on a desert island. Tick.

How much have you learned from watching TV? I learned that vinegar is a good stain remover. It's something I picked up from watching Kim and Aggie off *How Clean Is Your House?*

A while ago, three British backpackers who got lost in a Malaysian jungle said they'd survived thanks to tips they'd picked up from watching the TV survival expert Ray Mears. They said they'd now watch every episode of Ray Mears in case the situation ever cropped up again! You'd think what they'd been through would have put them off the programme, as it would bring back bad memories of their near-death experience. It would be like Anne Frank watching *Cash in the Attic.*

The advice that saved the backpackers from being lost was that you should follow a watercourse downstream and that would lead you to the coastline. I'm just glad it was Ray Mears the backpackers had watched. If it had been Bruce Parry they'd still be lost but would now probably be off their tits after licking the back of a toxic toad. But this left me wondering if anyone had ever opted for the survival tactics offered up by Bear Grylls. Bear is a bit more extreme than Ray. If you said to Bear, 'I'm so hungry I could eat a scabby horse,' he'd probably say, 'Too late. I've eaten it all.' In one show he was covered in blood and guts after stripping a camel. He went on to explain that the carcass makes an excellent makeshift sleeping bag! I don't want to come across all Goldilocks here, but how much sleep are you going to get inside a camel? It must be the worst animal to use as a bed. It's got a hump on it, for a start. I have the feeling that if Bear missed the last bus home when in England he'd probably break into London Zoo and strangle a giraffe for a sleeping bag, then kill a couple of koala bears while he's at it to make a pair of slippers, rather than just get a cab. Anyway, if you ever find yourself in this situation, having killed a camel to sleep in, and your clothes are covered in bloodstains, try vinegar.

I've never been in a position where I've had to use proper survival techniques. My brother and his mates took over the house when me mam and dad were on a holiday once. I came home from working nights to find some bloke and a woman in me bed, another pair of strangers in me mam and dad's bed, and a couple on the sofa, so ended up sleeping in the car. That's about as tough as it's got for me, so this is why I picked a night on a desert island from the Bucket List. I thought it would test me a little, plus, of all the things on the Bucket List, I'd say this is the one most people would like to do. I was imagining the TV advert for the Bounty bar. For anyone who hasn't seen the advert, it involved a woman on a really nice paradise-type beach. Nothing like the beaches we all spend our holidays on. There was no washed-up seaweed, plastic bottles or dead jellyfish, no donkeys leaving shit everywhere, or seagulls making a racket. It was just the perfect beach with light blue sea. A coconut drops from a palm tree and cracks open to leave a Bounty bar, which is a bar of coconut-filled chocolate. Now, by rights, I doubt the woman would have been up for eating chocolate on such a hot day. I think she'd have been more in the mood for a Magnum lolly, but putting that aside I reckon most people who have seen the advert would be imagining this same image as me if they were to pick this for their Bucket List.

Luke the director said I could take a few bits and pieces with me that might come in handy for my night on the island. I ended up packing a lighter, a roll of gaffa tape, a Stanley knife, a crossword/wordsearch book, some string, biscuits, toilet paper and a small shovel.

I would be staying on an island in Vanuatu, a place in the South Pacific. I'd never heard of the place. When I told people where I was going they hadn't heard of it either. Suzanne bought me a globe when I started travelling so I could put little stickers on all the places I had been to, but this globe didn't even include Vanuatu.

I was told that it wasn't possible to get a direct flight to Vanuatu due to a massive ash cloud from a volcano in Chile that was causing problems, so we ended up flying to Sydney and then on to New Zealand where we stayed the night. I thought we'd be getting on another flight first thing, but that was not to be the case. I woke up to a voicemail from Stephen.

STEPHEN: Hello, Karl. I know you're probably waking up in Queenstown and thinking what's going on here. I tell you what, Ricky and I were talking, and we just thought it would be mad for you to go all the way to the desert island and not stop off in New Zealand to experience what probably is the ultimate Bucket List classic – the bungee jump. Now, before you start screaming and shouting going, 'No, I'm not going to do it', just think about it. We've got a couple of dudes – adrenaline guys, you know, they know all about it – and safety is their optimum concern. I know you'll be reluctant, but I'm saying go with them, see what you think of it, don't judge it straight away. It's something that Ricky and I want to see, I know it's something the viewers want to see, so, just go with an open mind, alright. Rip off the plaster, it'll be over in seconds. And it will be painless and safe. Alright, so don't let us down, mate. Enjoy it. Bye.

This really annoyed me. He was the furthest away he'd ever been from me and yet he had still managed to annoy me more than ever. I'd made it clear to them at the very beginning that this was exactly the thing I was not up for doing. I remember being sat in their office when they told me about the Bucket List idea and Stephen mentioned bungee jumping, and I said, 'If that's the sort of things you'll be surprising me with, you're wasting your time 'cos I'm not interested.' If it's over in seconds, what's the point? I don't like party poppers 'cos the amount of enjoyment versus the time it takes to clean them up is not worth it. Same with confetti.

Luke the director tried to reinforce what Stephen's message had already said about it being safe and that the 'dudes' who would be taking me do it all the time and would help me beat my fears, which pissed me off even more as it's not a fear that needs to be beaten. I'm happy that my brain doesn't think it's a good idea to jump off ledges that are high up. To me that means it's doing its job, that's the reaction it should have. I know my brain isn't very interested in maths or politics, which annoys me at times, but that doesn't put the rest of my body in any danger, so as far as I'm concerned it's not a 'fear' that needs fighting. I've heard of koumpounophobia, which means your brain is scared of buttons. There was a woman on the news who had it so bad she couldn't even sit and watch the kids' TV programme *Button Moon*. It was like a horror movie to her, and she couldn't turn the TV off, or over, because that would involve more buttons. Now, that's a fear that needs beating.

#32 Paraglide from a mountain X

#34 Skydive from a plane X

#35 Experience base jumping X

#92 Jump from a cliff into the sea X

I'm convinced the reason they don't make James Bond movies like they used to is because the stunts he used to do no longer impress us as people do that stuff on a wet Thursday afternoon in an office team building session. Even sweaty Pete from IT manages to get his fat arse into a jumpsuit so he can do a tandem jump with his head of department. I also blame medical advancement – would people still risk injuring themselves if they knew no doctor would be able to repair their broken arms and legs? If I worked at A&E I would put anyone who has an accident doing any of the above at the back of the queue and sort out people who have had a genuine accident first.

I was arguing with Luke about my reasons for not wanting to do it when a few car beeps stopped my flow. I looked outside where two young fellas in a camper van were shouting my name. I went out on to the balcony.

> **BLOKES:** We got a call from your mates Ricky and Stephen, and they want us to look after you today, show you a few sights in the adventure capital of the world, Queenstown.
>
> **KARL:** Yeah? Well, I've just been saying, I'm definitely not bungee jumping.
>
> **BLOKES:** We know you're not bungee jumping, but, hey, you'll be alright, mate. Just head on out. Come on, we'll show you around, mate. You're in this beautiful place, so come on down, bro.

Their names were Sam and Kyle. They stood looking up at me from their graffiti-covered camper van. They seemed friendly enough, but if there's one thing that doesn't work with me, it's people trying to force me to do something. The more they force, the more my brain fights against it. I've tried to teach my brain new things but then it just forgets them. Yet, I can remember postcodes of old addresses from years ago. My dad once bet me that by the time I got home I wouldn't remember the number plate of a car in front of us. I can still remember it now. It was a maroon Ford Orion, registration D189 ONB. Why has my brain chosen to store that bit of information? What use is it? I can't even remember my National Insurance number. My brain does what it wants.

SAM: I know you're not that keen on bungee jumping, but we'll tell you a little bit about it because it's fantastic – you'll love it!

KYLE: Safe as houses, mate. Nothing can go wrong.

SAM: Nothing can go wrong . . . most of the time.

KYLE: It's an absolute rush, total adrenaline rush – you'll love it.

KARL: I don't like it. I don't need it. Honestly, I'm not messing. I don't need adrenaline rushes.

SAM: Why is that?

KARL: Because I have enough stress in me life.

KYLE: This will ease all the stress out.

SAM: And that is the whole point. To take that shit out of your life.

KARL: No, it won't ease it, it'll make it worse.

SAM: It won't.

KARL: It will! You know nothing about me. You've just turned up here telling me what I like. You don't know. I don't like that kind of danger.

I came in from the balcony. Luke told me that Sam, the taller of the two, was a doctor, which surprised me, but then I suppose doctors and surgeons do have to have a bit of a mad streak in them to do the jobs they do. Normal people wouldn't be able to remove lungs from someone's chest and remain calm.

Luke the director asked me to go along for the ride with Sam and Kyle and witness them do a jump. As we drove we talked about my concerns. They tried to sell it to me by saying that it would all be over in eight seconds, but that isn't a good enough reason to do it. Eight seconds of joy isn't worth having. It's the same reason I don't understand why people eat oysters. They're only in the mouth for a second. Sam said I could discover who I really am by doing a bungee. I hope by now, aged 38, I know who I am. If I'm actually someone else what a waste all these years have been.

SAM: There is a point of madness to it, and that's it, just embrace the madness, and admit there's something wrong with me here.

KYLE: Embrace the idiot inside.

SAM: Yeah.

KYLE: Let the idiot out.

KARL: Maybe that's it though, maybe my idiot is always out – it doesn't need to do bungee.

KYLE: What you thinking, man?

KARL: Okay, I'm happy to stand on the edge 'cos I want to give myself the chance to do it if my brain wants to.

#31 Complete a bungee jump

I agreed to go out onto the ledge to see if my brain got the urge to leap, but first I had to be weighed so that they knew the right sort of bungee cord to use, and I had to sign a waiver form. We made our way over to the bungee platform in a type of cable car that was suspended 134 metres above the Nevis river. The minute we stepped off the cable car, back it went to pick up more people – the idea being that by the time it got back to the platform I would have jumped off and be ready for my return. Loud rock music was playing out of speakers, which I presume was to get you pumped up ready for the jump. I stood in the middle of the platform like a trapped fly in a spider's web.

I was introduced to Phil, a pony-tailed instructor, who was in charge of safety. He had me sat on a chair in no time, strapped my ankles together and hooked me on to the massive bungee cord. At this point I still didn't know if I wanted to do it or not. I'd stopped saying 'definitely not' and was willing to see what happened.

Phil explained the process. 'So, we're gonna put you in a set of ankle cuffs, go out to the edge, and you've just got to listen to us, okay? Nothing bad can happen once you leave that edge. You're gonna get the best feeling you've ever had in your life. Guarantee it. So, the idea is you're gonna do a nice big forward dive out, just like going into a swimming pool, okay? A belly flop. Can you do that? You're gonna go down, you'll enjoy a couple of bounces, and we'll bring you back up.'

Phil said all this very calmly in the same tone that a negotiator would use to change the mind of someone who was thinking about committing suicide by jumping off a bridge, the difference being he was trying to get me to jump. He shuffled me to the edge with my ankles bound. I'm not afraid of heights – I was quite happy looking out at the mountains and taking in the fresh air – but it was the idea of leaping that I couldn't get my head round. At this stage, I still wasn't sure if I was going to do it or not. My heart was pounding and I was now aware of my heavy breathing. The platform shook as the cable car dropped off more people.

KARL: There's a queue over there of people waiting to do this! I've been in New Zealand for under 24 hours, I've hardly seen any people, and the most people I've seen are queuing up to do a bungee.

SAM: That's what people come to New Zealand for. Travel to the top of the world to jump off it, man. This is the point.

KYLE: I believe you can do this, bro.

KARL: Yeah, but don't be saying that. Are you going to be disappointed if I don't do this?

SAM: No, but we'll be stoked if you do.

KYLE: Yeah, we'll be over the moon if you do.

SAM: There's only you, it's not about anyone else. It's not about who wants you to do this. You're the only person that can make you jump off the edge. It's just you and that space between fear and total excitement.

KARL: My brain is saying no.

SAM: Of course it is.

KARL: My stomach's saying 'don't be stupid'.

SAM: Your entire being is saying 'this isn't making sense'.

KYLE: Yet there's a little bit in there that's saying do it.

KARL: No, I haven't got that bit. I'm not hearing that.

KYLE: You're out here now, aren't you?

SAM: It's that little element that wants to kill the tiger, that wants to ride the lightning . . .

PHIL: Okay, you ready?

KARL: Errmm, hang on a minute. Errmm . . .

KYLE: COME ONNNN! YEAHHHH!

SAM: It's proving to yourself that you can quieten that voice in your head that says don't do it.

This is the part I don't understand. Surely you should listen to the voice in your head. It's when you stop listening to that voice that you get yourself into trouble. If I didn't listen to it at this point, would it ever speak to me again? I wouldn't if I was it.

The problem is, these days you have to listen to too many parts of your body. Sometimes I go with my gut feeling, some say go with what your heart says – it's only a matter of time before my appendix will have an opinion. This is probably why there are so many helplines these days. No one knows who to bloody listen to!

My left leg started to shake uncontrollably like it was trying to walk away from the ledge.

KARL: Look, me left leg is moving and me right leg isn't doing anything.

KYLE: That's normal, man. Push down on your heel, that'll stop it.

KARL: Yeah, but what's it saying to me? Why is it getting involved?

KYLE: Your left leg is going 'cos the adrenaline is pumping and coursing through your veins right now.

KARL: Right. I'm getting the rush of adrenaline without stepping off, so why go further?

PHIL: When you leave that edge that's when you get it, that's when the endorphins kick in, that's when you get the reward. So, what you've got to do is take a couple of deep breaths again. You can do this, work with me. We're going to go to the edge, look up, you've had a look down, you know what it's like down there. I want you to look up, I want you to find that mountain out there, the sunshine, focus on it. We give you the countdown, it's gonna be three, two, one, short countdown. Go for it. Once you leave that edge, boom! that's it, job done. You're gonna be absolutely giggling, I promise you. Karl, stop thinking about it!

KARL: But I've got to think about it.

PHIL: Don't think too much!

PHIL: Just let go, stop listening to that thing in your head.

KARL: No, because that's what you should listen to in life.

PHIL: No, you shouldn't, not always. You'll never get anywhere if you listen to that all the time.

The mood started to change. The other bungee jumpers were getting impatient and shouting, as they were getting tired of waiting. I suppose they'd hyped themselves up to do it and now I was getting in the way and giving their inner voice more time to make them reconsider, which isn't good when you've probably paid around £130 to do this. I asked them to shut up, as I couldn't think straight with all the noise.

PHIL: Don't think about it too much! You're gonna go for it!

KARL: No.

PHIL: Yes, you are.

KARL: No.

PHIL: You have got it, mate.

KARL: No.

PHIL: It's all yours. Look up, focus.

KARL: No.

PHIL: Just let it happen.

KARL: No.

PHIL: We're gonna count you down.

KARL: No, stop pushing me.

PHIL: I want you to say yes! I'm holding on to the back of you . . .

KARL: No, no, I wanted me to say yes, I'm not saying yes, it's everyone else saying yes.

PHIL: Okay, well, say yes.

KARL: No!

SPECTATOR: Strap on a pair of balls and get out there!

KYLE: You're being Welsh about it, aren't you? Go on, get out there, mate!

SAM: Can I get you a tissue for that vagina?

KARL: Say what you want, it doesn't bother me.

KYLE: Toughen up.

In the end I decided to listen to the voice in my head and not do it. Sam and Kyle did though. They didn't hang around as long as me and think about what they were about to do. They got hooked up and jumped without looking down and didn't give time for their inner voice to get a word in. They came back up woooohing loudly, but nothing made me want to do it. In a way I was proud of the fact I said no. To this day, there is not one bit of me that wished I had done the bungee. I wonder how many people end up doing it under pressure from spectators standing by yelling at them the way they did with me. How many of them are brave enough to say no? How many of these people would do it for themselves if no one was watching? I've always been quite good at not doing things I didn't want to do. When I was younger I had loads of mates who did daft things like sniff glue and gas but I always said no. I had a friend whose ambition it was to work in a cobbler's just for the free smell of glue. The only time I took drugs was by accident at a pub quiz. There were loads of chocolate brownies on the tables. I wandered about from table to table eating them. When I left I hailed a taxi, but when he asked where I wanted to go I couldn't remember. It turned out I'd been eating hash cakes. I had to sit on the pavement for ages before my address came back to me. But I can still remember the bloody reg plate of that maroon Ford Orion though.

Sam and Kyle said they knew I was never going to do the jump and had set up another activity. They took me to a golf course, but not for golf . . . No, that would be too boring for a person in this part of the world. They wanted me to experience zorbing. I'd never heard of it. They had a huge rubber ball sat in the rough, close to the fourteenth hole. They asked me to climb in. Kyle then started pouring in water from a big drum. I wasn't expecting this, so I quickly zipped up the hole. They started to roll it. I was being thrown all over the place. It was like being in one of them balls you put in the washing machine that has softener in it. The water swished about drenching me. This must be what it feels like being a baby in the womb. It was hot in there, and the smell of warm rubber on top of being chucked around made me feel really sick. It's not even as if it looks cool. Some people might do bungee jumping and sky diving 'cos they think it gives off a macho look, but zorbing doesn't even give you that. It's the sort of thing you wouldn't brag about. I felt like a hamster in a wheel.

I was worried I was going to be sick, which could be dangerous while trapped in a moving ball, as I could end up choking. So, I yelled all the swear words I knew at the top of my voice. They eventually stopped it rolling. Kyle said I shouldn't have closed the entrance as the more water that's in the ball, the smoother the ride. That's some information I may as well forget about, as I'm never going zorbing again. No one should go zorbing. I think the ball should be used for shifting furniture that's too heavy to carry. Shove in a big telly and then roll it down the road.

Before they left, Kyle gave me a blow-up kiwi (the national bird) as a memento. I watched a programme on these birds ages ago and remembered that they mate for life. Some have been known to be together for 30 years, but I don't know why they make such a big deal about it. I put it down to them all looking the same. I'm pretty sure if all men and all women looked the same there wouldn't be as many divorces. While I'm on kiwi facts, even though it has wings it's a flightless bird and prefers to keep its feet on the ground like me. And it sleeps during the day, which was something I wished I could do as the jet lag was killing me by this point.

I called Ricky and told him I didn't do the bungee and I wasn't happy about being put in the situation. He made some chicken noises: £1.50 a minute and he's doing chicken noises. But he said I had a chance to redeem myself because he'd arranged for me to go to another island where bungee was actually invented. He said the island was known as the happiest place in the world, and to stop moaning.

We were up early the next day to catch a small private plane that would take us to another airport to catch another plane that would take us to the island of Pentecost in Vanuatu. A woman was scraping frost off the windscreen as we loaded up our kit into the six-seater. It's the first time I've ever had to ask the pilot if he could move his seat forward so I had room for my legs. We flew really low, so low that the woman co-pilot seemed to be using a normal road map. I'm surprised we didn't stop at traffic lights we were flying that low.

#59 Learn to fly a plane

I sat next to so many pilots in small planes during this trip that I reckon I've picked up the basics. I'm not a fan of flying so maybe it would be a good thing to do as it would help me understand how it all works and take away my anxieties. I worry on my flights that something will happen to the two pilots and no one else will be able to land the plane. If I learnt to fly, I could step in. I find it a bit odd how they have more subs on a bench in a football match in case of injury than they do on a plane carrying 300 passengers!

We got to Pentecost where I met John. He took me from the landing strip through the woods where I could hear whistling and singing, and through the trees until we came to a massive tower that looked like it was made of scaffolding poles. As I got closer I could see it was a structure of wooden poles all bound together with rope. It looked like a giant game of KerPlunk.

Men and women were dancing and singing while others were climbing up the side of the wooden frame. John explained that they were looking forward to seeing a white man do a land dive. As he explained why they do the land diving, men were jumping from various heights with nothing but vines wrapped round their ankles. Somehow, they measure the vines so that the land divers just brush the ground before being whipped back up by the vines.

The highest jumping platform was around 30 metres high. When one of the men jumped, the whole structure shook violently, as if it could come down at any moment. As each man landed another two blokes ran up and cut the vines free to clear them before the next man dived, like a kind of air traffic control.

As soon as the jumpers were released from the vines they ran back up the tower to have another go, like kids in the park playing on a slide. I imagine it would be difficult to refuse to do the jump if you lived here. It might lead to being shunned in such a tight-knit community. I think most people in life just want to fit in so follow suit rather than questioning things. It reminded me of the bungee jumping situation . . .

John said that if the divers brushed the land with the hair on their head, it blessed the land. 'No chance of me doing that then,' I thought. I'd have to plant my head in the earth like an ostrich for my hair to brush the land. He explained that the higher the jump, the more plentiful the harvest.

There were no St John's Ambulance people on stand-by if things went tits up. Even in the professional set-up in New Zealand I had to sign a waiver to say if anything happened it wasn't their responsibility, so I doubted if this village had any sort of cover. They didn't even cover their bollocks, so Life Cover wasn't going to be on offer.

The men wore a nambas, which is a small bit of material worn over the knob. The bollocks are left free. I didn't see the point of the material. It didn't really cover anything. It's like when you wrap a bottle of wine for someone at Christmas. There's no surprise there, and it was the same with the nambas – it wasn't hiding anything.

But, as with everywhere else in the world, you'll always get someone who wants to be different. There was a man who was walking around dressed in a right load of foliage. He was the Lady Gaga of the area. Maybe this was his way of getting out of doing the dive, by getting camouflaged up. The odd thing about the clothing was how the tradition had carried on and yet the odd villager had a mobile phone or wore a quality watch. The watch just didn't look right. It was never designed to go with a knob sheath. If anything I'd probably wear the watch round the nambas as a belt to stop it falling off. Surely if they accepted mobile phones and watches they might as well wear underpants or a pair of trunks.

A young lad who looked about six years old did a jump from around twenty-five feet. Kids of his age in England are being told not to play conkers at school due to little injuries, and yet here's little Billy diving to his imminent death just for the sake of growing some cabbages. This is what happens when people don't have enough to do. No jobs, no paperwork or bills to pay, no washing of clothes, no sales calls to answer, or windows or cars to wash, so they turn to arsing about.

There was no way I was going to do it from the top. I told John it was too risky. I explained that I have a mortgage and other responsibilities that I wouldn't be able to sort out with a broken neck. He told me: 'Not a problem. It safe. Been doing for many years, no accidents. No worry.' Yet, one after another, men continued to hurl themselves off the tower like lemmings. These people need wings more than the kiwi bird.

Everything seemed to be going well until a man whose vines were too long went and planted his head in the ground. He lay on the ground shaking like a baby sparrow that had fallen out its nest with his eyes rolling about in the back of his head. The singing and dancing continued as two men went over and slapped his face. Eventually he came back round with a big smile on his face.

I didn't want to let everyone in the village down, and I knew Ricky and Stephen would moan at me if I didn't get involved somehow, so I came up with an idea. I agreed to do the lowest possible land dive. I pointed to the lowest rung on the structure and asked everyone if jumping from there still counted as a land dive. They said it would. Two men prepared the vines for my dive. They definitely looked too long for the distance I was going to jump. They tied them around my ankles. I got up on the ledge to find it was a lot higher than I thought. Just as on the bungee platform in New Zealand where loud rock music blasted out of speakers, here the singing and whistling puts you in a kind of trance. I held onto the wooden frame with one arm and leaned as far forward as possible. Now I just had to let go. I remember having the same feeling when I was learning to swim as a kid, when you know you have to let go of the side of the pool and push away. This was like letting go of the edge of a pool, except there was no water. No one was shouting at me like the jump in New Zealand, no one was counting me down – I just had to wait until my inner voice said, 'Release'. The thing Sam kept saying to me on the bungee in New Zealand was in my head: 'Coach, pass me the ball, and I'll make the play.' With everyone wearing a nambas, now wasn't the time to be asking for any ball to play with. I let go.

The vines they had attached to my legs were far too long. I faceplanted the earth. Given the distance I'd jumped I'd have been better using shoelaces instead of vines, but the villagers loved it. The chanting and whistling got louder, and they lifted me in the air in celebration. I felt good, not from the dive, but because I felt they had appreciated my effort.

I called Ricky.

KARL: I did the land dive. I did it.

RICKY: Did you?

KARL: Yeah. I spoke to Stephen, and he was a bit down on me and that, and you were calling me a chicken, but I got there. I did the proper land dive.

RICKY: What, the thing with the vines?

KARL: Yeah. I was getting on with the locals, and they sort of . . . I dunno, I dunno how they did it 'cos when I got there and I first saw it I was like, 'Not a chance!'

RICKY: Right.

KARL: I don't know where it came from. I did it. Wasn't an amazing feeling, but after it they were all throwing me about in the air. They were loving it. The people who were sorta pushing me the other day were annoying me. I don't like being forced into things, whereas these people were a bit more, I dunno . . .

RICKY: Hold on! Did you do the real one or did you do the child's version? Let's get this straight because I've seen five-year-olds do it, and they just jump off and it's only about ten feet. Which one did you do?

KARL: It was, it wasn't the child's one, but the thing is, you've got to remember that I . . .

RICKY: How high was it? How high was it?

KARL: (*to director*) Luke, how high was it?

LUKE: I think you've got to be honest with him.

KARL: Yeah, I know, so how high, how high?

LUKE: It was the one below the child's one, about four foot, Karl.

KARL: It was about . . . about five foot.

RICKY: Five foot!?

KARL: Yeah, but . . .

RICKY: Sorry? Five foot! I've high-jumped higher than that.

KARL: No! Ricky, I think it was about five and a half foot. You jump and you land on the ground. It's not a bungee. You hit the ground.

RICKY: How do you hit the ground?

KARL: With your head!

RICKY: You just jumped five foot. You didn't even jump your own height basically!

KARL: Yeah, but I landed on my head! When you see it, you'll understand. Apparently I'm the first white man to do a land dive. Now that's a lot better than that other bungee jump. I've broken a record here!

RICKY: Right. So, you're the first white person to land on their head? Is that what the record is? Do you want me to ask Guinness World Records UK if you're the first white man to land on his head? Basically, you fell over and hit your head. (*Karl laughs*)

RICKY: So, if I punch Stephen in the face and he falls over and hits his head, he's broken the record 'cos he's done it from two foot higher than you! You fucking . . . terrible! (*Laughs*) Right, since you've been so brave and so brilliant, you've won the night in a half-decent hotel so enjoy that. Well done! You've been through a lot of trauma here, boy.

We boarded another plane and made our way to the nice hotel that Ricky had promised. It was decent – a posh place that made the towels in the room into animals. I had two rabbits on my bed made with hand towels and a couple of swans by the bathroom sink made with flannels. I suppose it gives some purpose to a flannel – something I've never got into using. I also found a funny egg cup in the room. It had two little legs and had EGGS ON LEGS written on the front. I packed it in my bag as it cheered me up and I thought I might be needing something like that on my island, the way Tom Hanks had that football to talk to in *Castaway*.

After a good night's sleep I got up and had a full English breakfast on the pier. As I ate my egg, sausage, beans and toast I watched loads of flying fish in the clear blue sea. It's odd how evolution gave fish wings. I wonder whether if people continue to chuck themselves off ledges and big wooden frames we will eventually grow a pair.

But I couldn't enjoy my little treat from Ricky and Stephen as much as I wanted to. I was worried about what they had planned for me next. It felt like being in a private hospital. It's nice having your own room and good food, but the fact is you're in hospital to have your legs off the next day so how can you really enjoy it?

A plane flew over really low and then landed in the sea and chucked out an anchor. It was a seaplane. The pilot introduced himself to me as Seaplane Paul. The plane was tiny, like a motorbike with wings. He said he was going to take me to see the many small islands that were dotted around to give me an idea of the sort of place where I might be spending my night.

We saw loads of islands. All different sizes. Like clumps of broccoli sprouting from the sea. Paul told me around 83 islands make up Vanuatu. I saw a few nice ones I'd have been happy to stay on. Nice white sand, clear blue water and bushes and trees for protection from the sun, just like the Bounty advert I mentioned earlier. He then took me to see a volcano. It was terrifying. I'd seen a lot of volcanoes when holidaying in Lanzarote, but they were all dead and just looked like giant ashtrays. This one was alive. I kept saying that it wasn't safe as we flew through the steam clouds that were gushing out of the top. We had to do extra flights on the way here due to ash clouds from Chile and yet here we were flying through the smoke like contestants on *Stars in Their Eyes*. I could see the red hot lava bubbling like beans do when you've had them on the stove for too long. We were being battered by the heat that was rising from it and being thrown all over the place. I wasn't happy. Paul was getting too close for my liking. He seemed to be attracted to it like a bluebottle in a chippy flying too close to one of those FlyZap electrocutors. I wasn't feeling great from the turbulence, but what made me feel worse was the smell from the volcano. It stunk. To me, the fact that nature has made this thing stink is a way of telling us that we shouldn't be anywhere near it.

The smell of sulphur is similar to rotten eggs. It's odd to think the middle of the earth smells of bad eggs.

We headed back and I quizzed him about Vanuatu being the happiest place in the world. Paul was from Australia and he told me he'd travelled a lot and he really thinks it is the happiest place he's ever known. He told me that the locals use a greeting that is a type of laughing sound.

KARL: But if everybody's doing that sound how do you know when they are really really happy?

PAUL: But they are really really happy.

KARL: No, they're not. They can't be – not all the time.

PAUL: Yes, they can.

KARL: So, you meet someone and go heeee and they go heeee, and then they say 'What's been going on?' and you go 'Oh, my gran's just died' and they'd go 'Why are you so cheerful?'

PAUL: Ah, you would know if their grandma had died 'cos you'd see they would have a beard. If someone dies no one shaves.

KARL: For how long?

PAUL: Ah, I think it's for how long they feel, maybe a couple of months either way.

KARL: So, 'cos I have a bit of a beard they'll think someone close died?

PAUL: Yeah, and they'll try and be even happier to you, so you may get a few more heeees just to stop you going into depression.

KARL: It's worth keeping it then 'cos they'll treat me better, won't they?

I like the idea of growing a beard when someone's died, as you wouldn't really be in the mood for shaving after hearing the bad news. It's also a way of showing respect without it costing anything. Death is a costly business at home. It's another way of getting money out of us, and they try to make you feel you're a better person if you spend more on the dead. My dad says it's all bollocks and he wants to be stuck in a bin bag and I should let the council get rid of him. The trend at the moment seems to be buying a bench with a message engraved on it. They're like the new gravestones. 'Arthur used to like sitting here. Missed by wife Betty 1936–2012.' I bet the councils can't believe their luck how much they're saving on not having to cough up for public benches.

It wasn't long before I was at the airport again to get on another plane to fly and meet a tribe that worships Prince Philip as a god on the island of Tanna. Luke gave me a few photos of Prince Philip to pass onto them and a limited edition

£5 coin that had been released to celebrate his recent ninetieth birthday. £5! That's a lot of money for a coin you're not going to spend. Why couldn't it be a special 10p coin? It's things like this that annoy me about Britain. It's a right rip off. We don't even have £5 coins in circulation. It's things like this that would stop us ever making it into the Top 10 list of happiest places in the world.

Anyway, the Prince Philip tribe . . . The story goes that the son of a mountain spirit travelled across seas to find a powerful woman to marry, and somehow the son turned out to be Prince Philip. He visited close to the island in the 1970s, which helped to back up their beliefs. I met two locals as I got off the plane who were holding a piece of wood with my name on it. One, who spoke some English, was called JJ. He introduced me to Albi, who was described to me as the happiest man in the village, as well as being the greatest dancer. They were both stood there wearing next to nothing. Just a bit of plant on their heads and wicker on their knobs. I got in the back of a van with Albi as JJ had claimed the passenger seat on the inside.

Most places I visit I do try to learn a few words like 'Hello' and 'Thank you', but during this trip it was hard to keep up as they say Vanuatu has over 100 languages in use among the 230,000 population. I don't know how a place can run like this. Surely a lot of people have to speak a certain language for it to qualify as one. If the Teletubbies moved here they'd have to add that language to their list, too. English is used a little, and so is French, with Bislama being the main national language. It was hard to understand when being spoken, but it was possible to work it out when written down. While driving to meet the rest of the villagers with Albi and JJ, I saw a sign that read SLO DENJA which meant SLOW DANGER. They write down words how they sound, which is good. It's how it should be, really. I don't know why we started using silent letters in the English language like using a 'ph' to sound like an 'f' in the word 'phonetic' or an 'x' in 'xylophone'. Why not 'zilofone'? Our words have become so long and complicated we've had to come up with abbreviations to help us use words we don't know how to spell. If I was in charge of the dictionary I would have a right clear-out of words. Words like 'necrophilia' I'd get rid of. If someone has that (attraction to dead bodies), I'd make them say, 'I fancy dead bodies'. Then, at least when they tell people, they might realise how mental it sounds rather than it being hidden in a posh word. And then they'll stop having the problem. The fact that it has its own word makes it seem more acceptable.

On the rest of the trip I spent most of my time looking at billboards and signs to work out what they were saying. It was like looking at those images that were popular in the 1980s where if you stared at them for long enough you'd see a monkey riding a unicorn. Some examples for you: 'Mi wantem' is 'I would like'. 'Mi wantem' sounds like 'Me want them', which equals 'I would like'. 'Bitwin' is 'between'. 'Bisnis' is 'business'. By now you've probably got the hang of it, so I don't have to tell you what 'Gud moning' means. If you're still struggling you're a 'dik ed'.

I gave Albi the photos of Prince Philip that Luke had cut from magazines and he was really really happy with them, so I gave him the coin as well. He was even more chuffed. Luke said I'd made a bit of an error giving Albi the coin, as I should have saved it for the main chief of the village. We didn't have any more coins, so I wanted him to hide it, but this is the problem with wearing nothing but a wicker knob coverer – there's nowhere for small change. I gestured that he should hold it tight in his hand and show no one.

#17 GambLe in Las Vegas

Suzanne doesn't allow me to gamble. Now and again I want to sign up to gambling sites online but she says, 'No, once you're signed up you'll be gambling all the time and lose everything.' She's probably right. I used to like fruit machines when I was younger but I find they've all got a bit complicated now. It used to be three pears or three melons to win the jackpot but now there's so many fancy fruits in the world they've had to add more reels to fruit machines so there's less chance of winning. They seem to have loads more buttons and lights flashing than they used to have too. I had a go on one in a service station recently that flashed and made so much noise I may as well have just stayed in the car park and kicked a car to set off its alarm. I would have got the same result and saved myself 20p.

We got to the village after an hour's drive. All eyes were on me as I got out the back of the van. They stared at me stony-faced and the only noise came from a pair of scrawny-looking dogs having it away and the flapping of a British flag they were flying high. I've never been a fan of flags. I don't think they're necessary anymore. When I see the British flag I don't feel it's important to me. Maybe before the invention of words they were handy to mark a territory, but now, what are they for? I see people waving them at sporting events, but most of the time I don't know what country the flag is from. When Neil Armstrong put a flag on the moon what would it mean to someone from another planet who landed and saw it? When he stuck it into the moon's surface it just stood there, like one of Suzanne's mam's towels when she's forgotten to use softener, all hard and stiff. The only good thing about a flag is, you can wash them and then put them straight back out to use, and they can dry while doing their job. The only proper use of our flag is that if you fly the British flag upside down it is a distress signal, but then not many people know that, and what are the chances of having a flag on you when in a distressed moment?

I think the whole of the village was out to greet me, but then I suppose when you live in mud huts any excuse to get out is a good one. Albi was definitely the happiest man in the village, but was that just because he was five quid up? JJ led me to see the collection of photos of Prince Philip they had hung on a piece of string. Some were cut from magazines, some were postcards. Then I came across one of JJ and Albi wearing dinner jackets along with a few others, stood next to Prince Philip. I don't like wearing suits as I always feel overdressed, but that saying has never been more apt than for JJ and Albi. They looked really different in a suit. JJ said they went to meet him at Windsor. Normally, to get this close to Philip you'd have to take part in the Duke of Edinburgh Awards. A lad at school climbed some mountain in Scotland and got the award, but I don't think he got to meet him. I thought I was getting involved in the DoE Awards when my school sent me to hand out biscuits at the local mental home, but it turned out I was just sent to help. To this day I don't really know why I was sent there instead of being in school.

#41 Meet your idol

There's a saying that you should never meet your idols. I tend to agree with it as when I was a kid I liked Gary Glitter, so good advice. But recently when I was in India I went out of my way to meet Ganga and Jamuna. They are conjoined twins. I never thought I would meet conjoined twins. They're less common than a four-leaf clover even though now is probably the best time for them, what with all the two-for-one offers that are out there. In a world where everybody looks the same it was good to meet Ganga and Jumuna and I will never forget it.

I like the way they have a god who they can actually contact and get answers from. People have lots of different gods, but how many of them can say they've had a photo with them like some of these lot have? They believed in something that made them happy, so what does it matter? A lot of people would be keen to tell them it's nonsense, but sometimes the truth doesn't matter. I think we're too keen to state the truth about everything. There was a programme on Channel 5 ages ago called *The Truth about the Killer Squid,* as if its lies were that important.

JJ asked me to join everyone for food. As we sat on the ground I noticed everyone that faced me had beards, which I remember Seaplane Paul had said was the sign of a death. Suzanne tells me I look like a scruff when I don't shave, but if I was walking about nude like this lot what's the point in having a nice smooth face when my hairy arse and back would be on show for everyone to see? I asked who had died, and they said it was the supreme chief who had reached 111 years old. Maybe he was – it's a healthy lifestyle – but when living like this I imagine it's easy to get dates wrong. Every day would feel the same. Why do they need to know if it's Thursday? They don't have bins to put out or bills to pay by a certain date, they do what they need to do when it needs doing. Simple.

My mam only needs to know what day it is so she knows which TV soap to watch, but since *Coronation Street*, *EastEnders* and *Emmerdale* seem to be on every night these days I don't think she has a clue what day it is.

#58 Stand on the international date line

I'd be happy to do this, if someone took me there – although I don't really see the point. What you wouldn't catch me doing is living there. Imagine trying to arrange for a builder or a plumber to come round. It gives them the perfect excuse to mess you around.

JJ said, 'And this is the son that is in place of the supreme chief. And his speech is: "I would like to take this opportunity to thank you and to tell you that we appreciate your presence here, and to tell you that it's the first time in our history that we the black people and the white people sit together here to share food. In the past, our ancestors and our elders never ate together with the white people, and we want this unity and the peace."'

#37 Research your family tree

The chances are, if you've got an interesting family tree you already know about it. If you were somehow linked to Einstein that information would have been passed down through the family. If you go looking for things you're more likely to find problems. It's like having a check-up at the doctor's or taking your car for a service – they'll find problems that weren't a problem before they started looking. Knowing my luck, I'd end up having to pay a gas and leccy bill for some old Pilkington who never paid it before they died.

I'd be interested if they could go really far back – right back – so they could show me a photo of an ape, jellyfish or slug and say, 'Karl, this is the earliest Pilkington we could trace. This is your great-great-great-great-great-great-great-grandad.'

We ate some chicken, and I asked if anyone had any questions, expecting to be asked about what food I like or what hobbies I have, but they kept asking questions I didn't understand or know the answers to about their prospects and future.

> KARL: You don't need to worry. Everything's gonna be good, I'd say. Everything's good.
>
> JJ: (*translates to rest of village*) Thank you for the message you give us confirming us not to worry, everything will be okay. It is a time when our elders have to decide on what they will do, but we depend on you now that you have promised everything will be good.
>
> KARL: I think it will be. I think it'll be alright. Things change, but, I think, I think it'll be alright. I'd carry on as you are.

I was guessing, but I do think they'll be alright. We then danced to some chants to celebrate the good news. It started off with a type of conga before moving on to some foot stamping that caused dust to fill the air from the dry ground like a natural smoke-machine effect. The men danced as the women sat and watched, some with their faces decorated in splattered colours as if they'd been to a paintball event.

If Suzanne wanted to do this to her face I'd have an issue with it, as she'd make a right mess of the pillowcases when she went to bed, but here they don't have pillowcases, so they don't have to worry about stuff like that. All the bright colours must attract wasps though, which must be annoying.

Albi and JJ wanted to take me to see Grandmother, so we got back in the van and travelled quite a distance. We ended up staying over at another village for the night. I ended up sleeping in a treehouse, with a headache from hunger, as I didn't bother waiting for tea after they showed me what they'd be serving up. It was fruit bat. It's a bat, and adding the word 'fruit' to it doesn't make it any more appetising. I don't think I could count it as one of my five a day, either. I asked how long a bat takes to cook, a question I never thought I'd ask. I doubt Ask Jeeves or Google would even know the answer. I said I'd skip tea, as the smell of the dead bat didn't grab me, and went to bed. You'd think they'd go to bed earlier, with them having no electricity, but it didn't stop them singing and dancing well into the night to the same song over and over and over again. I kept waking up, but I couldn't tell if I'd been asleep for hours or just a few minutes as the same song was being sung. It was like when Bryan Adams was number one with '(Everything I Do) I Do It For You'. You couldn't escape it.

I was woken again when Albi and JJ came into the treehouse to sleep. The good thing is, they wear so little, there was no messing around getting undressed. They just got straight into bed. It felt like I'd just got off to sleep again when the next thing I knew Albi was waking me up to go and see Grandmother. It was 4 a.m.! Why so early? Are we helping her do a paper round or what? I felt sick from tiredness as I tried to get dressed in total darkness.

As we drove up a mountain I could hear explosions and see a red glow in the sky. JJ pointed and said, 'Grandma.' It was a volcano.

#88 Climb an active volcano ✓

It didn't really surprise me that they call a volcano 'Grandma'. Remember, I was in a place where Prince Philip is god. As we got closer, the road we were driving on had steam coming through it. The volcano was acting like underfloor heating. The noise of the explosions got louder as we got closer. Funny how their grandma makes a lot of rumbling noises; it's my auntie who is known for her explosions. She once broke wind for five minutes. She said it doesn't happen anymore, but I just think her hearing isn't what it used to be.

It was difficult to know if we were in any danger as Albi continued to smile. He seemed so relaxed with it. My car insurance costs a bomb just 'cos I have on-street parking. What would it cost me if I had one of these on my doorstep?

We made our way up a makeshift path with a handrail that had been battered and broken in places by smouldering rock spewed out from the volcano. I asked JJ about safety and which way to run if this thing started getting more active. JJ explained, 'If you are running, you keep on talking or speaking to her (Grandma), telling her to be careful and to take care of you.'

This place has got enough languages without me having to learn to speak Volcano. I was worried about a lump of it landing on me as I can't be doing with burns. I was always burning myself as a kid on kettles and hot plates. I don't like frying an egg as I don't like the way it spits out hot fat at me. This was like that but on a bigger scale. It was like one big dodgy firework that was unpredictable. The longer the silence, the bigger the explosion seemed to be. Standing on the edge, looking down into the churning red magma made my heart pound more than when I was on the edge of the bungee platform. It didn't seem to bother JJ and Albi. The loud echoing booms didn't even make them flinch.

74 Visit Angel Falls in Venezuela

Apparently Angel Falls was named after a US aviator called Jimmie Angel who was the first to fly over the falls in a plane. Even though it already had a local name, Kerepakupai Vena, he re-named it. I think the name Angel Falls works better to attract the tourists as it's a lot easier to remember so it was a worthwhile change. I don't know why they ever bothered changing the kitchen cleaner product name from Jif to Cif though.

I had an empty plastic bottle I'd been drinking from all morning that I wanted to chuck into the bubbling lava, but JJ said I wasn't allowed. As far as I could see, this would be the only advantage of having one of these things on your doorstep. It would be great to get rid of old sideboards and mattresses by just tipping them in. Surely much better on the environment than landfill. If we had one of these in the UK they probably wouldn't allow tipping either, but it would have nothing to do with upsetting Grandma, it would just be because they'd lose money, as it's £25 a time for them to come and collect big pieces of rubbish. It would also be a good place to put dead bodies. A lot more efficient than burying, and each time you heard it exploding it would remind you of old family members who had passed away. Their ashes would eventually go back into the ground.

JJ said they don't throw anything in out of respect for Grandma as she fertilises the ground with ash for good produce. Then he said we should move. The wind was changing direction, and there was more chance of the big hot rocks coming our way.

He wasn't wrong either, as moments later, while making our way back down, we saw two huge big steaming rocks the size of cooler boxes land where we had been standing. We got back down to the van. Then Albi and JJ got out two bits of wood and asked me to go back up the side of the volcano with them.

JJ explained the plan: 'Karl, you must struggle to survive in hot places like this, in the desert, and learn to enjoy yourself, so arse boarding is one of the things that can make you happy when you are in the desert.'

Arse boarding was something they used to do when they were younger. They'd sit on a type of homemade ski and then slide down the side of the ash-covered volcano as if it were snow. I thought JJ and Albi would be the last people up for this kind of activity wearing what they were wearing. I could feel the sharp glass-like ash getting into my shoes, through my socks and under my skin, so God knows how it would feel on their arses.

I tried it but I seemed to be too heavy to glide. So I tried using my feet to push a little bit but I ended up just looking like a dog wiping its itchy arse on grass.

Three middle-aged blokes arse boarding on the side of a volcano: it was like a scene from *Last of the Summer Wine*. Albi was laughing to himself and loving every minute of it. All this did was back up my opinion that if people don't have much to do, most will opt for arsing about. Literally.

#94 Take part in a fire-walking ceremony

This act of walking on fire has existed for thousands of years and is practised by cultures all across the world as a rite of passage into adulthood. I imagine most of the people who do this are like JJ and Albi who wander about all day barefoot which means their feet are tougher. When I got in the back of the van with Albi I noticed the skin on the bottom of his feet had hardened from having no protection from shoes. His toes were nice and straight though. I reckon Albi could walk on broken glass and not flinch. I tickled his feet when he wasn't looking and he didn't even notice. Another example of how modern living is making us a little bit weaker. My feet can't even handle under-floor heating.

Thinking back, even though I was a bit worried on the edge of the volcano I'd say it was my favourite thing on this trip.

STEPHEN: Alright, Karl, by now you should have met quite a few of the happy islanders in Vanuatu, and I hope you're starting to get a sense of what it really means to be an island dweller because it's time to take it to another level, mate. One more plane ride to the remote island of Malakula where we've found you your very own Man Friday who'll take you to your desert island and teach you all the survival skills you'll need.

Another plane, a long drive, a pick-up of a pig from a farm (a payment for the tribe teaching me survival skills), and a boat on quite a rough ocean later, I was in Malakula.

Since being back at home I've found out that Malakula was named by Captain James Cook. It comes from the French *mal au cul* which means 'pain in the arse' after Cook found it difficult to deal with cannibals, volcanoes and other annoying features. It's good to know proper explorers sometimes share the feelings I have on my travels. I remember feeling a bit like Captain Cook at this point in the trip. The whole reason why I picked the night on a desert island was because I like peace and quiet and my own company. I hadn't really had any time to myself since leaving England, and it was difficult to have a bit of 'me' time while being here as the people of Vanuatu never seem to spend time on their own.

I got off the boat, and there was the chief stood with a stick, feathers sprouting from his head, wearing a nambas with flip-flops. Again, if they can buy flip-flops, they can buy a pair of pants, surely. The chief's nambas was not made of wicker like Albi's and JJ's. It was made of leaves and looked like a cross between some sort of Thai starter and a spec case. Clothes normally help you to guess the age of people, so I was struggling to guess the age of most people while in Vanuatu. I tried to see how low the men's testicles hung as a guide. The lower they hang, the older the man. For women I used the same technique but with their breasts. By using this guide I'd say the chief was around forty.

As he led us up to where he lived the the rain came down. We walked and talked. He told me they speak the language of Ninde. He said everything begins with the letter 'n'. It's at times like this I wonder if they make things up to joke around with tourists like me. A palm tree he pointed to was called a Nimdimdip, we saw Naho, which is a fruit, and he pointed out a leaf that was called

Nooholee. I said that playing I-Spy here would be tough as you'd be guessing all day. He agreed.

We then stopped at an area where he explained that people lay. At first I thought he meant to relax or to have it away with their partner, but then I saw a load of bones and realised he meant where dead bodies lay. I saw a skull and asked whose head it was. Quick as a flash, he said, 'Nicola', as if showing me a photograph. I would've understood it more if it had been the head of some ancient chief or something, but the name Nicola isn't usually the name of a leader. Maybe having everything beginning with the letter 'n' makes it easy to remember things. I thought it would be odd to see the skull of someone I knew.

We got to the village. It was really nice. The gardens were like something in a royal park. The chief took me to a wooden hut where I would be staying the night. It was basic but would do the job of keeping me dry. They had also installed a wooden toilet over a pit, which I think was built especially for me as it looked unused. This was how they showed their wealth. It wasn't about how much they had for themselves, it was more about how much they could give to others. He told me meat and kava would be served soon. I set out my sleeping bag on the floor, put up a mozzie net while there was still light and hung up my socks and trousers to dry before joining everyone at the communal eating area.

All the men were sat around chatting. A few set about making some kava, a drink made from the kava plant roots. They ground the plant with some water from the stream. After an hour of bashing the root with a wooden pole they had created a washing-up bowl full of grey kava. They poured me some first, as I was the guest. It tasted like soap and made my tongue numb, which at least made it easier to drink the rest. My taste buds were off their tits.

#23 Drink a beer at Oktoberfest ✗

Apparently 5 million people attend Oktoberfest every year. I like the odd beer but not with 5 million other people. Imagine the queue at the bar. I'm happy having a night out with maybe three others but soon as you're having to push tables together and use a notepad and pen to make a note of what people want to drink – it's too many. I've only done it once or twice but I didn't enjoy it. The saying used to be 'two's company, three's a crowd'. I wasn't sure if I was on a night out or on some sort of protest march. I remember having to announce I was going home forty minutes before I wanted to go to allow time to say goodbye to everyone even though I hadn't actually had time to say hello to them as there were so many bloody people. Never again.

No women were present. In all the time I was there I didn't see the men and women mix. Nicola's dead head was the closest I saw the chief get to a woman.

The chief was sat on a log chatting on his mobile phone, a sight I'd still not become accustomed to, even though each tribe I'd met since being here seemed to have them. It struck me as odd that a man who's a chief, wears feathers and has skulls of friends in his garden has a pay-as-you-go mobile. He must get sales calls from people trying to sell him things he doesn't even know exist.

I ate some meat that I'm sure was nice, but I couldn't taste it 'cos of the kava. I went to bed.

I remember waking up and feeling impatient. I just wanted to be introduced to my Man Friday, get to my island and experience what I had come to experience. It was the same feeling you get the day after a wedding when you've stayed in the same hotel all the other guests have stayed in and you feel like you have to continue the celebrations over breakfast with strangers you're never likely to meet again.

I had a wash in the freshwater stream, and then Luke told me that I had to go and meet the chief who would introduce me to his son. He was the man who would be teaching me the survival skills on my remote island. He then said the chief would be expecting me to wear the traditional dress of the nambas. I said, 'Not a chance.' It annoyed me that he expected me to wear one. I'd been keeping myself well covered and taking malaria tablets all week, and now he wanted me to walk about with only my knob covered? It didn't make sense with all the mosquitoes around. I wanted to learn skills like Ray Mears and Bear Grylls, but this was turning more into *How to Look Good Naked* with Gok Wan.

Luke said it was a sign of respect, but I didn't understand why getting my bollocks out would show respect. At home it would be classed as anti-social behaviour. I'd already shown respect by not upsetting anyone and taking them a pig. That's a big gift to give someone, isn't it? I think some top-up time for his mobile should have been enough. I went to see the chief.

CHIEF: We have to give your nambas to you.

KARL: I'm not too worried about that, don't trouble yourself. I'm quite happy. You've made me welcome, I've stayed the night, you gave me kava, I had a really good night. You don't have to give me any more. So, yeah, we can just . . . I just came to meet my friend who is going to help me to survive on the island.

LUKE: It's traditional, Karl. If one becomes an honorary tribe member, it is an honour for the tribe if you don the nambas.

CHIEF: It is a tradition thing when we go fishing.

KARL: I think it's more important to have a rod and bait when fishing. Fishing tackle is important. Not my tackle! I'm not going to pull off that look. What sort of rule is that? If I don't wear a nambas they won't teach me to fish!?

CHIEF'S SON: It is a kind of respect.

KARL: It's just . . . (sighs) . . . wearing the nambas, a friend's winding me up back at home. He is making me wear these nambas. I didn't know that was going to happen, you see. It's a bit of a surprise for me. I thought I was just coming here to have a look, observe with eyes and then go. Now everybody's keen to get me in a nambas, and the longer this goes on, the more embarrassing it is.

CHIEF'S SON: You have to be in the nambas.

LUKE: It's just for a short while. I think it would be the right thing to do.

CHIEF'S SON: After you put on nambas, then we have to do a dance here.

KARL: See! They're adding a bit more now. Pop these on, then we're going to have a dance. That's when things pop out – when having a dance.

CHIEF'S SON: It is a short one.

KARL: What do you mean, it's a short one?

CHIEF'S SON: Short dance.

KARL: Oh, short dance. It's just, you see, this is normal for you, but for me, this will go on the TV, and me mum, me dad will be saying, 'Oh, what's Karl been up to?' I'm dancing around with stuff on show. It's different at home. People don't dress like this, so it's a bit of a bigger deal for me. To be, you know, having it all out there, moving around, then something falls out.

LUKE: It's a taboo you're messing with, something symbolic here, you know.

KARL: Yeah, well, they're messing with my symbollocks. How can we move this on because this is getting more and more awkward as time goes on?

We were getting nowhere, so we came to a compromise. I would wear the type of nambas that the children wear, which was more of a grass skirt than a knob wrap. I don't understand why they don't all go for this option. It must be easier to go for a quick pee wearing the skirt than it is when wearing a nambas, where you have to learn the art of origami to wrap it back up again.

Two fellas measured me up like tailors on Savile Row. They made a type of band that tied round my waist and then attached big leaves to it. Once I was dressed, the chanting started. We danced around a tree. Then, I was told that John, who was the chief's son, would be taking me over to the island where I would be staying.

John said we had to get some leaves. This time, it wasn't for clothing but for shelter. He got out his machete and hacked down some big leaves the size of surf boards and we carried them to two little boats we would be using to get over to the island. The weather was chronic. The rain was heavy, and there was a cold wind. Luke pointed out the island. It didn't look as big as any of the ones I had flown over in the seaplane with Paul. It looked like a tiny muffin, but I thought it might be big, maybe it's just far away. Luke said it was called Ten Sticks Island. During World War Two the American military used the island for target practice.

It took about twenty minutes to get across the choppy sea as the current was dragging the boat out into the ocean. One or two of the big leaves blew away but I wasn't going to start trying to retrieve them. I was proper pissed off now. Everything I had been through and this was the pay-off! This was nowhere near what I'd pictured when I picked this trip off the Bucket List. It was nothing like the Bounty advert.

I got to the island to find it was just as small as it had looked. I suppose the fact that the US military used it for target practice should have been a clue. I'd seen roundabouts bigger than this. It didn't even have sand. Sharp rocks and broken shells covered the ground. There was no point in me showing my disappointment in moaning. John was struggling to understand me, and by the look on his face he wasn't very happy either.

I found quite a good spot to make the shelter. It was a little bit protected from the howling cold wind that was whipping in off the sea. John had started to build a frame for our shelter, and I used my anger energy to shift some big boulders that would help to keep it in place.

#64 Build your own house

Building my own home has never been an ambition of mine. Me and Suzanne fall out when we have to work together on picking a shade of carpet, so there's no way we'd still be together if we took this on. I watch the TV show *Grand Designs* quite a lot. It's a programme where you see a couple go through the whole house-building process from the design on paper right through to moving in. It begins with a happy couple who are excited and full of positive thoughts and eager to get the project going, and then you witness them age over a year as they end up having to live in a caravan as the project runs well behind schedule. The wife, who at the outset is full of smiles, wearing lots of make-up and hair freshly done for TV, ages overnight as you see her sat with her kids eating Pot Noodles, wearing a hard hat as the builders bring more bad news that the ship carrying the special environmentally friendly tiles they wanted from Sweden, rather than the normal ones from the local Topps Tiles, has sunk and has now delayed the project a further three months. Music from Coldplay is used as we see the wife crying because she hasn't been able to have a bath for four months and Kevin the presenter telling us the build has now gone 35% over budget. The budget always goes over. I don't think they ever take into account the money spent on tea bags whenever builders are around. They can get through a box in three days.

John was cutting up leaves to use as a type of natural rope to tie the frame together, but it was taking too long for my liking. I got out my bits and pieces that I'd brought from home. My big ball of string and roll of gaffa tape really speeded the job up. At this point, Luke the director and the cameraman disappeared off in their boat. I thought they'd just gone to film from a distance or something, but they'd gone right out of sight. I got the Stanley knife out of my bag and found the egg cup that had made me smile in the posh hotel. It didn't make me smile today. A part of me wanted to knock it on the head, but my inner voice – the one that wasn't keen on me doing the bungee at the start of the trip – was telling me I'd got this far, so I may as well follow it through. I listened to my inner voice a lot, as John wasn't saying much and it was the only company I had.

27 Spend a night in a haunted house

I visited the most haunted house in Britain a few years ago but I didn't see anything. The bloke who owned the gaff said that there was a ghost that gets in his bed at night and rubs his legs. That never happened on *Scooby Doo*, did it? The thing that is weird with ghost sightings is that people always describe seeing them float down a corridor wearing Victorian clothing. Why do they never see a ghost wearing a tracksuit and trainers? And no one ever reports seeing a black or Asian ghost, do they?

KARL'S FACTS

VILLAGES ON VANUATU HAVE MEN-ONLY AND WOMEN-ONLY SECTIONS.

WHEN PRINCE PHILIP VISITED THE ISLAND IN 1974 SOME OF THE VILLAGERS THOUGHT HE LOOKED LIKE A MOUNTAIN SPIRIT FROM A MYTH, AND NOW THEY REVERE HIM AS A GOD.

THE ULTIMATE DESERT ISLAND MAN IS ROBINSON CRUSOE, INSPIRED BY A SCOTTISH SAILOR WHO REALLY WAS STRANDED ON AN ISLAND OFF THE COAST OF CHILE FOR FOUR YEARS AND FOUR MONTHS.

VANUATU WAS DECLARED A REPUBLIC AFTER THE COCONUT WAR OF 1980.

THE OLDEST MESSAGE IN A BOTTLE SPENT 92 YEARS 229 DAYS AT SEA.

While he was doing the last few touches to the roof, I walked round the whole island to find wood to burn on a fire. It only took about a fifteen-minute slow walk to get round it, but in this time I came to realise the island shouldn't be called Ten Sticks, as I could only find half that amount to burn on the fire. I tried to get them burning with the lighter I had brought from home, but it didn't work due to the amount of rain that had got into my bag. John ended up using his skills and rubbed his special sticks together to get the fire going inside the shelter. I sat and ate my biscuits with John. There was something about the fire that put me more at ease. John seemed happier now, too. I think all men have some attraction to fire. Let's face it, you don't get many women arsonists, do you? Maybe it's something inside that goes way back to cavemen times.

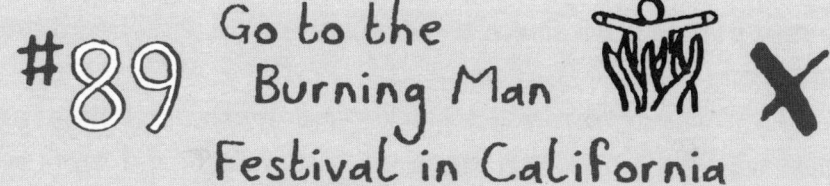

#89 Go to the Burning Man Festival in California

I think this is like Guy Fawkes Night. I remember using this night when I was a kid as a way of getting rid of a pair of shoes that I didn't like. They were really hard leather with edges round the ankle so sharp that they could slice cheese. Me and my mates managed to get a lady mannequin from the back of a woman's clothes shop called Jasmine's that had closed down. The plan was to dress it using our own clothes, go door to door for a penny for the guy and then remove the clothes before setting fire to her, except I saw this as a chance to get rid of the shoes once and for all. We put the nude mannequin that was wearing nothing but an old man's cap and my shoes on the bonfire. The next morning on the way to school I stopped off at the fire to see if it was still burning and there was the mannequin, slightly charred, still wearing my shoes. They looked totally undamaged. I was about as successful as Guy Fawkes blowing up Parliament.

John didn't rest for long. He was up with his bow and arrow aiming at fish for food. He made a few attempts but had no joy. He came running over and gestured that I go with him. He pointed to my boat. I thought he'd also had enough and wanted to go back to the mainland. I got in my boat and followed him. It turned out that he'd spotted two coconuts floating by and needed help dragging them in. He reacted quickly to avoid missing the chance of food. It reminded me of the way I used to rush putting my trainers on when I was a kid and I heard the tune from the ice-cream van.

John was right to react quickly and get the coconuts, as there was nothing else on this island that I could eat. I suppose this is how he lives. There's no shop or home deliveries round here, which is no doubt why they stay in groups. They help each other to survive. At home having friends isn't the same as here. People are obsessed with how many friends they have on Facebook or followers on Twitter, but none of them are there to actually help.

I was sat by the fire trying to dry my trainers when Luke and his team came back. They had all eaten and seemed fairly upbeat, which can be quite annoying when you're fed up. John produced something from his bag for me to eat, which he said would get me through the night. It was taro, a potato-like thing. I found it hard to be grateful at the same time as being so disappointed. I think even Ainsley Harriott on *Ready, Steady, Cook* would struggle to make something decent out of a taro and a coconut. John then told me he was going home.

Luke handed me a gift from Ricky, to rub more salt into the wound. It was a football with a face drawn on it like the one Tom Hanks had for company in *Castaway*.

#55 Explore the Galapagos Islands

Charles Darwin visited this place in 1835 on his travels round South America and it helped him come up with his idea of how we evolved from apes after studying all the animals and plants on the islands. It still puzzles me. I don't like thinking about the evolving process as it hurts my brain. The way nature worked out we needed eyes and made it happen is too much for me. I do wonder though if we'd be more advanced now if we didn't have eyes as they're too happy watching telly which means the mind isn't being used to think about important things in life. Evidence of this is how I have to close my eyes when trying to work something out. I reckon HD TV might stop our eyes improving any further and now cars have sensors to keep an eye out for things which means we don't have to use them as much. I think we've stopped evolving now and we'll start devolving. We'll end up as blobs in jars with a mobile phone and a TV remote.

I put the taro on to cook and tried doing some of my crosswords by torchlight, but my brain wasn't working as well as it normally does. I enjoy working on these at home, but it just wasn't the same in these conditions. I struggled to answer the question 'American version of prawn (6)'. I tried the taro. It was pretty tasteless and burnt.

Just as I was thinking of having an early night to get this experience over and done with, I heard the sound of a boat engine and saw someone pointing a flashlight at us. Luke went off to see what they wanted. He then came back with a couple of slices of steak he had sorted out for us earlier. He thought it was only fair, as the day had been a total wash-out. I used the shovel I had brought to cook them on. At the time it tasted like the best steak I'd ever eaten.

I was finally dry, warm and full. That's all I need to keep me happy. I knew I was happy 'cos my brain even worked out the answer to the crossword question. It was 'shrimp'.

CHAPTER TWO

#12 Travel the Trans–Siberian Railway ✔

RICKY: Travel the Trans-Siberian Railway. That's the stuff of dreams, isn't it? This is known as the greatest railway journey in the world. That's its nickname.

KARL: But is that because most train journeys aren't that great anymore? I never get on the Pendolino from Euston to Manchester going 'I'm looking forward to this', I do it because it's getting me from A to B.

STEPHEN: Well, I've always wanted to do the Trans-Siberian Express. I'm fascinated by Russia, amazing place. The history alone.

KARL: It's grim though, innit, Russia?

RICKY: What, all of it? It's the biggest country in the world and all of it's grim?

KARL: The bits you see on the telly are people queuing for spuds and stuff like that. Now maybe it's a good journey to them 'cos their other trains are worse than ours.

STEPHEN: What if I told you that the luxury carriages of the Trans-Siberian Express have all the mod cons? It's like luxury stuff.

KARL: What's the toilet situation on the train?

STEPHEN: I mean, as I understand it, I've never been on the journey, so I can't say for certain, but there's toilets.

KARL: Well . . . As long as there's toilets.

RICKY: How long are you on the toilet?

KARL: Ages.

RICKY: Why? Why are you on the toilet for ages?

KARL: It's a bit of me time, innit. I like to sit in there. It's me, and there's no one else coming in annoying me when I'm in there. Everywhere else I go in the house, Suzanne's there going, you haven't done this, haven't called them yet, that needs fixing . . . She doesn't come in there. Shut the door, sit there, me legs go numb. That's the thing for me though. I've gotta get up in a minute because otherwise she'll have to come in and help me off.

RICKY: What a life! What a life he's carved out for himself.

KARL: This isn't one that jumps out for me. I'm not over the moon with it, but it's better than the others. That's the problem with this list.

STEPHEN: Can we sign you up for this one?

(Karl nods)

STEPHEN: Enjoy it.

People always use the 'Is the glass half full or half empty?' question to find out if you're an optimist or a pessimist. I think it's hard to tell how full a glass is these days with the amount of ice most pubs put in your glass, but Suzanne tells me I'm a half-empty sort of person, which makes me a pessimist. I agree, I am a bit of a pessimist. I've been one from a young age. Me mam said I learned to frown years before I could walk. The first time she saw me smile she thought I had wind.

When I was told stories as a kid the pessimism was there even then 'cos I never believed me mam when she finished a story with 'And they all lived happily ever after'. 'No, they didn't. I don't believe it,' I'd say. I preferred Humpty Dumpty – nice and short, and a realistic ending. He never hurt anyone, but he had a little accident and died. Shit happens. That's life, innit. No great life story, or love interest, just a dead egg. But I heard they've messed with this story now, as I have mates with kids who sing a new song that goes:

> Was he pushed?
> Did he fall?
> Was there such a crime at all?
> Why did Humpty Dumpty fall?
> It's a mystery. It's a mystery.
> The courts assembled here today,
> To see that justice has its way.
> The guilty one will have to pay.
> Let's start proceedings right away.

What's going on! Kids are struggling with basic spelling and maths, and yet they're putting more effort into the Humpty Dumpty case than they did with OJ Simpson. I don't know how Humpty Dumpty ends these days. I'll have to buy the box set.

Anyway, me being pessimistic, I just expect the worst, so when it happens I'm prepared. Isn't that the right way to live? Why else do we all wear seatbelts when we get in a car? I mention being pessimistic as I imagine this is how most Russians would be. It's not a country where you hear about people going off to for a good laugh, is it? I read that when McDonald's opened branches in Russia they treated it like all their other shops and asked the staff to smile at the customers, but it didn't go down well as people in Russia don't smile at strangers. It's something saved for friends and family.

The flight to Moscow only took three hours, but then we were held for a further six hours because we had to write down a list of every piece of equipment the film crew were bringing into the country. Even though I'm a pessimist I thought the day couldn't get any worse, but then I met Pascha, a bearded man who spoke in a breathless, irritated way. He would be giving me a quick tour of Russia in his old Range Rover that was covered in mud and had dodgy brakes. I told him my reason for being in Russia and asked if he had been on the Trans-Siberian Railway.

PASCHA: No. Why would I want to do something that's totally predictable? I'll leave that to you British. So, anyway, what do you want to see? Red Square?

KARL: Yeah, you can show me that if you like. Errmm, I mean, whatever you think is worth seeing here.

PASCHA: Nothing.

KARL: Right, well, that isn't very . . .

PASCHA: Red Square is a place of execution. The ground is saturated with blood. We would be walking waist deep in blood.

KARL: Do you do this as a living, this tour guide thing?

PASCHA: Occasionally. It's not really my main service product, but, yes, I do these things. The more I do it, the less I like it.

I never understand why people stay in a job they really hate. Yes, we all have to make money to pay the bills, but if you hate your job so much you've got to get out.

KARL'S FACTS

THE TRANS-SIBERIAN IS OVER 9000 KILOMETRES LONG AND CROSSES 10 TIME ZONES.

IT TAKES OVER SIX DAYS TO TRAVEL ALONG THE WHOLE TRANS-SIBERIAN.

 SIBERIA COVERS 13.1 MILLION SQUARE KILOMETRES AND HAS MORE THAN 25% OF THE WORLD'S FORESTS.

THE WORD 'SIBERIA' MEANS 'SLEEPING LAND'.

hit by a bush

 MORE THAN 1.6 MILLION PEOPLE DIED IN THE SIBERIAN GULAGS (PRISONS) BETWEEN 1929 AND 1953.

#49 Leave a Job you hate

The worst thing would be to have a job that you can't leave. I've always thought that with doctors and surgeons. If they left and became interior designers or butchers I'd imagine they'd feel guilty. It would be like Superman knocking it all on the head to become a financial adviser.

I'm always surprised when they ask if a doctor is on board a flight. There they are trying to have a holiday from their stressful job and now 'cos someone in seat 47b is choking on their bag of free nuts, they have a call of duty. The closest I've come to having to do a job I really didn't like but couldn't leave was having to do jury duty. There is no getting out of it. Having to sit there for weeks in court judging a stranger. I felt like Simon Cowell. The most annoying thing was that you're not allowed to eat or drink when doing jury duty. I don't know why as I watch *Midsomer Murders* while eating a Twix and having a brew, and it doesn't affect me working out who did the murder. If anything, eating helps you to think. Kojak solved plenty murders while sucking a lollipop.

I offered Pascha some of my Revels as a way of bonding, but he wasn't interested. So I tried to be friendly by showing interest in his car.

PASCHA: It's the worst car I ever bought, and it's British. I never thought a car could be that bad.

KARL: But you've got to look after cars. You can't expect it to just run and run. You've got to service it if the brakes have gone. You've got to get the brakes fixed.

PASCHA: How many times do you think I've had the brakes fixed this year?! You want to guess?

KARL: You say fixed. Do you mean replaced?

PASCHA: Replaced the whole system. I would take to a qualified Land-Rover dealer and say, fix it, I don't want to think about it, four times!

KARL: Four? But maybe it's just a bad garage then.

PASCHA: Uh, how many garages do you think I went to?

KARL: (*pause*) Four?

PASCHA: What do you think I was doing this morning?

KARL: Fixing your car?

PASCHA: Attempting to.

KARL: Well, get rid of it. If I'm annoyed about something I get rid of it.

PASCHA: That's what I'm trying to do!

KARL: Are you fed up at the moment?

PASCHA: Yes, I am. With car, with job and, frankly, with you British.

KARL: What? Me? I haven't done anything.

PASCHA: No. You're not my usual type of client. Before you I had a British couple come to my cottage to do horse riding. They signed up for two days. I told them it is important to inform me once they left Moscow, but they won't do that, because the Brits, um, you have the mentality of slave owners. You expect people to wait on you.

KARL: What do you mean? We don't have slaves. Where did you get that from?

PASCHA: You speak a different language. By now I would have called another driver. I don't understand you.

I think I moaned less when I was with Pascha. His pessimistic approach made me more optimistic. This hasn't happened much to me before. Suzanne very rarely moans, and I wonder if it's 'cos I do it all for her, as Pascha was doing for me. If someone is happy I tend to look at the negative. There's no fun in moaning if it isn't getting the opposite reaction. The longer he was with me, the more he moaned. If Pascha was a dog I'd have had him put down.

Other than his tuts and huffs we drove in complete silence until the police pulled us over. Pascha spoke to them in Russian and then we drove away again.

PASCHA: The fine for this is 300 roubles.

KARL: What, for having a dirty car?

PASCHA: But they can't be filmed while fining us, so no fine.

KARL: But they would normally?

PASCHA: They would. They would if they had nothing better to do. Three hundred roubles. About ten dollars.

KARL: But, still, it's only a dirty car. What about the brakes then? You told us the brakes were dodgy. What would they do if they knew about that?

PASCHA: Ah, technically nothing, because Russia is more concerned about appearance. It's consistent with the general Russian pattern – form and appearance. If you have errors, factual errors, in your document they will not be noticed. If you cross something out and correct it yourself, it will be noticed and you will be required to fill out the entire thing again.

KARL: Yeah, we had that at the airport, with all the equipment. We had to write it out, someone made a mistake, and we had to do it all again.

PASCHA: Now this is the kind of discussion I do welcome, because it has to do with the essence of the country.

I got out of the car while I was on his good side. The director took me to an old-looking place that I thought was going to be for food. I entered the main room where old dark wooden furniture soaked up any light. Me mam bought some old antique furniture like this once, but me dad found it depressing so he stripped it and painted it in white gloss. Me mam went mad. He did that sort of thing a lot. He washed an old ornament with a Brillo pad 'cos he thought it was dusty, and all the paint came off, so he tried painting it himself. It ended up looking like a garden gnome. There's a song by Daniel Merriweather with lyrics that go 'took something perfect and painted it red' – I'm sure Daniel must have met me dad.

Men sat around talking, some naked, some with very little on apart from a towel and a white bell-shaped hat. I sat down on one of the hot leather high-backed chairs. Not the sort of chair to sit on naked 'cos it sticks to your skin. It took me back to when my dad had a Ford Cortina with a dark PVC interior, seats that on sunny days could heat up to temperatures close to that of molten lava. People always talk about the summer of 1976 when it was so hot you could fry eggs on your car bonnet. Well, in my dad's Ford Cortina we could have slowcooked a leg of lamb. Baby seats were not needed back then 'cos the hot plastic kept young kids stuck to their seat. Everyone had car seat covers in the late 1970s, not for comfort but 'cos they were needed to stop drivers getting third-degree burns and oven gloves were used as driving gloves the steering wheel got so hot.

I picked a row of seating where nobody else was sat and pointed at some food from the menu, which I thought was sausage. A plate turned up with thin strips of dark meat. It could've been bits of burnt arse skin scraped off these leather sofas, but it turned out to be horse meat, and going on the amount of meat on the plate I'd say it was the whole horse. It was dried, quite spicy and tasted alright, but I didn't get to eat much as a man threw me a towel and asked me to get undressed. This place wasn't just a restaurant, it was a banya, which is a traditional Russian steam bath. Blokes were wandering about in the huge tiled area wearing the little white felt hats but nowt to cover the bollocks. If you're hot, surely the hat comes off before the pants! It's not a good look. It's like being naked with socks on – it looks bloody stupid. It always seems to be the people you don't want to see naked that are happy to be naked. The man said that the hat was worn to protect the head from the intense heat in the sauna. It was roasting in there. I was asked to lie on a bench where another man then took it upon himself to batter me with a shrub. It was twigs from a birch tree that they use to help blood circulation. As I was being whacked, other men in the sauna sat and cheered and laughed. There was not one bit that was nice about the whole experience. It felt like walking through an automatic car wash.

I've had quite a few different styles of massages around the world, and they're getting madder. In China I had some woman rub my legs wearing gloves that were set on fire. In Thailand I had a woman prisoner bending me about. I saw something on the internet recently where they pile a load of snakes on your back to wriggle about! There's even some procedure that involves smearing bird poo all over your face to take off dead skin. I experienced this once when my pet magpie poo'd on my ear and I didn't have anything to wipe it off with. I thought I'd leave it until I got home, but I ended up forgetting it was there. A few hours later, it was pointed out to me, so I cleaned it off to find it had burnt away my ear. But what's the world come to when a relaxing day is having snakes all over your back and your face smeared in birdshit? I remember when a posh face wash was using Imperial Leather, an expensive bar of soap that we only got out when we had visitors.

After I'd been battered by the bush I was told to pull a chain on a bucket that then tilted and poured a gallon of freezing water over me to finish off the relaxing process: hot to cold, back to hot and then freezing, a bit like Pascha's personality.

Later, we made our way via Red Square to where I would be boarding the Trans-Siberian Railway. It was the first time I'd seen tourists while being in the country. They were all busy getting photos of themselves stood by St Basil's Cathedral. When I think of Russia this is the building I picture. It's not your normal design for a cathedral. It looks like something a Lottery winner or a footballer might build. The amount of different colours on it, you'd think the whole thing had been done using Dulux sample pots. The story goes that Ivan the Terrible was so impressed with the building, once completed, he gouged out the eyes of the architects so they wouldn't build another one like it. Seems a bit harsh, but then his name says it all.

The biggest queue in Red Square seemed to be of people who wanted to see the dead body of political leader Lenin. He died in 1924 and was embalmed and then put in a glass box. I think I quite like the idea of this. People will never forget him while he's there to be seen. Statues kind of do this job, but you can't beat having the actual person, can you? I wonder if we'll get to a point where we do it with loved ones. I can imagine having Suzanne waxed and stuffed in the front room. I'd just have her sat reading a book. That seems like the most normal thing to have her doing. If someone came round to read the meter or decorate they wouldn't say anything to her 'cos people don't interrupt people who are reading. They wouldn't know she was stuffed. I'd just change the book now and again, so they didn't think she was a slow reader. I think it would be nicer having her there like that than not at all.

We got to the station early, which was just as well, as it wasn't easy working out which train I needed to be on. No one spoke English, and the signs didn't help in the slightest. Russia has the angriest-looking font in the world. When email first came about I used to get told to stop writing everything in capitals as this comes across as though YOU'RE SHOUTING. That's what all the signs in Russia look like. A love note would look like a warning on a bottle of bleach.

After a lot of wandering around trying to make sense of the departure boards, we eventually found our train. A stern-looking woman who had a face like there was a bad smell in the air checked my ticket and gave me a nod. My little cabin wasn't as fancy as I thought it was going to be. I was picturing the Orient Express, where the carriages have bright white tablecloths and silver cutlery. This had worn red velvet seating like the type you see in an Aberdeen Angus Steakhouse in London, and an off-white net curtain. Still, I had my own space, and that was more important than the decor. When on a train at home it's nice to get a table, but it's a gamble, as you never know who you'll be sharing it with. It's like going on *Come Dine with Me*.

I sat and played Patience, and made my way through another packet of Revels. Things were going well until about two hours in when guards came to my door and asked to see my ticket. It only gave me the first-class coach for so many stops, and I should have moved a while back. I said I would move but I needed some time to get my stuff together. They waited to make sure. I followed them as we made our way down through the carriages that got smaller, smellier, smokier and busier. We stopped. The same space I'd had to myself in first class was now shared with five others. It was like one of those mad charity events where they try to squeeze as many people as possible into a phonebox. The guard pointed to a bed. I say bed, but it was more like a shelf. This was third class. I don't even send letters third class.

The people below gestured that I sit with them. The way they were crammed together I presumed they were a family, but they weren't. The man of the group looked tough. He had a black eye and some cuts and bruises on his face. He offered me a beer, which I took. Richard the director told me I should give him something in return, as this is what travellers do when using this train. I offered the bloke some Revels, which he declined. Just as well, as they're not to everybody's taste. I like all the flavours, but some people don't like the chocolate-covered coffee or the chocolate-covered orange ones. In a way, it's the equivalent to Russian roulette in the chocolate world. I got my cards out and tried to teach them the higher or lower game.

I didn't have to sleep in third class in the end, as the guards moved me into second class after it started to kick off between some drunk Polish people and some Russians. I guess they didn't want us to film it. Second class was like first class without the velvet.

I slept like a baby. When I say slept like a baby, I mean I was up all night. The toilets didn't work. They were locked half an hour before getting into a station, but then some stations were half an hour apart, which meant they were never open. They also have a rule that you can't use the loo while at a station, as the toilet had a pedal that empties the loo straight onto the track. I think they should allow you to use the loos while in the station because if human waste was all over the tracks it would stop kids messing about on them. Putting up signs saying 'Danger' doesn't stop them, but if there was a chance of getting shit on their trainers I'm pretty sure they wouldn't be as keen to mess about on the lines.

#5 Ride the Rocky Mountaineer train in Canada

This sounds like the nicest train journey of all train journeys – passing impressive views whilst travelling in proper comfort – but I don't think it would be as memorable as the Trans-Siberian because that was pretty grim, and bad memories seem to hang around in my head for longer and are a lot clearer than the happy ones. Maybe it's because when I'm comfortable in a situation my mind thinks about other things, whereas if I'm not enjoying something I can't think about anything else. So, if you want an unforgettable holiday, don't bother with the Caribbean, go to Rhyl for a fortnight.

The next morning Ricky called to tell me that it was fifty years since Yuri Gagarin became the first man in space. To celebrate he suggested I visit Star City, which is home to the Yuri Gagarin Cosmonaut Training Centre. A teacher at my school said he waved to Yuri Gagarin when he visited Manchester in 1961 after his trip into space. He said Gagarin drove through Moss Side, which some would say is more dangerous than travelling to outer space, and hundreds of people came out in the rain to show their appreciation. He said he was a true hero who had risked everything to make history for his country. I remember not being that impressed at the time, as I knew monkeys had been launched into space before him. He was basically taking over a monkey's job. How hard can it have been? Plus, there was so much more that needed inventing back then. What was the rush to get to space? You know, we landed on the moon before someone thought about putting wheels on suitcases!

The teacher then asked us to write a story about doing a heroic act and the speech you would make afterwards. I made up a story in which I had one of my tonsils out to give to my brother. I wrote that I couldn't do a speech about how I felt about my heroicness afterwards as my throat hurt. The teacher wrote 'Lazy' in red pen.

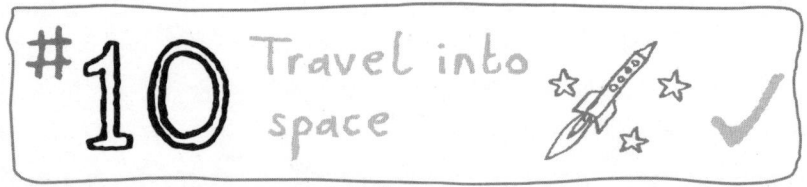

#10 Travel into space

I wasn't really interested in space when I was younger. It was something that was a big deal before my time. I liken it to how Benidorm was a popular place to go in the 1970s, then Tenerife in the 1980s. Space was all the rage in the 1960s. Since Armstrong landed on the moon it seems everyone has lost interest after seeing there wasn't much there.

I got to Star City. There was a statue of Gagarin not far away from the apartment he used to live in. The head of the statue was good and looked like him, but the trousers were not so good. Maybe this is why most statues are of naked bodies. Sculptors find it easier carving out a knob and bollocks than getting the creases in trousers to look real.

#83 See Mount Rushmore, USA

I'm pretty impressed by the heads that have been carved into Mount Rushmore. More of this should be done. There's loads of mountains all over the world and we don't do much with them. Rather than taking a chunk of rock down from a mountain and making a sculpture and then sticking it in a town centre where it just gets in the way, leave the rock where it belongs and sculpt it there.

Also, people get lost when they're out climbing in mountains in Scotland. What could make life easier for rescue people than being able to pin-point where you are by saying whose face you're climbing up? Also, maybe kids would get off their arse more and go walking if they could go and see the faces of One Direction cut into Ben Nevis.

I was greeted by a man called Andre kitted out in cosmonaut overalls. He was going to show me around the place. First stop was at the centrifuge. This is a bit of kit they use to give cosmonauts the feeling of G-force, which they experience on taking off in a rocket. The centrifuge was thirty years old and looked it. Andre took me down below into the big hall, so I could see the scale of the thing. It's the biggest centrifuge in the world. A huge sixty-foot arm sat on a massive motor with a type of cockpit on the end where the cosmonaut would sit as it spun. Imagine a giant swing-ball, with a seat in the ball.

We went back upstairs to the control room where loads of staff were standing around. Andre said I could have a go in the centrifuge. I wasn't keen on the idea, but he reassured me it would be fine. I got into a large dentist-type chair where a few men in jumpsuits buckled me up as if I was getting on the waltzers at a fair. I kept asking who was in charge, as I wanted to get across that I wasn't an adrenaline junkie and don't even like rollercoasters, so don't make it go too fast, but it seemed like no one was listening to me as they were all concentrating on their job. My heart was pounding. This must've been how Yuri felt before his space trip, with the extra pressure of knowing he couldn't back out due to the whole world watching. I'm a good driver and can reverse park quite easily, but once I know there's a car waiting for me to park before he can pass I can't do it. Having an audience changes things.

They wheeled me in the chair and slid me into the cockpit like a chicken being slid into an oven. I was now horizontal.

KARL: I can't wait to get out. Honestly, I'll be so happy. You'll see the biggest smile you've ever seen when I get out of this. I'm not happy.

ANDRE: *(laughs)* Don't worry.

KARL: What's the reason for having to be in this position? 'Cos this isn't even comfy.

TRANSLATOR: Because this is the position of the cosmonaut during take-off. This way, the G-force influences you in the best way. You will not black out because the blood will be spread all over your body.

> DOCTOR: Calm down, Karl. It will be less than 1G.
>
> KARL: It doesn't mean anything to me, that. I didn't pass science. I got an E in history, that's all I got.
>
> DOCTOR: It will be even less than when your girlfriend is on you.
>
> KARL: You haven't seen her!
>
> *(Doctor laughs)*

It looked even older on the inside. Light blue and grey metal everywhere with a few worn switches and a bog standard office fan bolted to the ceiling to keep the place cool. They pulled at my belts a few more times to make sure they were safe and then locked the door. I had headphones on and could hear everyone doing their last-minute checks. I felt really helpless sat there. Is this how it is for spacemen? I didn't even get to hit a start button. It started to move. I tensed up. The woman in the control room asked me to calm down and breathe normally. Is there anything more annoying than someone asking you to calm down? It was an odd sensation, as there wasn't really any sound or feeling of movement, but I could feel pressure pushing me down as it spun. The ride didn't last very long, but I guess that's 'cos it must be an expensive thing to run. Once that was over, I was off to a briefing on details of a zero gravity flight that would be taking place the next day at 7 a.m. This is a flight where you experience floating around like you would in space. The instructor explained that the plane doesn't actually go into space but instead gets to a height that allows them to basically plummet down to earth, giving the impression of floating when in fact you're falling.

He said we must eat breakfast but to avoid coffee from now until after the flight and that if we felt sick it is best to be sick in the bags that would be provided. He went on to say that there would be parachutes on board for everyone in case they were required.

A video then played, showing a group of cosmonauts floating around. Then it started getting silly. They showed lit matches floating around and men spraying cream from cans and eating it. No wonder they get sick.

Then there was David Coulthard, the Formula 1 driver, floating about with his car onboard, which was also floating. What was going on?! Was all this pissing about really part of the space programme? I've always doubted the seriousness of it all after I heard about an astronaut who hit a golfball 2,400 feet when he was on the moon. No wonder they always put a flag up when they land, they're playing bloody pitch 'n' putt up there!

#40 See a space shuttle Launch

When I was on holiday years ago in Florida we paid to go on a NASA tour which involved us going to a spectator platform. We could just about see the shuttle in the distance. It didn't take off though, it was going to be another two weeks before it got off the ground. 'What's the point in us being here then?' I asked. It's like going to the Thames a few days before New Year's Eve to see where the fireworks will be going off.

I stayed the night in one of the blocks of flats that were built for the cosmonauts to live in before and after their trips into space to work on the space station. They were nothing fancy, similar to the sort of room you get in a Travelodge. I was sat in the communal kitchen eating some biscuits when I met Sergei. He had just got back from being in space. He had been away for a few months and was glad to be back. I asked him what it was like to see earth from up there, but he said they were all too busy to be looking out of windows. To him it was just a job. I asked him what the worst thing about his work was, and he said the taste of bread. He said bread in space doesn't taste as nice as it does on earth. Not exactly the speech I was expecting. It doesn't have quite as much clout as Neil Armstrong's, but I guess everyone's different.

Sergei noticed my biscuits, so he offered me some of his space food. I was surprised to see that half of it was in tin cans – and not the modern sort where you get a ring pull, which means before lift-off it must have been someone's job to check they had a tin opener. The tinned food didn't look very appetising. They were very plain cans that reminded me of when I worked in Cordon Bleu supermarket and we used to sell cans of things cheap that didn't have any labels. It was a bit of a gamble at ten pence per can. It could have been beans, soup, stewed meat or dog food.

He went off to his room and came back with a cosmonaut nappy for me as a souvenir. His English wasn't great, but I think he said it's what they wear during the trip to the space station. I took it, as I thought it might come in handy on the train seeing as the toilets are constantly locked.

The next day I didn't feel too good. I was really tired and had a sore throat. I had to have my health check before getting on board the zero gravity flight. The doctor asked if

I had any problems. I told her I got headaches and have had kidney stones, a bad back, sinus problems, a bit of eczema and have quite flat feet. After checking my throat and ears she said I was not well and that my glands were swollen, and that it wouldn't be good to go flying as I could damage my hearing. Now, if I'm being honest, I wasn't that fussed. I was glad to get out of doing the zero gravity flight. Experiencing weightlessness seems like the ultimate lazy thing to wish for. There are times when I wish it was possible, like when I have a ceiling to paint, but other than that I didn't see the point. The director went white when he heard I couldn't go. He looked more ill than I felt. He explained that it had cost a fortune to get on this flight. What could I do? I wasn't willing to do my ears in.

I called Ricky to let him know.

KARL: I can't do it. I'm gutted.

RICKY: Why not?

KARL: My health isn't good enough.

RICKY: What do you mean?

KARL: Well, I had a medical. They have to give you a medical before you get on it. I saw the doctor and she said your neck's all swollen, your nose is glowing and your ears are wet or something.

RICKY: You sound like a fucking Labrador! What do you mean?

KARL: Well, I'd love to do it but I can't. She said it's not worth it, I could cause myself more damage if I go and get in. I said I'm gutted, but it's too dangerous. But I can just chuck something else in there. I know we've paid for it, it's cost a lot of money. I'll just give them something else to go in, and they can film that floating about.

RICKY: What do you mean give them something else? Who wants to see a toaster floating around? The viewers want to see Karl Pilkington floating around.

KARL: But they've booked it now, haven't they, so they might as well do it, because it's paid for.

RICKY: (sighs) Right.

I saw another doctor to get a second opinion, and they said I had tonsillitis and gave me some antibiotics. The prescription featured the same angry font I'd seen a lot during my trip. It looked like a box of rat poison.

The director and film crew went on board. I gave one of the cosmonauts a family pack of Revels to throw about in zero gravity, as I was sick of them. I went on to see what it looked like. It was basically a jumbo jet with no windows, all the seats taken out and mattresses tied to the floor. Three men were strapped to a control area. I guessed they were there to signal what to do, 'cos I'm pretty sure they weren't there to serve nuts and duty free during the flight.

The film crew looked worried sick. I was happy not to be going on it. I went and sat at a table next to the runway for about an hour before they all returned with small bags of sick. Most of them said it was good but they wouldn't want to do it again.

#1 Fly a fighter jet

You just shouldn't be allowed to do this unless you're prepared to join the RAF and go and fight in a war. It should be a perk of the job for the professionals, not something that anybody can arse around with. I blame Jeremy Clarkson.

Back on the train I was upgraded to second class.

Ricky called to let me know he'd arranged some company for me. He said I was going to meet Magnet Man. (As his name suggests, he is a man who is magnetic.) I enjoy weird stuff like this, it's what makes the world interesting. I made my way to his carriage. Mikhail was a dead ringer for Bez out of the Happy Mondays. He was bare-chested and he didn't speak English, so there was no small talk. He went straight into sticking cutlery to his chest. It's a strange one, 'cos as much as it is a type of superpower it's not one that you think might be a useful one. I remember seeing a bloke on the TV who had a good superpower. He could mess about with live wires without it killing him, but like Mikhail he didn't do much with it, just used his power to cook sausages in his hands.

I was trying to think of positive uses for a magnet man but I struggled. Finding a needle in a haystack, maybe. I think I came up with more reasons why it was more of a weakness than an advantage. If he lay on a metal-springed mattress would he have been able to get out of bed?

DESERT ISLAND

DESERT ISLAND

I LOOK LIKE BLOODY HUMPTY DUMPTY!

I FELT LIKE A BIT OF A WEED – BUT THIS FELLA TAKES THAT EXPRESSION TO ANOTHER LEVEL.

I FLEW LIKE A BIRD . . . IF IT WAS A KIWI BIRD, THAT IS.

DESERT ISLAND

DESERT ISLAND

> Three middle-aged blokes arse-boarding on the side of a volcano: it was like a scene from Last of the Summer Wine.

I'VE SEEN ROOMIER COFFINS.

THEY DON'T EVEN KNOW EACH OTHER . . . THE SEAT'S BEEN DOUBLE BOOKED.

THE HAPPIEST FACE I SAW IN MY WHOLE TIME IN RUSSIA.

#21 Get into the Guinness Book of World Records

I'm already in there for the podcasts. The most downloaded podcast in the world in 2007. But I can't say I've got much to show for it (Ricky kept the certificate).

I was in Macedonia recently – a place that takes getting into the record books quite seriously. I think it's 'cos their country is quite new so it's important for the people to be recognised for doing something. I met a man who broke a record for running for 36 hours whilst listening to the same song over and over again. I decided I'd take this challenge on whilst I was there. I didn't bother with the running part but I listened to the Mr Men theme tune over and over again. I had it in my headphones from 10.15 a.m. until gone 11 p.m. at night. Ricky called my phone about five hours in which stopped the music for a few minutes so the director said it didn't count, but I carried on. I listened to the theme tune over 1,500 times. It won't get in a book but I know I did it and that's all that counts really.

As I was thinking these things over, he continued to stick forks, knives and now plates to his body. He was more of a human pot rack. I thought it would be useful for being hands-free when using a mobile phone, but his ears didn't seem to have magnetic power. I asked if he had been a magnet baby, and he showed me photos of his kids who were also magnet kids. The photo showed them lined up with bits of metal and plates stuck to them. They didn't look particularly happy, but that was no surprise. They can't be a close family because magnets repel each other.

He then passed some of his magnet powers onto me by rubbing the various eating utensils on himself and then placing them on me. They did stick for quite some time, which makes me think it must be down to him being sweaty. It's a superpower that could be beaten by talcum powder. Talc is like his kryptonite. After half an hour we had to stop, not 'cos using his powers wears him out, but because it was close to lunchtime and the train's kitchen wanted its cutlery back.

#39 Try a jet pack X

Everyone at some point has thought about which superpower they would like to have. Teleporting is a good one, but Suzanne has enough holidays as it is. If we could do this I'd never get anything done, as she'd have us going all over the shop. Shapeshifting sounds good, but I don't know how often I'd choose to be me. Flying must be overrated, as pigeons have the ability to do it, but most of them choose to walk. I'd be happy to have the flying power of a chicken, so that if I fell off a roof I'd have the ability to flap down to the ground safely. I did have one idea of a superhero I'd like to be. I'd be Bullshit Man. There's a lot of bullshit being spouted all the time. When builders or mechanics tried to rip people off I'd like to have superhearing that is sensitive to bullshit talk. I'd fly in and shout 'Bullshit!', and they'd have to take back what they'd said and not rip people off. There wouldn't be any violence. I'd just state the fact that what they had just said was bullshit and they would have to change their ways for their business to survive. Maybe I'd let them bullshit once or twice and send a letter of warning first, but after that I'd fly in. I wouldn't bother with a superhero costume, as that is bullshit. There's no need. Superman used up valuable time finding a phonebox to change in instead of getting on with the job in hand.

Stephen left a message about me going to visit a traditional healer after hearing that I wasn't too well. I can't imagine Russians being into traditional healing, as they seem like a no-nonsense country (I doubt Bullshit Man would be needed in this part of the world very often), but I was happy to get off the train, as I was suffering with motion sickness. I met with another man named Andre, same name as the fella at Star City.

#28 Meet someone with your own name

I think it has to be surname as well as first name for this to count, but I don't know why this is on the Bucket List. It'll just end up being a confusing day. And I wouldn't want to speak to the bloke anyway, as it would be easy for him to steal my identity once he got a few more details off me.

Andre and his friends were in the middle of nowhere digging holes in a forest. I was handed a shovel and asked to dig. I kind of guessed by the size of the hole that it was being dug for me to get into, but what I didn't realise was that my whole body would get covered, including the head.

KARL: So your head's under? I didn't realise that. I thought you meant just lie in it with your head out. How do you breathe?

TRANSLATOR: You use a pipe.

KARL: A pipe?

TRANSLATOR: Yeah.

KARL: How do you know if I'm panicking then if I'm under there going mmm mmm mmm? You can't hear me!

TRANSLATOR: There are some safety rules and some safety precautions. We've been doing this a long time, and everything went fine every time. Just remember that you're able to stop it at any moment you wish. There is a specific set of signals underground that we can hear.

KARL: How are you picking up signals? This is mental! Honestly, this is daft, this!

(Andre blows into pipe three times)

TRANSLATOR: You see?

KARL: What?

TRANSLATOR: Three beeps, we immediately take the person out of the ground. Like this. *(three beeps)* It's really easy to do. If you feel you want to stay a bit longer there – this happens a lot – use the second signal. Two beeps.

KARL: Two beeps to leave me alone? Wouldn't it be better to do two beeps to get out 'cos that's quicker? Three beeps takes longer to do.

TRANSLATOR: We can do whatever you want.

KARL: We need a system here!

Apparently, this is an ancient form of self-enlightenment that was used by shamans. I quite enjoyed the digging of the hole – there was something therapeutic about that part, that's why people do gardening – but I've never seen Alan Titchmarsh get in a hole after planting his petunias.

The translator tried to explain why I should get in the hole: 'In extreme situations the thing that kills people is panic. And it's really difficult to create a state where the state of fear is around you every single moment. In some everyday situations, for example, parachute jumping, it lasts only a few minutes, so it's not that hard. Here you feel uncomfortable a bit longer, so it gives you more of a chance to learn to communicate with it, with your own fears. We just need to learn to communicate with the fear.'

I tried calling Stephen to see if he was aware of what I was being asked to do, but it went to voicemail. I called Ricky. No answer there either.

I thought I'd give it a go. I don't know why. Maybe it was because I felt guilty about not doing the zero gravity flight, but I like a bit of peace and quiet, so how bad could it be? Andre told me that to stop the panic it's best to count slowly to calm myself. This keeps the brain busy and stops it from worrying. This doesn't make sense to me. If counting helps to calm you down why was I worried all the way through my maths tests at school? In the end I decided to strap me iPhone to me head and listen to 'Stranger on the Shore' by Acker Bilk on repeat. It's a calming bit of music I never get sick of. They laid a sheet of plastic in the hole, and I lay on it and made a little mound of earth for a pillow to rest my head on. They put the sheet over me like I was a chicken wrap, stuck a bit of garden hosepipe in my mouth that was long enough to stick out of the ground, and then they started throwing earth over my legs. They were over my face in no time. Here I was getting buried, yet Lenin who's dead is above ground. The music in my headphones seemed a lot louder now that I was underground, but I was unable to move to turn it down. I also felt really cold. I was fine with it, but I had a little bit of a panic when it came to swallowing my saliva, as I'm always waking up in the night choking if I lie on my back. I've wrecked pillows with the amount of saliva that escapes from me. We have to replace our pillows a lot, as they get stained with light brown saliva patches. They end up looking like I've made a pillow out of a giraffe. I was busy focusing and swallowing when the music went off and the phone started ringing. I let it go to voicemail. I moved my legs slightly, and the earth quickly filled any gaps that were there before, so I felt more pressure from the ground above. I gave the three beeps signal. They dug me out. I'd done about fifteen minutes. They'd been busy digging another hole while I was under there, and a woman had turned up for a session. I asked why she was doing it. She said she suffered from claustrophobia and thought this would help her beat it.

I enjoyed being under there. It was the most relaxing thing I'd done since being in Russia. I listened to the message I got when I was underground. It was Ricky.

RICKY: Alright, boy. Got your message. Yeah, that sounds horrible. I wouldn't do it. But, the thing is, if they bury you and just leave the head out that's more dangerous because someone would definitely use you as a football and give it a boot. Don't panic. That'll make it worse. If you don't like it and you get down there and it's horrible just say, 'I'm a celebrity, get me out of here.' That's how it works. That's what Kerry Katona did, and she was Mother of the Year.

We got back on the train. It wasn't as long as it had been at the beginning of the journey. They had detached a few carriages, as there didn't seem to be as many people travelling the last leg.

Stephen called.

STEPHEN: It sounds like you have been chilling, relaxing and sitting on your arse which is great. It's important for you to have a little Karl time. But we're worried about your health, your cardiovascular system, so we've managed to arrange a little sporty excursion for you. It's got a sort of, ya know, exercisey Olympic vibe. I don't want to give too much away, so, you've got to do a quick tour of Mongolia, and then you're all set.

I don't know why I couldn't do some Olympian activity in Russia. That country is full of Olympians. I've never heard of a Mongolian Olympian.

I met two Mongolians called Otgonbayar and Balag who picked me up and took me by horseback to their homes. They lived in nowhere land and had three gers, a type of big round tent. They were really roomy. As far as I could work out one was a lounge, one was to sleep in and the third was for guests. They welcomed me in and I met the rest of the family. There were quite a few kids knocking about, who I guessed belonged to them, as no one else lived round these parts. But then, I think if I lived in a place like this I'd probably have a few kids. I haven't bothered having them 'cos it seems like a lot of stress having them in Britain. I know people at home who have them, and they have to totally change their life to run around after them. They get treated like gods.

#72 Continue your gene pool

While I'm living where I live there's pandas that are more likely to bring a kid in the world than me doing it. If there was a kind of 'try before you buy' so I knew what I was gonna end up with it wouldn't be bad but there's no guarantee it wouldn't be a right lunatic and then what do you do?

You need a house with enough bedrooms and that costs a fortune, too. You can't let them play out in case someone takes them or they get run over, which means you get dragged into sending them to ballet or violin lessons to keep them busy and away from getting into trouble. You've got to get them into a good school, and there's pressure for them to do well so they can go on to get a good job, but they don't seem to have any of those problems here.

I was given a cup of tea, but you'd never have guessed it was tea. They'd overdone it with the milk, and I can't stand milky tea. Just writing 'milky tea' makes me gag, plus I always worry about drinking milk abroad after having a tiny bit in India that made me almost shit out a lung. I drank a little drop and was hoping to get it to a level that wouldn't seem rude to leave, but the lady of the house kept topping it up. She had also brought out a plate of cheese, so many blocks of cheese I could have built them a conservatory with it.

Otgonbayar passed me a leaflet with photos of wrestlers in it. This was the sport that Stephen was talking about. The village wanted me to represent them at the Nadeem Festival where the prize would be five million tugrik, which is around £2,500. I explained through a translator that I'd done a lot of wrestling around the world and had never won, so it was a pointless exercise, but he said Otgonbayar could no longer enter as he had a head injury from a motorcycle accident and they would be grateful if I accepted the challenge. I agreed to it. The family seemed really happy, but I knew I wasn't going to win.

They brought out more cheese in celebration. It always amazes me how welcoming some of the people are in these foreign countries (Pascha excluded). At home I don't even know my neighbours. Years ago, you got to know them from borrowing a cup of milk or a little bit of sugar, but since shops like Tesco Local are open virtually 24 hours a day it's got rid of that little interaction. Neighbourhood Watch to me is checking my neighbours aren't outside their house before I leave the flat, to avoid getting into long discussions.

#26 Master a musical instrument ✓

After a small amount of training for the wrestling they put the kids to bed and we sat indoors. A friend of the family did a little bit of traditional Mongolian throat singing. I liked it a lot. He produced amazing sounds from his throat that I haven't heard a machine or an instrument produce. He was making notes that sometimes sounded like they were coming from someone/somewhere else. It was a proper skill. After a while I felt the urge to join in. I couldn't get the tones that this man could but I produced some different ones. Otgonbayar and his family looked impressed, and I thought I performed well, as I did it with confidence – a confidence that I knew I wouldn't have at the wrestling the following day. If I lived somewhere like this I'd spend time trying to learn throat singing. At the moment, I'm learning to play the ukulele, but I don't practise enough, as there's always something else that needs sorting at home. There are so many things you can do when you haven't got other things that need sorting. An example of this is the mimic octopus. It's an octopus that's learned to do impressions of other stuff living in the sea. I'm sure it picked up these skills 'cos it's got nowt else to do all day.

I slept well for a good four or five hours before being woken up by a rat-type creature scratching about on my rucksack. I then couldn't get back to sleep. I wasn't sure if it was because I was nervous about the wrestling that faced me or from all the cheese I'd been eating earlier. I still wasn't feeling too good, and my glands were swollen.

I got up when I heard movement outside. Otgonbayar's friend was dealing with the goats. I had a wash in a sink on a nice wooden unit with a mirror placed in the open ground between two of the gers. It's at times like this I realise how mad all this travelling is. I'm miles away from home, far from anywhere, in a spot I'll most likely never travel to again, brushing my teeth. It's an odd feeling.

The director said my wrestling clothes were on my bed ready to change into. I had never seen such a mixed-up outfit. There was a pair of small red shorts with beads sewn on, an odd off-the-shoulder cardigan that mainly covered my arms and lower back, a pair of boots with curled-up toes like something you'd expect a genie to wear, and a hat that looked like it had the neck of a champagne bottle on the top. These weren't clothes designed to fight in. If anything, they were clothes that would start a fight. Lady Gaga would struggle to get a dafter look. I was sure the cardigan belonged to one of the kids in the family and had become mixed up in my pile. I felt really irritable from the discomfort of the clothes. Maybe this was the idea, as they made you feel more up for a fight.

We got to the festival where there were thousands of people. The Mongolian president launched the event, which featured singers and dancers of all ages, and I got my first glimpse of the kind of people I would be wrestling. They wore the same outfit as me, which was a relief, as I honestly thought I'd been set up. These fellas were massive, similar in size to that of a sumo wrestler. To make things worse, I had to wait five to six hours before it was my turn to fight. I had that feeling you get when you're a kid and have arranged to have a fight with someone after school. All day it preys on your mind. I won't go into long wordy detail about what happened 'cos there's nothing to say. I lost, as I predicted. Otgonbayar and his family didn't seem too bothered though.

And then, as if none of it had ever happened, I was back on the Trans-Siberian Express for the final leg of my Bucket List challenge. There were more Chinese passengers now. That made me look at the guidebook for the first time since I'd been here. I saw the distance I had covered and noticed we were going into China. After visiting China to see the Great Wall, and not enjoying it, I didn't like the idea of visiting it again. I spoke to Ricky who said that was the reason he thought it was a good idea to go again – to give it another chance. Now, last time I got back from China, I spoke to a mate who is into the same sort of odd things in life as me, and he mentioned a place that I was gutted I hadn't visited. So I told the director about it. I was worried about it being not very politically correct, but the place existed and ignoring it wouldn't change anything. He began sorting out permission to go and film there. I thought it was in keeping with the aim of the programme: meeting different types of people and seeing how they live. It was Dwarf Village.

It's a proper village whose hundred or so dwarf residents run its fire service and police force. Some of the dwarfs had nothing before this place: no work, no money and nowhere to live. But now, because of Dwarf Village, they do. They perform twice a day singing, doing magic and dancing. The show wasn't due to start for another hour, so I had a walk around the place. I saw behind the scenes where they all hung around in little mushrooms. One dwarf was doing some art by carving into wood. Dwarf builders were busy building an extra tall mushroom that would eventually be flats (the number of dwarfs coming here is on the increase). A group of women was sat around chatting while repairing clothes. The mood was good.

I would prefer to be a dwarf than big like Stephen (Merchant). What are the advantages of being tall? Take away any health issues dwarfism may cause (which I don't think there are many of, as I've never seen a dwarf in a doctor's waiting room) and I'd much rather be small than tall. I was the height of a dwarf when I was about six or seven, and I never struggled that much. I would have been a lot happier on the shelf in third class as a dwarf. Other positives are that king-sized Twixes would be massive, clothing would be cheaper and there would be more leg room on planes.

Around 250 to 300 people turned up to watch the show. It lasted around an hour and was hosted by two compères – a man and a woman who were like the Richard and Judy of the dwarf world, a few singers (a Peter Andre and Lily Allen) and loads of dancers. There was a little bit of magic where a dwarf with a Mohican ate nuts and bolts and then coughed them up again, and then the show finished with a big song-and-dance ending with what looked like seventy or so dwarfs on stage as the king of the dwarf empire came out and waved to the spectators.

Richard, the director, was worried about featuring this in the programme. I texted Ricky to get the number for Warwick Davis to run the concept by him. He was in the film *Star Wars* dressed up as some little bear thing. He's played a leprechaun and probably a gnome in something. To me there's no difference in what he does to what they're doing here.

KARL: Hey, Warwick. It's Karl, Ricky's mate.

WARWICK: Yeah? You alright? What you up to?

KARL: I'm doing this travel thing, and, uh, I'm in China. I'm looking at a dwarf village and I was just saying you're the only dwarf I know at home, and I wanted to run the whole concept by ya, 'cos I know that people at home might get a bit funny about it, saying 'Oh, you shouldn't be having a little dwarf village' and all that. But, it's really good, the people are dead happy, uh, nice little show they put on, and I just thought it would cover me if I spoke to you and said, 'I'm at a dwarf village', and you went, 'Yeah, I've heard of that. It's nice. Good on ya.'

WARWICK: Yeah, I have heard of it. Definitely. But I don't think it's nice.

KARL: Why not?

WARWICK: Well, it's like going back to the days of the freak show, really. I mean they're all in there together, and you're all going in there to gawp at them, basically.

KARL: Uh, well, yeah, I did, and, you know, there are blokes in little funny outfits and all that, and you do sort of smile, but they're smiling. I think it's alright, innit?

WARWICK: I think it's terrible, Karl. I can't believe it. How would you like it if I and everyone else watching the programme popped round to your house and watched you do the washing up?

KARL: No, they're alright, honestly. You're as bad as everyone else, going 'They're not happy'. If you weren't in *Star Wars* and all the pantos you did, what would you be doing?

WARWICK: Well, I dunno, but I'm complicit. I actually want to do what I do. These people in the dwarf village in China – they might have no other choice, and that's what worries me, 'cos there's exploitation going on there. You don't know who's behind the scenes running it all. Did you meet them?

KARL: Yeah, there's a king.

WARWICK: And is he little?

KARL: Course he is.

WARWICK: But that might be a show king.

KARL: No, no, it was the head man. He was at the top. He had a little cloak and a crown on, shades, and you could tell he was in charge.

WARWICK: But he's just a performer, and it could be an act. These people, they might not want to be there. Seriously, I think it's a bad thing. You're just encouraging more of this sort of thing, by showing it and, basically, enjoying it.

KARL: So, if all your work dried up – they're not making a new *Star Wars*, you can't dress up as a little monkey, you've got no money coming in – you wouldn't think about coming here then?

WARWICK: Definitely not, that would be the last thing I'd do. I'd just get a proper job.

KARL: But you wouldn't get a proper job. I've never seen a dwarf with a normal job. When I've had plumbers out time and time again for my knackered boiler, a dwarf has never turned up.

WARWICK: But that's not to say there aren't any dwarf plumbers.

KARL: I haven't seen any. I'm 38, Warwick, and I've never seen a dwarf plumber.

WARWICK: But dwarfs do have regular jobs. There will be a dwarf plumber out there somewhere, but what's happening out in China is segregation. It's exploitation, seriously.

KARL: You haven't been. See, this is what annoys me about people. I'm in the thick of it here. I'm stood by their houses, and they're all happy. There's a woman I met who's a little dwarf, she's only been here four months, and she's already got her own mushroom to live in. Now you tell me that's wrong.

WARWICK: You actually asked her, did you? Are you happy living in this mushroom? And she said, Karl, I'm having a wonderful life . . .

KARL: She looked happy.

WARWICK: That's it, that's the key word. She 'looked happy'. It's a performance. They might be miserable once you've closed that mushroom door. You know, she's in there and she might be miserable.

KARL: I just wanted your backing. I thought you'd be up for it.

WARWICK: I'm a bit disappointed in you, to be honest.

I know I was only there a few hours, but the only dwarf I saw who didn't look happy was the one who did the magic. But I think that was just his onstage persona, which considering there were over one hundred of them wasn't bad going. When you think of Snow White there was a grumpy one, and there was only seven of them. I'd go so far as to say, compared to Pascha, the first man I met when I got to Russia, this lot were all ecstatic.

CHAPTER THREE

#20 Swim with dolphins ✓

STEPHEN: When I think Bucket List I think swimming with dolphins.

KARL: Isn't it more about where they are?

RICKY: Well, if you choose this, it is a beautiful place. It's not in the Thames.

KARL: I think that's all it is. It's about being in a nice place. The dolphins are neither here nor there.

RICKY: Well, it is because they're fascinating creatures. They're highly intelligent.

KARL: Everyone says they're intelligent . . . They aren't.

STEPHEN: You don't believe that?

KARL: It just annoys me when everyone else says Karl's a div, and yet they think dolphins are so intelligent. What have they done?

STEPHEN: Why are you not convinced by their intelligence?

KARL: It's not that I'm not convinced, it's just it annoys me that everyone says that about dolphins, saying they can cure people and all that.

RICKY: Who says that?

STEPHEN: You think dolphins are trainee doctors?

RICKY: Yeah, they can't even scrub their flippers.

KARL: They just say anyone who's ill, stick 'em in a bunch of dolphins and it'll make 'em better.

RICKY: No, it doesn't. It's not to do with making them better, it's like a wish list. It's like a little dream for people who are ill.

STEPHEN: Are you worried that they're gonna show up your level of intelligence if you hang out with them?

KARL: No, they're nowhere near my intelligence. I've read about them, they've got the intelligence of a three-year-old, so that's what I'm saying – they're not even that bright.

STEPHEN: What if we told you, you were going to Australia to swim with dolphins?

RICKY: Wow, what a lucky man he is. Yeah, look at him smiling at the thought of that.

KARL: I'm just worried about getting a little snidey one.

RICKY: Definitely won't, mate.

KARL: It's the sea in Australia that worries me.

RICKY: Why?

KARL: Just . . . It's where all the weird stuff hangs around. There's a lot of mental stuff in that sea and you can't see it. It's all hiding away under rocks.

RICKY: You'll be with trained people, telling you where to get in and what to do.

KARL: Alright then. Yeah, dolphins.

The plane wasn't direct to Australia. It stopped at Thailand. Not sure why, planes can hold enough fuel to fly direct these days. Maybe the pilot wanted a fag break. Ricky and Stephen said that seeing as it stops there, you may as well see the place. I was fine with the idea. I like Thai food, or, as I call it, 'posh Chinese'.

Suzanne told me not to be going to any rude shows. She said the women do things with ping-pong balls. They should introduce that as a way of 'Releasing the Balls' on the National Lottery, it would make it a lot more bloody interesting. I don't know why the Lottery is televised. Four people it takes, as well. A presenter, an adjudicator, a bloke who hits the start button and a fella who does the voiceover telling us 'The lotto machine is named Lancelot and has made 52 appearances'. Who wants to know that! Four people to select six numbers, yet cutbacks on staff at the council mean I can only get me bins emptied once a week.

I arrived in Bangkok on 13 April, the day of Songkran.

Imagine arriving in London on New Year's Eve around 11.30 p.m. and your hotel is in Trafalgar Square. That's what I was faced with. The festival of Songkran involves the locals chucking water over everything to celebrate the start of the rainy season. They believe the water will wash away any bad luck from the previous year and bless you with good luck for the next. Jesus, if that's what makes them happy they should move to Manchester and enjoy the rain. Nothing and no one is safe from the water while this festival is on. Not a place to be if you're a Gremlin. Policemen get splashed, shop fronts, cafés, every car gets a bucket of water thrown at it, and people on mopeds don't escape from it. They get a face full of water from people armed with water pistols, hosepipes and buckets.

I found it odd that the country had only just dried out from the 2004 tsunami yet here they are drenching everything.

Ricky had a go at me years ago when I said people from this part of the world seem to age quicker than Western people, but now I realise they just look old and wrinkly 'cos they're constantly wet from this festival. The traffic was gridlocked, so Krish the director said we should get out and walk. I took my suitcase with me on the off chance that this would make the locals realise I was not there to celebrate Songkran and that I was just trying to find my hotel, but it didn't work. I got wet through.

As well as getting wet someone rubbed some kind of clay in my face. Not sure if that was part of the celebrations or just a local lunatic potter. Songkran can last for three to four days. What is the point in me turning off the tap when brushing me teeth to help the environment when this lot are wasting gallons of water over three days. I tell ya, if they ever install water meters in people's homes here in Thailand, Songkran will be over.

#24 Participate in La Tomantina Festival in Spain

I saw this being promoted on the telly during one of the flights I was recently on. Some presenter was in a town in Spain being pelted with tomatoes as she harped on about how much fun she was having. I'd like to see if she would be as cheery if I bumped into her at her Tesco Local and chucked a tomato at her head from the veg aisle.

The video showed a truck turning up and dumping off thousands of tomatoes, and locals and tourists throwing them at each other. I'd hate to live in this town 'cos it must make a right mess. I can't be doing with unnecessary mess. It's like confetti at weddings. I don't understand how confetti isn't classed as littering. The other thing is it's a waste of tomatoes. If they have to do it they could at least use one of the less useful fruits, like kumquats.

I got to the hotel and had a shower.

I got a call from Stephen telling me that I was going to get some training in one of Thailand's national sports, Thai boxing. After doing series one of *An Idiot Abroad* these little surprises don't shock me as much. I've come to accept these mad little diversions but I'm still always on edge. It's like waiting for a jack-in-the-box to pop out, you know it's gonna happen, but you're not sure when. I used to have the same problem when I visited Ricky in his old flat. He used to jump out of the bin cupboard as I walked down the corridor on his floor, but I used the jack-in-the-box example, as I'm guessing more people could relate to that, as most of you won't have mates who jump out of bin cupboards.

#70 Run with the bulls in Pamplona

What is it with Spain? If they're not throwing tomatoes at each other they're running down alleyways avoiding rampaging bulls! It's like they're living in a computer game. I suppose this is what happens when you live in a place that has good weather most of the year round – people come up with daft outside events. We only have a bit of sun each year and a group of people in Gloucestershire came up with the idea of rolling cheese down a hill.

#53 Be part of a flash mob

This is when a group of people take over a public place for a short space of time and dance, sing or have a pillow fight. My problem would be getting to the right place. I'm always arranging to meet Suzanne somewhere and then getting it wrong. The amount of supermarkets I've walked around in trying to find her, to then realise I'm in the wrong one.

I don't need this sort of thing in my life. I don't really like taking part in group activities. Suzanne always reminds me of the time she took me to a party when we first met and she got involved in doing the conga. Everyone at the party joined in and went round the pub and into the car park before coming back into the pub. When she came back in there I was doing the conga but on my own by the bar.

#45 Learn a martial art

I did a little bit of boxing when I was younger after seeing the film *Rocky* starring Sly Stallone. Films did this to me. I tried joining a dance club after seeing *Flashdance* on VHS, but I didn't get that far with it, as when I got to the dance studio, it was shut and was being used as a warehouse to house toilet rolls. A storyline *Fame* never went for. My boxing training was at the youth club and it wasn't very professional. It was once a week and it was run by a big fella who owned the Chinese chippy. I think his main reason for doing it was to get tough young kids as his mates, so he didn't have to pay protection money to some local gangsters to look after his chippy. He was hardly like the trainer Rocky had. Instead of thumping frozen meat, he battered fish.

I arrived at the Thai boxing venue and met my trainer. His name was Ming. He seemed a little bit annoyed that we were late. I told him it was 'cos of Songkran. He wasn't wet. I doubt anyone would be chucking buckets of water at this fella. He was an ex-champion. Ming didn't speak much English, so there was very little talk, but lots of training. An hour of press-ups, star jumps, kneeing a punch bag and sit-ups while his pet dog jumped all over me, then into the ring to spar with him. He gave me a head guard. I tried to explain I wouldn't need a head guard if he just didn't hit my head. He didn't understand. I had a sweat on and felt dizzy. I don't really do any fitness stuff, but if I did I think I would do something like this. Learning self-defence might at least come in useful if you got into any bother. Suzanne tried to get me to do Pilates where they teach you how to stretch, bend and balance, but apart from when I'm tying my shoelaces I don't know when those skills would come in handy.

I think, because we have got lazy as time has gone on, we've introduced exercises for lazy people. I'll never forget being on Carnaby Street in London a while back and a woman asking me if I wanted to join to do breathing exercises! Who is so lazy that they can't be bothered to breathe? She told me it wasn't like that and that she would teach me to breathe properly. I told her I was 37 and I thought I had the hang of it.

Later I got a text from Stephen:

> STEPHEN: Alright, Karl. Hope you enjoyed the Thai boxing training. We've organised a little fight for you this evening, so you can put your new skills into practice. Good luck with that. PS: It's blindfolded Thai boxing.

I didn't understand why this would exist. The whole thing with Thai boxing is using all of the body to fight. Fists, feet and knees, so why not use the eyes? It's ridiculous. Blind people don't get into many fights for a reason. I remember being in an aquarium watching two seahorses have a fight, and it was rubbish. Certain things aren't made to fight. The great boxer Muhammad Ali had a saying, 'Float like a butterfly, sting like a bee'. He didn't add 'Eyes of a mole' on the end.

It didn't help that we arrived early, as it meant we had time to see a few fights first. I wish they'd blindfolded me before I got to see how it worked, as the contestants really go for it. There were all ages – eight-year-old lads, nine-year-old girls and fully grown men. I was called up. Blindfolded. The bell rang. I swung my arms around and kicked out. I found after a while being blindfolded actually gave me more confidence, as I couldn't see the crowd. I did two rounds. After which I was announced the winner, but they only let me win because I was a tourist and was filming it for the TV. You might be thinking, 'Karl, don't put yourself down. Why are you always so negative? Maybe they thought you were the best fighter, so announced you the winner.' Well, if that was the case why didn't they give me one of the aluminium pressure cookers that the other winners got?

The next day we headed over to Bangkok. I was to meet some local lady boys. This was the side of Thailand I was worried about. Suzanne told me they have some proper dodgy stuff going on here and to avoid the seedy areas. I'd heard of lady boys, but didn't really know much about them. I thought of them as transvestites, just blokes who like wearing lipstick and knickers, but aren't kidding anyone. They don't even try and be women. They still go to the local and play darts and drink pints, so on meeting Vivian, a local lady boy, I was blown away. If I hadn't known, I wouldn't have known. He had his hair pinned back, had leggings on with high heels and not that much make-up. Even the way he held himself and the way he walked you'd have put money on it being a woman. I shook his hand. Not just 'cos I knew he was a bloke, but 'cos I'd only just met him. I'd do the same if it was a woman.

 # 46 Get a complete makeover ✓

Viv took me to a nail parlour where we met his mates Jip and Nam. They were also lady boys. I sat and got me nails done on me feet while we chatted. I didn't ask the person doing me toes if they were a man or a woman 'cos it might have offended her/him, but after seeing Viv I now have me doubts about everyone here in Thailand. The work they can have done is like modernday Frankenstein stuff.

KARL: So, is that it for life now? You're not going back?

VIVIAN: To being a man? No, of course not.

KARL: Why have you, eh, why have you had it all done? Everything gone?

VIVIAN: Yes.

KARL: Oh . . . Right. Okay.

VIVIAN: How can you go back?

KARL: Bet there's some way.

VIVIAN: This is the way I love to live.

There's no way I'd follow something through like that. I wouldn't even have a tattoo 'cos I don't like the idea of being stuck with it, so having me knob off is not gonna happen. The person moved from me toes and starting hacking away at the hard skin on my heel with a type of potato peeler.

VIVIAN'S FRIEND: Are you gay?

KARL: No, I've got a girlfriend . . . sixteen years.

(They all laugh)

KARL: It's a good question though. I'm sat here having my nails done. You know, fair play.

VIVIAN'S FRIEND: If you want to be a gay you must try.

KARL: I don't think I'm right for it. Honestly. The lifestyle isn't me.

VIVIAN'S FRIEND: You must try.

KARL: I believe that if I did give it a go I'd get into it. It's like olives. I never used to try olives. Then I had four, and I was, like, what's wrong with olives? But I don't want to give it a go. I'm quite happy.

VIVIAN: You be more happy tonight.

KARL: No.

VIVIAN: Yes.

KARL: Nah . . . no chance.

VIVIAN: No, no, no. I mean to see the show.

KARL: Oh yeah . . . I'll have a look. I'll come and see what you do . . . at the show.

Viv's mate Jip told me he has breasts, but isn't planning on removing the knob and bollocks. Now that I don't understand. Even now I'm back home and have had time to think about it, it still makes no sense. Who is looking for that? That's like moving your bathroom downstairs, when it comes to selling your house – it puts people off.

But Jip just said, 'It's like this because lady boys are not girls. Everybody loves me in this way. So. I am what I am. Love me, love my dong.'

Viv told me she talks to men and goes on many dates. He will tell his dates he has had the operation only if they ask. Made me wonder how many blokes are married to blokes without knowing. Suzanne could be a bloke for all I know. It's odd that this can happen in a world where we are told everything. A label saying 'May contain nuts' has never been more required. At this point Viv showed me a photo on his phone of his boyfriend. He looked a bit like a cross between John Barrowman and Peter Andre. Jip told me he has a straight partner.

KARL: I can't get my head around it, makes no sense. You would get a gay man, wouldn't you?

VIVIAN: Jip, gay man, straight man. Jip can accept everything.

KARL: I don't understand how you can get a straight man if you have still got a knob?

VIVIAN'S FRIEND: Gay not like lady boy. So, I go out with straight man.

KARL: Are you going out with a straight man at the moment?

VIVIAN'S FRIEND: Yeah.

KARL: A straight man?

VIVIAN'S FRIEND: Yeah!

KARL: But he's not! He's not.

We had to agree to disagree. Years ago it wouldn't have been possible. But now people say 'I'm a woman trapped in a man's body' and they can make it happen. Science means someone

one day will wake up and decide they want to be a gerbil and it'll be possible.

Ricky asked me once what would I be if I could be anything in the world, and I decided I would be a sloth. At least if I didn't like it they tend to sleep a lot, so I could just dream about being something else.

#69 Protest at a demonstration

As I'm not a fan of large crowds you would never get me going on any sort of protest march. To be honest I don't know why there have to be so many people involved. Just one person walking about with a placard does the same job without taking over streets and blocking traffic. An example is that fella off Oxford Street who has a 'Golf sale this way' sign. If you've ever been to London you will have seen him. Point proven. There was also the religious scouser who was down from the 'Golf sale' man who shouted on a tannoy, 'Are you a sinner or a winner'. Again, on his own but he got his point across.

If you're doing a group march, participants should get their march sponsored like a sponsored walk so that when no one listens to their point at least it hasn't been a total waste of time 'cos they'll have raised some money for a local hospital or something.

Viv and his mates then took me to the theatre where they perform their nightly show to around eight hundred people. There was a running order of songs on the wall including 'I Am What I Am',

Mariah Carey's 'Hero' and Madonna's 'Papa Don't Preach'. It wasn't long before they had me sat in one of their chairs applying make-up. While Viv piled on the foundation I was still looking for any signs of man-ness but couldn't see any. Maybe if I spent more time with her, there would be certain things she couldn't help. Being practical, for instance. Men are more practical. Suzanne is always asking for a dog, but she doesn't think about the other problems that come with it. The pain in the arse it causes when you want to go away, taking it for walks at all hours . . . Maybe lady boys still have that bit of man-ness to them. That's when Viv's friend whipped her dog out. It wasn't a manly dog either. It was one of them small pug dogs you can stick in a handbag.

They finished transforming me. I don't think I'd be kidding anyone. It did make me wonder what I would do though if Suzanne turned out to be a bloke. After sixteen years together you can't just end it. I came to the conclusion that I'd still let her live with me, but I would get her to do more around the house. No longer would I be the one carrying all the heavy bags from the supermarket on me own. She could also clean the windows.

I asked for a couple of breasts, from KFC I mean, ate them and left.

I had the afternoon free to roam, so I went to the Siriraj Medical Museum. It was not your bog standard museum. It was full of weird things and nicknamed the 'Museum of Death', and to make it weirder, it was on the second floor of a hospital. There were plastic boxes containing arms, a sliced head suspended in a clear plastic box like a novelty ice cube. 'Bollocks!' you say. Yeah, they had them, as well. There was a 75-cm-diameter scrotum resulting from contact with the Mansonia mosquito. When I was in the jungle in Peru last year, no one told me to rub Deet there.

Everywhere you look, box after box of births gone wrong, tiny bodies in formaldehyde, conjoined twins, swollen skulls and cyclopia – all of which were real. I turned a corner, and there was the body of a man called Si Ouey Sae Urng, mummified. He was the first serial killer in the modern history of Thailand who was convicted, executed, mummified and then put on display as a type of deterrent to anyone who may have been having similar ideas. He was displayed in what looked like a telephone box. He was leaning against the glass like a pissed-up Clark Kent.

It's quite a good idea having a museum in a hospital. It's annoying when you visit someone but arrive early before visiting hours with nothing to do. Or if you're waiting for your girlfriend to give birth but you don't like the idea of seeing it pop out, go and look at half a head instead.

It's weird how quickly you can get used to looking at pretty gruesome stuff. When I first looked at the head that had been split in two I was thinking, 'Oh, that's pretty brutal', but after a few minutes I was wondering what tool they used to get such a perfect cut. Suzanne has a go at me 'cos of the state I leave the bread in after cutting meself a slice, so I'd like to see how they made such a perfect cut. I even thought about how I'd quite like the two bits of head in my house to be used as bookends. Let's face it (no pun intended) it's no worse than having someone's ashes sat on your fireplace, is it?

After seeing the baby with two heads I wondered if this is the way we are meant to evolve. Maybe they've got it right, and it's us one-headed people who have got it wrong. People aren't as sociable as they once were. If you have two heads you're never alone. More stress in our lives, two heads are better than one. 2 for 1 offers in supermarkets. Crossing busy roads and being able to look both ways. It all makes sense. We always interfere with nature. I think if tennis players continue to wear headbands they will end up killing off eyebrows, as they're there to catch sweat. No headband needed.

It turns out this wasn't the last bizarre exhibition I was going to see. The hotel we were staying at was quite good. It had good food, wifi, balconies, a swimming pool and a knob garden. Everything you need. What? What's a knob garden? It's a garden full of knobs. They don't call it the Knob Garden here though, they call it the Chao Mae Tuptim shrine. It's a fertility shrine. There must have been two hundred or so wooden penises all over the place. All different sizes, from the size of a cream doughnut to the size of a canoe. I don't mind the concept – they're not harming anyone – but why have so many? It was like a warehouse for knobs. It would look classier if they just had one big main one. It would give it more of a Ye Olde Powerful Knob impression. Maybe it started off with just one knob then whoever is in charge got carried away. Me mam did the same with gnomes. People collect anything, don't they? Never understood why people collect thimbles, but I'd rather have them on a shelf than a two-foot knob. And the weird thing was, for a fertility shrine you'd think the bollocks would be the bit that was important, but there wasn't a pair of bollocks in sight.

We went out for some tea. Bangkok is busy at night. If I wasn't looking at the women to work out if they were women or not, I looked at the billboards. They have so many of them on the motorways, one after another. The biggest I've ever seen. Thirty metres across. Laptops, cars, cameras and TVs. It's like driving through an Argos catalogue.

As I said earlier, I'm quite happy eating Thai food. It's spicy and tasty, but the amount of dishes they bring out gets a bit silly. You just help yourself from each plate. I didn't know what I was eating most of the time. I think at one point I might have eaten a fag end out of an ashtray. The problem is, you lose track of how much you've eaten. We had a change from the usual Thai food this evening though. We went to a place called the Flying Chicken. It's a place not really known for the way the food tastes but how it's delivered to your table. I can get a bit annoyed at times when out having a sit-down dinner if there's too much faff. I've been to fancy places in London where you put your order in then they bring it and spend five minutes explaining where the carrots were grown and what the chicken liked to do in its spare time. I'm not joking. I went to a fancy place for a steak and they told me the cow my steak came from liked listening to rock music. Going on the price of it, I think I was covering the cost of a front row seat at the last gig it went to.

At the Flying Chicken, the way it works is like this. You order chicken. A bell rings once the chicken is ready. The chicken is then placed onto a lever. The bell rings again. From nowhere comes a man on a unicycle wearing a helmet with a spike on the front. The boy at the lever catapults the chicken through the air then the man on the unicycle catches it on the spike and brings it to your table. Imagine Britain's Got Talent delivering your KFC.

Once all the chickens had been delivered, during a quiet spell, the bloke on the unicycle showed his skills off by catching smaller objects like grapefruits, oranges, plums and finally something the size of a grape. He let me have a go. Four dropped chickens later, grease streaming down my face, I managed to catch one on me head. The Flying Chicken – where the food is headable, not just edible. I didn't stay for pudding.

If visiting a place called Monkey Town had been one of the 100 things on the Bucket List, I would have picked it. I love a monkey, me. So, when I saw that there was a place called Monkey Town we were passing by anyway, it would have been mad not to stop off and see.

I was expecting to just see the odd one sat in a tree. I couldn't have been more wrong. There were hundreds of the bloody things. Everywhere you looked there was a monkey. Some big, some small, some healthy, some not so healthy, some swinging on telephone lines, some sat on fences and high up on balconies. A gang of them were sat on a car. Who knows, it might have been their car. It was like some odd cartoon town. I don't know where they have all come from, but they've made this place their town. There were definitely more monkeys than people. We went into a temple where at the gate a man (may have been a monkey in a human outfit) didn't sell leaflets on the history of the temple, he sold bags of nuts and fruit. I bought a bag of nuts and was about to enter the temple gates when a monkey climbed my shorts, grabbed the bag and ran off. I bought three more bags. Monkeys circled me, so I hid them in my pockets.

I sat down. I had about four or five monkeys all over me. They picked at my head like they were looking for tics. One worked out that no hair meant it was just easier to lick my head for any passing tics. I slowly pulled out another bag of nuts. A monkey jumped from behind me, grabbed them and left. This was getting silly now. I wasn't feeding the monkeys, I was just being mugged.

I had a packet of Monster Munch in my other pocket, so I thought I would use them to teach the robbing sods a lesson. They were spicy flavour. Maybe this will stop them nicking food off other people in the future. I was about to open the packet to hand a monkey one crisp when the whole packet was grabbed. They are so quick. I turned to see the monkey climbing the side of the temple like when King Kong climbed the Empire State Building. So, is this why nature gave them the opposable thumb, is it? So they could open bags of crisps! You might be thinking, 'Karl, stop moaning. They're probably just hungry and this is their way of surviving.' Oh really? Well, what are the reasons for another monkey to nick me hat and another to have me glasses away? They're robbing bastards. Simple as that.

The guide told me that the oldest monkey there was over forty. So I asked to go and see it. It was resting while drinking one of those Yakult probiotic drinks! I don't even have them. As it sat there necking it, it looked so human: the way it sat, the way it looked around. It's just their arse that is un-humanlike. These had a similar arse to chimps. Horrible big red bulbous arses. What went on there? I'm glad we evolved to get a better arse. Goes to show even nature realised that that arse design was not good. Sore red arse. The one that nicked my Monster Munch might have ended up with an even redder arse.

#18 See orang-utans in Borneo

It would be good to see some orang-utans but I think I'd enjoy seeing one walking through London more than having to go all the way to Borneo for it.

Someone will probably complain and say I shouldn't even be trying to give a monkey a Monster Munch. I watched a programme on TV once when a bonobo was making itself a Pot Noodle, and some people complained about it, as Pot Noodles are not very good for you. But that's what it was eating the night they filmed it. The night before, it was probably knocking up roast chicken with new potatoes and asparagus.

I called Ricky.

KARL: I went to Monkey Town, thought I would love it. They were doing me head in.

RICKY: Why?

KARL: Part of it, I think, is looking forward to something a lot, but I got there, just buying some nuts outside off a bloke, monkey came up, nicked them straight away, attacked me, scratched me leg, grabbed a packet of Monster Munch out of me back pocket, ran off up in the temple.

RICKY: (laughs) This sounds like a weird sort of animation or a dream. The fact that you are somewhere with Monster Munch in your back pocket and a monkey is nicking them and running into a temple, it's like something out of the *Beano*.

KARL: They're on the roof and on the balconies. The problem is, you know how you say you shouldn't give monkeys jobs? I think, honest to god, they've got to, they've got to give them something to do. They used to have them in films. They had them in tea bag adverts. Now they've got nothing to do.

RICKY: No, Karl, we've been through this. Remember you saw that thing on YouTube, a little news story where there's a monkey dressed as a waiter in a bar? That's a stunt. He hasn't really got a job, he hasn't beaten people to that job. It's a trick, okay? Those chimps in the PG Tips advert? That was fake for the cameras. It was just stunt. They didn't really have those jobs.

KARL: But you're contradicting yourself. Because on one hand you go, 'They don't like working in bars', and on the other hand you tell me they're 98% human. Well, if they're 98% human, that's the bit that they like working from. The other 2% is when they are a chimp.

RICKY: This is so mixed up. This is amazing.

KARL: You're always saying opposable thumbs and all that, and we come from monkeys and blah, blah, blah. Well, I'm just saying everything is evolving, everything, all the time. You've told me that, haven't you? Everything is changing.

RICKY: Okay, okay, right. We didn't come from monkeys, we came from a mutual ancestry, so we are similar genetically. We're 98% genetically identical to a chimpanzee. Okay, that doesn't mean that percentage is dedicated to liking working in bars. Otherwise you could say that chimps are close to Australians because Australians like working in bars. That doesn't mean they like to. What am I saying?! Chimps don't like working in bars. It's exploitation. If you tell them to do what they want, it won't put on the uniform and start pouring a pint of ale. They do that, they are inquisitive, but they have got all these things that . . . You don't give them a P45 to fill out.

KARL: But, we might as well be, because I was in there giving them nuts. They don't even have to go and get them. If we're not going to interfere, let's stop all the free nuts that they're getting. You can't on one hand say, here you go, have some nuts, but do you have to do anything for that? No, because that's cruel. Either they get free nuts or you chuck them out in the wild. But they were acting like they were human. They've taken over a temple. People can't use it as a church anymore there are so many monkeys.

RICKY: It's our fault because we interfere with the species. But the thing is though, once chimps start working there will be unemployed people going, 'Why has that chimp got my job? I'm unemployed!!!'

KARL: Work harder then. You've got competition, which then makes us better at what we do. Who would want to be replaced by a chimp?

(Ricky laughs)

I had a bath back at the hotel. My legs were covered in monkey scratches. When I saw the Seven Wonders of the World last year I had to have injections before I travelled, one of which covered me in case I was bitten by a dirty monkey. I never thought it would come in handy. I lay in the bath feeling a bit disappointed after visiting Monkey Town. I thought I'd really enjoy it. Just goes to show that you don't really know what you're gonna like. I think I enjoyed dressing up as a woman with Viv more than visiting the monkeys. Bit of a worry, innit?

Next day I woke up to a message on my phone from Stephen. He said I'd be visiting Snake Village! What is it with this country letting animals take over places? I asked the director if they are dangerous. He said they are king cobras and they're very dangerous. That's when I noticed an ambulance was tagging along with us for safety. It's mad to think this whole trip was meant to be me swimming with dolphins in Australia, but here I am in Thailand piss-arsing about with king cobras.

When we arrived I was given some protectors to put round my ankles, so they couldn't bite me. Last time I wore something like this they were leg warmers. It was a trend in the 1980s. I think *Fame* made them popular. I didn't buy any, as they were too expensive, but me dad made me some from an old shirt of his. He just cut the sleeves off and then rolled them down me legs. I was the only kid in Manchester who had leg warmers with cuffs.

There were three paramedics. Don't know why three. I'd have preferred just the one. If I got bit they'd all be discussing who was gonna suck the venom out instead of just getting on with it. I was told I would be fine because the medics carry anti-venom. Who knows? It might not work. I suffer from a bit of eczema, and the chemist keeps flogging me E45 cream for it. It doesn't work. I need something stronger. When I have headaches I need to have Nurofen Extra 'cos normal paracetamol doesn't work. It's 'cos everything is constantly evolving as we make it stronger by fighting it. It's like bacteria. Years ago bacteria was bad, but now we have friendly bacteria that we have in yoghurt drinks. It's like it got sick of fighting and became friendly, but then in a few years it will become so friendly we'll have groups of people saying, 'Don't eat friendly yoghurt, its cruel!'

We got to the village. There was a small gathering of about twenty people. There was also a type of priest. It was a funeral. For a snake. They worship the snake, as they bring tourism to the area. This was the first funeral I've ever been to. I've always avoided going to funerals. I avoid weddings, as well, but I have been forced to go to a couple of them. I don't really like get-togethers. My dad says I would prefer funerals to weddings, as it doesn't take all day and you don't have to take a gift, but you still get fed well.

The dead snake was in a glass box, and a live one was slithering about on top of the box just a metre away from us (must have been related). I never found out if they bury, cremate or stuff 'em to make a draught excluder, as a man called Bualee came and said hello. He was a snake charmer. I shook his hand. It felt odd. I looked down and noticed it was lacking fingers. I was gonna ask him how many times he'd been bitten, but I'm guessing he's not good at adding up with so many fingers missing. He ended up telling me anyway.

'I've been bitten twenty-one times,' he said. I don't think he's cut out to be a snake charmer. Twenty-one times! He's clearly not charming enough. The snake charmers I've seen in cartoons normally play a flute to the snake, but I suppose Bualee's lack of digits would mean he wouldn't exactly be able to knock out a good tune on a recorder.

He took me to his home where there were boxes lined up outside, but they weren't for recycling like all the boxes we're given from the council. They were for his snakes. Six or seven big boxes. It was like *Deal or No Deal* with Noel Edmonds. He lifted the lid on the first box. It wasn't even locked shut. He got a snake out. It must have been about five feet long. Of all the people to show me a killer snake I wish they could have got me someone with fingers to grip hold of the snake tightly. I wouldn't trust this fella to hold a vase on *Antiques Roadshow*, and yet here he is wafting a king cobra in my face.

He then got out an even bigger king cobra. It must have been eight feet long.

The ankle protectors I was wearing were a little bit pointless, as once the snake is upright it could easily have me by me neck. It's like when people wear bulletproof vests. They don't protect you from a bullet in the head, do they? Bualee wanted to show me how the king cobra eats. A young lad who seemed quite upset came along with a snake in a jar. I managed to work out that it was this lad's pet snake and they wanted to feed it to the cobra because they didn't have any rats. I said I didn't want the kid to lose his pet, just so I could see how a cobra eats. So the pet snake got to live another day.

He then let the king cobra loose. It's amazing how quickly and quietly they move. I didn't move. Bualee was down low on the ground shifting from left to right, getting up close and then moving quickly when it got too close. It just seemed like a pointless risk to me, like having a chunk of radium as an ornament. I don't think there's enough for people to do round these parts and that's when you get people doing silly things like this. They need a local youth club with table tennis or something. Everyone watching was deadly silent. That's when I heard a fart noise. I thought it was Bualee. It wasn't. It was the snake. I didn't know they did that. I had to tell Ricky about it.

RICKY: Are the snakes happy? They're not stressed, are they? They're not keeping them in horrible cages and poking them?

KARL: I don't understand why you're worrying about them. They could kill me within fifteen minutes.

RICKY: I'm worried that these animals are being annoyed or teased or exploited in any way.

KARL: I don't think they were that stressed. They're too relaxed if anything, and I tell you why, while one was sort of dancing about . . . it farted.

RICKY: (laughs) I've never ever experienced a snake farting.

KARL: That's exactly what I said. I mean, I was blown away by it. I had no idea they even had an arse.

RICKY: *(laughs)* Wait a minute, course it's got an arse. If it eats rats, something's gotta come out.

KARL: But I kind of thought it might gag it up or something. I didn't know.

RICKY: Hold on. Snakes aren't thin because they're bulimic. They're thin to get through the undergrowth. What do you mean 'gag it up'! Hold on a minute, you sure it wasn't the fella who farted and went, 'Ooh, that's the snake'?

KARL: Well, that's the thing. He's an old fella. He's only got about four teeth, but that's still more than the amount of fingers he had. Listen, I've watched all the Attenborough programmes, and nature stuff where they cover snakes, and you see them eating hippos and attacking stuff, but I have never heard a snake fart. That's what's good about this programme though, innit? Broadening my mind, teaching me new stuff.

RICKY: Yeah.

KARL: Attenborough has never shown that a snake farts. I think we've hit on something here. On YouTube that clip with the panda farting got about 40 million views in a week, so . . .

RICKY: One, it was a panda sneezing, not farting, and, two, there's a reason why Attenborough doesn't show a snake farting on his shows. I mean, I don't know if he's that interested in one.

KARL: Yeah, but I didn't know. I thought the fart was a human thing. It's something to do with arse cheeks or whatever. The snake is smooth.

RICKY: (*laughs*) What are you talking about, you thought the fart was a human thing? What does that mean? So, something really important in our evolution, as soon as we're upright, we've got language, we've got forward-facing eyes, we've got total dexterity, we've invented the wheel, we've got imagination, we've got a knowledge of the future . . . Something missing, and someone farts, and they go, that's brilliant. What are you talking about, you thought farting was a human thing?

KARL: I think it just surprised me 'cos I was really scared. I was worried about it and then once it had done that – it's that thing of being scared of your boss, imagine them naked – I wasn't scared of the snake. Once it farted, it was, like, why am I worried about this?

RICKY: Karl, how many times have you imagined your boss naked then? Because your boss is Rupert Murdoch. So, how many times have you imagined Rupert Murdoch naked?

KARL: No, I haven't. I'm just saying it's a well-known thing that people say.

RICKY: Okay, okay. Are you imagining it now?

KARL: Well, yeah, 'cos you've put it in there.

RICKY: What does he look like?

KARL: Like a tortoise without a shell on.

(*Ricky laughs*)

It was time to leave Thailand. After a flight to Sydney, another one to Adelaide and then a small plane to Port Lincoln, I eventually arrived at a harbour for the main event. Except that's when I found out I wouldn't be seeing any dolphins. Ricky left a message saying that they had changed the plan a little bit. I would be swimming with sharks instead. I don't think the Make-a-Wish Foundation ever changed plans at the last minute for the sick kids like this.

The boat I would be spending my time on was called *Princess 2*. I didn't want to ask what happened to *Princess 1*.

I met Rodney Fox and his son Andrew who were going to take me out to see the sharks. Rodney knows everything you need to know about sharks. He was a surfer when younger and was attacked by a shark in the 1960s. It tore open his side, broke half his ribs, punctured a lung and exposed the main artery to his heart. I don't know what he's playing at wanting to be anywhere near a shark after that, but I guess they do say, 'Whatever doesn't kill you makes you stronger'. Unless it's polio.

The plan was to lower me in to the water in a cage. It turned out that Rodney was the one who came up with the original idea of using a cage to get close to sharks, which made it difficult for me to slag off the design when I saw it. There was nothing to it. They might as well lower me into the ocean in a shopping trolley. Luckily he said I was going into a bigger cage. I still wasn't that happy. I felt like Goldilocks. Maybe if I say I'm still not happy they would have the perfect third option. But he didn't. This was the cage I would be getting in. There were big gaps between the bars. Rodney said the sharks might be able to get their heads in the gaps, but they wouldn't be able to open their mouths, so I shouldn't worry. Rodney took it upon himself to show me a photo of his shark bite. It looked like a jam tart, bright red with a ragged edge.

Rodney told me not to worry, as the chances of that happening were slim. I'm sure the chances of having Monster Munch nicked off you by a monkey were slim, but it happened to me.

It wasn't long before I started to feel seasick. What made it worse was, a woman who worked on the boat let it slip that I would be staying on the boat for two nights, when I thought we'd be back first thing in the morning. I was shown my room. It was a nice enough room with bunk beds and a little toilet, but it stank of fish. I lay on the bed where the sound of the chugging engine put me to sleep.

I woke up in the night when the boat took a bit of a bad knock from a wave. We must have been anchored up, as there was no chugging engine. The only sound was coming from the sea sloshing about outside. I felt sick. My stomach was churning. I went and sat on the toilet. I remember being sick into the sink, as seawater was landing on my back from the open porthole. I was pretty fed up although apparently I shouldn't have been. This experience is on the list of things to do before you die. I crawled back into bed. What's annoying is, I'm putting meself through this and I might not even see a shark. I sometimes find it hard to find Suzanne in Tesco if she wanders off, so what are the chances of seeing a shark in this vast ocean?

A few hours later I could hear movement on the boat. Friendly chatter between boat crew and film crew. I was in no mood for friendly chat. The smell of fish seemed worse. After lying there for an hour I thought I best get up, as feeling sorry for myself wasn't doing much good. I stood up and felt really sick again. I went and saw everyone. Rodney was full of beans. I didn't want to seem ungrateful, so I sat and had some toast and scrambled egg. Rodney told me that he worked on the film *Jaws*. He told me how they used a dwarf to play the part of Richard Dreyfuss in some of the sea scenes, so the real shark looked bigger than it was.

I went out onto the deck to get some fresh air. It was freezing, and the sea was quite choppy. There was no fresh air, as Andrew was already out there chucking in big pieces of tuna the size of house bricks to attract the sharks.

I was told to get a scuba suit that fitted me. Feeling sick, rocking side to side with the smell of fish in the air while trying to climb into something as tight as your own skin isn't easy. I've never liked tight clothes. I've never understood skin-tight jeans, and this outfit was even tighter, to the point that I couldn't really stand up straight. I reckon this is how it would have felt if one of those king cobras had swallowed me.

I sat on the edge of the boat as the cage was lowered down into the sea. I then had to wear a belt of heavy weights to keep me under. Andrew continued to throw out bait. The director, Luke, got in the cage first with a small camera to film me. I climbed down. The sea was bashing the cage about. I clung on for my life. It was strange to put my head under water while breathing normally. It was difficult to know where to grab as looking through the glass mask made things seem nearer than they actually were. The only fish I could see were chopped-up tuna chunks floating about.

The pressure on my body made my sickness seem worse. I couldn't believe I'd travelled to the other side of the world for this. I got out.

KARL'S FACTS

DOLPHINS CAN SWIM AND SLEEP AT THE SAME TIME. FOR 8 HOURS, THE ENTIRE BRAIN IS AWAKE. THE LEFT AND RIGHT SIDE THEN TAKE TURNS SLEEPING FOR 8 HOURS.

karl

DOLPHINS CAN STAY UNDERWATER FOR UP TO 15 MINUTES.

DOLPHINS HAVE NO SENSE OF SMELL.

A DOLPHIN'S FLIPPER HAS FIVE DIGITS — ALMOST THE SAME BONE STRUCTURE AS A HUMAN HAND.

THE US NAVY USES DOLPHINS TO FIND UNDERWATER MINES.

Luke got out to find his camera's protective casing hadn't worked and the camera was now knackered. It wasn't going well. I stood in the shower and let warm water into my wet suit. I read the messages other people had scribbled on the wall of their experiences.

I was a bit confused by Michelle's message about having a 'major chubby' the whole trip. Thought only men could have 'major chubbies'. Maybe Michelle was a woman from Thailand. One thing for sure though, I didn't have a major chubby. The outfit I was wearing would have shown it.

I was brought a hot mug of veg soup while the hot shower warmed me up. This was the happiest I had been since being on the boat. All this just proved I like the simple things in life. Being warm with a Cup a Soup. Isn't that the best way to be?

The director said he wanted me to give it another go tomorrow, as the weather was going to be calmer, and they had another camera to film with. I had another mug of soup and then an early night, so the time would go quicker. I used to do that as a kid at Christmas, so the big day would come sooner. I used to make myself sick with excitement at Christmas, but here I was feeling sick for a different reason.

Freddie the sound man woke me up in the morning to say we were going for it a second time. Once I was awake he got out pretty quickly. I found it a bit odd. Over breakfast Freddie said he didn't know how I could sleep in that room with the smell. I thought everyone's room had stunk like that. Turned out it was just mine. No wonder I'd been feeling ill. I asked Andrew about it. He said, 'Oh, the fridge we put the bait in is above your room and it leaks in through your porthole.' Typical.

I got ready again and got in the cage. I was determined to get this done, as there was no way I wanted to be forced into another night out at sea. It wasn't as choppy. The cage wasn't rocking as much. I got myself in a corner and waited. Rodney spoke to me in my ears via talkback and calmed me down, then warned me a great white shark was getting close. Then there it was. Not a sound. It drifted past like a ghost. It was massive. Like a three-piece suite with teeth. Its eyes looked dead. Sort of a bored expression, as if scanning biscuits in a supermarket aisle, looking for Custard Creams. Rodney said a large female was close by. He wasn't kidding.

The female was huge. It was an odd feeling being so close to something that could rip me apart. The last time I had this feeling was when I was on jury duty and was stood facing a lunatic that was just a metre away.

For some reason I remember reading somewhere that if sharks attack they don't like being punched on the nose. Weird how the brain remembers certain things. I have no other skills on how to tackle any animals, like how to get a bear in a headlock or drop-kick an otter.

I was down there for 45 minutes and although I never felt completely relaxed, now that I'm safely back on dry land I can say that it was an amazing experience. We even managed to see dolphins on the way back to harbour.

SWIMMING WITH DOLPHINS

SWIMMING WITH DOLPHINS

SPOT THE DOG?

GIRLS ALOUD HAVE LET
THEMSELVES GO A BIT.

THE MOST NATURAL
BREAST IN THE ROOM.

SWIMMING WITH DOLPHINS

THAT . . . IS NOT A DOLPHIN!

THERE'S A SAYING THAT THE FACE WILL BE MORE HONEST THAN THE MOUTH WILL EVER BE.

Thanks to the crew—Jen, Jess, Josh
Remember—you h
have looked death
shark cage! The
time I come I
my open water

RODNEY PUTS HIS HEART AND SOUL INTO GREAT WHITES, QUITE LITERALLY AND HAS 462 STITCHES TO PROVE IT.

COLD WET FEET. ONE OF THE MOST DEPRESSING THINGS IN LIFE.

I THOUGHT I WAS NERVOUS.

HAPPY CHRISTMAS.

CHAPTER FOUR

#97 Go whale-watching ✓

STEPHEN: You want to see a whale?

KARL: Yeah, I would like that.

RICKY: Amazing. Biggest creatures that ever lived. Some whales are twice as big as the biggest dinosaur. A blue whale is regularly 100 feet long, 150 tons plus. Their tongue is as big as an elephant.

KARL: Well, it would be, wouldn't it? It would be weird if it had a human-sized one.

(*Ricky laughs*)

KARL: But that's their problem in a way, that's why they're sort of endangered, 'cos they're so big. Easy to see, easy to catch.

RICKY: But who's catching them?

KARL: The locals.

RICKY: But they shouldn't be, should they?

KARL: Well, you say that, but what else they got out there? They have one to last them a year. They do a big catch, drag it in, chop it up and stick it in the cellar or something. They've got nothing else to eat, so you can't really moan at them when we're here wasting stuff, binning food. They've got a whale, let them have a whale.

RICKY: They haven't only just got whale.

KARL: Well, what else have they got?

RICKY: Alaska? It's the biggest state in America.

KARL: If they live in the middle of nowhere, they can't keep nipping out, can't get Tesco home delivery. It takes days to get somewhere. I saw some kid crawling on an ice lake on the telly going to school. It took them six hours or something.

(Ricky laughs)

KARL: So, they're not gonna just nip out for a loaf, they're gonna eat what's around them. What's around them? Whale. I don't want whales to die out – I think they're really nice, don't want to kill them off – but if some little fella's in an igloo saying 'I'm hungry', would you be that person to go in and say 'You're not having whale, you can starve'. That's all they got.

RICKY: It's not all they've got, not in Alaska.

KARL: They haven't got much more because it costs so much to get stuff to them. Seen it on the telly. There's a supermarket with nothing but old apples and bananas. Now if I lived there, I might go, okay, you can't kill a whale, they're lovely creatures and they're dying out, so I'll have this old banana. After a week of that I'll go, okay, I'm sick of bananas, give me whale meat. I'm sure they don't want to kill off whales, but they've got no option. So, I want to see them before they're all gone.

STEPHEN: Would it interest you to spend time with Eskimos, or Inuits as they like to be called?

RICKY: Yeah, don't say Eskimos. That's a derogatory term now. Say Inuit.

KARL: Who's come up with that little problem for them? I've never heard an Eskimo moan about that. They've got bigger worries than that. They've got mouldy old bananas and no proper food. It's someone else in London, that, in an office saying 'Oh, they don't like that'. They're not bothered!! I bet if I called one 'Eskimo' they wouldn't get upset about it.

(Ricky laughs)

KARL: People make up little rules. You can't call a midget a midget. They prefer dwarf. And leprechauns . . .

RICKY: Leprechauns don't exist. Leprechauns do not exist.

KARL: Well, if they did, they would go 'Don't call them that'.

RICKY: What do leprechauns prefer to be called?

KARL: Gnomes or something.

Have you ever been given an item of clothing that has stressed you out? I was given a big coat to wear for my trip to Alaska that made me worry. There was a label inside where I was to write my name, an emergency contact number and . . . my blood type. I'm all for writing my name and phone number, comes in useful if I leave my coat somewhere, but why blood type?! I didn't even know my blood type. I couldn't believe I'd been asked a question I couldn't answer by a coat! I called up the doctor's and made an appointment to get a blood test. When I got to the clinic the doctor asked why I needed a blood test. 'Because my coat needs to know,' I said.

I had to pack more for this experience than for any of the other trips. I had big boots, thick socks, gloves, scarfs, hats, extra-thick trousers and heat packs. I ended up wearing the massive coat to the airport as it was too big to pack in my case with everything else. It was like a continental quilt with a hood. It had eleven pockets. I made use of all of these by putting chocolate bars in each of them.

Our flight from London arrived late at Anchorage so we stayed at a hotel for the night. Nice place, but there were stuffed animals everywhere you looked. Grizzly bears, brown bears, black bears, polar bears and moose. Bloody big things, they were. I've never understood the point of stuffed animals. Years ago I suppose this was the only chance people had to see most animals as they didn't have zoos or TV to watch nature programmes, but now, unless you're planning on using a moose head as a clothes' horse, I really don't see the point in taking up room in your house with a dead animal. Years ago, I had a mate called Ryan who had one of those rugs that still had the animal's head attached. It was a bear. He said his dad had won it in a card game. To think of all the trouble Noah apparently went to saving all the different species and yet here was one of the strongest animals on the planet with Ryan's mam hoovering its back with a Dyson. I went round to his house again to find that they had cut off the head as his dad got sick of tripping over it and almost falling into the coal fire. His dad said it was probably less dangerous when it was alive.

The next morning we set off to meet a local man called Marty. The plan was for him to show me how beautiful the area was, while also teaching me how to survive in these cold conditions. We got to the meeting place early. No one was around. All this snow and not one snowman in sight. I could already feel a headache coming on, not from the cold but from the white of the snow. My eyes aren't good at dealing with brightness. If heaven does exist and I make it up there I hope it's not as bright as people always paint it. If it is, I hope there's a Boots up there where I can get an aspirin. I put it down as a side-effect of growing up in Manchester and having a dad who didn't like wasting electricity on bulbs. As soon as a light was turned on he would be there to hit the off switch. It was like he was playing that 1980s computer game *Simon* before it had been invented. We didn't even have bright white walls when I was a kid, it was always magnolia, so my eyes are in no way trained for this. I took two Nurofens to try and ease the pain. My headache certainly wasn't caused by any noise. It was strange how quiet it was. It was as if the deep snow soaked up every sound. Mind you, why would there be any sound? If we hadn't been filming, I wouldn't be out in these conditions either. I'd be staying in watching a *Columbo* box set, drinking tea and making me way through a pack of biscuits. Maybe that's why taxidermy is big here; apart from Sir Edmund Hillary, who would wanna take a dog a walk in this weather. As I waited for Marty I had one of my chocolate bars from one of my eleven pockets. It was a Twix. I'd basically turned this coat into an advent calendar.

Marty turned up. He was a big man wearing a cowboy hat. Imagine Burt Reynolds in a fleece. He was dragging two sleds full of gear. I wasn't sure if we were going for a trek into the mountains or I was just about to help him move house. I've seen bag ladies carry less than what Marty was lugging with him. He had axes, shovels, skis, ropes and a gun.

KARL: Where we going? Honestly, do we really need all this? I think we're carrying a lot of extra stuff.

MARTY: No, we need that.

KARL: Why?

MARTY: What if something happened to me? What if I got hit by an avalanche? Are you ready for this? I am not joking. This is a very serious business. I'm not kidding you. My friend died in an avalanche on Saturday. What is today? Tuesday. Four days ago. They triggered an avalanche, all three of them get washed down, one guy breaks a leg and the other guy is buried. Not kidding, not joking. Didn't find his body. Nightfall came. Sunday morning helicopter rescue, fifteen feet below the surface of the snow.

KARL: Dead?

MARTY: They found him . . . dead. I'm not kidding. I wouldn't have brought any of this equipment up here if I didn't think it was necessary for your safety.

KARL: Did your mate know what he was doing? Was he a proper climber?

MARTY: Yes, they were all very experienced. One of them, I know for a fact, climbed Mount McKinley before. So, they were totally experienced, trying to enjoy the back country, like you and I are going to do. We're going to be on the very same mountain they were.

KARL: Why are we going to that one?! Why are we not doing another one?

(Marty laughs)

#33 Go ice-climbing ✓

I told Marty I'm not really into dangerous fun. I love having a nice stroll, but if having a stroll involves carrying guns and shovels I'd rather stay in. He said we were going to have 'an awesome time'. Awesome seemed to be one of his favourite words. He used it a lot. I asked him if it's so 'awesome' why was he carrying a gun. He told me he brought it for my safety. 'We're in bear country,' he said. I asked him where my weapon was, as all I had to stop a bear attacking me was ten bars of chocolate. He handed me some pepper spray. A lot of people who live in these parts don't like carrying guns but need protection from bears, so they carry bear spray. He said it could spray pepper up to thirty feet. I remember thinking that that wasn't a great claim. A thirty-foot spray is nothing. I may as well throw it from a pepper pot. I would have been happy to carry a gun. I was carrying so much stuff already I looked like a contestant on *Crackerjack* so what harm would one more item do, but he said if I wasn't used to shooting a gun the chances are I would miss my target and end up hitting one of the film crew, so I would be best just using the pepper spray as a form of defence. The idea of the spray is that bears have an amazing sense of smell and they don't like the pepper. I took the lid off, and Marty kept telling me to be careful. The problem was, Marty was hard to read as he was an excitable person and spoke like one of those voiceovers you get on kids' nature programmes who say things like 'Woooowwwww' and 'Loooooook outtttttt, duuudddeee', so I never knew if he was kidding or not. It was like one long game of Call My Bluff with

Marty. I sprayed it. Marty started screaming while squeezing his eyes. I thought he was messing about. Richard the director told me to put the cap back on the spray as if he was some sort of hostage negotiator. I then noticed Freddie the sound man's eyes were streaming, and a gust of wind sent some of the spray into everybody else's eyes. It wasn't long before we were all stood there crying, like we'd just been eliminated off X Factor. My eyes may not be good at dealing with the brightness, but they handled the pepper spray quite well. I put this down to the fact that I grew up with my mam using loads of Silvikrin hairspray. If I had to go in the bathroom after she had been in there spraying her head I had to learn to keep my eyes open. If I closed them the amount of lacquer in the air would stick them shut. Marty told me I needed to keep the spray in a location I could get to quickly if a bear appeared, so I moved a KitKat I had in my right-hand front pocket and put it where the Twix I'd eaten earlier had been. Another tip that Marty gave me, if I was to get chased by a polar bear, was to strip while running, as the bear would stop to sniff each garment. If I had to do this, with the amount of layers I was wearing, there would be more clothes on the floor than at Primark when a sale's on. And the chocolate would probably help too.

Marty asked if I had any back problems or health issues. I told him I'd just taken some Nurofen to stop a headache. He seemed concerned and was worried about me doing a trek if I wasn't fully fit. Again, I wasn't sure if he was being serious. Here he was being worried about my safety after having a couple of tablets for a headache, and yet a few minutes ago he'd given me some pepper to protect myself from a bloody big bear. I told him I would be fine, and we started our trek. It wasn't long before we were wading in five feet of snow. Never mind pepper spray, salt spray would've been more handy to melt ourselves a path. I thought these sorts of conditions were meant to have died out with the woolly mammoth. I was knackered. I didn't know how deep the snow needed to get before Marty would think about using the shovels we were both dragging with us. He kept saying how beautiful everything looked, but everywhere looks nice when covered in this much snow. It's a good place to fly-tip 'cos after a few hours in these conditions anything you tip will be covered.

I asked Marty if he had any water as I was thirsty. He didn't, but he said the snow that surrounded me was the cleanest snow in the world, so it would be safe to eat that.

As we walked we talked.

KARL: Have you walked around England?

MARTY: I've never been there. Do you know the Beatles?

KARL: The Beatles? Most of them are dead.

MARTY: Oh, don't talk like that.

KARL: They are though. Well, 50%.

MARTY: What's that place called, the Cave, Liverpool?

KARL: The Cavern? It's not a cave, you know. It's not somewhere to climb. It's a bar.

MARTY: Is it still there?

KARL: Yeah.

MARTY: You've been there?

KARL: No.

MARTY: You've never been there?!

KARL: No, it's in Liverpool.

MARTY: Well, how far away's that?

KARL: It's about forty miles.

MARTY: Forty miles and you never went there?

KARL: Well, I'm from Manchester. The two cities don't get on.

MARTY: What does 'two cities don't get on' mean?

KARL: Well, you know, kind of, football rivalry.

MARTY: Hold it! Stop! Woah, when you gonna put your gloves on?

KARL: My hands feel alright at the moment.

MARTY: Are you sure? Keep an eye on it. Know anything about hypothermia, frostbite?

KARL: Um, yeah. Your fingers fall off.

MARTY: Yeah, well, I've seen a lot of frostbite. I've climbed Mount McKinley thirteen times, four-week expeditions to the tallest mountain in North America. You know of Mount McKinley?

KARL: No.

MARTY: You never heard of Mount McKinley?

KARL: No. I'm not a mountain man.

MARTY: You never went to Liverpool, and you've never heard of Mount McKinley?! Dude, we need to get you out more.

KARL: It's just no big deal for me. Have you ever heard of Snowdon?

MARTY: No.

KARL: Right, and you're a mountain man. Now who's embarrassed?

The sun was starting to go down, and so was the temperature. We got to the top of the small mountain where we would need to ski down to get to the place we would be staying at for the night. I've never skied before. My school did a few skiing trips but they were really expensive things to go on due to the amount of kit you had to hire, plus my dad said I should learn to spell before I learn to ski, so I used to stay at school and sit in a class with a few other kids and draw, so skiing was a new experience for me. One I won't be doing again. I was useless. I can understand why kids do it, but not fully grown men. People look at me strange if I start trying stunts on a BMX, but I don't see the difference. I couldn't get the hang of it. I was on my arse more times than Norman Wisdom, so I ended up sitting on the sledge I'd been dragging around for the last five hours and made my way down that way. The temperature must have been around minus ten, so I was looking forward to a hot bath. We got to the hut I would be staying in. The bath wasn't going to happen as the hut was basically a shed with a bed in it. It was freezing. There was a little room I thought was the bathroom. There was nothing in it apart from a tiny sink with no taps. Marty told me it was a room for privacy for changing in, but we were in the middle of nowhere. A toilet was needed more than privacy. But he said pipes would burst in these temperatures so there was no plumbing.

He told me if you needed to go to the toilet you had to do it outside. He then showed me a piece of ice he had shaped like one of those Jubbly ice drinks and told me this would be used as toilet paper. Makes no sense. Earlier, Marty had me eating ice after saying it was the cleanest snow in the world, and now here he was telling me that mountaineers wipe their arse with it. I understand that you have to use what nature gives you and they have snow, lots of it, I understand them making igloos out of it, slush puppies, even have a go at making a frappuccino, but not wiping your arse with it! No wonder kids don't make snowmen round here if that's what they do with it.

Marty sat and sang a few songs on his guitar. Funny how he didn't have room in his bag for a few bottles of water or a toilet roll, and yet he managed to bring his guitar along. Here are the lyrics to his song 'I Really Caribou You'.

> I really caribou you,
> I'm a loon when you're a whale,
> It's hard for me to bear, because I love you so deer,
> I really caribou you.
> You're salmon special to me,
> You give porpoise to my life,
> I dolphin thinking of you, I wolf forget I love you,
> You're salmon special to me.

He had a few good songs and a nice enough voice, but I couldn't really enjoy it knowing that if I needed to go during the night I would be wiping my arse with what was basically a choc ice. To think he was worried about my hands getting frostbite. Marty gave me a copy of his CD *Strummit from the Summit*. Something else he managed to carry. I went to bed. Normally I sleep in just my undies as I don't like pyjamas – I don't like being too hot – but on this occasion I went fully clothed apart from my boots. But I still didn't sleep as it was too cold. I must have spent a good hour making smoke rings with my breath like smokers do in the cold air. At around 4 a.m. I got up. You might be thinking the reason was to get a drink or have a wee – that's normally the reason you get up in the middle of the night, isn't it? – but it was neither of those things. It was to put my hat on 'cos me head was so cold. When I was a kid I stayed in a caravan that was as cold as this. I ended up waking up with my eyes frozen shut. My mam and dad crept about the room thinking I was having a lie-in when I wasn't, I just couldn't open my eyes so didn't know they were there. I was worried they would freeze together again here. The shed didn't even have curtains. It had blinds. Blinds are all very well for a flat or an office for giving some privacy, but they're useless when you need to keep the heat in a place. There's that saying about good salesmen being able to sell snow to Eskimos. They should change the word 'snow' to 'blinds', as the same applies. The hut needed a little blow-heater of some sort but all there was was a vacuum cleaner. Maybe the idea is to do some housework to warm up, but I was worried the noise from the vac would wake everyone else up next door, or, worse, cause an avalanche.

#43 See the northern lights

Until a few years ago I honestly thought when people talked about the northern lights they were talking about Blackpool illuminations. When I heard people rave on about how it was such a must-see mystical sight and how they got goose bumps from it I'd tell them I'd seen them a few times and that I took Suzanne to see them on our first date and she wasn't that impressed and one of them said, 'Ohhh she is so lucky.'

'Yeh, I know, and I bought her fish, chips and peas after,' I said.

I eventually needed a pee so did it in the little sink that didn't have any taps. Let's face it, a sink with no taps is a urinal. What other use does a sink with no taps have? I had a game of Patience with a set of cards I had taken with me and then thawed out a Mars bar by rubbing it between my hands. After that I looked through a few magazines I found on a shelf, hoping to find a word search or crossword I could have a go at. Unfortunately, the magazines were all about guns, so not the sort of publications to have 'fun tea break puzzles'. They were just full of pictures of hunters sat on bears they had shot. Like all magazines there were adverts on every other page, but not for collectable thimbles or commemorative plates. Instead, they were all for guns with slogans like 'For when you need something bigger'. It was at this point I found a weird scribbled note on one advert. It said 'Cathy, MK (crossed out), Card, Flowers, Gift, Dinner'. Using skills I've picked up from watching *Columbo* I deduced a couple had come to stay in this shed for a weekend away. I reckon the man had booked it and planned on a shooting weekend, which probably didn't please the woman (Cathy), and they had an argument. It looks like the bloke then thought about doing her in by buying an MK (type of gun), but then he must have thought about trying to save the relationship one last time by buying her a card, flowers, gift and a dinner. I might be miles away with my conclusion, but whatever it is, you have to admit that it is a weird list.

After a sleepless night, I made a call to Ricky who told me to make my way over to a place called Barrow. It's one of the northernmost cities in the world, and I was to get a taste of how Eskimos live. Part of my journey towards Barrow was covered by being dragged by huskies.

#95 Drive or 'mush' a dog sled

Ricky asked me to make sure the dogs were happy. He's always worried about animals, which isn't a bad thing, but then he goes too far with his cat. I moan about it a lot, but it's 'cos it really does swan about like it owns the joint. Even when it scratches him he doesn't slap the little shit. It gets away with murder and does nothing for its keep. He keeps showing me photos on his phone and asking me, 'How can you not love that?' But I can't, and anyone who ever meets it will agree with me. I wish there was some kind of pet swap TV programme, which would allow me to give it to some family who had a big dog and five kids for a week, as it needs a bloody wake-up call. It would be good for it. It's good for animals to work. It gives them a purpose to be on the planet. Dogs have loads of jobs – from leading blind people to sniffing out bombs and drugs. There was one I saw recently which had a job of sniffing out bed bugs in hotels. Thinking about it, no wonder there's high unemployment. People always say it's foreigners stealing the jobs. It's not, it's dogs. I read recently how even bees are now helping out in the workplace by detecting bombs. They've got jobs in airports and ports after scientists have taught them to stick their tongues out if they get a whiff of any explosives. At the end of the day, I suppose there are fewer gardens in the cities, so rather than pollinating, bees have found other work to do. It's only a matter of time before the long horned beetle that can carry over a thousand times its own weight will start up a removal business, and yet Ricky's cat will still be sat with its paw up its arse.

I met the husky's owner. He was called Bill. He was a champion husky racer. Racing is the main job of huskies these days, though back in the day they were the only way to transport goods in these regions before snowmobiles came along. Bill was a softly spoken man, which wasn't good, as I had a problem hearing him due to his dogs making a right racket. There's something about dogs barking that does my head in. We had a neighbour who had a Dobermann pinscher that never shut up. It just sat in the garden all day barking. Why is it that it never seems to bother the owner? It's the same with car alarms and babies. Bill told me I'd have six of his dogs dragging me. Woodrow was the main dog in charge, and after Woodrow there was Olive Oyl. Stupid name for a dog, but then I suppose when you have as many dogs as Bill you're bound to start running out of options. The barking got louder, and I couldn't hear any of the other names. It was a bit pointless anyway, as there was no way I was going to remember all of them. It was similar to being at a wedding when people introduce you to cousins and aunties. You never remember their names, and what's the point in remembering names of people you're never likely to meet again anyway. Bill showed me where to stand, how to slow the sled down, and how to use the snow hook, which is a type of anchor that stops the dogs running off when you're not on the sled. After that quick lesson in dog mushing, I was off. The dogs shot off at high speed. I yelled at Woodrow to slow down, but I doubt it could even hear me, as it was right at the front, which was about forty feet away from where I was stood. Thinking back, Bill should have started me off on some smaller dogs. This is the equivalent of popping a lad who's just passed his driving test in a Porsche. Bill could have started me on five pug dogs or eight chihuahuas. Let's face it, there are so many breeds to choose from now. When I was younger, it was a Jack Russell for a small dog or an Alsatian for a big dog, but now it's like coffee – too many variations. I heard they crossed a Labrador with a poodle to make a labradoodle, so you can get the temperament of a Labrador with the tight hair of a poodle. They should cross a Labrador with a husky for blind people who're in a rush to get somewhere.

I was yelling at the dogs to slow down, as the ground was getting bumpy, but they were taking no notice. They just ran and ran. I'd say they're good pets for lazy people, as you don't have to walk them, they take you for a drag. Bill told me they retire the dogs once they get to a certain age. I can just imagine someone picking one up from a dogs' home, having no idea of the dog's history, chucking a ball for it and then never seeing it again. I tried the 'whoa' command Bill told me to use with no joy, so moved onto the 'slow down, you twats' command, which had no effect either. Bill told me he has raced using sixteen dogs so God knows how fast he went with them. The dogs didn't even stop to poo. They just opted for the Paula Radcliffe skill of doing it while running, which I suppose is a good thing if you're in a husky race, as you wouldn't want them to keep stopping whenever they see a lamppost.

After about an hour and a half my arms and legs were really aching from holding on tight, but Bill said he was impressed with my skills. He said he had once taught the actor Steven Seagal to mush for the film *Dangerous Grounds* and Steven had come off loads of times, so that made me feel pretty good. I put it down to the fact that it was quite similar to riding a supermarket trolley. I often push myself off in Morrisons while holding on tight and using the weight of my body when cornering, but then I guess Steven Seagal doesn't do his own shopping, so he won't have these skills.

We flew the rest of the way to Barrow, as that is the only way to get to the place. I remember looking out of the plane window thinking we were flying above cloud until I saw a big dark crack. We were actually above frozen sea. There was literally nothing until we came over the airport where there was a couple of thousand homes all bunched together in the nothingness. We got off the plane. It was freezing. Colder than I've ever been. It was now around minus twenty-five. It hurt if you took in a deep breath, as the cold air seems to burn your lungs.

We stayed at a university camp where they study the Arctic ecosystem amongst other things. It looked similar to the base that was in the film *The Thing*. We had a type of small hangar/ shelter close to the sea front. It was basic, but it had everything you might need, including heating.

There were seven of us in total, so we had to share bedrooms, which wasn't a bad thing, as more body heat per room would warm the place up. I was given some long johns and quilted trousers to go over my normal trousers. I was now wearing three pairs of trousers, two pairs of socks and a thin pair of gloves to fit under my gloves. Washing baskets must be massive here to deal with the amount of clothes being worn on a daily basis.

We went for a walk by the sea, and then had a walk on the sea itself, as it was totally frozen. There were big walls of ice, as if the cold had frozen a wave mid-break. I was reminded of the reason of this trip when I saw whalebones lying about everywhere, as popular as scaffolding poles are in London. The locals obviously still hunt whales for food in these parts. They strip them and then leave the carcasses for the seagulls to feed on. I suppose that is the problem with eating whales, the leftovers are such a pain to get shut of. I couldn't be doing with it. It annoys me when Suzanne makes gravy so lumpy I can't pour it down the sink and I end up going outside to pour it down the grid, so having whalebones to get rid of would really do me head in. They disposed of them quite creatively by stacking them up like pork chops on a Gordon Ramsay dish. Some bones were on roundabouts. I'm not sure if the council had put them there as a feature or if someone had fly-tipped them. Maybe people go out in the darkness of night and dump them. I tend to do that with the Christmas tree every year.

I had a feeling that this wasn't a place I'd be seeing a living whale. I didn't see many living people out and about either, apart from a man who was shifting the snow off the road, which is a job for life if you live here. Another job that needs to be done in the area is the emptying of honey buckets. Honey buckets are used in the homes of some elders who can't afford a septic tank. A honey bucket is a five-gallon plastic bucket with a toilet seat on top. I met up with a fella called Rob whose job it was to empty them. I was asked to help. He suggested I popped on some of their overalls, as there was a chance of splash back occurring during the emptying of the buckets. Nice, innit? Rob was given a list of addresses that needed their buckets emptying.

We got in his truck, which was similar to a UK dustbin lorry, except it had a hopper on the side which you poured the contents of the honey buckets into. You then pulled a lever, which sucked the waste into the tanker. There was a massive crack across the windscreen, which seemed to be the case on four out of five vehicles here, either caused by bumping into things on black ice or the cold temperature on the outside as the car's heater is pumping out warm air on the inside. We got to the first address where my first bucket was sat waiting on the step. I picked it up and carried it over to the truck. It was heavy. I asked if the contents were a week's or a month's worth, but Rob wasn't sure when this bucket was last emptied. He and his team are out emptying six days a week.

The plastic bag in the bucket had been fastened and was full to the brim with pee and poo. It was like a balloon full of water where the slightest pressure could burst it. Gillian McKeith, that woman off the TV show *You Are What You Eat* would love it here. She's always looking at people's stools. I'm no doctor, but I'd say whoever this bucket belonged to was not well. It was similar to the lumpy gravy I was talking about earlier. I took my time carrying it, as the paths were slippy. As I poured it into the hopper, the bag split and the smell hit me. Rob said that was normal and he's now used to the stench. He seemed quite happy that this was his job and just said, 'That smell is my money.' I put the bucket back onto the porch, and away we went to the next house where there were two full buckets next to some legs that Rob said looked like caribou legs. I don't think they worry about the kerb appeal of their homes in Barrow. One of the bags was split. I asked Rob what the rules are on split bags, and he just said, 'Be more careful.' It's funny to think at home my binman doesn't take a bag if it's not in a proper bin bag, never mind a split bag full of shite. Rob's walkie-talkie went off. It was the base passing on four more addresses of people who needed their buckets emptying. They don't recommend leaving the buckets out too long, as they attract polar bears. If this stench attracts bears I really don't see how the pepper spray Marty gave me is supposed to scare them off.

19 Spot a polar bear on the ice

Polar Bear on Ice sounds like some ITV reality show. I'm not sure if I would have been that happy to spot a polar bear while out on the tundra. Spotting should be saved for the safer things like trains or planes, or just get one of them *Where's Wally?* books. It's odd how kids are given bears as toys and brought up thinking they're nice cuddly friendly creatures like Paddington Bear, Pooh Bear, Yogi Bear and SuperTed. I think kids grow up being more scared of the damage salt can do to their bodies than they are of bears. I think there are slugs with fewer worries about salt than some humans, 'cos we're constantly told it's bad for us.

The main problem is there's nowhere to hide in these places, which means if you spot a bear, the bear will also spot you, and being spotted by a polar bear isn't on the Bucket List. Rob told me I shouldn't have been wandering about on the frozen sea, as that's where the bears tend to be. I told him it would have been nice to see something that was living. I hadn't even seen many people since being here. I'd only seen bones or stuffed animals. He said Barrow is frequently visited by the polar bear even though there are only about 25,000 of them left on the planet. I think there could be loads more than that, but they're difficult to count due to them being hard to spot. Let's face it, a white bear on white land isn't an easy thing to see. Rob didn't seem that concerned about the number of polar bears left on the planet, but then if I lived here I suppose I wouldn't want numbers going up.

We carried on with the honey bucket collections. It's an odd name, isn't it? I think they give jobs nice names to try and make the people who have to do them feel better. A mate who worked at Subway said he was given the title of Sandwich Artist when he worked there. Mind you, if Rob's job title was Buckets of Shit Removal maybe not as many would apply.

Rob noticed the next address on his run was his cousin's place. I asked if it was odd picking up buckets of poo from people you know. He just laughed and said not really. I asked 'cos I know my mam wouldn't like it if she knew the person picking up her honey bucket. In all the time I've known her I've never heard her announce that she is going to the loo. I normally know she needs to go if she tries to get me and me dad to go out for a walk.

The more I emptied, the more I came round to the idea of the honey buckets. It means you can use the toilet in any room of the house. I hate it when I'm expecting a delivery, and they say they could come any time between 9 a.m. and 6 p.m. They always turn up just as you're sat on the toilet. With a honey bucket you could sit by the door.

After emptying the buckets I went to meet Roz at her house. She was a local elderly woman. She had a fairly decent-sized bungalow, not much of a garden, but then what would be the point of having a garden, anyway? Animal skins hung on her washing line looked frozen solid. I don't know what a good weather day is for hanging out washing here. She invited me into their home where I also met her sister Janey. The heating was blazing. It was similar to walking into a department store when you've been out in the cold on Oxford Street, so I took off a few of my layers and sat on their sofa. I explained that I was in Alaska to see a whale. At this point Roz went off and came back with a bag similar to the size of a bag of Oven Chips.

'Muktuk. A layer of bowhead whale,' she said. I explained that I wanted to see a whale swimming around in the ocean, not in a carrier bag. I don't think they could grasp why I wanted to see one, to them it was just food. They offered me a piece, so I tried it. I felt a bit bad, as I'd come all this way to see a living whale before they become extinct and here I was snacking on one. Muktuk is part skin and part fat, eaten raw. It wasn't horrible, but it wasn't that great, either. The fat broke up fairly easy, so you were just left chewing on tasteless skin. I'm sure if they had other options they wouldn't eat it, but they haven't, so they do. A radio was sat on the kitchen sideboard that would broadcast news from whalers when they had a catch. Roz and Janey told me how they help out with the whaling. It's their job to cut it up and divide it into pieces. The whale I was eating was caught last April. It was now March 2011, and I'm guessing if it was all this consistency they could be chewing on this well until 2015. The problem is, Barrow is not a place to be a vegetarian as fruit and veg can't be grown here due to the conditions, though, saying that, Roz's place was so hot due to her heating being full on I'm sure she could have grown tomatoes in her lounge. I told them I wasn't keen on the muktuk. Roz then got something else from the fridge for me. It was a chunk of caribou meat. It didn't have any taste, as it was frozen. At home, fancy restaurants give you an option of the meat being either well cooked or medium to well. Here in Barrow I think the options are slightly defrosted or frozen. It's the first time I've had to suck meat to soften it before I was able to chew.

The time that is saved on the cooking is definitely taken up with chewing. I asked why she had an oven in the kitchen. She just laughed. But, honestly, why have an oven when everything seems to be eaten frozen? Maybe it was a gift. I've got an ice cream maker that someone bought us that we've never used.

KARL'S FACTS

WHALES MOVE ABOUT 5 MILES PER HOUR, OR THE SPEED OF A CHILD ON A BICYCLE AND CAN SPOUT WATER 5 METRES HIGH.

A SINGLE BREATH FROM A MATURE BLUE WHALE CAN INFLATE UP TO 2,000 BALLOONS.

A WHALE'S PENIS IS CALLED A DORK.

sick here

THE HIGHEST TEMPERATURE RECORDED IN ALASKA IS 37.8 °C AND THE LOWEST WAS −62.2°C.

Stop!

ALASKA IS THE BIGGEST STATE IN THE US – LARGER THAN TEXAS, CALIFORNIA AND MONTANA COMBINED – AND HAS MORE THAN 3 MILLION LAKES.

#56 Spend the night in an igloo

I tried building an igloo with Janey when I was in Barrow. Igloos are little dome huts that are used mainly as emergency housing. If you're out hunting in the middle of nowhere they offer a little bit of protection from the mental weather. Janey started by getting me to dig a hole about 6 foot across, so I could lie down. I decided to dig a hole for a toilet and made a lid. We then made the bricks by using a normal saw to cut blocks of ice on the ground and then using a spade to lift them up. Janey got a neighbour and a young chubby lad, who didn't seem to have a clue, to help out. It was going well until it got to the roof. It's a tricky part as the blocks of ice have to be cut to slip in place.

Janey said she had to leave to go to church. The other two used the same excuse. They'd basically made a big bowl for a polar bear to eat me from. I didn't bother staying in it.

Roz said she would like to take me to a place called Point Barrow. We put our layers back on and off we went. I'd never heard of Point Barrow, but she seemed so excited about the thought of going I thought it was the local shopping arcade – a place to have a drink, a game of bingo, maybe. Roz gave me a lift on her snow bike. I tried to chat as we went along. I asked how many words for snow they have here 'cos I'd heard there were hundreds. I think they invented them just to make it more interesting for weathermen here. She said there were a few, but she seemed to be busy concentrating on riding the snow bike. I don't know why 'cos there was nothing for her to hit. Stevie Wonder could have given me a lift in these parts, and it would have been safe.

I ached from tensing up from the cold wind as we travelled along. I felt the cold more, due to the fact that I wasn't doing anything. I never liked waiting for buses at home for the same reason. I always used to walk to the next stop until one came along. An hour into the journey, she pointed and said, 'There's Point Barrow.' I couldn't see anything. I kept asking where, and she kept pointing.

Roz eventually pulled up and turned off the engine, and said, 'Karl, welcome to Point Barrow.' There was nothing but a 20-foot pole. It was like everything else I'd seen since being in Barrow. Honestly, go to Google maps and type in 'Point Barrow'. If you haven't got the internet just stand in front of a white wall. That's what I was faced with. She then explained that it was the northernmost part of Alaska and we were on the top of the world. I didn't feel on top of the world. My headache was starting again, my nose was running, and my feet were going numb. No wonder seals don't have hands or feet. It's nowt to do with evolution. They probably fell off with frostbite. I explained that I didn't think this was the top of the world, as heat is supposed to rise. I think we've got the world the wrong way about and that Australia isn't down under but up over, but she didn't understand my point.

We were the only ones there, but I guess that was no surprise. It was really really cold now, as the sun was starting to drop. I asked her what do we do now, and she said she usually brings a thermos with her but she hadn't bothered today. I took a bottle of water from my coat pocket. It was frozen solid, and my Galaxy Ripple was brittle. Even my layers weren't keeping me warm now. Some locals stay warm wearing skins from animals and big trousers made from polar bear fur. This wouldn't be for me. I don't like wearing white, as I seem to have more accidents spilling things when I wear white shirts or T-shirts 'cos I'm trying so hard not to stain them. I'm guessing polar bear pants aren't the sort of clothing you can just chuck in the washer either, so that's another reason I wouldn't want a pair. Any clothes I have that say 'dry clean only' means they will never get washed. I was dying for a pee. For some reason the cold makes you want to pee more than normal. No wonder honey buckets get so full. The problem was there was nothing to pee behind. There doesn't seem to be one tree in Barrow. Maybe that's what the 20-foot pole is there for. Roz said she hardly comes here but when it's open water (not frozen) this is where they come whaling, but there would be no whales round here for a few months. Brilliant.

8 Explore Antarctica ✗

51 Stand at the North or South Pole ✗

After being to Barrow I don't think I need to visit Antarctica. I imagine it's quite similar in the way that I wouldn't waste time debating to go to either Tenerife or Benidorm. It's the same stuff.

Barrow in Alaska was worth seeing just 'cos it's a place that no one should be living in. It's odd to think as I write this people are pottering about that place chewing on whale blubber. I think the best way to see Antarctica is by watching

David Attenborough on the telly. Let him do all the exploring. There's nothing but snow for miles, the landscape doesn't change and when you see footage of the penguins marching across the place even they look pissed off with being there – and they're from there.

As for standing on the North or South Pole I think it's just one of those things that you do so you can tell people you've done it. It's not an experience; it feels no different from standing anywhere else on the planet. I've stood on the equator when I was in Africa seeing the gorillas and the memory I have of it is a nice coffee and muffin we got from a café there.

#44 See the glaciers before they melt

The next day I got a message from Stephen. He wanted me to head over to Prince William Sound to go and see some glaciers. He explained that glaciers were melting at an accelerated pace. I told him I was sick of seeing snow and ice but went anyway. I'm not sure what Stephen wanted me to learn from my trip to the glaciers. I'm aware that the earth is warming up, but what can I do about it? I think I'm quite good when it comes to using energy. I'm always telling Suzanne to put a jumper or a coat on rather than the heating, or to walk to the supermarket rather than me driving her. As I'm bald I don't use hair dryers or hair straighteners like she does, so I'm much more energy-efficient. She also buys plastic products that aren't needed, like kitchen roll holders. A kitchen roll is quite happy stood by itself without any help from a holder. Also, I'm happy to wear the same socks a few days on the run if I haven't walked much. It's Suzanne again who takes them off me to clean. Then there's the kettle. When she's making my dinner, she'll ask me if I want a cup of tea with it, and I'll say yeah, so she boils the kettle then gets on with making the sausage and egg or whatever, then forgets about the tea and has to boil the water again when she's remembered. She says she can multi-task, but she can't. That kettle boils the water three or four times before it hits the tea bag. I tell you, Greenpeace shouldn't be chasing oil companies, it's Suzanne they need to sort out.

As the boat made its way towards the glaciers the director pointed out big chunks of ice that had broken away and were floating about like little pontoons. He was telling me that some of these glaciers are millions of years old, but I can't get excited about old ice. Ice is ice. You never see someone on *Antiques Roadshow* turning up with a block of ice for a reason. When things get into millions of years old I struggle to get my head round it. Ricky and his girlfriend bought me and Suzanne a fossil of some fish that is dated at 35 million years old. It's a bit older now, as that was two Christmases ago, but there it is just sat next to the Nintendo Wii.

As the journey went on, the amount of ice in the water increased. Big chunks the size of a Mini Cooper rolled and broke up as the waves hit them. The director wittered on about how if all the glaciers melted, coastlines could get flooded. I think this is why we are now advised to drink more water every day. They recommend at least two litres a day now, maybe this is to try and get rid of some of the water. Thinking about it, bottled water must solve some of this problem. When I was a kid there wasn't such a thing as bottled water, whereas now there's gallons of the stuff in warehouses ready to be sold, so that must help a bit. Like

I said, I think I do my bit towards saving the planet, but I think we'll always have to change and some stuff will die out. I've said it before about the dodo. They went extinct, and we carried on. Ricky moans at me, saying that everything has its job and its place, but I don't think it does. I recently read there is a koala bear that sleeps twenty-two hours a day! Now, unless it's running round doing stuff like a blue-arsed fly when it's awake for them two hours, I struggle to see what that is contributing to the world. It must be groggy for at least forty minutes when it first wakes up, which leaves an hour twenty, which it probably uses to make a fresh new bed for its lazy arse.

Like I said, I save energy 'cos I don't think it's good to waste anything. The standby light on the TV could go, as it's using energy. Instead of having adverts telling us to make sure it's off, why don't they just get rid of it? The light in the fridge could go (we don't have them in freezers), use by dates make people throw stuff away when it's perfectly fine, and we're encouraged to buy new instead of getting things repaired. I would also put a stop to Christmas crackers and Kinder eggs, as the amount of crap they bring into the world is unbelievable. That's all the stuff that ends up in landfill. It's funny to think how in Egypt they dig and find jewellery and vases made of gold from years gone by. When people in the future dig they'll find a plastic kitchen roll holder.

I was out on the deck of the boat when there was a massive cracking sound that was louder than thunder. It was caused by ice breaking off a huge glacier, probably caused by Suzanne boiling the kettle again. The boat pulled up, and two fellas who were on the boat started getting dressed into wet suits. They were there for my safety and they were experts on dealing with cold water. Normally, they're dealing with men deep down in freezing cold waters working on oil rigs, but today they were assisting me touching some ice. I was handed a red suit. They said this was the safest colour. Turns out I was expected to actually get in the freezing cold water to get even closer to the glacier. The red colour would stand out, if, for some reason, I drifted out. I put it on. They were right about me standing out against the white. I stood out like a boil on Snow White's pale face. It looked rubbish on me, as it wasn't tight fitting. The other fellas' wetsuits looked good, like the Cadbury's Milk Tray man or that bloke out of the *Bourne* films, but I had the look of a bloody jelly baby.

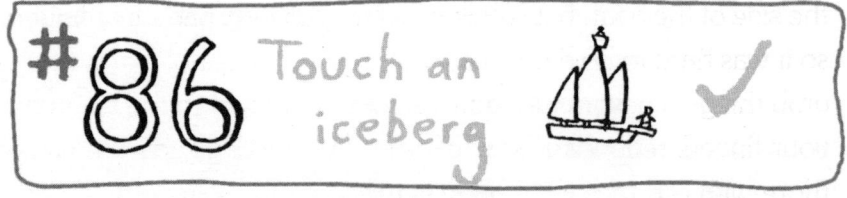

#86 Touch an iceberg ✓

I could see the glacier and was happy with that. Why touching the ice was going to make the experience any better I don't know. I can't believe anyone would really want to do that. I can't imagine if the question on *Family Fortunes* was 'What would you like to do before you die' that 'Touch some old ice' would be a top answer. Why? I really doubt any of the passengers on board the *Titanic* felt the need to reach out and rub their hand on the berg before they went under and drowned.

The two safety men asked me for a code word that I was to shout if I felt water getting into the suit, as it's so cold it could kill me. I went for a word that I used on my last lot of trips for the first series of *Idiot Abroad,* which was 'Congress Tart'. I picked that word, as there was no chance of me accidentally saying it, unless someone asked me what my favourite cake was. But that didn't seem the sort of chat the men in black would bring up. The two men said, 'Con what?!' 'Congress Tart,' I said. 'It's my favourite cake. Almond crust with jam inside.' They continued to struggle with the name, so the director said I should choose another word.

'Well, how about the word "help". That suggests I need help. That's what it was invented for.' In the end we used the word 'apple'. I know it sounds daft, but no matter what the word is, it will always sound ridiculous being yelled in an emergency. Seems pathetic that if I'd ended up drowning to death and Suzanne asked them if I had any message for her as I took my last breath, they would have to have said, 'No. He just said "apple".'

Once the safety word had been established, they took me out in their little boat and pushed me overboard. I tried to hold on to the side of the boat, but I couldn't as my suit only had three fingers, so it was hard to hold on to anything. I don't like not being able to grab things. I never wore mittens as a kid 'cos of this. They made your fingers redundant. I wonder if we would have evolved to do more with our toes if we hadn't started to cover them with shoes and socks. Oven gloves are also daft. When dealing with a heavy chicken in a roasting tin with hot juices floating about you need a proper grip. Why take your fingers out of action at such a critical time? I told Suzanne she should get welders' gloves, but she said they don't look nice hanging off the utensils rack in the kitchen.

The two men pushed me away from the boat. I floated around like a turd in a honey bucket for about ten minutes, as people on the boat watched. No one spoke. It wasn't enjoyable, and it wasn't a great spectator event either. All I could hear was the rain coming down on my wet suit. After a long ten minutes, one of the men in black said, 'Time's up.' Their work was done. I doubt this is the sort of work they had put in all the training hours for. They lifted me out. I would live another day. I just hope it will be more interesting than that one.

We headed over to a place called Kodiak where I got a call from Ricky. He told me that this is where I would be getting to see a whale. He said I wasn't going to be on a busy touristy boat with lots of other spectators, I would be on board a proper fishing boat. I met the small crew of four and off we went. Brian was the captain. He said he sees whales all the time, so everything seemed promising at this point. I think the fact that they are an endangered species made the trip more worthwhile. That might seem mean, but these things could be extinct in years to come. It's like making an effort to see your gran when she's ill. You don't know how much longer she's gonna be around, so you make the effort to see her. I also find the sea the most interesting place on the planet. The world is 70% water so, really, I think the planet is here more for sea life than it is for us. I always like to watch TV programmes about the oceans, especially if they're looking at the stuff that lives deep deep down in the dark. There are some odd things down there. The lantern fish is one of my favourites. It's a fish that has evolved with a type of light bulb hanging off the front of its head to help it find food in the darkness. I heard that a man had one of these in a fish tank and he read his newspaper by it at night. You can't get a more energy-efficient pet than that, can you? Suzanne is always saying she wants a fish, and I've always said they don't do much, but if we could get a few of them for in the lounge I'd be up for it. I'm always having to walk about switching off lamps that Suzanne leaves on. Starfish are also amazing. There is a type that if it loses an arm a new one will grow back, and, even weirder, a new starfish can grow from the detached arm. You can't get more alien. I don't know if you can eat them, but if you can, they could be an everlasting snack.

#30 Scuba dive at the Great Barrier Reef

Because I'm not very good at swimming (and after experiencing the shark diving) I don't think this one is for me. I'd be happier just going to the fishmonger's in Selfridges. They have a pretty impressive collection of fish. Okay, they're dead, I know, but this means you can get really close and even prod them without worrying about a shark coming along and taking your leg off.

Narwhals would also be good to see. These are whales that have a big horn sticking out the top of their head. It always puzzles me that the narwhal actually exists, but then people talk of the unicorn as this made-up mystical creature. All it is a horse with a horn. If you're gonna make up a mystical animal why not go for it a bit more than that. A bald-headed llama with wings and human feet would be weirder, and I just made that up there and then off the top of my head.

As well as them being endangered, the other reason I wanted to see a whale is that it's not something you can get to see in an aquarium. I went to see a washed-up one in Kent last year, but by the time I got there the council had shifted it. Typical. When I tried to get them to move an old kitchen for me they said I'd have to book a date, yet a whale gets washed up and they move it straight away. They said in the news you shouldn't go near Bruce – they named it Bruce for some reason – 'cos you can catch TB from it, but I had a jab for that when I was at school, so I thought it was worth the risk. There was another whale in London in the Thames. Apparently, it had got lost. Happens to me all the time, that. Whether you're using sat nav or sonar, London is still a tricky place to get around.

I stood looking out for whale tails, as the crew were getting on with their jobs on the fishing boat, until Brian suggested I put some overalls on so I could help out. I didn't want to seem rude. If it hadn't been for him, I wouldn't be seeing a whale at all. Eric then told me that they would be out fishing all night. This worried me, as seas tend to get more lively at night. I hadn't prepared myself for a night out at sea. I thought it would just be a few hours. I put on the overalls. They stunk of fish. Not just fish, but rotten fish. In fact, I just gagged again now, at the thought of how bad the smell was. Eric asked me to go into the bait room to help cut bait. I was given an octopus to cut up. I wouldn't have known it was an octopus if he hadn't told me. Because octopuses have no bones they had obviously shoved it into some type of cool box and flattened it into a pose that Houdini would have been impressed with. They then threw the 'flat-packed' octopus on the deck a few times to defrost and soften it a little. If Roz had been there she would have thought they were serving a starter.

It was my job to cut chunks the size of potatoes. Octopuses are really brainy. I was telling Eric about the octopus called Paul that was able to predict the winners of each game in the 2010 World Cup. I wasn't impressed with it knowing that England would lose though. I reckon a starfish knew that was gonna happen, and they ain't even got a brain. I managed to get through about five of its arms when I had to stop. The chugging of the engine, the smell of my overall and the sight of fish being cut up started to affect me, so I went outside to try and get some fresh air, but they asked me to carry on with my work and kept shouting 'Chop chop'. I made my way through the never-ending supply of arms. Knowledge can sometimes make things worse. Ricky told me ages ago that the testicles of an octopus are in its head. I said, 'Course they are. Where else would they be? They're just a head with legs.' That fact stuck with me, so when they asked me to chop the head up and gunk oozed out, that was it. I couldn't do anymore. I went and sat outside on the deck and heaved.

The director came to talk to me, but not for long as the smell from my clothes was too much for him and he walked off to be sick. Freddie the sound man offered me some pill that he said I should put against my gum to help fight the seasickness, but it didn't seem to work. Richard the director said I should try going inside the nicer area away from the bait. Thinking about it now, he probably said that because he wanted to escape it, too.

I tried to take my mind off the sickness by watching one of the DVDs they had onboard. I opted for *King Kong*, but because I felt so ill I couldn't stand for long enough to get the disc in the machine and select the correct channel on the TV. I really wanted to get off, but I was trapped. That was the worst thing about this experience – not being able to escape. I made my way to the very front of the boat. There was hardly any space there for other people, which was good, plus it was the place furthest away from the fish smell. I just wanted to escape and be on my own. I sat breathing deeply with my eyes closed. Brian the captain shouted that there was a sperm whale ahead of us. I looked and just caught the tail as it went back into the water after breaching. I thought we would be getting up close, but that never happened. As I sat still with my eyes closed I could hear the moaning sound from the whale. People say the moan is a whale communicating, but I'm not convinced. Maybe, even though they went from being land mammals over 50 million years ago, they still ain't got used to seasickness and that's why they're moaning.

Richard the director had gone inside to try and sleep off his sickness. The pill still wasn't helping me feel any better, so I tried the Fisherman's Friend sweets I'd brought along with me. They did no good whatsoever, either. I don't know why they're aimed at fishermen if they don't help against seasickness. It's not even as if the fishermen market is a massive market. They may as well make sweets aimed at lollipop men.

I was sat in the darkness now. It was freezing, but at least everyone left me alone. Eventually, Brian came out to the front and said he was going to head back to let us get off, now that I had seen a whale, which was decent of him. I think the rest of the film crew were also glad we didn't have to stick it out for much longer. We got back to the harbour around 1.30 a.m. I was so happy to be back on land.

Me and Richard were starving, as we hadn't eaten since lunchtime, so we thought we would make use of the 24-hour McDonald's next to our motel. The idea of a quarter pounder, fries and an apple pie was just what was needed. The front door was locked, so we walked to the drive-through counter.

DRIVE-THROUGH GUY: Sorry, this is a drive-through. You have to be in a car.

KARL: We haven't got a car.

DRIVE-THROUGH GUY: Sorry, it's company policy. If you're not in a car, I cannot serve you.

KARL: But we're starving.

DRIVE-THROUGH GUY: Sorry, sir. I could be fired for serving you.

KARL: But who will know? It's two a.m. How will your boss know?!

DRIVE-THROUGH GUY: Security cameras, sir. We're being monitored.

No wonder the world's ice is melting when we're forced to use a car instead of our legs.

CHAPTER FIVE

#16 Come face to face ✔ with mountain gorillas in their natural habitat

RICKY: Look at this one – come face to face with mountain gorillas in their natural habitat. What a privilege that is. One of the most endangered species on the planet, one of our closest living relatives. Ninety-eight per cent genetically identical to a human, a gorilla.

STEPHEN: Even more so than you.

KARL: They are close to us, but they don't follow the same rules. They say they're 98% human, but if I'm there and it rips my head off, the human rules don't apply. They'd get away with it.

RICKY: Well, they are about six times stronger than the average man.

KARL: Well, there you go. I wouldn't want to come face to face with that. Although I have seen one in a zoo and it did impress me.

RICKY: Why did it impress you so much?

KARL: They're just very human in the eyes. I watched one in a zoo for ages once.

RICKY: I think it would be a meeting of minds your coming face to face with a mountain gorilla in its natural habitat. Both naked amongst the foliage.

KARL: I'm in the nude again, am I? What is it with you and being nude?

RICKY: They don't like clothes, and you're hairy all over, and I think you'd have more of a chance of them seeing the similarities.

KARL: I'm not wandering around in the woods looking for apes in the nude. There'd be a point when the woods would end and suddenly one would creep out and you'd get me legging it out of there nude.

(*Ricky laughs*)

'What have you bought that shite for?!' I heard my dad say while I was visiting. This is always my dad's reaction when my mam has been out shopping.

'You said you wanted a smart address book. You can't get a smarter one than that, it's wearing a tie.'

'Yeah, but I meant a leatherbound one, you silly sod.'

My mam had bought an address book that looked like a suit and tie from a charity shop. These are the only shops she tends to go into these days. Once a week my dad takes her into town, and she goes on the hunt for tat in Oxfam, the Heart Foundation shop, the RSPCA and Barnardo's.

'Why can't you find some decent stuff that's actually worth something?' my dad said. 'Like the people on *Antiques Roadshow*. Put it in the bin!'

She's said that when she dies she wants all the stuff she's bought over the years to be buried with her, like some kind of Egyptian king. Except with that much garbage being put in the hole I don't know if it would be a classed as a funeral or landfill. My dad probably thinks he doesn't do much towards helping charities, but he does. He's the one who gives me mam the money to spend in Oxfam and ends up taking the crap she's bought back to Oxfam, which is then resold (sometimes to me mam). He's running one big charity cycle single-handed.

I mention these acts of charity, as this is what Ricky and Stephen want to get me involved in while I'm in Africa. The gorillas I would be seeing were in Uganda, but my first stop was South Africa.

STEPHEN: Karl, things to do before you die can include helping others for once in your life.

KARL: Hang on a minute. What do you mean, 'for once in my life'? I do loads of charity stuff.

STEPHEN: Right.

KARL: If I showed you my bank statement you'd think it belonged to Mother Teresa.

I signed up to a lot of these charities years ago when I lived on a high street. There were so many charity collectors on it I'm sure road accidents went up, as people had to keep crossing the busy road to avoid them. I should have started a campaign to raise money for the much-needed zebra crossings. I'd nip out on what should've been a quick errand to get a pint of milk and end up back home twenty-five minutes later with the milk I went out for and a copy of a direct debit I'd set up to help save a limping snow leopard. I think this is why ordering food online and getting it delivered has become so popular. It's a way of avoiding being hassled by people with clipboards. And once these charities have got your number they don't leave you alone. Whenever there's a disaster in the world I avoid answering my phone, as I seem to be the first person they get on to for help. If Red Cross ever went on *Who Wants to Be a Millionaire?* I'm pretty sure they'd have me as their Phone a Friend.

#93 Swim the English Channel ✗

Primrose Hill or Hampstead used to be the place to go celebrity spotting, but these days they tend to hang out in the English channel raising money for charity. You can't turn the local news on these days without hearing about someone off TV swimming across the channel. No wonder immigrant numbers are going up. It's obvious how easy it is to swim over to our country when chubby celebs are doing it for fun.

The problem is, it's hard to know what to give your money to. I read that money was raised for an elephant that needed a pair of slippers for its sore feet, and another story was about a man in America who had testicles so big he almost played keepie uppie with them as he walked down the street. They were so swollen they weighed seven stone, but he couldn't afford to get them sorted, and yet there's an elephant wandering about wearing slippers!

#81 Do some charity work ✓

Once we had arrived in South Africa, we headed for a place called Diepsloot, one of Jo'burg's most densely populated and poor townships. As I stood by the road waiting for a man called Sepo to pick me up, there were shacks as far as my eyes could see. They were built like bonfires, with any materials they could get their hands on used to put a roof over their head. I wasn't too shocked at the sight, as it's one we're shown on TV again and again. I was ready for it, but what was different from the TV coverage of places like this was that not everybody was ill and fed-up. The mood was similar to the estate I grew up on, where the people knew they hadn't had much luck in life but were just getting on with it. The atmosphere was surprisingly upbeat and had more of a community feel than the street I live on.

I met Sepo, a man who helps raise awareness and money for the townships. He gave me a handshake that was so long and complicated I'd seen less effort go into a dance routine on *Strictly Come Dancing.* If this is how everyone shakes hands, no wonder it's taking so long to get stuff sorted out here.

I got in his car and we started talking.

KARL: How many people are in this area?

SEPO: About 600,000.

KARL: 600,000!

SEPO: Yes. Statistics will tell you we have 300,000, but we have proven that it is not 300,000. We did a walkabout. We did some research. It's more than that. And it only has two clinics.

It would be a nightmare to try and do a proper count of all the shacks. Everything is crammed in so tightly and there's no proper numbering system. Sepo told me that once they think they've finished counting one area more people have moved in, so it's an impossible task.

Sepo said the first stop would be at a school where I would get to teach some local kids. The thought of it terrified me. I didn't know what I could offer them. I haven't really got a specialist subject. I was rubbish at school. I think I learned more from the questions I heard on *Bullseye* every Sunday night than I learned all week at school. Learning needs to be done in an interesting way for me to take it in. I think kids learn too much these days, and the basic things like maths and spelling get left behind. Basic arithmetic is something I never learned, as they were too keen trying to teach us algebra and Venn diagrams, and how to ask for a fish in French – never going to be useful as I'm not keen on eating fish.

Again, I did more arithmetic adding up the scores from the players on *Bullseye*. If it hadn't been for *Bullseye* I don't know where I'd be. It wasn't that I didn't try in school, my brain just couldn't take it in, and so I couldn't enjoy learning and then I got left behind. Most lessons were spent correcting all my mistakes with bottles of Tipp-Ex. I found one of my schoolbooks years after I'd left and the pages were as stiff and brittle as a poppadom 'cos of all the Tipp-Ex. The teachers didn't always know how bad I was at things, as a lot of the marking was done by handing your book to some other kid to scan over as the teacher read out the answers. Thinking about it, it was treated more like a pub quiz.

We passed a couple of BMX bikes on the way into the school, so I said I could teach them a few tricks I used to do on mine – a type of PE lesson is what I was thinking – but Sepo said I had more to offer than that. I knew I didn't. Ben, a director working with Luke, suggested that I tell them what I had learned from my travels around the world. But most of these kids would never leave this area. They needed useful skills. Turning up and telling them that in China they don't have doors on their public toilets would hardly shock them. Some of these kids didn't have front doors on their homes.

Sepo said the kids had already picked a topic for me and wanted to hear me speak to them about Risk. I didn't know where to start. I didn't have a clue about the risks kids in this area would have to watch out for. I doubt the Green Cross Code would be that important here.

I entered the classroom. There were around ten kids waiting for my arrival, which didn't seem like many to me. My school classroom was packed. I think I went to the only school where the classrooms had standing room only.

I went in hard at the beginning so the kids wouldn't be cheeky to me.

KARL: Alright. Stop messing about at the back. Right, will someone shut the door, please? Because that's very risky, leaving the door open. Right. Good. So, you want to know about risk. Does anyone here have any risks in their life?

CHILD: Can I try?

KARL: Yeah. Course you can.

CHILD: Some teenagers fall pregnant. That's a risk.

KARL: How old are you to be worrying about that?

CHILD: Thirteen.

KARL: Thirteen! I didn't worry about having kids when I was thirteen! Honestly, I thought I was coming in to talk about Humpty Dumpty. Do they honestly want to know about risk?

SEPO: Yes.

KARL: In sex? Do you understand that? That's what we're talking about here.

CHILDREN: Yes.

I tried to remember what I was taught in school about sex education, but I could only remember the whole class sat around a small portable telly as a worn-out VHS played footage of some really hairy nude people having it away. It didn't really cover any risks as such.

KARL: Right, let's see. Does everybody in here want kids when they're older?

CHILDREN: Yes.

KARL: Errmm, I haven't got kids, just so you know. I'm 38 now, haven't got any kids.

CHILD: So why do you not have kids when you are old?

KARL: I'm not that old! But I haven't had kids because they're trouble. I was a kid once. And I was hard work. You can't just say, 'Oh, I'm gonna have a kid.' It's not like a dog that you can sort of kick out when you've had enough. You've got to look after that kid for years.

CHILD: It means you don't have a wife!

KARL: No, I have. I've got a girlfriend, not a wife. Girlfriend, for seventeen years.

(*Children gasp*)

CHILD: That's too young.

KARL: No, no, she's not seventeen. I've been with her for seventeen years.

CHILDREN: Oooh. (*Laughter*)

KARL: Right. I sort of said to her, if you want kids, I'll let you have a kid, but I don't want the hassle of it. Because someone in the relationship has to look after that child, don't they? Either the dad or the mum. And I'm busy, working.

CHILD: With what?

KARL: Well, look at me. I'm in Africa. If I had a kid at home living in London, who's gonna look after it? A kid needs feeding, shoes on its feet. So, I've got work. This is my job.

CHILD: You have a wife that's going to sit with him at home.

KARL: No, honestly, you don't know what she's like. At the beginning she'd say she'd be happy to look after it, but a year in, she'd say, 'I want you to do it. I'm sick of it.' That's what she's like.

CHILD: She can beat you.

KARL: She can beat me?

CHILD: Yeah, because of when you tell her that she must stay with the baby.

KARL: She won't listen. It's all very well sat there. You don't know what she's like. She'd go, 'No, you made this, as well. I'm going out with my friends. You stay and look after it.'

And I'd be there with a baby that I didn't want. It's not good, is it? So, that's what I'm saying. Don't rush into having kids. It can be a tough thing to take on, you know? It's one of the toughest things in life, having a baby. People say moving house is tough. It's nowt compared to having a kid. So, think about it. Do you all have brothers and sisters?

CHILDREN: Yes.

KARL: Most people do. See, it's normal here to have big families. At home it's very expensive. If you need a two-bedroom house in London it costs, like, half a million.

CHILD: You can stay in the small house.

KARL: I don't want to. I've worked hard. I don't see why I have to live in a small house to have a kid.

CHILD: Live in a shack. You can stay in there. Many people can stay in the shack.

KARL: I know, but don't you want more than that? Are you happy just to grow up and stay in a shack in Diepsloot?

CHILD: No, but you can make a house after you have your child.

KARL: It's all the wrong way round, though. Get a job first. Do you all have an idea what you wanna do when you're older?

CHILDREN: Yes.

KARL: You all have a rough idea? Concentrate on that. Focus on getting a job. Get that job, meet a woman, meet a man. Have a good time for a bit . . . but be careful. Wear a condom.

And then once you've got the house together, and you've been with them for a while and you know they're the one for you, maybe leave the condom off. Have a little kid. Don't rush into it, though. Right, we've covered that. What else do you wanna know? What else can I tell you about? Tell you another thing: before you have a kid, learn to drive. That's useful.

CHILD: We will have a kid before we will learn to drive.

KARL: No! Why are you in a rush to have a kid? Are you not listening to me? What's wrong with you? How old are you?

CHILD: Thirteen.

KARL: If you're thirteen, you don't wanna have a kid until you're twenty-one, twenty-two. No rush, just slow down!

CHILD: Who cut your hair? You?

KARL: No, it's not cut. This isn't a style. I'm bald!

I could see they were getting a bit bored so I asked if they wanted to play on the BMX bikes I'd seen on the way in. This news perked them up. I taught them a few tricks I used to do when I was their age. I thought I gave them some good advice. I suppose if even one or two take any notice maybe I've helped them. I could still do the tricks I used to do twenty-odd years ago, so it goes to show my brain remembers how to do things I enjoy doing.

Sepo said my day wasn't over. My help was needed to build a new home for a local resident. We picked up a new £500 shelter that Ricky and Stephen had paid for, and now they wanted me to build it. We drove deeper into the township. The deeper we drove, the tighter and rougher the roads seem to get and the closer together the shacks became. The fella I was building the shack for was ill, but Sepo said he was on the mend. He lived in a single-roomed shack, eight by twelve feet, with a woman and three young kids. They had already removed their few possessions – a bed, a couple of cupboards, blankets and plates – so that three builders who were donating their time and I could get to work demolishing the old shack. It was held together with only an odd rusty nail here and there. It wasn't built too long ago. I knew this as I found a copy of the *Sun* from 2008. Cheryl Cole's problems with her husband Ashley was the main story. Odd to imagine people here reading that. The ill fella was lying on his mattress at the side as we were pounding with hammers on the corrugated sheets. I can't imagine anything worse. Being ill isn't good as it is, never mind having builders in knocking your home down. When you're not well you just want to be left alone. I can't be doing with visitors when I'm in hospital. It's annoying how people visit you more at the time you're feeling your worst.

As we put up the new structure a few English girls came to help knock in a few nails. This is the part that didn't seem right to me. I know they were only trying to help, but more nails were getting used as they couldn't hit them in straight, and the job was taking longer. This is probably why the last hut didn't last very long. It reminded me of one of those DIY shows where someone's husband has lost a leg and not been able to finish off the conservatory on his house, but then a film crew turns up and suddenly neighbours they don't even know come and help so they can get on the telly. The actual finish of the work is no good 'cos it's been done by amateurs.

I didn't feel that good about what we'd done. Yes, it was a shiny new shack, but it was built on the same spot as the old one, right next to a river of sewage and rubbish.

As we were leaving I asked what would happen to the old destroyed shack that was left by the road. Sepo told me the bits would be used by other people who needed to make a shack. So, the problem wasn't getting smaller. If anything it was getting bigger. I think the lesson I gave to the kids, as useless as it seemed at the time, might have been more useful than building that new hut.

I told Sepo my thoughts, and he said he wanted to take me to Soweto, a township that has improved a lot since money was ploughed into the place. Old shacks have been replaced with brick-built homes with gardens and drainage. I remember thinking, Hold on, brick-built and drainage is good, but gardens? I ain't even got one of them. They'll have hot tubs next.

He pulled up at two huge cooling towers, 90 metres tall, which had been painted with loads of colourful images that represented Africa. It had been done back in 2010 in time for the World Cup. Seven local artists painted the murals over 75 days using 3,500 litres of paint. He said it was now used as an entertainment venue. It was a good idea. I grew up in a house with a bedroom that faced a chemical plant and the cooling towers are normally big grey ugly-looking things. I used to sit by my window as a young kid waiting to see if any UFOs would land there, as I imagined it would be the sort of place that aliens would want to explore.

I got out of the car and was about to ask what sort of entertainment took place here when I heard a scream. I looked up to see someone falling from a platform that hung in between the two towers. Bloody bungee jumping again.

I told Sepo there was no way I'd be doing it, that I'd tried it before in New Zealand and it wasn't for me, but he said it was Ricky's idea and I would get a great view of Soweto from up there. We got in a cage that ran up the side of the tower. I called Ricky to ask him what he was playing at sending me to a bungee jump again.

RICKY: How's it going?

KARL: I'm a bit pissed off 'cos I'm on the edge of a bungee jump again.

RICKY: Yeah, I think you'll feel really good about yourself if you have one more go and do it this time.

KARL: But I told you last time, when I was in New Zealand, I don't want to do it. It's not part of my Bucket List.

RICKY: I know, but it's weird you don't want to do it. I mean, you wouldn't admit that you were scared. It's OK to be scared, but I think deep down you wished you'd have done it. Like all fears and phobias we wish we could overcome them, but to do that you have to face them. All the things I've regretted in my life are those I've not done, not tried my hardest at. I just think you'll feel great if you jump.

KARL: Yeah, but when I didn't do it last time and I got back to the hotel, I had no regrets. It's just not me. You know what I'm like. You've known me for ages. I don't like getting a buzz, and that's what this is. It's pointless. I don't want to do it. There's no reason for me to do this.

RICKY: Okay then, what if I gave you a reason to jump? I'll buy a hut for someone if you jump. How much are they?

KARL: They're £500. I'd rather pay the £500 out of my own money than do this jump. I'm being honest, if that's what it comes down to, if that's what all this is about . . . getting another hut.

RICKY: £500 not to jump.

KARL: Definitely. I'd much rather do that.

RICKY: Okay, I'll raise you. I'll buy two huts if you jump.

KARL: I'll pay the grand. Let's leave it there. Two huts, they'll be over the moon with that. Let's leave it there.

RICKY: No. Three. Three huts.

KARL: Fuck's sake.

RICKY: And that third would make someone's life so different and so much better if you jumped.

KARL: You're making me look a right twat here.

RICKY: No, I'm not.

KARL: You are, 'cos I don't wanna do it, and I've been in the huts and helped build one. I was teaching kids about sex and bunny hops . . . I really don't wanna do this. I'll pay it.

RICKY: You'll pay £1,500?

KARL: Yes.

RICKY: Not to jump?

KARL: Yeah, if that's what this is about, if this is about raising more money, I'll do that.

RICKY: I'll tell you what, mate, this is my last offer, okay?

> I'll buy five huts if you just jump. Then you've done it, you've raised the money, you've bought five huts, basically, five huts for your new friends, and you'll feel good about yourself, and you've made me look a twat. Think about it . . .

I did think about it. I had exactly the same feeling I'd had when I'd stood on the edge of the bungee platform in New Zealand. Luke the director really wanted me to do it this time, and so did Sepo. I was willing to pay for the five huts myself but was more worried that Ricky would keep bidding me up to the point where I would have no choice but to do it. While I was thinking it through, Luke said he would take my place, as it had cost us to go up there so someone may as well do the jump. This was when I came up with a plan. I said he might as well wear my hat, so it could be filmed to look like me doing the bungee, and then I could call Ricky, say, 'That's it. I've done it,' and then I'd pay for the huts when I get back home. Job done.

    I called Ricky back.

> RICKY: How was it?
>
> KARL: Mental. Proper mental, it was.
>
> RICKY: Did you do it? You jumped?
>
> KARL: Yeah. I had to, didn't I?
>
> RICKY: How high was it?
>
> KARL: Well, I mean, it's weird because when you're falling it's hard to tell. I don't know. It's like you go blank, like it's going

on forever. But, it was off a cooling tower, so you know how high they are. But, it was kind of different because I knew I was doing it for some good. It pushed me a bit.

RICKY: Excellent. Well done.

KARL: Never again though.

RICKY: Well done. No, you don't need to do it ever again. You did it. You know what it's like. They're going to get five huts, so what do I have to do?

KARL: Well, we'll sort it out when I get back.

RICKY: Okay. Wow. Well done. Were you scared though? You can admit it now you've done it. Were you scared?

KARL: No, not really. Just thought, Right, is the tape rolling? I'm doing this. Bang. Done. Bosh. Get those five huts. Let's get these people happy here.

RICKY: Brilliant. Well, I'm proud of you. Well done.

He was well done. Ricky was happy, I was happy, and Sepo was happy, as he was getting the five huts paid for. It was a lie but not a bad lie.

As a treat Ricky said he'd arranged a little caravan for me to use that would come in handy as I drove across Africa. It was little, but caravans are good at making the most out of the space. We had one when I was growing up that could sleep loads of people even though it only had two bedrooms. The sofas flipped out to make single beds, and the table dropped down to make a small double. I think they even sold the oven as a place for a baby or a dwarf to get their head down.

Seeing as Ricky and Stephen wanted me to see and get involved in acts of charity while in South Africa, it gave me a good enough reason to go and see a couple who had taken in a wild animal they had found. I pulled up to their home to see a sign on the gates warning me of the animal I had come to see. Toni and Shirley met me and took me down to the bottom of their garden by the river where Jessica the hippo was keeping cool in the river. Her ears, eyes and nostrils were the only give-away signs that she was there. Shirley called her over in Afrikaans.

SHIRLEY: She's not in captivity at all.

TONI: She was orphaned on 11 March 2000. One evening, there was a flood and she was shipped away. Fortunately, I found her in front of the house, and found her before the crocodiles. There are many crocs. The authorities have been saying to me her whole life, 'Did you raise her?' No, I saved her.

KARL: So, without you, she would be dead, then?

SHIRLEY: She would've been taken by a croc, definitely.

KENNY: Yes, we've lost thirteen dogs to crocs.

Shirley was making Jess a drink of tea and asked if I'd like one. While I went for a normal English Breakfast tea, Jess had some fancy redwood tea from a two-litre plastic bottle. Strange to think a hippo had fancier tastes than me.

It was hard to imagine that hippos are classed as one of the most dangerous animals on the planet as I stroked her on the head and gave her a drink. It didn't even touch the sides. It just went down her throat like I was like pouring water down a grid.

Jessica was now eleven years old and hippos have been known to reach the age of forty.

SHIRLEY: I'm her mother.

KARL: Is that how you feel?

SHIRLEY: I am her mother. Definitely. After I miscarried I actually felt that nothing good could happen to me in my life, and while I was pregnant Jessica actually licked my belly. And after I miscarried I went through a traumatic experience in my life where I got addicted to tablets and alcohol very badly. And I slept with her every night, and when she became interwoven with my life, and licked my belly and accepted me, I could actually kick the habit. So, Jessica cured me.

KARL: So, you saved her and she saved you.

SHIRLEY: Yeah.

I went into their home through a doorway that had a big steel security gate fitted to the doorframe. But unlike the bars at a zoo it wasn't designed to keep an animal in, it was to keep Jess from roaming into the house when she pleased. Shirley called to Jess. She made her way out of the river and up the steep garden and into the front room. It was at that point I first got a proper idea of the size of her. It was a mad sight, like something in a cartoon or dream. And to think I'd asked if I should take my shoes off when I entered a few moments earlier! They didn't have many ornaments dotted around, but then this wasn't really a home for Toni and Shirley to live in, it was more hippo-friendly. I doubt any insurance company would cover the costs of breakages if it was reported that a pet hippo knocked over a Ming vase. But this is the problem with having such a pet. It would take over your life. It's bad enough when you have a dog or a cat and you have to get someone to look after it when you go on holiday.

When I was about twelve I had a pet magpie that was fun to have at first. I would throw small glittery things like Coke can rings and rolled-up tin foil and it would fetch them. On a few occasions it came flying into my bedroom window with bits of jewellery that it must have either found or nabbed from going into other open windows. I would ride around the estate on my bike with Maggie (the magpie) sat on my handlebars or shoulder, and it would hang around the school so I could play with it in the breaks. But after a while it seemed to get quite aggressive. It got to the point that I'd look out of the windows before leaving the house to check it wasn't around. I'd think the coast was clear, but it seemed to know the sound of our door opening and it would swoop down and peck at my head like a scene from Alfred Hitchcock's *The Birds*. The final straw was when it popped the tyres on my Raleigh Grifter, so I rode to the water park with it and then sneaked off as it was trying to steal some bait off some fishermen. I never saw it again.

Shirley told me Jessica hangs about with other hippos downstream for a few hours a day but she always returns. She sometimes brings her pals back, but they aren't allowed in the house. It reminded me of a childhood mate who lived in a flat on our estate. His mam was obsessed with keeping the place spick and span and wouldn't let me in, so I used to have to stand outside his bedroom window, and he'd have to stretch the joystick over so I could play him on his computer. It was just as well he lived on the ground floor.

Shirley gave me a carrier bag full of green beans and got me to stand behind the worktop in the kitchen as she called Jessica over. She opened her mouth 160 degrees as I threw in handfuls of beans. She never really chewed or tasted the food, just swallowed them as if they were hundreds and thousands and then flipped open her big mouth quickly like a lid on a pedal bin for more. I suppose it's a good way of getting rid of scraps.

While we had been feeding her, Toni had dragged in a mattress off the porch and put it in front of the plasma TV. Shirley announced it was time for her massage. Jessica did a five-point turn to get out of the kitchen area and headed for the mattress. Once she was lying down she looked even wider. It's funny to think Suzanne won't let me have a 50-inch telly 'cos she says it would take over the room!

Shirley got out some cream and all three of us sat round Jessica and rubbed it into her back. She was really relaxed and nodded off as we massaged her. It was similar to polishing a car. Wax on, wax off. The skin felt like hard rubber. I suppose that is one good thing about hippos as a pet. No hairs on the sofa. Just a few days ago I was building a hut for a family of five. Now, here was a hippo in a house getting a back rub while nodding off watching the telly.

Later that day Stephen called to explain that I'd be visiting the Ndebele tribe as the next stage of my trip:

STEPHEN: The Ndebele tribe, they're a disappearing culture. They're fading out, so they're quite keen to pass on their heritage to people like yourself. You've already got your own kitchen in your caravan, so I thought it might be nice if you pop by and cook something up for the king of the tribe using the caravan we sorted for you. More sharing, you see.

I don't really do cooking. Luckily, Suzanne likes to do it and I like eating, so we work well together. If I have to sort myself out it's never anything nice, it's just something to stop my hunger. Suzanne makes really nice butties with loads of extra bits like tomato, cucumber and lettuce, but I never think about putting those layers on. Once I've put the cheese on it's ready to eat as far as I'm concerned.

I stopped off at a Spar supermarket and bought some bits and pieces that were going to be easy to cook using the basic cooking implements I had in the caravan. At home I suppose you'd have to ask if anyone had any allergies to anything, but I don't think people in this part of the world worry about things like that. I've never seen Lenny Henry turn up to a poor town in Africa on Comic Relief and someone saying, 'Thanks for the bread but I have a wheat allergy.'

#79 Have Lunch with the Queen of England

I like to have a pasty with some bread and a cup of tea, but I can't see the Queen being up for that. Plus, the Queen wouldn't want to be wasting time with me either. It's a right rubbish gig she's got. I'm glad I wasn't born into the royal family. Your life isn't your own. I had a mate who had no choice but to be a butcher 'cos his dad wanted him to carry on the business. The Queen's job is the same in a way.

I can't be bothered going to weddings of people I know 'cos I'd have to chat to long-lost cousins. The Queen has to speak to total strangers she's never going to meet again. Always being the centre of attention must be annoying for her, as well. Never being able to be left alone – it must be like sitting in the front row at a comedy club.

I know someone who got an invite to some lunch do with the Queen. They said some fella called the Master of the Household tells you the rules on how to speak to her. Apparently she is given biographical notes about you so she can lead the conversation. I just hope that if I was ever invited they don't use Wikipedia, as someone once asked me if it was true that I knocked an old woman off a bike and killed her as they'd read it on there.

I bought some nibbles for a starter. Crisps, biscuits, two apples and some sour wiggly worm sweets. For the main I went for the English classic of cheese on toast with beans, with chocolate cake and custard for pudding.

I got to the Ndebele village. They're known for their brightly coloured buildings, which are painted by the Ndebele women by hand with no help from tools or rulers. The designs are complicated triangles, diamonds and zigzag patterns that would give a chameleon a headache. The bungalow-type homes are painted in a variety of reds, yellows, blues and greens with a thick black outline. They look like a game of Tetris.

Stephen told me it was an art form that was dying out. Because it's not done to be sold, it's more of an opportunity for the wives to express themselves with the choice of colours and designs and set themselves apart from their neighbours.

The artist I met was a woman called Francina who is famous for her work. She was sat with a few friends and family on the floor in the shade. Some of them wore clothes that were as bright as the walls they were leaning on. Francina wore metal rings round her neck.

KARL: How many have you got? One, two, three, four, five, six, seven, eight, nine, ten, eleven, twelve rings round your neck!

NATIVE WOMAN: These ones are the original rings.

KARL: You can't take them off?

NATIVE WOMAN: You sleep with them, you bathe with them, you work with them.

KARL: Oh, I couldn't be doing with that. Why can't you take them off?

NATIVE WOMAN: It's our tradition.

KARL: So is it like a wedding ring?

TRANSLATOR: Exactly.

NATIVE WOMAN: You are supposed to wait until your husband dies, or you yourself die.

The story goes that the rings show their faithfulness to their husband. I don't know why so many rings though. Her neck was like a curtain rail. I didn't like wearing polo neck jumpers when they were trendy as they'd give me headaches, so I couldn't put up with this. The only positive I could think of is that she would never be strangled by anyone.

The younger woman had something different round her neck. It wasn't tight to the skin or made of metal. It was a plastic temporary one that looked like the big rubber seal you get on a washing machine. Her version was like the baggy loose-fit compared to Francina's skin-tight rings.

KARL: So, if that means you're married, what does that one mean? (*Points to softer big ring around another person's neck*)

NATIVE WOMAN: Married also.

KARL: That looks a lot comfier than the brass ones.

NATIVE WOMAN: Nowadays you can't find that type in any shops.

KARL: You can't find these metal ones anymore? That's because she's wearing them all! You have them on your arms, as well. You must have to use a lot of muscle to walk around with all that. Can I lift your arm up?

NATIVE WOMAN: Yes.

KARL: That is heavy. Like the weight of a bag of sugar. Jesus, you've got them on your legs, as well. What does that mean?

NATIVE WOMAN: Married.

KARL: I know she's married from looking at her neck!

The others had plastic covers on their legs that gave the impression they were wearing rings but without the weight. It wasn't easy for them to get up from the seated position as the rings got in the way of their knees bending.

61 Get a tattoo and/or a piercing

I kind of understand tribes having tattoos – it's their way of letting other tribe members know of their position. But we've got business cards, so I don't think it's really necessary over here. When I was growing up I used to see a lot of my uncle, Tattoo Stan. He used his body like it was a post-it note – little doodles all over it. But the trouble was, he did them all himself, so he used to have good tattoos on his left arm but crap ones on the right as he was right handed.

The king that I was waiting to cook for was running late, so they said they wanted to paint my caravan. I explained it wasn't mine and that I had hired it, but they insisted and said it would easily wash off. They wandered over with a bucket filled with what looked like mud, but it turned out to be cow shit. I was already £2,500 out of pocket from the bungee, and suddenly I had caravan vandalism to pay for too. They said it would be fine. Francina stuck her hand in and started spreading it on the caravan. It was nothing like the art they had on their walls. It was like some kind of dirty protest. Luke said I shouldn't cause any upset, as using diluted cow dung was the traditional way of finger painting. Back in the day it acted as a natural bug repellent. I suppose if you have shit all over the outside of your house it keeps the flies out the kitchen.

I stuck my hand in and copied the squiggly lines in a triangular shape that Francina had done. It took me a lot longer than it took her. The phrase 'She ran rings around me' has never been more apt.

The King still hadn't turned up. Just as well, to be honest, as it gave me time to get all the cow shit from under me nails. I then put some crisps, shortbread biscuits, wiggly worms and a couple of apples on a plate. At this point he turned up. So I popped the beans on to warm up.

I went to greet him and put my arm out to shake his hand, but he just nodded his head in a way that suggested I was not allowed to shake his hand.

#87 Shake hands with the Pope X

Because I'm not religious it wouldn't mean anything to me. I think I'd get more joy if I could arm wrestle him.

He wasn't your bog-standard-looking king. He was wearing the skin of what looked like a cheetah and carrying a shield that was covered in lionskin.

KARL: Busy day?

KING: Yeah, busy.

KARL: Alright, fair enough. Well, I don't know, errmm, I'm just preparing your food.

KING: Yes.

KARL: How many people are you eating with tonight?

KING: I think there is only . . . this people.

KARL: All them are eating as well?

KING: Yes.

(Four tribe members walk over to the King, and walk in a line back with the King)

KARL: One, two, three, four, five, six and yourself? Seven?

(Tribe member speaks native language)

KARL: Okay.

(Tribe member speaks native language)

KARL: Okay. You go and do what you've gotta do. One, two, three, four, five, six, seven, eight.

(Tribe member speaks native language)

KARL: It's all of 'em, Luke. It's all of 'em. Eight in total.

LUKE: You're supposed to follow here. It's tradition.

I joined in and danced but I couldn't enjoy it. Dancing isn't something you can do when you're fed up. It's the same with whistling. I then remembered I had left the beans on the gas, so I did a moonwalk back to the caravan.

That was when I realised I had no toaster. I had to cook the bread directly on top of the flame on the hob. I tried a bit, as all chefs should. I could taste the gas, but seeing as they'd never had this before I didn't think it would be a problem. It would be like me eating stale hummus, I wouldn't have a clue. I was struggling to open the cheese slices when they flew everywhere, the beans were bubbling and the toast was burning.

I'm not that good at multi-tasking. Multi-tasking to me is sending emails while sat on the toilet.

I asked Luke to take over the plate of starters. He said he wasn't taking it over as he was embarrassed by it. 'You created it, you should take it,' he said. I took the crisps, wiggly worms, shortbread biscuits and the two apples over. They all tucked in. Luke wanted me to explain the dish, but I said they should just be left to eat it. I hate it when chefs come up and start telling me where the chicken lived and what its name was. Just let me eat it.

KING: Meat?

KARL: Meat?

KING: Yes. Beef.

KARL: I couldn't cook. There's not the facilities for meat.

KING: For meat.

KARL: Why? You eat meat a lot?

KING: Yes. You must put the meat in. Man always eat the meat.

KARL: Oh, right.

KING: We're strong and big.

KARL: It's just in England where I'm from . . .

KING: Yes.

KARL: This is a sort of popular dish.

KING: Yes.

KARL: We do eat meat, but mainly on Sundays. But this isn't all there is. There's also a pudding.

I finished off the meal for the King with the chocolate sponge and custard.

I hated the whole experience.

I was knackered and wanted to go to bed. But I had to wash all the cups and pans I had used. I wanted to get it sorted rather than have to face it in the morning. Plus, there were loads of insects knocking about due to the shit on the side of the caravan. I didn't want to have my crockery caked in ants after leaving them out all night. Ants have an ability to hunt down any sweet stuff, so I washed up in total darkness using some VO5 shampoo and a toilet roll to dry up.

#50 Become a vegetarian for a week

I could easily do a week, in fact, I have done – not 'cos I wanted to though. It was when I was in China and someone served me dog by mistake. I decided to just have soup and rice for the rest of my time there. When I got home I felt like I actually needed meat. My body does that. It gets urges to eat certain fruits that it obviously requires. I'll be sat watching telly and suddenly want a plum, an orange or a banana. There was a lad at school who ate the teacher's chalk. I think his body was telling him he needed calcium.

#84 Go on an African safari

Ricky left me a message the next day. He wanted me to get involved in a major animal conservation project. I'd be helping to relocate a wild rhino at the Entabeni nature reserve. Rhinos are one of the most endangered species. The main problem seems to be poachers killing them for their horns, which seems really wasteful, like killing a human for their tonsils. The list of endangered species seems to be getting longer all the time.

I wonder how many of these species are still doing something useful for the planet if there aren't many left. Maybe they were important many years ago but are now just hanging around, a bit like Ceefax.

Pandas have been in the news a lot recently. I don't know what to make of them. They don't seem to help themselves. I keep hearing that the main issue is that humans are ripping up all the bamboo they eat, so they struggle to find food, but maybe they just have to find something new to eat. They seem really stubborn, a bit like Suzanne's dad who has a strict routine when it comes to his eating habits. He's in his sixties but he's never had Indian food, Chinese food or pasta. Maybe as well as us changing our ways to save the planet, pandas have to change a bit as well. Badgers have that white line down their back. They always seem to be found dead in the middle of the road, so did this happen so they fitted in with road markings. Makes you wonder, doesn't it?

Something that keeps cropping up is cloning and how in the next few years scientists may be able to bring the woolly mammoth back to life using DNA. This is all very clever, but I think it's wrong. If it didn't work first time round why bring them back? It's like a Steps reunion tour.

#7 See elephants in the wild

Elephants are one of my favourites. It's their memories that are most amazing.

Some people say their memory is better than that of a human, and they have been known to recognise a family member even though they had been separated for over twenty years.

I do wonder if that's because they don't change much, whereas humans can really change.

I heard this story off a mate who went to a school reunion:
'Have you seen Barry? He's changed a lot.'
'Has he?'
'Yeh . . . He's got a lovely pair of tits.'

Also I can recognise people but totally forget where from. I once almost went up to someone at Piccadilly train station in Manchester who I thought I knew from school until Suzanne pointed out I knew the face because it was David Beckham.

Maybe our long-term memory isn't as useful as it was years ago as things change so much these days. No point remembering where the biscuit aisle is in the supermarket as they keep moving the aisles about. In a way, having a good memory can be annoying as it means we constantly harp on about the good old days instead of just getting on with it. So go and see elephants in the wild but the elephants might remember your meeting a lot longer than it sticks with you.

#98 Live with the Masai people

When I was on safari with Suzanne in Africa and found lions wandering about outside the tent, I suggested to Suzanne that we should put a half-filled plastic bottle of water outside as my auntie Nora does this to keep cats off the lawn. It works, apparently.

Suzanne said it was a stupid idea and and told the manager of the place that we didn't feel safe so he sent down two Masai people to be on security. The lads who turned up looked about 17. Their dress was quite interesting, with braided hair, lots of beads and tight laces strapped round their lower legs. One also had an elastic band around his head. I don't know if that was part of the traditional dress or if he was just keeping it on his head so he knew where it was. I couldn't ask as they couldn't speak English.

They stuck feathers to certain parts of the tent. Suzanne said that it must work 'cos they are the experts. It annoyed me she thought three feathers could save us from lions and yet she pooh-poohed my bottle of water idea.

#99 See the wildebeest migration in the Masai Mara ✗

Over a million wildebeest migrate every year with another half a million zebra, gazelle and impala. What's mad is, this migration only started in the 1960s when the population of the wildebeest increased after vets stopped them dying out. Now there's so many of them they have to move for food and water. I've always said how sorting out problems just creates new problems. The example that springs to mind is the way hospitals used to say they didn't have enough beds for patients. By the time I went into hospital with kidney stones they had sorted that problem and had plenty of beds, but were short on pillows. I was eventually given one that still felt a bit warm, as if it had been removed from underneath a dead head. I can't sleep without a pillow. I reckon that will be the next evolutionary step. Humans will evolve to have a big

WHALE-WATCHING

SQUIDDLY ~~DIDDLY~~ DEADLY.

HAVING A WHALE OF A TIME!

MEET A MOUNTAIN GORILLA

MEET A MOUNTAIN GORILLA

WHAT DO YOU MEAN, THIS ONE ISN'T JESSICA!!!!

I THINK I'VE PULLED.

QUICK! HIDE IT, THE LANDLORD IS HERE!!

SUZANNE - WAKE UP!

THE CAB FIRM WERE NOT HAPPY.

MEET A MOUNTAIN GORILLA

MEET A MOUNTAIN GORILLA

I HAD A RIGHT BAD HEADACHE
AT THIS POINT.

LOOK AT ITS RED EYES. NOT
'GORILLAS IN THE MIST', 'GORILLAS
BEEN ON THE PISS' I RECKON.

bulbous bit at the back of our heads to stop us needing pillows. Think about it: whenever you see images of aliens, the backs of their heads are normally quite big, and I'd say they're more advanced and more evolved than us. Just Google the image of the Roswell incident and look at the alien on the bed. No pillow, but it looks perfectly comfortable. After that, Google the wildebeest migration on YouTube.

I met Lee the ranger who took me out in his Land Rover and got talking about the rhino I was here to help with.

KARL: Why have we got to shift it?

LEE: This particular rhino is a bull. He's holding territory which is full of young females – many of them are his daughters – so purely and simply from a conservation perspective, as soon as you manage a reserve, you need to assist with the management of the animals. The idea is that we're going to move him to a new territory in a part of the game reserve where he's never had access before, and we're gonna replace him with a bull from that territory where we have the same problem.

KARL: It's like a wife swap?

LEE: Yeah, very much so. Well, husband swap, really.

KARL: What would happen though if the fella mated with the daughter. What's the result?

LEE: The first generation wouldn't be a problem, but the second or third generation there would probably start to be problems. Genetic weaknesses might come through, and from the perspective of managing our animals we do not want to end up in a situation where we must manage the animals because of the contrived environment. We have to find ways to manage them and make sure that what we do is best, and obviously the more DNA you've got mixed in there, the stronger these animals are gonna be at the end of the day.

He pulled up at a pile of dung. I thought he may have been collecting it for the Ndebele tribe to paint their front room with, but he said to hunt the rhinos down he used an old-fashioned technique of following tracks, which involved tasting their droppings.

LEE: What I am doing is determining the freshness of the droppings. It can be determined just by taste. A fermentation process takes place with herbivores, so as it builds up more alcohol, it becomes a bitter or sweeter sort of taste.

KARL: Is that a last resort?

LEE: You don't want to follow the wrong set of footprints, do you?

KARL: How often each week are you licking shit?

LEE: It isn't a bad taste. It's very dry. Just a little taste, very quickly. Lick it.

KARL: There's no sort of germage in it?

LEE: No, no. If there was anything like that, I wouldn't be doing it. I wouldn't be here to tell the story. (*Asks driver Sandro to pull over*)

There was a big pile of dung, or, to Lee, an All You Can Eat buffet. I understood what he said about tasting it, but I'm pretty sure just squeezing it could give you clues, like people do with melons in supermarkets.

LEE: Let me show you what's going on. We have a whole bunch of droppings together. This is normally an indicator that we are dealing with a male rhino. They make these big droppings that are full of grass. Some are clearly quite old. You can see that.

KARL: Yeah, I can see that.

LEE: But over here there's one I can determine the freshness of. The scrape marks of the male. Look at these two bare patches on the ground. He kicks it backwards. He kicks his dung like that. It's all spread out. Okay, so now we know we are dealing with a male. This is the rhino we are looking for.

KARL: I would say that's fresh just by looking at it. It looks quite moist. Yeah, it definitely is.

LEE: Taste it. Get that freshness. You'll pick up how sweet it becomes if it's not too fresh. It's experience that you have got to build. We'll find an even fresher one later, and you'll taste how sour it is. You want to try? Just put it on your fingertip and have a taste. It won't hurt you.

KARL: You know what's weird? This is the second time in three days I've had my hand in shit.

LEE: Get your finger in there and get a little bit of it. Taste it. I think you'll find it's slightly sweet.

KARL: 'Things to do before you die': stick a finger in a load of shit. (*Sticks finger in shit*)

LEE: Did you taste it?

KARL: Yeah. It's like Shredded Wheat.

LEE: Yeah. It's a little bit sweet.

KARL: Mmmm, it's like a wine tasting.

LEE: Did you just get the smell?

KARL: That's why we're given noses, isn't it? We know it's fresh 'cos we can smell. Taste buds for food.

LEE: Well, it's the combination. You need to use both skills.

KARL: Say there were piles of shit, and I blindfolded you and went, 'What's that?' Could you tell just by smell what type of animal it is?

LEE: I would give it a go.

KARL: It's not a skill to be proud of.

We headed off looking for fresh rhino poo and saw giraffes on our travels. This is the animal that impresses me the most. It's the best example of evolution to me, the fact that it grew its neck to help it reach for food. The Ndebele women might one day evolve to have longer necks with all the rings they wear. They'd be able to look in an attic without using ladders.

News came in on the radio that they had tracked the rhino by helicopter, so us licking rhino shit all morning had been a bit unnecessary. By the time we got to the scene the rhino had been tranquillised and was starting to slow down in its tracks. The mission now was to get the rhino in a place where it could be easily transported into the back of a big metal container and then shifted quickly before the drugs started to wear off.

Its walking was similar to that of a pissed-up old fella stumbling home from a Sunday afternoon drink. The vet who had administered the drugs was guiding it towards the truck but first he wanted to take some blood samples. He managed to walk it into a tree trunk that was perfect for it to rest against without lying down. The rhino's head perched perfectly between the branches of the tree. He then covered its eyes with a scarf to stop it stressing out. This was a chance for me to get up close. They're weird-looking animals. Its skin looked too big for its bones.

Lots of people were there to help, which was just as well, as it took fifteen people to steer it over to the truck. They eventually got it in and drove it to a new area. When it was released it seemed a bit annoyed and groggy, like a kid who's just been to the dentist and been given gas.

Finally, it was time to go in search of the mountain gorillas. The journey to the impenetrable forest took twelve hours on rough bumpy roads. I spent my time sleeping and watching the film *Gorillas in the Mist* to get myself in the mood. Sigourney Weaver plays the part of Dian Fossey, a woman who dedicated most of her life to saving gorillas from poachers and showed the world that they weren't as aggressive as people thought.

After a bad night's sleep in a hut at the edge of the forest, we set off on our trek to find the gorillas. I picked seeing a gorilla as it's something me mam said she would have liked to do, so I thought I'd do it and then report back and let her know if it was any good. But beyond that, I hadn't really given it much thought.

DIRECTOR: Have you thought about what you're going to say to the viewers when you're out there with the gorillas? How you're going to express it?

KARL: No, because that would be wrong, wouldn't it? If I've pre-planned it, then I'm not really expressing what I'm feeling at the time. Let's see what happens. I mean, did Attenborough plan it?

DIRECTOR: Well, famously, no. He ad-libbed.

KARL: Did he? Because they said that about Armstrong and his 'One small step' thing. But he had a long journey to the moon, sat there doing nowt. It must've been going through his head. But at the end of the day it's more about the gorillas, isn't it? Just film it. I've seen Joanna Lumley do this sort of stuff, and you just go, 'Oh, my word! Oh, gosh, look at the head on it!' That sort of thing. I don't know, just see how it goes. Why are you worrying about that? You do your job, film it, get it on the telly. No one is expecting a great speech from me, anyway, are they? Everything's been said that can be said about gorillas.

DIRECTOR: Well, why are we doing it?

KARL: I just wanted to see one . . . Well, my mam did.

I was looking forward to seeing them but I'd be lying if I said I wasn't a little bit worried about wandering through the woods and coming face to face with a big gorilla. These things are massive and could rip me face off. It's not a way I want to go, to be honest. It wouldn't be good for Suzanne having to tell people.

'Oh. Sorry to hear that. How did he die?'

'A gorilla battered him.'

We had been walking for forty or so minutes when David, our guide, pointed out some gorilla poo. He knew it was the poo of a silverback, as it's always six to eight centimetres long.

DIRECTOR: Do you have to taste it to see how near they are?

KARL: No. You don't need to do that!

DIRECTOR: Remember, that's how Lee tracked the rhino.

KARL: This is fresh. I don't have to taste it. You can see it's fresh. The leaves are wet. Why are you jumping straight into me having to stick my finger in it? This is what annoys me with you. You want me to be like Attenborough, and get all classic and everything. But, at the end of the day, you're just saying, 'Stick your finger in a pile of shit.' I don't know what you want anymore. I'm trying to do a proper interview here and you're going, 'Touch the shit!'

It wasn't long before I was out of breath. The path soon disappeared. We were clambering through bushes and we had to cross rivers. The enthusiasm that was there at the start soon started to wear off. No wonder gorillas didn't evolve to walk upright. They couldn't in these conditions. I was on all fours half the time, and on my arse for the other half.

It started to rain, too. My feet were wet through, I was getting bitten by insects, and I had a headache coming on. Dave said he did this walk three to four times a week. Thinking back, I should have asked why the path wasn't more flattened if that was the case.

About three hours in and Dave kept saying that some trackers up ahead had spotted some gorillas and that we were getting close. I wanted to stop for just a few moments to have some food, but he said we had to keep going as the gorillas were constantly on the move. I couldn't argue with his logic except on a few occasions when he stopped to show me more fresh gorilla shite. He kept saying, 'We're just five minutes away,' and then five minutes later he would announce, 'We're just seven minutes away.' It was like when you order a cab and call the firm when it hasn't turned up. They always say, 'Yeah, it's just coming down your road now.' It never is.

Twenty minutes later we were still trekking. It wasn't getting any easier, as the rain was now bouncing down. In the film I watched, Sigourney Weaver only had to deal with mist. I'd like to see if Dian Fossey would have been as keen to save the gorillas if it had been pissing it down like this. There's no way my mam would like to do this. If there were charity shops to nip in and out of along the way, maybe, but she isn't a fan of walking. She even leaves it to me dad to put the bins out.

I suppose this is the problem when going on a search for an endangered species. They're not going to be easy to find, are they? It's like trying to win a Willy Wonka golden ticket.

We'd hear Dave up ahead of us sounding excited and shouting something, only to find it was just more gorilla shit. Even Ben the director was worried. He was concerned about the daylight and having to make our way back in total darkness. I suppose that was one good thing about all the gorilla shit. We could use it to find our way back like Hansel and Gretel.

In the end, we did turn around. Dave announced that somehow we had gone past them. I wasn't happy. We're meant to be more evolved. Yet here we were being outdone by a group of gorillas. We would have been better off just staying still somewhere and waiting for them to come to us.

Just under five hours in and Dave told us to *sssh*. We had finally caught up with them. Suddenly everything was a bit of a rush. Ben didn't want to miss the chance to film, so he pushed me into shot. Dave said that we'd be lucky if we got 25 minutes with them before they started moving again. Ben told me to speak and give a quote, but I had nothing. Nothing was springing to mind. My feet were throbbing, and so was my head, and the thought of having to do that return trip was getting in the way of me enjoying the moment. I've never been that good at quotes. The only ones I remember are 'It's not the cough that carries you off, it's the coffin they carry you off in' and 'The cat crept into the Kremlin, crapped and crept out again', but these were more tongue-twisters than useful quotes.

The director told me I had had five hours to think of something to say.

Neil Armstrong had time to come up with his 'One small step' quote as he was sat on his arse on his way to the moon, whereas I'd been concentrating on not slipping on my arse into rivers and on avoiding wasp nests.

I looked at the gorillas. The mother was sat under a tree feeding its kid. The male silverback was sat on his own forty feet away from the mother. Two others were high up in the trees. I watched as the young gorilla ate grass using its feet.

KARL: Their foot is well useful. I tell you, we've gone backwards. We can't do anything using our toes. All we ever do is stub them on the end of the bed. I always think, 'Get rid of 'em.' More trouble than they're worth, toes. But, gorillas can actually grab stuff with them and use them. They have better feet but the same hands. They have little ears, which we might as well have, because people don't listen anymore, do they? Too busy talking. The little ears are good. Long arms. Short legs.

DIRECTOR: Is this your speech? Because all you're doing is describing their body parts.

KARL: Yeah, I know. But I'm just saying, look at how we have changed. We have longer legs and shorter arms. They have shorter legs and longer arms. Why has that happened?

DIRECTOR: Because we don't swing through trees, Karl. We have evolved.

KARL: Yeah, but look at supermarket shelves now. You go to Tesco now, you can't reach up. So, we need longer arms. Look, you're not going to get a speech out of me! I told you, everything has been said. Sometimes you can say it best when you don't say anything at all. Ronan Keating said that. There you go.

DIRECTOR: Is that going to be your line?

KARL: 'Life is a rollercoaster', he also said that. 'Living every day as if it is your last.'

DIRECTOR: It's just that this is quite a big moment, and you're quoting Ronan Keating.

KARL: Who else can I quote? I don't know any other quotes.

DIRECTOR: Don't quote anyone, come up with your own quotes. That's what I've been saying to you.

KARL: What would you say if you were sat here? What's going through your mind?

DIRECTOR: Let me . . . just wait. I've got what David Attenborough said here to help you: 'There is more meaning and mutual understanding in exchanging a glance with a gorilla than with any other animal I know. Their sight, their hearing, their sense of smell is so similar to ours that they see the world in much the same way as we do. We live in the same sort of social groups with largely permanent family relationships. They walk on the ground as we do though they are immensely more powerful than we are. So, if there was ever a possibility of escaping the human condition and living imaginatively in another creature's world it must be with the gorilla.'

KARL: I sort of said that.

DAVE: We have to leave now.

DIRECTOR: We've got to go? Just one last go, Karl.

KARL: I haven't got anything. I've got nothing there. I've let you down, but I thought the Ronan Keating line was good. We don't have to say it was Ronan Keating.

KARL'S FACTS

THE WORD 'GORILLA' MEANS 'TRIBE OF HAIRY WOMEN'.

NEVER STARE OR POINT AT A GORILLA.

GORILLAS' ONLY ENEMIES ARE CROCODILES, LEOPARDS AND HUMANS.

GORILLAS BELCH TO SHOW THEIR CONTENTMENT.

GORILLAS AND HUMANS HAVE ALMOST THE SAME DNA, AND THEY CAN LIVE FOR AS LONG AS 55 YEARS.

We walked back and did it in just under five hours. The rain was biblical. We walked in silence. I preferred seeing Jessica the hippo to this. That was the best way to see a wild animal – in somebody's front room. I got the chance to get up close while having a cup of a tea and a biscuit, and Jessica was happy too.

I spoke to Ricky when we got back.

KARL: It was the gorillas thing today. It was mental.

RICKY: Oh, yeah, of course. Did you see one?

KARL: Yeah. I saw a family of them. They wanted me to give some quote of what I was feeling like, but I couldn't think of anything. What would you have said in that situation? With a gorilla seven foot away holding its kid. Quick, we've got the camera on, gotta do this quick, 'cos he's gonna piss off in a minute . . . what would you say?

RICKY: This is one of the greatest privileges of my life.

KARL: Is that it?

RICKY: Well, yeah, what else would you say? What a privilege to see that. My God, you're one of the luckiest people in the world, Karl.

KARL: Yeah, but it was a nightmare to get there. This is the thing you didn't see. You don't see people on the telly having to go through the trek and by the time you get there you can't be arsed, honestly, because your mind's thinking,

'I've gotta walk back.' Um, I just remembered a fact – that the word 'gorilla' means, um, 'hairy woman'. I think I heard that at some point.

RICKY: It means what?

KARL: Hairy woman. I don't know what language it is, but apparently that's what it means.

RICKY: I didn't know that. Is that true?

KARL: I think so, yeah. So, there's that, and, um, they've got thumbs and that, and, um, their feet are good.

RICKY: Brilliant. You are just like Attenborough. 'They've got thumbs and that.' 'Hairy women.'

KARL: No, but when the pressure's on ya . . .

(*Ricky laughs*)

KARL: They shit a lot. There's another fact. They've got little ears . . .

RICKY: Yup, okay, don't blow it. Quit while you're ahead. (*laughs*) Let's not get into too much detail. Let's not get too biological.

KARL: I know the trip was all about the gorillas, but I reckon I've done a lot more since I've been here. I've made a lot of difference. You sorted that thing out for me to build a hut. I've done that for them.

RICKY: Yup.

KARL: I've taught kids how to ride a bike. I . . . what else did I do? I cooked for the King and his mates. I shifted that rhino. That's another charity act. What else have I done?

RICKY: You finally did the bungee jump, which is pretty amazing, considering how adamant you were at the beginning about not doing it.

KARL: But, yeah, listen . . . I want to finish this trip and I'll pay the money when I get back and then that way it's all . . .

RICKY: No, no.

KARL: No, I don't mind. That's what I'm gonna do.

RICKY: I'll do it.

KARL: No, I wanna. Honestly, I wanna.

RICKY: I tried to get you to do it, and you've tried it. You've done it.

KARL: No, but . . .

RICKY: The bet was . . . the bet was that I paid it if you did the jump. You did the jump, so I'll pay.

KARL: I know, but I just feel like if I pay . . .

RICKY: No, because then I should do something. You did the jump, so I should pay.

KARL: I didn't do it! I didn't do the jump!

(*Silence*)

RICKY: What do you mean, you didn't do the jump?

KARL: I didn't do it.

RICKY: You didn't do the bungee jump?

KARL: Hmmm.

RICKY: What, you just lied and said you did?

KARL: Yeah, because you and Stephen kept going on about it.

RICKY: Hold on a minute, when were you gonna tell me you didn't do it?

KARL: Well, I wasn't gonna bother telling you because . . .

RICKY: But I'd have seen the footage of you not jumping.

KARL: Yeah, but I got Luke to put my hat on and do the jump, but his hat came off, so you can see he's not bald, so it didn't work.

RICKY: Right, so, you didn't. You got a stunt double. You got Luke to do the bungee jump and you thought that would fool me?

KARL: Well, he's not a double, is he? That was the problem. The hat came off. He's got a great head of hair.

RICKY: (laughs) Have you got the footage then, that you wanted to put in the show?

KARL: It's recorded, but it's no use because his hat came off. Well, my hat came off.

RICKY: You are the worst. Like one of those dumbest criminals ever. I can't even be angry with you because you're so useless.

KARL: Well, we can split the money then.

RICKY: No, no, no. You're paying it. You didn't do the jump. That's hilarious. Not only have you made a complete twonk of yourself, showing that you're a coward and a liar, you're £2,500 down. (*Laughs*) That's amazing. This is my best day ever. But, listen, you saw the gorillas. I'm not gonna get the footage back and it's Luke in a fucking fur coat?

(*Karl laughs*)

(*Ricky laughs*)

When we left the forest on our journey back home I passed a big gorilla sitting at the bottom of a tree just off the main road. It was sitting there like it was waiting for a bus. Typical.

CHAPTER SIX

#48 Drive a Cadillac along Route 66 ✓

STEPHEN: What else takes your fancy, Karl?

KARL: Um, Route 66?

RICKY: Well, it's a long one – two and a half thousand miles across eight states. You go through three time zones, from Chicago to LA – two of the greatest cities in the world.

KARL: Is it America that's made this seem like it's a good thing to do?

RICKY: What do you mean?

KARL: I just think they're excitable people. They're the ones you see in crowds whooping and stuff. When I was at Disneyland I went past some fruit and veg on a boat, and there were three old women getting excited about an eggplant. Now I sort of think, am I miserable?

RICKY: Yeah, you're fucking miserable.

KARL: But I get excited about stuff you should get excited about. I'm not gonna start whooping at an eggplant.

RICKY: And what's the last thing you got excited about?

KARL: I'm happy inside. You don't have to let everyone else know. And that's what I'm saying. In America it's all about show. 'Oh, look at him, he's miserable.' 'Oh, look at your head. It looks weird. Have some plastic surgery done.' It's all about how people look over there.

RICKY: Would you ever have plastic surgery?

KARL: No. I think it would freak me out to look in the mirror and not see me any more.

RICKY: Okay, what about a hair transplant?

KARL: No, it's not a problem. I didn't like having hair when I had it. I had rubbish hair. I had the hair of a Chinese man, that's what the barber said. 'You can do nothing with this hair.' 'What do you mean?' I said. And he said, 'You've got the hair of a Chinaman.'

RICKY: Right, I don't know what that means.

KARL: He just said you cannot style this type of hair.

RICKY: Are you saying that Chinese people can't ever style their hair? You've been to China.

KARL: Yes, and it's all the same. They don't do anything, they just let it grow very bowlish. And that's what my hair was like, and in the end it fell out and I've never looked back.

STEPHEN: So . . . Route 66. Get your kicks on Route 66. You must've heard of that?

KARL: I've heard of that.

STEPHEN: And the image is always the open-top Cadillac cruising down the highway, stereo blasting, beautiful girl by your side, hair blowing in the . . . So?

KARL: Well, people rave about it, but I've been there and never liked it that much. I went to LA and New York, and hated it.

RICKY: Why did you hate New York?

KARL: It's just so noisy. You can't get away from it.

RICKY: But it's the greatest city in the world.

KARL: It's not. They say it's the city that never sleeps, and there's a reason for that. It's a racket. I was just off Times Square. Sirens all the time. I saw a mugging within about a minute of being there.

RICKY: Why Times Square? Why did you do the touristy things? You've been to America, and you went to Disneyland and Times Square?

KARL: Yeah, but it's where everybody goes.

RICKY: Well, don't go there then if everyone goes there!

STEPHEN: The good thing about Route 66 is it travels through lots of smaller towns – the ones you wouldn't visit normally, the ones that aren't on the tourist map. You'll see the real America.

KARL: What is the real America?

RICKY: Good question.

STEPHEN: You'll find out . . .

I can't imagine anyone ever singing about a British road in a positive way, not like they've done in America for Route 66. Americans seem to have a positive attitude about driving and have the songs to prove it. I'm thinking of Steppenwolf's song, 'Born to Be Wild' for starters. I've never got in my car and thought I'll go looking for adventure. All I'm looking out for are speed cameras and potholes. Westminster Council have dug more holes in London's roads than archaeologists have dug in Egypt.

I haven't always had these feelings about driving though. When I was a teenager my driving test was more important than any other exam I took. I always thought that once I'd passed my driving test the world would be my oyster and I would finally have control of my destiny. Maybe that's a bit over the top, but at least I knew that I wouldn't have to wait any more at the bus stop for the 261 to Manchester Piccadilly with Mad Rita. Rita was the local nutter who would always ask for help with her pram when she was boarding the bus. 'You should always help a woman with a baby!' is probably what you're thinking. Well, there wasn't a baby in the pram, just a bucket with a face drawn on it. The clue was in the name: Mad Rita. Scruffy Sandra was normally there, too, taking up three seats with bin bags stuffed with clothes from secondhand shops, and John from the care home who sat at the back of the bus showing his knob to anyone who was interested.

I passed my driving test twenty years ago. It took two attempts. I've had seven cars in total, three parking tickets, been clamped twice, got three points for going through a red light, and been involved in one crash (that wasn't my fault). I think I'm quite a good driver. I sometimes get annoyed when other drivers are being indecisive, but I'm nowhere near as impatient as me dad. He has one hand poised on the horn like a contestant and their buzzer on *The Weakest Link*. I've covered a lot of miles in the passenger seat with me dad as he delivered papers or did courier work or drove his black cab. I used to sit on an empty bottle crate in the front of the cab and get tips off his customers. But there was a downside, too. If he ever gave me a lift somewhere in the cab he'd often pick up passengers along the way who'd want to go in the opposite direction, so it was often quicker to walk. The thing that used to wind him up more than anything was if a passenger asked to go somewhere and me dad knew exactly where he was going and he headed there – seven miles out of town, or wherever it was – and then just when we were moments from the drop off, the passenger would say, 'Just next on your right here, mate.' And that would do me dad's head in. 'I know where it is! I've brought you this far without directions, haven't I?' And I'd be sat there thinking, 'No tips from this one then.' Me dad takes great pride in his knowledge of the UK's roads. He often nips off to the toilet, not with a newspaper like most of us, but with an *A–Z* tucked under his arm. We call it his 'shat nav updates'.

The most important thing for me when packing for this trip down Route 66 was my iPod. I like listening to music when I'm driving. For me, it's music, mirror, signal, manoeuvre. I also made sure that I packed some pear drops, kola kubes and a hot water bottle (I'll explain that later). In the end, the only thing I realised I'd forgotten to pack when I reached LA was my driving licence. Still, at least this gave me a bit of time to explore the place, while Suzanne FedExed it over.

On the first day I went for a walk on Santa Monica beach. For me, the beach is a place to relax, but that wasn't the case in LA. Women were jogging, men were lifting weights or doing press-ups or sit-ups. Even the pigeons had bigger chests than the ones in London. A lot of people looked as if they'd had plastic surgery, too. It never looks right to me. Fair enough, if you've been scarred, but that's the only reason I can understand for getting surgery. I caught the end of a TV programme once where this person had something called mirrored-self misidentification. Apparently it's where you don't recognise your reflection in the mirror. Now, if everyone had this problem then no one would call anyone ugly or make anyone feel depressed about how they looked, because you genuinely wouldn't know what they looked like themselves. Sorted. I can't think of any situations where I've had to know what I looked like. I don't have to find me, because I'm always with myself.

While I was down at the beach I got a call from Ricky about taking part in an activity that was popular with the young generation over here. It's called Glee Club. There's a TV show that sparked the craze a few years ago involving kids at a high school who smile a lot and have great lives and sing and dance about how great everything is. The show covers kids' issues, but nothing heavy like drugs or pregnancy, just how to cope when you wake up with a spot on your neck. It annoys me how many singing shows there are on TV now. We have too many kids growing up wanting to be professional singers. Nobody wants a normal job. I never hear a kid say they want to be a builder or an electrician or a plumber. When I was having problems with my boiler recently I had to wait a week before a plumber was available 'cos there just aren't enough of them. But if I wanted someone to come round and do a dance routine in my front room, they'd probably be round within the hour.

I guess Ricky had suggested it because he knew I did a bit of dancing when I was younger – body popping and robotics was my thing. I even performed once or twice at the shopping centre, but mainly it was something I did at home in my bedroom. I don't dance as much these days. There's too many 12-inch remixes that go on for ten or twelve minutes. No wonder drugs started to be used in clubs. I need a couple of Beroccas just to get me through one song, let alone a whole night.

#68 Be an extra in a film ✔

Tick. Done it. I was in Ricky's movie, *The Invention of Lying.* It's basically a lot of hanging around for two seconds on screen, except Ricky then went and cut my bit in the edit. I was an extra in another of Ricky's films, *Cemetery Junction*, and made it through the final cut in that one. I wasn't originally planning on going along though. Ricky called me up and asked if I'd like to have a part and I said no, but then he said that the catering were doing pork chops that day so I said, 'Alright, I'll see you in twenty minutes.' That's the best bit about being an extra – the lunch is always good.

My tutor at the school was a woman called Gail who seemed to really know her stuff and seemed passionate about it. When I was growing up music lessons at my school were never taken that seriously. There wasn't the budget to buy proper equipment. In fact, it was probably my school that came up with the idea for *The Trash Musical,* where they use the bins as instruments. I'm sure it was the only school in the country that taught 'whistling', but even that was tricky 'cos so many of the kids were missing teeth. The Performing Arts weren't really what our school was about. The main stage was only used once a year for the Nativity play, and that was a joke. There were too many kids in the school, and not enough roles to go round, so most kids only got the odd line here or there. It must've been the only Nativity play that had Seven Wise Men.

Back in Santa Monica, Gail gave me a few lines to sing in one of the numbers they were rehearsing. It was 'Jump' by Van Halen. The thought of it worried me. I'm under no illusion that I can sing. Whistling and humming are more my thing. Plus, remembering words doesn't come easily either. I only know about three songs off by heart: a couple of Elvis songs – 'If I Could Dream' and 'In the Ghetto' – and 'Ain't No Pleasing You' by Chas and Dave. Still, I practised my lines to 'Jump', and then Gail said I would also have to remember a dance routine to go with it. I have never done a routine before. My dancing as a kid at the local shopping centre was basically improvised. I let my body decide what it wanted to do. But Gail wanted me to do exactly the same routine as the twenty other kids on stage. I really don't understand the point of this. If everyone is doing the same dance you might as well just have one person doing the dance. The same goes for synchronised swimming. Let everyone do their own thing, that way the audience has different things to watch.

I rehearsed for an hour while Gail kept reminding me to smile. I struggle with this. Smiling isn't my face's default setting. I smile when I'm really happy and only 'cos that's what my mouth wants to do. So, remembering to put on a false smile was hard. Gail kept saying, 'You're having fun! Let people see you're having fun!' And that's when I understood why 90% of the kids I was dancing with were wearing braces on their teeth. If you live in a place where smiling is so important I guess you want straight teeth.

An hour later, there I was standing at the side of the stage waiting for my cue. I did the first part of the dance routine fairly successfully, I think. I was a split-second behind everyone else, but I thought this was okay because if anyone blinked they wouldn't miss anything. I was sort of providing a catch-up service. I then shuffled off the stage to wait for my singing bit. But, as I was standing at the side, I realised I'd forgotten my three lines. There was a woman there with headphones on talking to Gail, and I told her that I'd forgotten my lines, but she was too busy to help me out. I got a right sweat on from the panic and desperately asked all the people around me to help, but they were in their own zones, quietly preparing for their next bits. And then I was being dragged back on stage by a young girl and handed a mic. The words that came out of my mouth were definitely in the wrong order, but I think I got away with it. And then I backed off the stage as quickly as I could.

But no sooner was it over than my director was telling me he wanted to do another routine, so that he had plenty of options when he was editing the final TV series. I wasn't happy about this. I was properly drained and had pretty much used up all my skills in that single performance. I couldn't tell if he wanted me to do another take because the first one looked too good, or too bad. Anyway, I agreed to dance to 'Everything She Does Is Magic' by the Police. It was a complicated routine with loads of hand movements. The rest of the kids seemed to do it smoothly, while I just looked like I was trying to communicate with the deaf.

Afterwards, Gail and the kids told me I was great, but deep down I knew I had failed. I was useless. And I didn't like the false praise. I just don't think it's healthy. People need to be told when they can't do something otherwise it gives them false hope. Nobody can be good at everything. But that seems to be the American way – everyone can be what they want to be, regardless of their talent. They can live the dream – which is another saying that I've never understood, to be honest. If you're living the dream then how do you know if you're awake or asleep? Also, the saying only works if your dreams are good.

96 Spend the Fourth of July in the USA

Using the same dates to celebrate things every year is a bit annoying. I'd prefer it if we were left to celebrate things when we were in the mood to. This would get rid of rip-off days like Valentine's Day when prices in restaurants double. It would also mean you'd get Christmas presents all year round as different friends and family celebrate it at different times.

I left the school absolutely shattered. We headed for a motel along the way to Route 66. Loads of motels in America seem to have novelty designs or themes. This one had concrete wigwams for rooms, which made the whole set-up look like a little council estate of teepees. It just confirmed to me that round rooms don't really work. Suzanne always says she'd like to live in a windmill, but round rooms cause problems. There was no corner to put the TV in, and pictures don't hang properly on the wall. Wallpapering would be a nightmare.

The next morning I called Ricky and told him about my Glee Club experience.

RICKY: Did you sing and dance?

KARL: Yeah, but it was annoying because the rehearsal bit was really good, but when it came to it, I was just stood on the side of the stage having a bit of a panic attack, forgot my words, forgot my moves, and ballsed it right up.

RICKY: I can't imagine you singing. I don't think I've ever heard you sing.

KARL: Well, I prefer whistling. Whistling's my thing. It's not as stressful.

RICKY: You can't whistle very well, to be honest, Karl. At least there are no words to forget with whistling. But you forget the tune and the concept of whistling.

KARL: No, but look . . .

RICKY: No, you can't whistle. It's pathetic.

KARL: Here you are. Here's the tune from last night (*Whistles 'Jump' by Van Halen*)

RICKY: Right. Okay.

KARL: See, you can tell what it is.

RICKY: Well, I couldn't tell what it was. I actually thought you were pushing a wheelbarrow at various speeds. It was out of tune.

KARL: I've never been that embarrassed. You know I always say to you that you give me anxiety dreams. I panic and stuff because of the things you set up. That time when I had a dream about being in a toilet, and you opened the door, and there was a big audience looking at me having a shit – it was exactly the same feeling I had in my dream as that. I just wanted to wake up and for it to go away.

RICKY: But the weird thing about that dream . . . it's not particularly Freudian or symbolic, right? 'Cos I often open the door when you're having a shit to annoy you.

KARL: Yeah, that's true actually.

RICKY: To be honest, I didn't think Glee was quite your thing.

KARL: Well, I don't like fun. That's what it's made me realise.

RICKY: Woah, hold on. When you say that's what it's made you realise, surely you must know you don't like fun by now, because you're the most joyless person I've ever met. You know, I've known you almost ten years, and if you're not aware of the fact you don't like fun then something's really wrong, because this is what I'm doing with this show. I'm putting you into situations that I know you won't enjoy. Possibly you will, but I think everyone already knows you don't like fun, so it's strange you should say that it's a revelation to you.

KARL: Yeah, but if you took someone else and put them in that situation they wouldn't be happy either. I'm 38, I'm on stage with kids whose average age was about 14. It looked like some daft old man had wandered in off the street. An old man with a bald head and a beard is suddenly dancing around forgetting words to songs. I mean, if I was a dad of one of the kids, I'd be saying, 'What is going on at this school? What's he doing here? That never happened in *Fame.*'

RICKY: Oh God.

After speaking to Ricky, it turned out that my driving licence had turned up at the reception of the wigwam motel, so I could finally start my drive. I was expecting a classic American car. Nothing too fancy, just something similar to the other cars I'd seen since arriving. But that wasn't to be. Ricky and Stephen had rented a Smart car for me. For people who don't know what a Smart car is, it's something about the size of a pram, with an engine. Never has something been so badly named since *Top Gear* (a TV show where three middle-aged men wear bad shirts and stonewashed jeans).

#4 Drive a Formula 1 car

I've had a bit of experience of this. I drove a Formula 3 car a few years ago and wrote it off, so I'm probably not best placed to advise people on this one. It was a freebie – a competition prize – but I was working nights at the time and I warned them before I got in the car that I was pretty knackered. But they didn't seem bothered. They said, 'You'll be fine, just don't push your luck.' But you do, don't you? You go round the track a few times and get a bit cocky and so I put my foot down but hit a bit of dirt and the car went in to a spin and ended up smashing up the front axle. They weren't happy. I wasn't even insured.

And I had a Go-Kart as a kid. It was motorised, but you had to be given a push to get it going. Fortunately, the British sprinter Darren Campbell grew up on the same estate as me, so I used to get him to push-start me – like a bobsleigh. In fact, I like to think I'm partly responsible for his future success. It was good training for a young kid, push-starting a Go-Kart.

I plugged in my iPod, opened my pear drops and put the hot water bottle under my seat. The reason I travel with a hot water bottle is for when I need to have a pee. I find it odd that we've got to 2012 and car designers still haven't sorted this problem. They still install cigarette lighters, even though most smokers carry a lighter, and glove compartments – glove compartments! Why is there an area reserved for gloves? It just helps impulsive murderers, doesn't it? Electric windows are all very nice but hardly necessary. And yet no one has thought about emptying the bladder. If you stop off at a service station you've immediately lost ten minutes' driving time. Which is why I started packing a hot water bottle. People don't really use them in bed these days, but they're great for taking a pee in (obviously not while driving – but you can pull over). Plus, they have really wide necks and can cope with spillage due to the reservoir. Just screw the top back on and continue with your journey. And if you were to break down and were forced to sleep in your car, your pee should still be warm, so you can use the hot water bottle for its original purpose. Good, innit?

We finally got on Route 66 and, to be honest, it didn't feel any different to the road I was on before, but it was good to know the reason I was in America had officially started. It's a lot nicer driving over there than over here. For starters, there are hardly any other cars on the road, which was just as well because my Smart car was slowing down the few drivers that there were. I didn't see another car as small as mine the entire time I was in the States. They don't do small cars. The fact that Prince sang 'Little Red Corvette' proves this, because Corvettes are massive. And Prince is only small, so the fact he calls them little, Christ knows what he'd make of my Smart car. There's no way that this car was made for a journey like this. It was designed for some posh mum to use to pick up Tarquin on the school run and then nip in to the deli to buy some couscous, not drive 4,000 kilometres across America.

Anyway, I picked some good American-style songs on my iPod to get the real Route 66 experience. First up was a country song by Kenny Rogers, called 'Ruby'. I like songs with good stories, and country songs are the kings of this. They're like little three-minute movies. 'Ruby' is about an ex-soldier whose legs are knackered and his wife who keeps going out leaving him at home on his own. It's not actually a feelgood song, but it's good all the same.

#52 Visit every USA state

It's just another example of people ticking things off. To me it's like ordering the taster menu in a posh restaurant, it's too much and by the end you're not enjoying the last few courses and they ruin the bits you did enjoy. I say skip the starter, have a decent main course and a pudding. That's enough.

Stephen sent me a text as I was driving saying that I should stop off to meet a local woman who was into some sort of New Age therapy. Her house was in the middle of nowhere – really the middle of nowhere – like those ones you see in documentaries about UFOs landing in people's back gardens. It was quite a big house, all on one level, but I guess land is pretty cheap round here. I knocked on the door and was greeted by Val. I said hello and put my hand out. Val said, 'You're a shaker, not a hugger? You don't want a hug?' I explained that I'd only just met her and that a shake was enough, thanks.

She walked me through the house where there were a few groups of men dotted about. We walked right through the house and out to the back where there was an expanse of rough ground and tumbleweed blowing by. Tumbleweed is something I associate with America. I remember watching an episode of *Sesame Street* as a kid, that featured a little film of a clump of tumbleweed being blown down various roads as a group of kids and dogs chased it. Cars almost ran into it, and every now and then it would get lodged in a fence or something, before breaking free and carrying on its journey to wherever the wind would take it. I remember thinking it would be good to have a tangled ball of tumbleweed to chase, but it isn't something you find on a council estate in South Manchester. And it doesn't really work with an empty crisp packet either. Believe me, I tried.

Val took me over to a large domed tent full of mats and cushions and a few lit candles. She then explained that I would be joining her at her evening Cuddle Party. Apparently it's a form of Reiki, which is a Japanese form of stress reduction.

VAL: Cuddle parties are designed around communication and boundary-setting skills that help us to become more empowered around touching and intimacy.

KARL: But, hang on, I haven't been here long and I've walked past four blokes and only one woman.

VAL: Yes?

KARL: So, how does that work?

VAL: There'll be more women. Don't you want to cuddle any men?

KARL: Well, I don't want to cuddle strangers really. How long do you have to spend with them before you have to have a cuddle?

VAL: You don't have to spend any time, or even have a cuddle. You can say no. And that's part of the workshop, for people to be able to say no – to ask what they want and be able to say no, or be able to say yes.

KARL: What's this all about?!

VAL: What we do when we meet is go over a set of agreements that set up a structure for the rest of the evening, so you won't be touched without being asked.

KARL: But if I'm saying, 'No, don't be touching me', they'll be going, 'Well, what are you doing here? You've come here for a cuddle, haven't you?'

VAL: No, maybe you've come here to learn to say no, not necessarily to cuddle.

KARL: I don't need to learn to say no! What's wrong with these people that they can't say no!

Therapy is something I associate with America more than the UK. I don't know anyone who has had therapy – or maybe it's just that they don't talk about it – whereas you read about Americans nipping off for therapy on a weekly basis as if it were a coffee morning. I wonder if it's because everybody's always smiling in America, so nobody knows if you're annoyed and you end up bottling it all up. Back home you walk around looking fed up, and your mates say, 'What's up with you, you miserable sod?', and then you talk about your problem, which turns out not to be a problem, and then you get on with your life.

I told Val that a hug shouldn't be wasted and that when Suzanne goes off to work I generally tap her on the head. I'll say, 'What's in the fridge for me lunch?', and she'll go, 'Oh, there's ham and cheese in there and a tomato that needs using', and I'll say, 'Cheers, see you later', and tap her on the head. I tapped Val on her shoulder to show her what I do, but she didn't like it. She said, 'I generally don't enjoy being tapped or patted, and I'll tell you why. Because I feel like a body of water, so if you slap me it's like a splash in the water, right, so my energy, it's like startling to me. But if you were to touch me and hold my hand or just give me a little squeeze, then I feel comforted and really in the flow of who I am. And also a lot of times, when we're expanding energetically, pats bring me down.'

I put on some all-in-one pyjamas that Val gave me, but I kept my cap on, so I didn't come across as too relaxed and look like I was game for anything. I went back into the tent where the cuddles would be taking place. Val was there, hugging another woman. It lasted ages. They were stuck together like two koala bears.

By this time more women had turned up, but they were still outnumbered by the men. I'm sure Val's heart is in the right place, but a lot of the men looked like they were just turning up for a bit of a feel. As we sat around on the cushions, Val thanked everyone for coming.

'Welcome to Soncco Wasi, Home of the Heart, Joshua Tree, where we are devoting life to love. I am Valerie Gill, and I feel honoured and excited to be able to hold this space with you all to create a space together where we can feel free to fearlessly explore, fearlessly express ourselves, fearlessly go beyond our comfort zone to fearlessly ask for what we want, and to fearlessly say no to what we don't want.'

I probably say no to more things than yes, and I think it's pretty easy to say no. Saying yes often requires more commitment. But maybe in America they just don't get as many cold sales calls or get stopped in the street by as many charity fundraisers as we do.

VAL: So, with that, I'd like to start the cuddle party with the 'no' exercise. The way this works is you're going to turn to the person next to you and make a request and the request is: May I kiss you? So, Karl, may I kiss you?

KARL: Err, no.

VAL: Are you sure you wouldn't like to kiss me?

KARL: Nah, it's okay, thanks.

VAL: Okay, thank you. And then you would ask me. That's how it works. So, you turn to the person next to you, choose A or B and ask, May I kiss you? But your job is to actually look them in the eye and practise saying no, and take turns, so do that now. Turn to the person next to you and ask, May I kiss you?

KARL: Can I kiss you?

VAL: No. Can I kiss you?

KARL: But that makes no sense 'cos . . .

VAL: Again.

KARL: Can I kiss you then?

VAL: No. Can I kiss you?

KARL: No.

VAL: Okay. Everyone, a show of hands: how many people assumed that when we said kissing, we meant on the lips? (*Everyone laughs*)

VAL: So, notice where we make assumptions about requests and invitations. So, throughout the night if someone extends an invitation or request to you, notice if you're feeling uncomfortable. And if you're feeling uncomfortable, maybe it's because you're making an assumption about what that means, so you can ask them for clarity. 'Do you mean on my lips? Because I'm a "no" to that.' And you can negotiate: 'But I would love a kiss on my forehead. Are you open to kissing my forehead?' So, you have room tonight to play. And the idea is to really feel safe enough to do some outrageous things.

I sat and ate a few free grapes and had a drink of Cava that somebody had brought along while Val handed out pens and paper. We were then asked to write love notes to ourselves. We had to write what we would like to hear from somebody – a letter that we'd really like to receive. Val asked me if I loved myself and if I enjoyed being me. I've never really thought about it. I don't really have any say in the matter. I'm me and I have to live with it. I've never understood it when people say they are proud to be American or proud to be English – it's not like we have any say in the matter. I'm English because my dad's testicles were in England. If I'd have come out of Ted Danson's bollocks, I'd be American.

Val then asked me if I felt good. But, again, that's a hard one to answer. I think I feel good. But unless some scientist comes up with a way of transferring feelings from one person to another how do I know if I feel good or not? To me, I feel fine. But if a healthier, happier person was put in my body they might say they feel like shite.

Everybody placed their notes in a teddy bear that had a hole in its back. Then we took it in turns to remove a letter and read it aloud. I picked one out that read:

SWEET WILD CHILD OF THE LORD, I LOVE YOU. YOU ARE MAGIC. WHEN YOU WEEP, FAIRY DUST FALLS UPON THE EARTH. WHEN

YOU LAUGH, ALL THE ANIMALS AND PLANETS SING. YOU ARE GRACE. YOU ARE LOVE. GOD IS WITHIN YOU AND EVERYTHING AND HIS LOVE SHINES FROM YOUR EYES WITH WILD ABANDON. I LOVE YOU.

The group seemed well impressed and responded enthusiastically, murmuring 'nice' and 'beautiful' in approval. Several more notes of a similar style were read out, and then finally a woman got to read my letter out:

ALRIGHT. HOPE YOU'RE WELL. ENJOYED OUR TIME TOGETHER AND ALL THAT. THE FOOD YOU COOKED WAS NICE. HAD A GOOD TIME. LOOK AFTER YOURSELF, AND LET ME KNOW IF YOU'RE AROUND NEXT WEEK. CHEERS.

My letter might not have been as poetic as the others, but I think I was clearer and to the point. I still stand by the fact that I would prefer to receive my note over any of the others. Personally, I always make an effort when sending birthday cards to Suzanne or me mam and dad. I normally do a little doodle or a poem that relates to them, but the letters people were writing at the cuddle party could've been sent to anyone – there was no personal touch there. Here's a card I sent to Suzanne for her birthday. The reference to the 20p is because that's how we met. Suzanne gave me 20p to buy meself a hot chocolate when I didn't have enough money.

I WONT REMIND YOU
    WHAT AGE YOU ARE,

AS IT MAY MAKE YOU
        FEEL GLUM,

BUT ITS BEEN FOURTEEN THOUSAND
    SIX HUNDRED DAYS,

SINCE YOU POPPED OUT OF YOUR MUM,

FIVE THOUSAND FOUR HUNDRED AND
    SEVENTY FIVE OF THESE HAVE BEEN
    SPENT WITH ME,

IT WAS DAY NINE THOUSAND ONE
    HUNDRED AND TWENTY FIVE WHEN
    YOU LENT ME THAT 20 P.

                        X X X

After the letters, we finally got on to the cuddle stage of the night. Val went through the rules.

VAL: The freedom here can be a little disorientating, so it's important to know what the guidelines are. It basically boils down to this: it's okay to like people at a cuddle party. It's okay to be attracted to people at a cuddle party. It's even okay to be aroused at a cuddle party. You're just not going to act on it. So, that means if you're cuddling and you become aroused, that's okay. That's a beautiful thing to acknowledge. Speak to your partner. You can excuse yourself. Have some grapes. Again, it's about using your voice and communicating. But it's okay to become aroused. It's not okay here, because this is a non-sexual event, to intentionally raise sexual energy. And there is a difference there. We do get questions here about erections, and they do happen from time to time, and women get them, too. They're just much smaller. It's a little more obvious for men. So, there's a level of discomfort and what we're aiming for here is to be comfortable with that. To be able to dialogue, to be able to talk about it.

At which point people started mingling, and it wasn't long before everyone was rolling about on the floor with each other. I'd say some of them were cuddling so hard I wouldn't be surprised if they had a kid between them now. No one came near me. I was like the fat kid at school waiting to be picked for the football team. But that suited me fine. I didn't need a hug, and if I did it would have come from someone who knew me. Plus, I once got ringworm on my leg. I went to the doctor's to get it seen to and asked how you get it in the first place, and he said 'by rubbing skin with strangers'. He told me that wrestlers get it a lot.

Val popped up and asked me to hug her – probably out of sympathy – but I said no. Then another woman asked me, and I said no to her, as well, and explained that if I hugged one person then the floodgates would open and I would have to start hugging everyone, or start explaining why I hugged some and not others. It would be too complicated.

It was the weirdest party I'd ever been to. Some people were in corners hugging each other as they cried. Some were hugging while laughing hysterically. I used to think it was odd when people in the 1980s held Tupperware parties where they would gather at other people's houses to buy plastic sandwich boxes and beakers and the like, but this was another level. I'd had enough, so I told them I had to leave, as I wanted to beat the traffic – which, looking back, wasn't the most convincing excuse with the tumbleweed blowing by outside.

#60 Go storm-chasing in Tornado Alley X

I like the idea of seeing a tornado. I dream about them quite a lot for some reason. I'm not sure I would want to chase one though. Using the word chase gives the impression that the people are in control, but they're not. Tornados go where they want to go and run from nobody. We humans like to make out we're in charge of things even when we're not. A good example is an orchestra conductor. Would the orchestra really not know what to do without the fella waving that stick about? It wouldn't be so bad if he played the maracas or tambourine whilst he waved the stick but he does nothing. If he got hit by a bus on the way to the gig, would it all have to be cancelled because he wasn't there? There's a band called Polyphonic Spree that has over twenty members and they ain't got a conductor. He's as unnecessary as the bloke who wears white gloves on the National Lottery programme.

The problem I had with driving Route 66 was the way I was continually thinking about getting to the end of it, instead of just enjoying being on it. I was treating it like I was running the London Marathon. I said at the time, it's the same approach I have to eating an orange – I'm so busy trying not to splurt it down my T-shirt or to stop the juice running down my arm, I'm not giving any thought as to whether I'm actually enjoying eating the bloody thing. The only time I can really enjoy eating an orange is when I'm in the bath, but I don't get to do that very often because the boiler overheats if I try to run a bath, and eating an orange in the shower isn't easy either. So, I've ended up opting for tangerines that tend to have a skin they're happy to get out of. But, looking back on it, I did enjoy driving through miles and miles of nothingness. It gave me a chance to ponder things without having to worry that I was going to run someone over, or drive through a red light, or get stuck in traffic, because there was nothing around apart from a random shack here and there.

#66 Run a marathon ✗

Some people take it seriously but others turn up dressed as a panda. I saw someone run one dressed as a hairy bollock to raise awareness for testicular cancer. Me mam thought it was meant to be Spongebob Squarepants. I lived on London's docklands for a few years and moved to a flat down the road on the day of the marathon. People clapped me as I walked past carrying a lamp as they thought I was doing a novelty run when I was just trying to move bloody house.

I stopped off at the occasional tourist attraction, mostly to stretch my legs, but there was one that has stuck in my mind – the bottle tree ranch. Like the giraffes at London Zoo, I could see the bottles without entering. Once in though, you really start to get a sense of how eerie the place is. I shouted hello, but no one replied, which was a shame because it was the sort of place that needs a tour guide.

The trees were made from scaffolding with metal branches welded on, and then bottles had been placed like leaves on each branch. The bottles were all different colours and shapes, and they were everywhere. In fact they had too many, so there were loads of bottles just scattered around on the ground. There weren't just bottles though. There were old shopping trolleys, broken toys, a sewing machine, a kids' go-kart, road signs, metal bed frames, broken clocks and watering cans. It was all these other things that raised my suspicions. Was this the home of an artist, or just a scruffy sod? Maybe he just got bored of waiting for the bottle recycling van to turn up.

Whenever the wind picked up, so did the noise. The metal clanked, and each bottle whistled and clinked. No wonder the fella was out. He'd probably nipped to the chemist to get some aspirin for his headache. It's odd how some people like to have some noise. Even though he'd chosen to live in the middle of nowhere where there was plenty of peace and quiet, he'd ended up creating noise. My mam did the same when she moved from Manchester to Wales. She couldn't handle the silence, so she bought a wind chime. But that drove my dad mental, so she replaced it with a rubber wind chime. I know – who knows where she finds these things. She has more shit in her house than this bottle guy had in his garden.

Was this art? Maybe. It did make me stop and look, and it was interesting walking around seeing old toys I'd also had as a kid. It felt a bit like walking round a car boot sale – something to do, something to look at, but I had no intention of wanting to take anything home with me. I came to the conclusion that he wasn't harming anyone. No weirder than people who collect thimbles. Maybe it was just his way of trying to meet people – getting them to stop and wander in and start a conversation. I can't say I've ever done something to my flat that expresses me like he has at the bottle ranch. I always decorate it and keep it simple, so it's easy to sell on. But this guy is doing what he wants. He's expressing himself, which is fine by me, just as long as he doesn't move next door to my flat in London.

I got a call from Ricky telling me to go and visit a country fair a little further down the road. He said I'd get to travel in something a bit bigger than my Smart car for a while. The last country fair I went to was at Heaton Park in Manchester a few years ago. I remember it was a really hot day and I had to be careful eating my jam doughnut, as wasps kept landing on it. The highlight was a fella who walked around a field carrying a Mini on his head. The crowd booed when they heard the engine had been taken out. Tough crowd.

It turned out I was going to drive a monster truck, owned by a bloke called Ronnie. He was a tough-looking fella with a shaved head and stubble and tattoos on his arms and legs. I'd seen these monster trucks on TV, but I'd never really understood the concept. Why have such massive wheels? It reminded me of the oversized shoes Elton John wore when he sang 'Pinball Wizard'. It just isn't practical to have such big wheels. Where do you keep a spare? Plus, you can't nip into Kwik Fit and get them replaced.

Ronnie's monster truck was called Nasty Boy. I climbed up from underneath, balancing carefully on its frame and hooked my arms in through the window. As I clung on, trying to hold my entire body weight, I realised there was one seat and Ronnie had beaten me to it. What's the point of that? A truck this big and only one seat? Ronnie started it up, and the noise was unbelievable. And then, as I was about to swing back down to the ground, Ronnie pulled away at speed. I almost shat myself. I thought he was about to do a circuit of the track and jump a ramp with me on it, so I was yelling at him to stop, but I was pretty sure he couldn't hear me over the noise of the engine. Finally, Ronnie put the truck

PURPLE RAIN, PURPLE RAIN

DANCING WITH GLEE!!

TAXI.

CLASS OF 2011, AND S...
OLD BLOKE.

ROUTE 66

ROUTE 66

MOUNT FUJI

YOU KNOW Y-FRONTS? THESE ARE WHY THE HELL FRONTS!!

BEING BREAST FED MADE A CHANGE FROM SUSHI.

THEY WAITED PATIENTLY FOR THEIR TURN AT THE GARAGE JET WASH.

MOUNT FUJI

The Pilko Pump Pant™

in a spin and came to a halt, and I got out as quick as I could.

I reckon he must've used a few gallons of fuel in the thirty seconds I was in the truck. That's another reason I wouldn't want one – the amount it would cost to run would be mental. I stayed on for the show and watched Ronnie demolish a few vans. He drove at the ramp at high speed, jumped twenty feet, and landed on them. The crowd were loving it. People say Americans like coming to England to see the old stuff 'cos they haven't got any old things in their own country, but they would if they stopped crushing it or blowing shit up.

#77 Sleep under the stars ✔

Everybody does this, don't they? Who's sleeping above them?

Next day I went to meet Joe. He was going to take me on the hunt for gold, which would be perfect, as I needed to find Suzanne a gift. I normally get her some sort of token of my trip. She likes necklaces and rings, but I very rarely buy her jewellery 'cos I don't see the point of it. It's just showing off, and another thing to lose. Plus, she's already got a few rings, which in my eyes are more than enough for the amount of fingers she has. So, I tend to buy her things that are a bit more practical. I bought her a bread machine for Christmas, which I think is far more useful and gives more satisfaction than a bit of metal. And it's cheaper. But if I could find some gold myself it would be a nice surprise for her, and it would mean more 'cos I personally found it. Plus, it's free.

#65 Skinny dip at midnight

Another one that doesn't appeal to me.

I'm sure there's a few things on this list that people say they want to do just because they've seen it in a film. What's at #85? Climb the Empire State Building with a giant gorilla? I did something similar to skinny dipping though when I was in Japan. I visited the hot springs, where people are dipping in the nude. Due to jet lag I woke up around 4.45 a.m. so I thought I'd give it a go, thinking that nobody else would be around. I'd literally just dunked into the hot bubbling water when an old fella came to join me. There were loads of hot springs but he came to get in mine! He had no shame and he stood 10 feet away facing me as he dipped his long hanging bollocks up and down as if dunking a teabag into a mug of hot water. I was up and out before the water had even touched his knob.

I knocked on the door of the trailer where Joe lived. A big fella with a handlebar moustache answered. He wore a whiter-than-white vest, black jeans, boots and a gun holster. It was Joe, looking like he'd just stepped off the set of *Die Hard*. The gun stayed by his side like a colostomy bag all the time I was with him. Didn't it bother him? I mean how often can you possibly need it?

Joe told me why he wore the gun: 'You never know, so I always wear it. I've been shot at before when I was younger, so ever since then I've carried a gun. I don't need a gun, but if someone else is gonna bring one out and take a shot at me,

I'm gonna be prepared, and I'll take care of it from there.' He went to get another gun from inside the trailer.

#85 ~~Climb Empire State Building with giant gorilla~~ X

See the statues on Easter Island

I haven't seen them but I bet they're covered in bird shit. Statues always are. I don't know what it is, but birds seem to use them as target practice.

What I like about these statutes at Easter Island is that no one really knows why they are there or even how they got there. It would be impossible to do something like this these days with all the CCTV or neighbourhood watch schemes.

I like to stop and look at most statues. There's a load in London. I always think that sculptors must have been well happy once soldiers no longer went to battle on horses as it must have made their job a nightmare, having to sculpt all them horses. It's tough enough drawing a horse on paper, never mind sculpting one out of stone.

The odd phase at the moment is that they've stopped putting them on plinths and started putting them on benches. It's barmy – there's not enough benches here for the amount of living people without giving them to statues.

JOE: Do you like these ones here?

KARL: Oh, Jesus . . .

JOE: Well, when you deal with gold you never know . . . Safety's on. That's an AK-47.

KARL: Yeah, I've heard of them.

JOE: I bet you have.

KARL: Bloody hell, you don't need this, do you? I mean, it's a nice bit of gold you've got, but you're not at risk that much, are you?

JOE: I dunno. Gold's getting to $1,500 an ounce.

Before we headed off on the search for gold, Joe brought out a box of stuff he'd found when out mining. There were all sorts of bits and pieces including a miner's lamp from the 1800s, a broken harmonica, pocket watches and old gun barrels.

JOE: I'll be out in the middle of nowhere, 100 miles from the road, and find a piece of a harmonica lying out there in the desert.

KARL: But what you gonna do with that? What's the point in keeping it?

JOE: It's a piece of history, man! Look, these were all found way long-aways from any roads, so it tells you there was a bunch of cowboys out there playing harmonicas, and they got shot by Indians or something, cause they lost their harmonicas.

My mam wanted a metal detector, but my dad put a stop to it knowing that she'd be like Joe – just collecting bits and bobs that are pretty much useless. She finds enough pointless stuff in the pound shops she likes to go in without her digging up more crap. Every time I go round, she's bought another odd thing like a gnome that whistles when you walk past it, or a banana holder (so you can unpeel it, eat half of it, and then put it back in a plastic case), a big sticker of pebbles for the toilet seat, and toenail cutters that come with a magnifying glass attached.

Joe then showed me a little pot that contained all the small pieces of gold he had found over the past few months that were worth a couple of hundred bucks. It turned out that his son Esra, who wandered out of the trailer, collected things, too.

ESRA: Dad, can I get some of my rocks and show him?

JOE: Sure, go get some of your rocks.

KARL: Is he happy just playing with rocks?

JOE: Oh yeah, he's got more toys than you can imagine.

KARL: That's brilliant though. Hard to break . . . don't need batteries. Most kids want Xboxes.

JOE: I'm not gonna give him a video game because he's just gonna be sat playing that all the time. That's his car there. (*Points*)

KARL: What do you mean, it's his car?

JOE: I gave it to him. I gave his brother a '71 Mark I, and I gave him a '88 GT HO. But that car will do 200 miles an hour, so I'm gonna take that engine out of it when he gets a little bit older. (*Laughs*)

KARL: How old is he again?

JOE: He's five. But he likes that car, so I gave it to him. I kind of spoil him, you know.

KARL: Yeah, it's one extreme to the other. One minute you give him rocks, the next you give him a car.

JOE: Oh, he's got everything.

KARL: Does he go to school?

JOE: Yeah, he goes to school. Pre-school on Tuesdays, Wednesdays and Thursdays, and then all the other time he has – what are they called? – T-ball practice and T-ball games, but other than that we're out in the hills or doing some work here and there.

KARL: Are there many other kids round here?

JOE: Not very many. I mean, he's got a few friends around here. Most of them are older than him, and, you know, they try to boss him around, but he's pretty good with it. He can take care of himself.

KARL'S FACTS

 ROUTE 66 STARTS IN CHICAGO, ILLINOIS, AND ENDS IN SANTA MONICA, CALIFORNIA.

ROUTE 66 WAS BUILT PARTLY SO THAT THEY COULD TEST THE USE OF CAMELS AS PACK ANIMALS IN THE US.

 ROUTE 66 IS 2,448 MILES LONG, AND CROSSES 8 STATES AND 3 TIME ZONES.

AMONG THE MANY ROADSIDE ATTRACTIONS ON ROUTE 66 ARE TEPEE-SHAPED MOTELS, FROZEN CUSTARD STANDS, REPTILE FARMS AND THE WORLD'S FIRST DRIVE-THROUGH RESTAURANT.

IN DOWNTOWN ALBUQUERQUE THERE IS AN INTERSECTION WHERE ROUTE 66 CROSSES ITSELF — YOU CAN STAND ON THE CORNER OF ROUTE 66 AND ROUTE 66.

Joe is a bit like my dad in the way he would turn his hand to all sorts to bring money home and get everyone fed. I can't ever imagine Joe using the Yellow Pages to call out a plumber or mechanic, as he would tackle any problems himself. You don't get many blokes like that, these days. That's probably why *Scrapheap Challenge* isn't on TV any more. I think it's partly due to the fact that if you take something apart to try and fix it, the warranty will no longer apply, so we're scared to give it a go.

We got in Joe's Ford Bronco, and he said we should do some off-roading. And with that, he put his foot down and hit the hill at speed, so the whole vehicle was in the air. When he said 'off-road' I didn't think he meant it literally. I was in the back, being thrown all over the place, shouting, 'Is there really no other route?!' But Joe just drove along chewing on a bag of jerky that was so tough he still had a use for his wisdom teeth. Twenty minutes later, we pulled up. Joe hopped out and grabbed a rifle out of the boot and some dynamite. He said he was going to show me how he creates big holes in the rocky mountain to make an entrance for a mine. He placed a tub of dynamite on the rock where he wanted to blow open a doorway, and then we retreated fifty or sixty feet back. Joe handed me the rifle to shoot the target to ignite the dynamite. I'd say I'm pretty good with rifles. I used to always win a prize at the funfairs on holiday, which was normally a coconut. I don't know why they gave coconuts as prizes. I never see coconuts in supermarkets, only at fairs. Saying that, right then, I'd have been happy with a coconut, as it would have made a change from all the meat.

I took aim. Fired. And missed. The noise from his rifle shocked me, as it was a lot louder than the ones at the fair. The funfair guns only shot pellets. This one had proper cartridges.

I took another shot. Missed. But, third time lucky, I hit. The dynamite exploded and blew a hole in the rock face. Joe then packed some more dynamite into the hole with a fuse. We lit it and ran. This was a new experience. The closest I'd ever been to doing something like this was throwing grit on the roof of metal caravans as a kid at our holiday camp and trying to get as far away as possible before the owners came out. Not quite as dangerous, to be honest.

Joe decided that we shouldn't go too far into the hole we had made, as it could have collapsed on us, like the song by Jimmy Dean called 'Big Bad John' (another song I'd been listening to on my iPod). We then headed to the river where we would be panning for gold. Joe gave me a panning dish. It's basically a rubber dish with grooves round the rim so you can scoop up soft ground and then use water from the river to wash through the finer gravel until any gold you've gathered up is caught in the grooves. Sounds simple, doesn't it? We did this for over an hour.

KARL: So what would you do then if you found a big bit?

JOE: A big nugget?

KARL: Yeah.

JOE: I'd keep it.

KARL: Why?

JOE: Well, once all the other money's gone, I think gold might have a little value still. But if I find a big one I'm gonna keep it. I'll keep the biggest one I ever find. Just as a trophy, you know.

KARL: Alright then, the second biggest one?

JOE: The second biggest? I'll give it to my son so he can keep it.

KARL: Okay, the third one?

JOE: Sell it if it's good enough to sell. What I like to do is take all the little ones and put them together and then sell them – you know, the real small stuff, like we find right here in these pans.

I don't think Joe was that bothered about becoming rich from his gold hunting. He just enjoyed the chase, a bit like my mam when she goes round those pound shops and Oxfams I mentioned earlier.

KARL: So you been down Route 66 much?

JOE: Oh, a little bit.

KARL: You like it?

JOE: What I like to do is go down Route 66 or any of these old highways here in Arizona and go off the highway and get on the dirt roads, off the side streets, 'cos that's where you find the places to pan for gold, or you find old cars, old dumps . . .

KARL: But if you're just having a day off though, forget the gold . . .

> JOE: If I have a day off? What would I usually do? Just go and look for an old ghost town, or an old dump or something. Just go out and relax, or come down to the river and just relax and drop the line in for the baby, let him go fishing.
>
> KARL: Quite a relaxing life then, isn't it?
>
> JOE: Yeah, sure, it's all good.

I know what he means about going off the beaten track to find new things. I had a problem with Route 66 'cos the journey is already set out for you. I had a good time looking for gold with Joe. It's like nature's Lottery ticket – each time I scooped the ground there was a chance of hitting the jackpot. Too bad I never found any. Suzanne's gift clearly wasn't meant to be.

Next day I heard from Stephen.

> STEPHEN: I know you're fascinated by people with different outlooks, different ways of seeing the world, alternative lifestyles. Is that fair to say?
>
> KARL: Erm, yeah. I always like to see different ways of living. In case there's one that suits me more than the one I'm living.
>
> STEPHEN: Well, this might be the one for you. I don't know if we've talked about this before, but how familiar are you with the Amish?
>
> KARL: Yeah, I've seen the Harrison Ford film, *Witness*.
>
> STEPHEN: You saw that film, you enjoyed that, right?

KARL: Yeah, it was alright.

STEPHEN: Well, I think we've sorted out a little treat for you then. It's spending some time with an Amish family, getting to grips with how they live life. What is the number one thing you can tell me about the Amish?

KARL: They're just into, sort of, basic living. It's like it's happening years ago.

STEPHEN: Yeah. You come from Manchester, so you're used to that.

KARL: Well, don't have a go. It's sort of a more simple life, innit? That's what I've seen of it, it's sort of making do with the basics.

STEPHEN: Exactly, and obviously quite a religious community, so be respectful. You know, they essentially live life like it's still the nineteenth century.

KARL: That old?

STEPHEN: Yeah, so, you know, things have not really moved on for the Amish. So, it should be interesting, shouldn't it?

KARL: So, I'll be going in like a future boy then? I can tell them stuff.

STEPHEN: Exactly, you're like a man from the future.

KARL: Alright. Well, that's fair enough then. I'm happy to do that.

Because America is so big, certain areas get left alone. That's my theory, anyway. I'd been with Joe who lived life like an old cowboy and was free to roam and set off dynamite in the mountains of Arizona, and now I was about to meet some people who live in an area where everyone pretends it's the nineteenth century.

I walked up to the family's house. It was a nice wooden-built detached house with farming tools scattered about outside. I knocked on the door. (They didn't have a bell but, then again, I haven't either. A bell is a bit of an unnecessary invention, to be honest, so maybe that had nothing to do with them being Amish.) I guessed that by choosing to live like it's the nineteenth century there are probably a lot of gadgets like doorbells that the Amish don't bother with – stuff that clutters up my life back home. Do they have tellies? I guessed not. Imagine if somebody played them a clip from *Antiques Roadshow* – it would be like *Tomorrow's World* to them.

A friendly looking man with the standard Amish beard (no moustache) answered the door. He introduced himself as Kenny and then introduced me to his wife Polly, who was wearing a bonnet, and their kids Joseph, Joanne, Loretta, Rosanna and Mini Marie, then his dad Laverne. I was hoping to go inside, as it was a really hot day, but Kenny said he was going to get me to do some work out in his garden. I asked if they had any suntan lotion. Kenny looked at me a little puzzled. They didn't have any. There was a bit of talk between Kenny, Polly and his dad about maybe getting me some lavender or vinegar, and then they offered a hat, which I said would be fine. I'm not sure if not having suntan lotion was to do with them being Amish or they just think it's too expensive. Suzanne's mam never brings any with her on the holidays we've been on together 'cos she says it's too expensive, and she ends up nicking it off us instead.

I didn't want to ask why they didn't have suntan lotion, as I'd only just arrived and didn't want to seem rude (plus I live in the twenty-first century and, thanks to Suzanne's mam, I didn't have any either). Maybe they were just out of it. As for the offer of vinegar, I was pretty suspicious of that. It doesn't sound healthy, does it? I ended up searching on the internet when I got back home why vinegar was mentioned, and apparently you can use it to calm down burns from the sun if you tap it on to your skin. It's amazing how many uses vinegar has. It can remove stains from clothing, get rid of smears on glass, get ink off painted walls, and you can even rub it in your cat to get rid of fleas. There's a different use for every day of the year, plus it's good on chips. Vinegar is one of the greatest inventions of all time.

Kenny took me over to his goats where I would have a go at milking. Virtually everything they eat they produce themselves. I went there thinking that I would be explaining how I live in the future compared to them, and yet it hit me that I'd never actually had goats' milk. Kenny and Laverne were surprised and said it's a lot better for you than cows' milk. Again, they're meant to be living in the past and yet they know more than I do. It wasn't doing much for my confidence.

The young girl taught me how to get milk from the goat, but I wasn't too good at it. I was worried I'd squeeze too hard and hurt the goat, so I let the girl get on with it. The kids were helping out quite a lot, but they seemed happy enough. They didn't go to school. Polly taught them from home. I'm guessing history lessons, for starters, would be easier because when you're living like it's the nineteenth century there's less to learn.

Kenny then showed me the tomatoes he was growing, the chickens that laid his eggs and where he produced cheese. I wasn't sure what all the fuss is about Amish life. To me, Kenny and his family just seemed like a decent farming family.

If I had more time I would live like the Amish. It would be good to grow your own food, but I haven't got any land. We're told we have to eat five fruits a day, but, short of joining a waiting list to get an allotment, I have no choice but to buy it. I admire their sense of community, too. I don't really know my neighbours that well. In fact, I only know their names 'cos the postman sometimes puts their post through our door. I guess it's because I think friendly neighbours can also turn into pains in the arse. I should go out my way to get to know everyone, though. I think this is why kids run riot. It's 'cos these days most people don't know who they belong to. If we did, we could go round and say, 'Your Tommy was smashing up a bus stop', and their parents would deal with it. But if you go round to a stranger's house to complain about their kids they always seem more defensive.

The only thing the Amish didn't have, that I would miss, is the internet. I could easily do without TV. Kenny said he and his family aren't as strict as some others in the area who wouldn't let me meet them, as they don't allow TV cameras anywhere near them. I was curious about other rules they had.

KARL: What is it that I might do that you would say, 'You shouldn't do that' or 'We wouldn't allow that'? What's the difference there? I mean, I know we've only just met, so you don't know much about me, but, say, I've got a girlfriend – I'm not married but I've been with her for seventeen years. Is that good? Are you happy with that?

KENNY: Let's put it this way – for me, that wouldn't be good. But, I'm not going to tell you what to do. I'd rather just show you a scripture for why I feel that way, and then you would have to choose what is right for you.

KARL: What upsets you about that, just so I can try and understand?

KENNY: What upsets me about it? Okay, Jesus taught that when you go together you should be married, and there's a union there. I guess it's kind of like when you get baptised. That's like a marriage to the church of Christ, and it's a union there, and I guess that's kind of the symbol of husband and wife, and then – how would you say? – there's a commitment there, and a tie there, like a foundation, for the children to follow.

KARL: I haven't got any kids.

KENNY: Right.

KARL: It's just me and Suzanne. Split costs on everything. Both work. Quite happy. I mean, we have arguments, but you must have arguments?

KENNY: Ha ha, you know we have our disagreements.

KARL: That's what I mean – it's the same.

KENNY: Would you consider raising a family like that?

KARL: I don't know. You see, it's different for you because of the way your kids are living. If these kids were in England, they'd be saying, 'Where's me trainers?!' 'I want a new pair of shoes!' Your kids haven't got shoes on, but they're quite happy. So, kids in the UK demand more. They're hard work, they stress their parents out, they're never happy, they always want something. Whereas these kids seem quite happy playing with the goats and playing around in the grass.

KENNY: Right.

KARL: It's easier for you to have kids, I think.

KENNY: I guess it's what kind of environment do we create for our children.

KARL: But it's hard to escape that environment, isn't it?

KENNY: It is. It is. I mean, as time goes on, you know they might choose not to . . . They might choose to step more into that environment. I've got family that kind of lives that lifestyle, so they . . . I mean, we have our family gathering, and they see it, but . . .

KARL: And they never think, 'Oh, I want that! I want that PlayStation, I want that computer game, I want that stereo, I want that album, that music'?

KENNY: Well, yeah, and we try and keep them active, you know. They've got their responsibilities. As they grow up, they get more. Just for an example, last night, my third, Loretta, came to me and said, 'I want more chores, Daddy.'

While me, Kenny and Laverne were chatting, Polly was inside cooking in the kitchen. Some would say that's a bit old-fashioned, but not here it isn't. It's the nineteenth century to them, remember? It also worked that way in Joe's house. I don't know why people moan about women who spend time in the kitchen while men are out working. Suzanne cooks, and I fix things. Now and again Suzanne will moan and say I should help out, but when I do she says I'm hopeless. I put a washing-powder tab in the dishwasher, and she moaned at me. It does the same job, and if she hadn't have noticed she wouldn't have known.

Kenny asked me to help with the ploughing. We carried on chatting while we worked. I was curious to know what Kenny did with his spare time.

KARL: What about relaxing? Do you know any James Bond novels? *Dr No,* something like that? Would you ever read something like that or can't you relate to it?

KENNY: Like a what?

KARL: James Bond. You haven't heard of James Bond? Seriously?

KENNY: Seriously. Is it kind of a mystery?

KARL: No, it's like a British agent. He's an undercover . . . He solves crime and . . . he's been around for ages, years . . .

KENNY: It doesn't ring a bell.

KARL: A movie – what was the last movie?

KENNY: The last movie? Like a real movie? I think it was *Home Alone.*

KARL: Did you like *Home Alone*? Could you relate to that or were you thinking, What's that kid doing at home messing about? He should be milking a cow.

KENNY: Ha ha. I guess, for me, it was entertaining, you know? But then afterwards, what good did it do?

KARL: It's just passing time.

KENNY: Yep, it's just passing time.

KARL: Well, that's life, innit, just passing the time until we die.

KENNY: But afterwards, I kind of feel like I was just . . . kind of idle.

KARL: Well, to be honest, it's not a great film, that one. There's a lot of better films you would've enjoyed more than that. Don't bother with *Home Alone 2*.

Polly came out and gave us some homemade lemon juice and chocolate brownies then took me into the cellar and showed me all the food they had grown and stored. There were jars and jars of all sorts of vegetables, more vegetables than I'd seen in all the time I'd been in America. I asked if I could take a pot for Suzanne as a gift, seeing as the gold panning hadn't worked out. They said I could, so I took a jar of garden peas for her.

I think the Amish community are doing it right, to be honest. I was only with the family for a short amount of time, but I think their way of life suits me. They're living an uncluttered life, unlike us. We fill our homes with things that entertain us for five minutes and then shove them in a cupboard and replace them with new stuff. The Amish haven't fallen into that trap. It's only really the beard thing that wouldn't work for me because when you're bald big beards look a bit daft. But apparently the beard is a sign that you're married, and seeing as me and Suzanne aren't married I wouldn't have to grow one, anyway. Thinking about it, Suzanne wouldn't look good in a bonnet. Her head's too big to carry it off, but I'd see her less, as she'd constantly be in the kitchen, so the bonnet thing wouldn't be that much of a problem.

Stephen sent a text.

> **STEPHEN**: Alright, Karl. Hope you've been enjoying Route 66. We understand you've been getting a little bit bored of driving, so we've arranged a flight for you to see the end of it from above. Enjoy.

I went to meet a man called Greg at an aircraft hangar. Before I'd even introduced myself to him, I couldn't help but notice all the small aircraft in the building, most of which looked so old they wouldn't have seemed out of place in the Amish village. Greg took me over to one and asked if I wanted to go flying. I explained that I wasn't a fan of flying. Even though I've done a lot of it for the TV show it's not something I enjoy very much – it just doesn't seem natural to me. The plane he wanted to take me up in had an open cockpit, which I hadn't experienced before. But that wasn't all.

'Well, you're not going to get to ride in the seat that much,' explained Greg. 'You're going to ride up on the top of the wing. That'd be your best view.'

What's the point of that? Airlines don't offer standing as an option for a reason. It ain't safe. British Airways never say, 'Sorry, all seats are booked, but we have some standing space on the roof if you're interested.' This is just more proof that the human race has gone daft.

Greg the pilot said he'd been doing this for twenty years, but I didn't want to hear that. It worries me more when people have been doing things for years because it often means they've become complacent. If he's so good, why hasn't he got a job as a proper pilot yet? Or, even worse, was he a proper pilot but was laid off for sending an air hostess out for a walk, mid-flight?

It's ridiculous. For days I'd been saying how much I'd love a walk after all the driving I'd been doing. Since leaving the beach in LA I hadn't really seen any pavements to even walk on. America is a place designed for cars, not walkers. In fact, they are so anti-walking that you can actually get arrested for jaywalking. Where's the logic in that? You can be thrown in jail for crossing the road at the wrong time, but it's okay to have a walk along an aeroplane wing!

RICKY: Hello?

KARL: I'm not doing it.

RICKY: What do you mean?

KARL: I told you at the beginning. I said it's Route 66 I'm here for. We had a chat, you talked about bungee jumping and all that other daft stuff, and I said I don't wanna do any of that. It's dangerous.

RICKY: No, no, fair enough. Bungee jumping, that's really dangerous, but you're strapped in for this. You just go up there, and it's, like . . . I mean, it looks worse than it is.

KARL: You haven't even seen what I'm wearing. It does look worse than it is. I look like a right fucking knobhead. It's not even a new plane, Ricky. It's a really old one.

RICKY: (sighs) You definitely not gonna do it? What are your worries? Is it safety?

KARL: Yeah! If this is a thing to do before you die, where are all the people who are dying to do it? Why isn't there a queue at this bloke's door? There's no fucker here, no one wants to do it, I don't want to do it. I told you I didn't want to do it.

RICKY: But, Karl, this is great. This can be a great ending to the show, where you're up there on a wing! Ahh! Just whizzing along. You can do it. If you do it, you'll be a hero. People love this.

KARL: No, no. Because the difference is, when I left England this wasn't on the list. It's not like I got here and then said I don't wanna do it. I told you before I packed my bag I didn't want to do anything stupid. I don't feel bad, I don't want to do it. You can't make me, I told Stephen. I don't feel bad . . .

RICKY: No, I can't make you, definitely not. I'm just thinking of you. You'll feel silly in the morning.

KARL: I feel daft now. I look like Spiderman at a funeral.

RICKY: (*laughs*) Well, I'll tell you what, it's a good job I'm a good producer because I thought you'd chicken out, so . . .

KARL: It's not chickening out.

RICKY: You are.

KARL: No.

RICKY: Listen, integrity is personal. If you're happy walking down the street with people going 'Puk! Puk-puk-puk!' then, you know, it's up to you. I don't want you to have to live with that. Whereas, I know if you went up there you'd feel great about yourself, that's all. But I did think you'd probably 'Puk! Puk-puk-puk!'-out, so I've got something else arranged for you. This is embarrassing 'cos now the crew know that I knew you'd chicken out.

KARL: Not embarrassing. I'm not bothered.

RICKY: No?

KARL: Not bothered in the slightest.

RICKY: Okay. Well, I've got something else for you, and it's no scarier than dancing on a stage with Glee, trust me. So, okay, do that instead, mate. But, remember, you've got to do one or the other. If you don't join in and get on stage you've got to do the wing-walk.

KARL: Oh right, where is it?

RICKY: The crew have got all the details. Look, I'm disappointed but . . . (*laughs*)

KARL: You can laugh away all you want. I'm not bothered. See you later then.

RICKY: See ya.

I told the director I wanted to do the other thing, but he told me I should do this, as I really wouldn't like the alternative. I said I'd be the judge of that, but he explained it would add more driving time to the trip if we got to the other thing and then I decided I didn't want to do it, and then we had to drive all the way back to the airfield, which he said we'd end up doing, as I wouldn't want to do the other thing. So I agreed to do it.

Greg talked me through it. He explained the toughest part is climbing up to the wing once we had taken off as – and I'll quote him directly here – 'it wouldn't be safe to be stood up on the wing during take off'. Thanks, Greg.

I practised my route from the cockpit to the wing a few times while on the ground. It wasn't easy as there were cables everywhere, and I also had to watch where I put my feet, as there were weak spots on the wing where I could easily go through the hollow fibreglass. And then we took off.

Once we were airborne, Greg wobbled the plane from left to right, which was the signal for me to climb up to the wing. As soon as I popped my head out of the cockpit, the wind hit me. It was difficult to breathe. It reminded me of being a kid and sticking my head out of the sun roof on my dad's car. I'd thought through my plan on the way up. I wanted to climb up and keep really calm and not even flinch, so Ricky and Stephen would get absolutely no enjoyment out of watching me doing it. So, I took my time and climbed up into position and was so focused on grabbing the right bars I wasn't even thinking about how high up I was.

Once I was up there, and steady, there was a moment when I thought, I'm loving this, brilliant view, peace and quiet. I could actually see the curve of the world I was that high up. All was good until Greg headed for the heavens. Direct. I remember hearing the engine working extra hard. We must have been doing 150 miles per hour. At this point, I had my eyes shut tight, but I could tell I was upside down, as the blood rushed to my head. The last time I had that feeling was when I was round at Uri Geller's house (the spoon bender) and he hung me upside down in a door frame, as he said it would help grow my hair back. It didn't work. If that's what made hair grow all men would have really hairy bollocks.

Back on the bi-plane I was screaming like a dying walrus, and my tongue was flapping about like a dog sticking its head out of a car window. I'm not sure if Greg could hear me though because he took me for some more barrel rolls and dives and steep climbs into the sky. In fact, it was pretty hard communicating with him at all. He'd told me to give a signal of thumbs-down if I wanted to land, but seeing as I didn't know which way up I was, that wasn't easy. I tried a thumbs-down, but he took me for another loop-the-loop. I tried again, and finally Greg wobbled the plane from side to side as a signal I could get back in the cockpit.

Once we'd landed I had to lie down for twenty minutes. Then I went mental at Jamie the director. 'I could have had a bloody heart attack up there!' It was at that moment that Jamie decided to tell me that the person who invented wing-walking died while doing it. It's not really an invention, is it? It's not the Breville machine or a food blender or $E=MC^2$. But Jamie didn't really understand why I was so angry because we'd ended up doing the stunt only a few miles from the airfield. He was keen to hear about it though.

'What was going through your mind when you were up there?' he asked.

'My arse,' I said.

I tell you what, if you ever get on a plane and you hear, 'This is Greg, your pilot speaking', get off.

#6 Fly in a helicopter over the Grand Canyon X

This is the one that has made me realise that this whole Bucket List idea is flawed. I like the idea of seeing the Grand Canyon but I just know it'll be heaving with tourists. There'll be helicopters whizzing round making a racket, there'll be people there who didn't really want to go but got talked into it by either a sales person at the hotel or a family member, and there'll be businesses selling tat to the mobs of people. People are working through this list trying to enjoy things that other people want instead of finding their own thing.

Some of these things on the list have lost what was special about them, by becoming special.

Once I'd finally calmed down, and my legs had stopped shaking, Jamie and the rest of the crew took me to see the alternative experience that Ricky had talked about. It was the annual Mr Leather competition in Chicago. If I'd done it, it would have involved me wearing leather pants and straps and dancing on a stage to some Hi-NRG music in front of about six hundred half-naked men also dressed in leather pants.

All I can say is, I'm glad I did the wing-walk.

CHAPTER SEVEN

#76 Climb Mount Fuji ✓

STEPHEN: Okay, what about climbing Mount Fuji in Japan?

RICKY: A free trip to Japan to climb one of the biggest, most beautiful mountains in the world. Clive James said it's the strangest place on earth.

KARL: Really?

RICKY: But he hadn't been to China like you have. You thought that was, didn't ya?

STEPHEN: Remember when you went to China, you thought you were going to Japan 'cos you thought you were going to a place of technology, and all the most advanced stuff? Well, that's Japan. Do you remember the other things you disliked about China were the bodily functions you always had to hear? People always coughing.

KARL: Spitting, gobbing.

STEPHEN: Well, in Japan it's the opposite. Something like blowing your nose in public, that's bad manners. Even gift wrapping in public is bad manners in Japan. So, already you're interested, aren't you?

KARL: Anything? Just opening anything is bad?

STEPHEN: If you're rustling a bag of crisps.

KARL: What, if you're outside, out and about, opening a bag of crisps, people will go, 'What's he doing?! You know the rules!' – is it that bad?

STEPHEN: Well, the key thing is, you're not going there just to experience politeness. You're going to climb Mount Fuji.

KARL: Yeah, well, it's a mount, as opposed to a mountain.

(*Ricky and Stephen laugh*)

STEPHEN: It's the most sacred mount in all of Japan.

KARL: If it's made for tourists I'm guessing it's not that bad.

RICKY: It wasn't made!

KARL: I like walking. I'm quite happy walking, but I almost died once because I started running downhill and I couldn't stop, so I kept throwing my arse on the floor, but I kept bouncing back up. It's not funny, I almost died. Could have gone into chips if I went into the slate wall at the bottom.

RICKY: Into chips?

KARL: Yeah, like smash into a slate wall. It would have cut me up into that sort of chip shape.

RICKY: Why would you have been cut into chips?

KARL: Because there was no cement in it. It was just a man-made wall. We were up there because I was getting slate with my dad.

STEPHEN: So you were thieving?

KARL: No, you can't nick off Nature, can you? So, we were up there nicking slate if you want to put it that way.

STEPHEN: Because it was owned by someone, wasn't it?

KARL: No, it was just on the hill. We wanted it for the caravan because we were going to put it on the top.

RICKY: You had a slate-covered caravan. Why?

KARL: So it wouldn't blow away in the wind.

RICKY: So, you were trying to weigh down the caravan?

KARL: Yeah, it worked. It was fine.

RICKY: What caravan gets blown away?

KARL: They do, as they're pretty light, the static ones. They move about when it's windy.

RICKY: Surely you bolt it down?

KARL: Well, you do have chains, but it can still move.

RICKY: So, what do you do? Put fifteen tons of slate on top to weigh it down?

KARL: No, not on top. On the sides. You just cement it on.

STEPHEN: So, you're running down a hill with slate in your pockets and in your hands?

RICKY: How many journeys were you making?

KARL: I think we did about five in the end. Had a trailer, loaded it all up, and then I had hold of it going down the hill, but it started to pick up a bit of speed. Before you know it, my dad's going, 'Don't drop it.'

RICKY: Your dad said, 'Don't drop it'?

STEPHEN: Yeah, I would rather you're made into chips than drop any of this precious natural slate.

KARL: My dad's mate Sid had to jump and grab my legs. I cut my face up and everything.

RICKY: This is gonna be a doddle for you. There's nothing on this list as dangerous as you running down a hill carrying slate with a risk of you being made into chips if Sid doesn't grab you round the legs. Right, off you go. Enjoy.

People used to make jokes about me wearing trainers with Velcro straps instead of having laces. They said Velcro was for kids, which I think is wrong, as kids have more time for tying shoelaces than adults. I don't understand why soldiers wear big boots with laces that could undo and end up tripping over them when they're on the front line. Velcro would be much better. Once fastened it never comes undone. It's one of the best inventions of the twenty-first century. What's strange is, Japan to me is the home of inventions, but I didn't see much use of the Velcro trainer strap. And yet they need it here on their shoes more than anywhere in the world, as you have to remove your shoes so many times a day when in Japan – when entering most restaurants, homes or any temple you go into. If you're a gas man in Japan taking meter readings you could be in and out of your shoes hundreds of times per day. They would love to have a Velcro strap instead of laces.

Most places have a large collection of slippers for you to pop into as you enter. In busy places the slippers you got were generally still warm from someone else's feet that had been in them just moments before. I don't like that feeling of someone else's warmth. Seats on buses are worse for it. The slippers they give you are quite smart. In all my time in Japan I never saw a novelty pair like we get at home with big pig heads or elephant feet or Simpsons characters on them. They were normally beige in colour with some flowers done in embroidery. As well as protecting the floor, I'm sure the changing into the slippers calmed me down and relaxed me mentally.

Mount Fuji is sacred, and it is Japan's highest mountain. It always seems to be wealthy people who have too much time on their hands who climb mountains. Evidence of its being a rich person's hobby is the fact that they once found an abandoned piano on Ben Nevis. Your average person doesn't get to own a piano. It's an instrument for people who live in big houses. To be able to take a piano up Ben Nevis and then leave it, that shows that whoever it was was made of money.

2 Climb Sydney Harbour Bridge

People just seem to climb everything these days. Is it because mobile phone reception is garbage in most cities and it's the only way to get a signal?

I looked online to see if this is even allowed, and it is. They've even had picnic events on top of Sydney Bridge. Other buildings and towers have started having outdoor extreme activities to pull in the tourists. I'm sure I read you can now pay to climb the roof on the Millennium Dome if you want!!

The company Woolworth's wouldn't have gone into administration if they had just thought about it putting the pick 'n' mix counter on the roof. People would have lapped it up.

It's odd how much praise climbers get, too. They always seem to be treated like heroes, but I'm sure a lot of people could do it. It's just that they don't have the time, as they need to be working to pay their way in life. I also seem to hear more about people who have died during a climb than the ones who make it back. The news normally features a family member saying, 'At least he died doing what he loved', which I don't think makes dying any better. I nearly choked to death on some of my favourite Happy Faces biscuits, but at no point did I think, Oh, at least I'm dying eating something I love.

I've never climbed a proper mountain. I've done long walks around the Lake District, sometimes longer than they should have been 'cos I got lost. I walk most places instead of driving or getting the Tube. I can walk and walk and walk quite happily if it's on flat ground. I could quite happily do the London Marathon if I could walk it, but climbing a mountain is tougher than doing the London Marathon, as once you're on that hill there's no way out of it. If you're doing the London Marathon and you get tired you can jump on a bus or use the Underground, with Mount Fuji all I have is my legs. I didn't train for it, as I didn't think it would be necessary. It's just walking, and I know how to do that. The main thing I would need is little treats to cheer me up for when I felt down, so I took a few bags of bacon-flavoured Frazzles and a big bar of Cadbury's Whole Nut.

Before I even left Tokyo airport I felt vibrations under my feet and a low dull continuous rumble through the arrivals department as the structure shook. I asked a woman who was working at the security point what it was: 'No problem. Minor quake,' she said. This was to be the first of many tremors I experienced while being in Japan. Apparently they get around 1,500 a year. I've been living in Britain for 38 years and have only experienced a single tremor, and it wasn't much of one. It was 1985. We were on holiday in Wales. We didn't notice it at the time, but the local news reported it. The only evidence we had of it happening was an ornament falling off the mantelpiece.

We went to get a coffee to try and help me with jet lag. We got to a café and were just putting on the obligatory slippers when the employee got quite animated with me about me leaving the door open. 'No, no, no,' she said as she pushed the door shut. She then got me to wash my hands before being taken to the ordering area. The director told me that it was a cat café. There are about forty of these cafés in Tokyo. For around £15 you get half an hour to have a coffee and stroke some cats. The reason these places exist is because most people live in apartments where landlords don't allow pet cats or dogs.

As if ordering a coffee these days wasn't complicated enough without adding more to the menu. 'I'll have a grande café latte with sugar-free vanilla and a big ginger moggy, please.' Luckily, the choice of cat wasn't an option, they were already roaming around the room like lap dancers at some seedy bar. This is why she was keen on me to close the door on the way in. She didn't want the cats to get out.

It's not a bad idea, but just like women in a lap-dancing bar, the cats weren't too keen on touching either and ran away whenever I got close. They were jumping high up on shelves or running into various boxes and tunnels that they have to play in. I didn't know at what point the half-hour started. If it's when your coffee turns up, or when you first stroke a cat. I tried to get hold of a big fat ginger one. Ginger ones are always fatter. It's as if they're unhappy about being ginger and turn to food. I got a few strokes, but it didn't hang around for long. It's not as if I'm not good with cats, as we had loads of them when I was younger. Me mam is a big fan. She doesn't own any at the moment, but she has a few regular wild ones. One is so cocky it steals food. Me dad got sick of it one day after it stole a full jam doughnut from his plate, so he shoved it in his car and drove about four miles, got it out the car, left it and drove back home. Me mam went mental. He said, 'I knew she would. She did the same when I tried the same with you.' A few days later, it turned up back at the house. He was that impressed with its navigation skills, he now lets it stay. He's just more careful with his doughnuts.

I called Ricky to let him know I'd arrived.

RICKY: Hello. What you up to?

KARL: Just in a little café with some cats.

RICKY: Cats?

KARL: Yeah, it's a cat café. If you want a coffee and a cat you come here.

RICKY: That's good, isn't it? That's nice.

KARL: Not really. Fifteen quid it is, for half an hour. They're not even friendly.

RICKY: Good for you, isn't it. Stroke a cat, it brings down your blood pressure. It's good for anxiety. You're always sort of stressed and moping around, and, you know, that just chills you out.

KARL: Well, I don't feel that chilled to be honest. I'm knackered!

RICKY: Well, exactly, that's what I mean!

KARL: No, but this isn't helping. They're not even being friendly. They're not coming near me. Your cat's friendlier, and you know how much that cat does me head in!

RICKY: Yeah, but that's because you're not friendly yourself. I mean, you know you don't make an effort really, do ya? You approach things with a certain attitude. You're stressed, you're moping around, that's why you're always tired, you don't do any exercise, you don't chill out, you get all angry . . .

KARL: I'd love to see your cat in here. It would get battered, the way you spoil it. Honestly, it would be like a posh kid going to a rough school.

RICKY: (*laughs*) I really don't know what you've got against my cat.

KARL: It's just the way you spoil it. You massage it all the time.

RICKY: We don't spoil it any more than any other cat.

KARL: You do, you spoil it.

RICKY: We put food down twice a day. It walks around.

KARL: I've seen you. You make a fuss over it when you come in, massaging its back. 'Ooh, it's stressed out. C'mere, Ollie.' It doesn't go anywhere near me.

RICKY: Yeah, because you're a miserable bastard, and every human being and every animal on earth knows that. I mean, listen to you now! You're in Japan. You're the luckiest man in the world but you're whinging because you don't do any exercise and that brings you down and that makes you ill . . . So, I've arranged some exercise for you. It'll make you feel good, okay? It's sumo. You're in the home of sumo wrestling, so I think you should do it. They're like superstars over there. There's nothing greater and more honourable than being a champion sumo wrestler.

#22 Watch a sumo match ✓

I didn't have the energy to argue, and I wasn't that fussed about having to take part in sumo anyway. I've always thought of sumo as a sport for fat people, so I wouldn't have a problem keeping up with them. It's good that they have something, as it's too easy for fat people to say there's no sport they can take part in.

I made my way over to where the sumo training took place. It was on the corner of a residential area. I found it just from the sound of thuds and grunts. I looked through the doorway to see two huge men smashing into each other like rhinos as others stood round watching.

Maybe it wasn't an earthquake I'd felt earlier, maybe it was one of these big fellas landing on their arse. They were big blokes with the traditional sumo hairstyle that they call 'chonmage'. I can't think of any other sport that actually has its own hairdo.

They must be the most unhealthy sports stars. There was no sign of muscles. The only six-packs these fellas see are probably Mars bar family packs. After watching for a few moments the main man pointed me to the changing room area. I explained that I didn't mind taking part but I wouldn't be wearing the nappy that the other fighter wore. He only spoke Japanese, but I could tell he just repeated what he'd said the first time but sharper.

Two sumo wrestlers followed me into the changing room. I told the director I wasn't happy about the loincloth they call a 'mawashi'.

The thing is, no one looks good in a nappy. Even babies don't look good in them. Clothing is designed to make you feel good and give you confidence. Whether it's a suit for businessmen or a uniform for policemen they're designed to give you a feeling of power. A nappy doesn't give you this feeling. That's why there has never been a super hero that flies about wearing a nappy.

I actually thought I'd get away with not wearing the nappy, as I didn't think they would have one that fitted, but it's kind of a one-size-fits-all design – one long strip of material that is then wrapped around the waist and bollocks. I complained earlier about having to wear used warm slippers. Things had got a lot worse. I let them put it on me as long as I could keep my undies on underneath. The young sumos kept saying no to this request, as their boss would not approve. I told the director there was no way I was going to wear one of these used rough canvas nappies on me arse without protection. Thinking back, it was an odd argument to be having. Eventually the boss man agreed to let me wear my undies underneath.

I headed out to the fighting ring where the floor is covered in a fine dark soil, which I presume is for grip on the bare feet. We did some stretching exercises. It was amazing how bendy the sumos were. I can't touch my toes, but these fellas had no problem. The closer I got to them, the bigger they looked. It was time to fight. The idea of the battle is to push your opponent out of the ring or push them over so another part of their body hits the floor. I ran at my opponent and hit him hard. He didn't budge. He just stood still as I tried tilting him. It was like trying to shift a wardrobe without taking the clothes out first. He then slid me across the floor as my feet skimmed across the dirt. I was out of the ring. 1–0 to sumo.

For the next round I thought I would use my strengths to beat him. I can run faster and turn fast, so I danced about the ring with the idea of a surprise attack, but he just stood still. I attacked again. This time it was like pushing a mattress up a narrow staircase. I almost suffocated, as my face was lost in his breasts. I now had sweat in my eyes, and what made it worse was it wasn't my sweat. It stung, and I could hardly keep my eyes open. It was at this point that he picked me up using the nappy as a handle and held me above his head. It looked like that classic nature programme scene when a killer whale chucks a seal pup through the air. I was shattered. I know I'm not that fit. I never have been, really. I've never been into any sport. I even played swing-ball sitting down.

I gave in. They were a lot fitter than they looked. While I sat by the side, they carried on pushing each other around like dung beetles. I still don't know why they have to wear a nappy though. What next, karate in a babygro?!

Afterwards, once everyone had stopped training, they invited me to lunch. A few junior sumos seemed to be in charge of cooking while the more senior ones relaxed. The bloke who had earlier held me like a handbag showed me round the place. From what I could make out they all lived above the ring in a place the sumos called the stables. There was another wrestler sat getting his hair oiled by the resident hairdresser ('tokoyama') who specialises in the chonmage. Again, how many sports have a resident hairdresser? It must get boring for the hairdresser when everyone has the same style.

We went downstairs where there was a massive spread laid on. There was everything on offer. It was as if the fridge freezer had broken and everything had to be eaten before it went off. This was as much part of sumo as the training. This is the stuff that makes them as big as they are. They also beat me when it came to eating. After course number five I left them to finish.

We got to the hotel where we would be staying. I was looking forward to having a nice shower as I stank of other men's sweat. I got to the hotel reception, popped on my second pair of slippers of the day, and the receptionist showed me to my room. But it wasn't a room. It was a capsule. It was a capsule hotel. Small boxes lined a corridor. Three boxes high and about ten across. It felt like a morgue. Opened at one end and contained a mattress, a TV, radio, blankets and a pillow, with just a blind between you and the corridor. Toilets and showers are shared. These hotels are mainly used by businessmen who work late, go for a drink and, rather than making their way home, stay in a capsule in town. I climbed in and felt like a hamster in a toilet roll tube.

I tried watching TV. I was hoping there would be a subtitles button. I'm used to having to read subtitles, as it's what I do when I go and visit me mam and dad, as me mam never shuts up. I don't think subtitles were invented for the deaf. They're for people with families who can't stop talking. It was hot in the cubicle, as there was no air movement. I thought I could smell everybody else sweating then realised it was the sumos' sweat I still had lingering on me. I ended up sleeping with my head sticking out the end of the box just to get slightly more air. I must have looked like I was some sort of magician's assistant in the box where the magician drops a blade to the neck.

I watched as the cubicles filled up with businessmen back from a night out drinking. Even though they'd probably had a few to drink they were still very considerate. I felt two more tremors in the night.

Next day, I spoke to Ricky who said he had organised some more exercise. It wouldn't be as strenuous as sumo. It would be more of a wind down after yesterday's activities. We headed to where it was to take place. A building site. I made my way to the top floor where all the builders for the site were congregating. There must have been around 1,500 staff: builders, electricians and plumbers. They all got into lines. I joined one. Music was then played from a speaker. It was quite a surreal sight, as they all started bending and stretching exercises that were led by the project manager. After the short twenty-minute work-out, a quick massage was given from the person stood behind, before the foreman gave instructions for the day's work ahead. They call the event rajio taiso (radio calisthenics) and most companies, work places and schools practise it. I suppose it's a good idea, it wakes everybody up so they're ready for the day. Mind you, the last thing we need at home are more reasons to slow down a builder's job. They have me making enough cups of tea for them without giving them more reasons to be 'gasping for a brew'. You wouldn't think doing crosswords is such thirsty work, would you? Whenever builders have called me saying they're having a problem, I always think they're going to say, 'The problem is 4 down, 6 across.'

Although I was in Japan to climb Mount Fuji I was mostly looking forward to seeing the gadgets. I've always associated Japan with the future. Growing up, I always watched the TV show *Tomorrow's World* where Maggie Philbin would show the viewer the future in technology. Everything seemed to come from Japan. Jet packs, vacuum cleaners that worked by themselves and compact discs that would replace vinyl records and were indestructible. The first bit of technology that entered our house was the TV with a remote control. It wasn't a proper remote control, as it was attached to the TV by a cable that wasn't quite long enough to get to the sofa, which meant we still had to get up, but not walk quite so far. I think the moment when proper wireless remotes were invented introduced evenings of watching nothing due to the easiness of just flicking channels all night. The first TV I remember us having only had five channel buttons. BBC 1, BBC 2, ITV and two spares for the unlikely event that two new channels were ever opened. Twenty-five years later there are over 200 channels, which means we go through batteries on the remote like there's no tomorrow.

I went to see the robot ASIMO (Advanced Step in Innovative Mobility), the world's most famous humanoid robot. I'd never heard of it before this point. Metal Mickey would have been top of my list, then R2D2 and C3PO. Short Circuit would even have come above ASIMO, but at least it was more along the lines of what I was expecting to see in Japan.

ASIMO performs to crowds in a car showroom a few times a day. I got there a bit early and killed time looking at the cars. Normally when you do this in a car showroom, sales people are onto you like flies on shit, but clearly they're used to people just coming in to see ASIMO.

Music came out of speakers to signal the start of the show. A little cupboard opened, and out came the million-dollar ASIMO to perform his show, which included a kind of 1950s dance, balancing on one foot, and a run from one side of the stage to the other, before he went back to his cupboard to get recharged before the next show.

I wasn't sure what I felt at the end. I mean, it was the best robot I'd ever seen, and we've got nothing like it at home. The closest we've got is probably Henry and Hetty, the vacuum cleaners that have faces on the front. The difference between the two being that Henry is a man vac and Hetty is the woman vac (she's pink and has eyelashes). I asked if it could do the robot dance, but the woman said it couldn't. How rubbish is that? A robot that can't do the robot dance! I suppose a robot that can run is very clever, but I don't want to see a robot running. I want them to come across as if they're in control of a situation. A robot should never have to run for a bus, as everything should be programmed to perfection, so that running about shouldn't be needed. And, as I've said before, we have enough dancers in the world. We don't need robotic ones. Years ago, I remember companies axing jobs in car manufacturers when robots were introduced, as they worked faster and cheaper than man, but now it seems the robots don't want manual work and have turned to the entertainment industry. Maybe this is why they have learned to run – it's for when they're late for their shift in the car factory after being to an *X Factor* audition.

The reason the Japanese wants the robot to evolve is that they're trying to get them to take care of the elderly who live alone. The aging population needs support, and they can't rely on humans to take care of them, so they want robots that can help around the house at a price cheaper than private care. I don't think I like that as an idea. I think they should work on robot arms that can be fitted to humans. The elderly wouldn't be weak then and wouldn't feel useless. We live in a world where we need to multi-task, so this would be ideal. In fact, these wouldn't just be aimed at the elderly, they would be aimed at people who are busy. No need for a hands-free phone when you have 'Hands Four'. That's what I'd call it – Hands Four –

with the strapline 'Hands Four Fun, Hands Four Work, Hands Four Help'. I like coming up with ideas like this, and while I was in Japan I decided I would try and create something useful. It must be good to come up with an idea that lives on after you're dead, something that goes down in history. After all, you're dead a lot longer than you're alive.

#62 Invent something ✓

I called Ricky and told him about my plan to invent something while in the land of the inventor.

KARL: Look at Dyson, he only came up with a new vacuum cleaner, yet he's up there with Einstein. I reckon I can come up with something better than that.

RICKY: Okay, I know the future of mankind is safe. I can relax. I mean, I don't suppose, you're not gonna find a cure for cancer or anything like that, are you?

KARL: Nah, that's interfering with nature. I want to come up with something useful for day-to-day life, something that'll either cheer someone up or something that is useful.

RICKY: Yeah, I mean a cure for cancer would be useful and would probably cheer someone up, but you're mainly thinking of things around the house, then?

KARL: Yeah. Look at that thing my mam bought, a gnome that whistles. Who'd have thought anyone would have brought that out, and who'd have thought anyone would have bought it? But now, because there's so many people in the world and online shopping, you bring something out like a gnome that whistles when you walk past it, and all you need is 1% of the world to buy it and you're made.

RICKY: Yeah, but hold on though, you started off this conversation with wanting to leave a legacy, something useful to change the world, not trying to corner a market of morons that will spend five quid on a load of shit. Don't just try and think of more tat. A whistling gnome? That's not an invention. It's just a whistling gnome.

KARL: Well, leave it with me.

I went shopping to see if any gadgets for sale would give me any fresh ideas. I noticed they used bird noises instead of the bleeping noise we have at traffic lights, which is nicer on the ears, but I couldn't help wondering how many blind people have been run over due to a low-flying chaffinch flying by.

Before I started my hunt I used a public toilet. It was the most advanced toilet I've ever sat on, and definitely the one in the best condition. You're lucky at home if there's a seat and toilet roll. The toilet had a selection of buttons at the side with images on them, but I didn't understand what they meant as I'd never seen the images before. You need to have the programming skills of Bill Gates just to empty your bowels. The thing should come with a manual. It would probably be the only manual I'll ever read, as I like reading when on the loo. The buttons also had Braille for the blind. I think, instead of teaching kids different languages at school, they should be taught Braille. If we're living in a world that's all about saving energy Braille books would mean we could read in the dark, which would in turn save energy. I see Braille everywhere now, at lifts, on food tins and on keyboards, the only thing I don't understand is how the blind know that the Braille is there for them to read in the first place.

I sat down. The first thing I noticed was the seat was warm. As I mentioned earlier, I'm not a fan of the warmth from slippers that have been worn and a warm toilet seat is another thing I don't like, but this wasn't caused by someone else's arse, it had a built-in heater. We don't need this in our house, as I'm sat on it that often it never has a chance to go cold.

I hit the first button. A noise came from a speaker. I thought it was an untuned radio. I later found out it was meant to sound like the flushing of the toilet. It's there to cover any embarrassing noises you might be making. It didn't sound like a flushing noise, it sounded more like people applauding me. The covering of embarrassing noises seems to be more of a problem here in Japan, as a lot of the walls are wooden frames with paper as a blind. This was the case in the toilet. You'd think it would attract graffiti, but while in Japan I didn't see any. In toilets at home you can't enter a cubicle without reading 'Sharon is a slag' or 'Call this number for knob action'. Maybe in Japan people are so busy programming the toilet they haven't got time for graffiti.

I hit another button and water pelted my arse. I moved to see where it was coming from and it shot up my back. It was a built-in bidet with built-in dryer. It was like an automatic car wash for the arse. It made me wonder if people ever use this part of it without having to use the toilet part. The bidet never really took off in Britain. I first saw one on holiday in Tenerife. I thought it was his and hers toilets, the same as the his and hers sinks they have in posh bathrooms. I tend just to use the bidet on holiday as a place to clean sand off my flip-flops.

I stopped hitting any more buttons on the toilet, as I was worried that it was so advanced it would end up ordering me a pizza. I've travelled a lot of the world now, and it's normally the toilet that is really basic, comprising a hole in the ground. Yet here in Japan the toilets have a higher IQ than me.

What was quite good was that it had a sink over the cistern, so the water you use to wash your hands then goes into the cistern to get used in the next flush. Quite an environmentally friendly good idea, except for the fact there's energy being used to warm the bloody seat up, so not that friendly.

I left the toilet in search for invention ideas in a large shopping centre. I found plastic boxes to carry your tie in, which seemed uncalled for. I found a small portable easy-to-carry arse cleaner. They seem obsessed with having a clean arse. At what point is it so important to have such a clean arse? I'm saying that like mine isn't, but it is, it's spotlessly clean, and I don't have a portable arse cleaner. I can't ever imagine leaving the house doing a check: 'Right, wallet, phone, keys . . . arse cleaner.'

I did find some good little gadgets though that included a crisp picker-upper. It meant you could eat crisps without getting grease on your hands, which is good if you're playing games on an iPad or something. And I also bought some little shoes and mittens you put on a baby's hands and feet, so that they can mop the floor while crawling around. I saw these years ago in a book, but they were designed for cats back then. I bought them for a friend who's recently had a kid. I think it's a good idea, as kids don't become useful around the house for years, but these change that. I also bought an everlasting ear bud, which was really good but I have since lost it.

There was also an aisle of small pets for people who wanted more than a fifteen-minute stroke of a cat in a café. They sold Triops. They're so tiny I really don't see how you can class them as pets. I stared at the glass bowl for about five minutes before I managed to see the small creature. You'd be better off buying an apple, letting it go off and breeding some fruit flies.

I did buy myself a pet. A stag beetle. They're strange things. Almost dinosaur-like with their huge antlers. They're really popular with kids. So popular, that as well as selling them in shops they also sell them in vending machines. Again, a bit like the portable arse cleaner, why sell them in vending machines? Why can't people just wait until the shops open? What's the urgency in buying a beetle? It cost 500 yen, which was about £4. I'm not sure if that's the going rate or not, as I've never bought an insect. I thought I'd play with it for a while and then release it into the wild when I left Tokyo.

By the end of my shopping I'd had a few ideas for my invention.

1) A BIGGER PILLOWCASE THAT COULD HOLD TWO PILLOWS INSTEAD OF HAVING TWO SEPARATE SLIPS. THIS WOULD HOLD THEM TOGETHER SO THEY DON'T MOVE APART IN THE NIGHT.
2) A SOLAR-POWERED TV REMOTE CONTROL. WHEN OUT AT WORK, PLACE REMOTE ON THE WINDOW LEDGE TO CHARGE.
3) EAR PLUGS WITH BUILT-IN ALARM.

I'd keep thinking.

It was time to catch a bullet train and head towards Mount Fuji. Bullet trains are really good and run to the second. They are big and roomy, and they feel more like the service you get on a plane with regular drinks and food served from a trolley. I really couldn't fault it. At home we like to complain about the trains as much as we do about the weather. It was a relaxing journey, as everyone respected each other and didn't make any noise. The fact we have a Quiet Coach on our trains says it all. I had my last bag of Frazzles using my crisp picker-upper. It worked well.

Now, you'd think with all the travelling I've been doing the past couple of years that I would be able to handle anything food-wise. I have got better at trying new things, but the food in Japan was tough, especially if you're not a lover of fish, which I'm not. I actually took to raiding the Strepsils from the medical bag, which are designed to soothe and numb sore throats. I found that they knocked out my taste buds enough for me to get through the odd necessary meal, so sucked on one ten minutes before the challenge. Not a normal aperitif, is it?

They served fish constantly in Japan for breakfast, lunch and tea. I think even penguins might have a more varied diet. I don't know what worried me more each day, being woken up by tremors or going down to face breakfast. There was so much fish on the breakfast tray you'd think there would be one piece that I enjoyed, but there never was. Facing a sea slug at any time of the day isn't easy, but first thing in the morning, I think even Bear Grylls would struggle. I ate very little during this trip. Everyone else was happy eating from bento boxes, which are nice little boxes with small compartments with different fish parts in them. The way it was displayed was like a piece of art or an expensive box of Thornton's chocolates, except instead of a coffee cream in dark chocolate, it's a squid bollock wrapped in fish arse. It's not a meal. It's bait.

I was taken to try funazushi. It's a delicacy, apparently. Whenever someone says this I always expect some dish that's bloody stupid. Traditions seem to keep idiotic things alive. I met a local man called Shin in a restaurant. He brought out the so-called delicacy in a wooden box. I removed the lid. It didn't look too bad. I'd been faced with worse most days since I'd been in Japan. I was expecting it to be alive, what with it having a lid on, as I've seen stuff on the internet where restaurants in Japan serve live octopus. I mean, why? Not only does it seem cruel, but why pay for that in a restaurant? The chef has done nowt to it.

Shin explained that funazushi is an ancient preparation of sushi that involves packing a fish with lots of salt, then fermenting it for up to six years. Six years it had been dead, and there's me thinking it was going to be alive. I reckon this fish's great-great-great-great-grandsons have been eaten by now, and yet this one is still waiting to be munched on. It could qualify as an exhibit on *Antiques Roadshow*.

I put it in my mouth. At first it didn't seem that bad until I bit into it and the taste was released, and it's a taste that should never be released. I can't believe anyone likes this. I think this dish is only still around 'cos the Japanese are too polite to say it tastes like shite. I know they say fish numbers are low, but if the only option is eating rotten old dead ones I'd rather not bother. It was like my taste buds had been mugged. Within 30 seconds it came back up, and I had to rush into the Japanese garden where I was sick on a bonsai tree.

I got to the hotel and called Stephen.

STEPHEN: What's going on?

KARL: Just in Japan, aren't I?

STEPHEN: You're just hanging out in Japan, yeah, and how you finding it?

KARL: It's a struggle. It's a proper struggle.

STEPHEN: I thought Japan was; sort of, you know, the future, and everything is sort of space age.

KARL: Yeah, it is. It's just the food that isn't the future. I ate something that was about six years old. New technology but bloody old food.

STEPHEN: Right.

KARL: It's all like ill-looking fish, just odd-looking sort of stuff. They make it look nice, it's brought to you on a nice plate, it's laid out like a piece of art, but that's to disguise the fact it doesn't taste good.

STEPHEN: What about all the sushi over there?

KARL: Yeah, well, that's what I'm struggling with. Me taste buds are just going, 'What you eating this for?'! They're not used to it.

STEPHEN: Have you never had sushi before?

KARL: No. Suzanne wants to go out for it, but it's a bit dear. It's about three quid for a little saucer of salmon, I'm not prepared to pay that. Other thing that's a struggle, and you would struggle, what size are your feet?

STEPHEN: My feet are size 14.

KARL: Right, well, if you were here you wouldn't be able to go in any restaurant.

STEPHEN: What?!

KARL: Because you have to keep taking your shoes off and popping slippers on that they supply. I struggle – I'm a size 10 – 'cos the people are smaller here. I doubt they'll have size 14 here.

STEPHEN: Yeah, I have that problem in England. Wow, I tell you this, mate, you've often portrayed these countries in a different light, but you've actually given me some genuine insight here. Normally, you've not thought it through, and it's a load of old bollocks, but this is genuine thoughtful stuff. One of the things I was quite keen for you to do, because I know that Japan can be quite stressful, it's a very busy place, and you've got to be in the right frame of mind really to go to somewhere as spiritual and calming and beautiful and meditative as Mount Fuji, so I've arranged for you to meet up with a Zen Buddhist monk called Matsuama. Now, are you familiar with Zen Buddhism at all?

KARL: Erm, not that much.

STEPHEN: Well, the sort of mindset behind Zen Buddhism is to kind of understand the meaning of life directly without getting bogged down by logical or rational thought or by intellectualism or by philosophy and . . . I know you're not into any of that, are you? You don't use logic, you don't use rational thought, philosophy, you're not an intellectual . . . It could be perfect for you.

KARL: Yeah, I suppose so.

STEPHEN: Great, well I hope it sort of just gets you in the right frame of mind for Mount Fuji.

I was fine with meeting a Zen Buddhist.

#36 Meet the Dalai Lama

Odd one, that. If he wanted to meet me, too, then I'm up for it, but if he's just doing it out of politeness I don't see the point, and, as nice as he is, surely it must get on his tits having to meet strangers all the time. It's like playing the part of Santa in a grotto but all year round. People say they'd like to ask him questions, but we have Citizens Advice Bureaux for that. He seems easier to meet than my bank manager.

After looking up why people want to meet him I also read that the Dalai Lama was found by Tibetan monks when he was two years old. The monks tested him to see if he was the reincarnation of the thirteenth Dalai Lama. He passed the tests, and had physical traits that the monks were looking for, such as moles in certain places and long ears. That was an easy job interview for him, wasn't it? You need more qualifications to be a lollipop man. Has anyone else ever said they fell into a job due to the length of their ears? What else did he do, try on a glass slipper? He took the throne at age four and became a monk at age six. I was just joining the Desperate Dan fan club at that age, and yet here he was trying to find enlightenment.

I think it's mainly other monks who look up to him and ask questions like 'What's the meaning of life?' and 'What are we here for?' because monks aren't allowed access to the internet. He's basically Google with long ears. The thing is, I reckon if I'd been taken at the age of six and had been protected from the day-to-day shite life throws at you I would be able to come up with answers. He can do it, because I bet he's not once been put on hold by his internet provider or had to sort car insurance or try and pay for parking using the new park and phone service.

I got to the temple where I was to meet the Zen Buddhist. I put on some slippers and met Matsuama, who gave me some Buddhist clothes to change into. I've always thought of myself as a bit of a Buddhist. I try not to upset anyone and I never kill anything, I save any insects from swimming pools when I'm on holiday, I like peace and quiet . . . and I've got a bald head. The clothes were my bag, as well: grey in colour, loose and roomy, and decent pockets. They were like pyjamas. Plus, with the slippers on, it was a look you normally have to be in hospital to get away with. I got a quick tour of the temple. Smart place with a relaxing atmosphere. Paper walls dividing the big space, spotless wooden floors and bells dotted about. The place was immaculate and minimalist. If Matsuama was to sell up and move, he could do it with one carrier bag.

I'd only been there a few minutes and thought this was the religion for me. It's like how they say when you walk into a house when house hunting, you know if it's the one. That soon changed though. I was expecting quite a relaxing morning, maybe doing some meditating, but that was not to be the case. He had me mopping the wooden floor within ten minutes of meeting me. Now, I'd been in Japan long enough to know that no floor needs mopping. No dirty shoe ever touches the floor. Even if they were to leave their house to go food shopping and then remembered they had forgot their bag for life and had to nip back in, they would still take their shoes off.

He handed me a wet rag from a bucket and showed me how to hold the rag and run along the floor in a straight line as if pushing a tiny moist go-kart.

MATSUAMA: Mopping, cleaning is the most important training in the temple.

KARL: I thought we would be sort of relaxing, meditating.

MATSUAMA: Oh.

KARL: I've just turned up and you're saying get the mopping done!

MATSUAMA: I'm sorry, but the main purpose is to keep cleaning.

KARL: Alright, when was this last cleaned?

MATSUAMA: Erm, this morning.

KARL: Well, why are we doing it again? What's the point in that if it's already done? Our kitchen floor only gets cleaned every other week, and I walk about in there with my shoes on!

MATSUAMA: To clean the floor is important. But to practise cleaning is more important for us. See it as kind of training.

KARL: What do you think about?

MATSUAMA: Nothing. I become the mop.

KARL: How do you become a mop?

MATSUAMA: You have to imagine that you yourself are mopping the floor, you run and you clean.

KARL: Right. Become the mop.

MATSUAMA: You're the mop.

KARL: I think me mam had higher hopes for me, to be honest.

MATSUAMA: So, errmm, just imagine, say, a football player. If you're very good at football, like Rooney.

KARL: Rooney. Okay.

MATSUAMA: If he can kick the ball with each foot, he practise every day, so it is something like that.

KARL: But I understand doing this if you're a cleaner, because practice makes perfect.

MATSUAMA: Yeah.

KARL: And Rooney, kicking a football, because he's a footballer. I'm trying to get my head around what I'm meant to achieve from this. When I am cleaning this floor, what am I meant to be thinking?

MATSUAMA: Nothing.

KARL: Absolutely nothing?

MATSUAMA: Nothing.

Buddhists believe in reincarnation. I think I know what Matsuama wants to be coming back as. I agree that we have taken away things in our lives that gave us time to think – like washing up and ironing, not shirts though, they're hard to do. Tea towels are good – and mopping is a good job for thinking, but not when doing it with a cloth. I got a right sweat on. I couldn't clear my mind and think of nothing, I was just thinking, why doesn't he have a proper mop? We're in the land of the robot yet no mop! Isn't it the Buddhists' mission to free Tibet? If they'd get some proper mops in, they'd have more time to focus on that.

After an hour's worth of mopping he had me raking his gravel garden. I thought this would be easy, but he wanted the lines perfect, so he kept redoing the areas I'd already done. Thank God he has a bald head, otherwise he'd spend half the day getting his parting in a straight line.

Matsuama then introduced me to a Buddhist puzzle.

MATSUAMA: Okay, so I would like to introduce the way of thinking of some Buddhism. Please tell me, how many stars in the sky?

KARL: Lots.

MATSUAMA: Lots.

KARL: Yeah.

MATSUAMA: But there is one single Zen answer to this question. So, please think about it. A lot is not the right answer in Zen.

KARL: Erm, as many as you can see with your eyes. That's good?

MATSUAMA: Closer.

KARL: How many stars in the sky. Oh, hang on, day or night?

MATSUAMA: Of course night.

KARL: I thought it was a trick question. Erm, let me think. I do like puzzles. Is the answer a number, is it a number? Is that what you want from me?

MATSUAMA: Yeah, a number. Please tell me the number. How many?

KARL: Well, I have read it, but I can't remember the answer. It's millions, it's trillions, isn't it? It's loads. Go on then, what's the answer?

MATSUAMA: The answer, as you say, the scientific answer is the trillion, billion. The Zen answer is just count one, two, three, four, five and so on.

KARL: What do you mean?

MATSUAMA: So, the purpose to answer this question is to just do it, start counting, right.

KARL: I don't know what you mean.

MATSUAMA: So, of course, there are lots of stars in the sky. But, if you don't start counting you never know, so just count. Start something is very important.

KARL: Surely though, you get one life, yeah . . . Who would want to do that? Say I'm going to dedicate my life to counting stars, then it becomes daylight, how do you know where to start again? It's impossible.

MATSUAMA: Yes, as you say, I am sure that it's impossible. But it is kind of an illustration, just example. Stars is example. In your everyday life, you have some problems. You think it's impossible, or out of the question, and . . .

KARL: So, you're saying, if you have a problem deal with it?

MATSUAMA: Yes, just go forward. I wanted to say that point.

KARL: Honestly, if you'd just said deal with your problems, I would have understood that, but the stars thing . . .

MATSUAMA: So, sometimes we think the problem is too much, and the job is too much. So, it is example. So, if you have very big jobs or works to do, sometimes we give up before we do anything, right? So I want to say that.

KARL: I understand that, people can do it, but they don't even try. They give up. That what you mean?

MATSUAMA: Yes, just try.

I prefer multiple choice when it comes to questions, then at least you have a chance of getting the answer right. I did a Mensa test and got 83%. Most of those questions were answered on gut feeling. My gut seems to know more than my brain at times. More proof is the fact that my brain thought it was a good idea to put the funazushi in my mouth whereas my stomach chucked it out.

I gave Matsuama a puzzle to work on, too, which went, 'What gets wet as it dries?' He didn't know the answer but said he would think about it.

Finally, we got round to doing what I came for. Some meditation. He told me the rules. I thought it would also be good for Matsuama to meditate and clear his mind. Maybe it would stop him forgetting that he's already mopped up.

MATSUAMA: So, now we sit in Lotus way, like this. So, the purpose in practising in meditation is to clean mind. For example, if this room is filled with many columns it may be very strong for the big earthquake, but if this room is filled with many columns you cannot come into the room. You can't meditate in the room, so you can't do anything in the room. So, the vacancy, the emptiness is very important for the room. So room should have room. It is the same with our heart. If you have very big trouble or very big problems, you go out for dinner with your friends, so the food itself is very tasty, but if you have very big trouble and you are worrying about something you cannot appreciate the conversation with your friends.

KARL: But I just wouldn't go out.

MATSUAMA: Oh really?

KARL: Yeah, really. If I was that bogged down I would know that I would ruin everybody else's night, so I would say 'I'm not in the mood. Have a good time. Bring me some pudding back.' Is that a sort of Zen way of thinking?

MATSUAMA: (*laughs*) Yeah, but this is example. So, if you are to appreciate something your heart should be vacant, right? This is a very important purpose to be practising meditation – to make your heart empty, vacant.

He told me that posture and the breathing technique were very important and said I must sit up straight and take no more than two to three deep breaths every minute. I had to keep my eyes looking straight ahead and clear my mind of thoughts and slowly count. I was just about to try and get in the zone when he showed me a big stick that is used by the master to whack Buddhists on the back if they flinch or fall asleep.

He explained what the stick was for: 'So, when I start the meditation I will hit this wooden stick once and this hum bell four times. After this hum bell please do not speak on any occasion, right? Even if a mosquito comes, or somebody is crying, or thunder is coming, please do not speak out.'

It's good to try and clear the head. It was the only thing left of mine that needed clearing as the funazushi had cleared my gut and the amount of Strepsils I'd been eating had cleared my sinuses. My mind has too much going on in it and needs sorting out. I think it's close to capacity, as I'm starting to forget a lot of things. I think this is the case for most people these days. People used to just need small reminders stuck on a fridge door, but now, look at the size of most fridges, they're massive. It isn't to hold more food, it's to hold more reminders. The amount of PIN numbers and account numbers stuck on our fridge looks like Carol Vorderman's been doing the numbers game.

The thing with my memory is, there's a part of it that remembers that I've forgotten something but then can't remember what it is. I just wish it would forget the thing altogether, so I don't forget more things because I've spent too long trying to remember the thing I forgot in the first place.

I was managing to keep still and quiet. I got bored of counting though and wondered if Matsuama had ever considered doing mime artist work. He could do meditating while making money from tourists. I don't know why we entertain the idea of human statues, the streets are busy enough without having people standing about getting in the way. I've always found it odd how tourists take photographs of mime artists. Everyone looks like a mime in a photo.

The meditation did help with my invention though, as it was at this point I had my eureka moment. All the time I had been in Japan I had been faced with sitting on hard floors, which is fine for a short while, but if you're out eating it could be well over an hour. I wonder if this is another reason they are more advanced. They do less sitting around on their arse than we do 'cos we have too much comfort. They'll get up and invent. So, the invention I came up with was a trouser with a cushioned arse. We don't need them as much at home, as we have chairs, but I still think they will have their uses. Good for people at church who have to sit on hard pews, good for festival goers who have to sit on damp grass as the cushion will offer a gap between ground and arse, builders on their lunch breaks, ramblers who stop for lunch on wet grass. I would have come up with more uses but was interrupted by an ant that crawled around on me ankle, which caused me to flinch a little bit. Matsuama stood up, got his stick and whacked me twice on my back. It really stung. I didn't speak 'cos I thought that would lead to more whacks. I thought we'd be clearing our heads. The way he was carrying on, he'd be lucky if he got cleared of manslaughter.

Fifteen minutes later, he hit the bell and the session was over, and while he was probably imagining being a mop, I had come up with my invention. Result.

#90 Partake in a Japanese tea ceremony ✓

Matsuama asked if I would like a cup of tea. I said I would love one. I'm a big fan of tea. On special occasions it's nice to have it out of a pot with some toast or a tea cake, but I'm quite fussy about the way I like it. If someone offers to make me one I normally find something in the room that is the right shade of brown that I want my tea to match, which can be difficult in this day and age as brown is not a trendy colour. In the 1970s I would have had the full range of brown shades on offer in most households. As we went for the tea we were followed by five women. He said they would be joining us. 'Great, innit,' I said. 'Where were they when the mopping wanted doing?'

We had to enter another room for the tea. As I went through the doorway I had to kneel down and bow and then make my way to the back. As always, there were no chairs. (Note: add tea ceremony to list of potential customers for cushioned pants.) I sat down next to Matsuama. One of the elders of the group of women then sat by some pots and utensils, one of which looked like a shaving brush. We sat in silence and watched as she prepared then mixed the tea powder. Every movement was very precise and calmly done, as if she was handling a newborn baby. Now, I'm a fan of not rushing the making of tea – there's nothing worse than a tea bag that hasn't had time to brew – but this went on for over twenty minutes. She could never have a café running at this speed, as the queue would be out the door. Maybe this is why they have cat cafés. You can stroke them to relieve the stress caused by pissing about hanging around for a cup of tea.

I was gasping. Matsuama told me it had taken the woman 25 years to learn this process of making tea. It felt like I'd been there with her for a good part of that time. I wanted to suggest that maybe she needs to switch from tea powder to tea bags to help speed up the process.

There was nothing in the room I could use to give my shade of brown, which was just as well. When she poured it into my cup, it was green. I am not a fan of green tea, but I didn't fancy waiting another 25 minutes while she brewed a different pot. She handed out some sweets to go with the tea before pouring. You then have to give a bow.

Matsuama then went through this procedure which I can't remember but involved turning the cup clockwise three or four times and then back a few. It was like cracking a safe. We then took time to enjoy the design of the cups we were drinking from. Then it was time to drink. It was quite bitter, but the sweet that came with it helped the taste. Once we'd drunk the tea we sat and talked about the blends of tea that I liked. Lipton's, PG Tips and, my favourite, Twinings English Breakfast. And Typhoo, that I have a box of, for when builders are round as they drink tea non-stop. I then reminded Matsuama that he had not answered my riddle: 'What gets wet as it dries?' He didn't know. I asked the ladies at the tea ceremony. They didn't know either. I told them the answer; it was a tea towel. The answer is normally just towel, but I thought I'd keep it in theme with the party. They seemed to like it. I really enjoyed the evening of drinking tea. I think it relaxed me more than the meditation. It's something we tend to rush at home. Sometimes I'm that busy doing something else I forget to drink my tea, whereas it was all about the tea here. I liked the way we didn't speak the same language and were from different parts of the world but tea brought us together. I left before they washed up though 'cos Christ knows how long that takes them.

It was the day of the climb. I hadn't slept well, as my room was really, really hot due to me not being able to turn off the heated toilet seat. It was hard-wired and none of the switches seemed to have any effect. I could have dried socks on it, it was so hot. I lay there for hours getting stressed about not sleeping, knowing I had a big day ahead of me climbing Mount Fuji. There was a plate on the wall with an image of the peak of Mount Fuji sticking up above the clouds painted on it. Maybe it wasn't an ornament. It could have been a plate rack making use of what tiny space the room had. I think the small living spaces are what make Japan so keen to create nanotechnology. The problem I have with smaller electronic stuff is that it's easier to steal. A robber can now walk into a home and take away your whole entertainment system in his pockets. We've made it easy for thieves. Big and heavy is good. That's why Stonehenge has not been nicked after all these years.

KARL'S FACTS

MOUNT FUJI IS 12,388 FEET HIGH – YOU CAN SEE IT FROM TOKYO ON A CLEAR DAY.

THE FIRST KNOWN ASCENT OF MOUNT FUJI WAS BY A MONK IN 663 – BUT WOMEN WERE NOT ALLOWED ON THE SUMMIT UNTIL THE LATE 19TH CENTURY.

JAPAN IS ON THE 'PACIFIC RING OF FIRE', AND HAS 108 ACTIVE VOLCANOS.

IN 2011 MORE JAPANESE PEOPLE SANG KARAOKE THAN PARTICIPATED IN TEA CEREMONIES OR FLOWER ARRANGING.

higher IQ than me

A WELL-KNOWN JAPANESE SAYING SAYS THAT YOU WOULD BE A FOOL NOT TO CLIMB MOUNT FUJI ONCE – BUT A FOOL TO DO SO TWICE.

13 Catch sunset over Ayers Rock

I like a nice sunset, or a sunrise, but I wouldn't go all the way to Australia to see one. It's the same sun no matter where you are. I guess some people do it for the romance, but that seems like a really cheesy, predictable thing to do. I think it can be just as romantic sitting in the car in the pissing rain looking out over the sea in Kent eating some Chicken McNuggets. I bet they haven't even got a McDonald's at Ayers Rock.

At around 4 a.m. I got up and made my prototype for my invention. I used cotton and thread from the hotel bathroom kit and sewed the blow-up neck brace I use on flights to the back of my trousers. It wasn't perfect, but when I sat down it was definitely more comfy.

It was a success.

I went for a short walk outside in them and sat on some dampish ground near a bonsai tree to test the trousers, as well as set free the stag beetles I had bought. Bonsai trees are tiny trees that are really difficult to grow. You need to care for and nurture them daily. I suppose it's like the Tamagotchi for the older generation. I'm not sure what they are used for though, as it certainly can't be paper. It would take an entire rainforest of bonsais just to make one toilet roll. I watched the beetles wander off on their adventure, now free from their box, and wondered how they'd get on in their new life. I don't know if it was the right thing to do. I'm always moving insects thinking I'm helping them. When I was on holiday recently I was taking beetles out of the pool as I thought they were drowning, but the bloke guarding the pool said they were giant water bugs that find food in the pool and are happier in the water. I had removed five or six of the four-inch things before he told me, one of which had given me a nasty nip. I shouldn't really interfere.

#82 Experience a full moon party

Seems an odd thing to have a party about but then I suppose when we use up a day to celebrate pancakes I guess it's fair enough to celebrate a full moon. This is a party they'll never have in China. It's so polluted there that they never see the moon at all, never mind a full moon. In fact, in China I reckon they don't even bother flying a kite as they wouldn't be able to see it due to the crap in the air lying so low. I know people moan in Britain, and say that we don't make anything anymore and all our factories have closed as most things are produced in the East, but honestly, I'd rather have a blue sky and have to get stuff imported than live in the depressing greyness that they have.

#29 Ride the world's biggest rollercoasters

Ricky had left me a message with the idea that I should go on a rollercoaster ride close to Mount Fuji, so I could get a proper view of my task in hand. I went on it and hated it and didn't really see Mount Fuji, as I had my eyes closed tight the whole ride. Not the sort of pre-climb preparation Ben Fogle does, is it?

There's not much to write about the climbing of Mount Fuji. I was a little worried when we were at the start, as an old Japanese man told me, 'Don't fuck with Fuji.' Was this an old Japanese proverb? Was I supposed to take these words of advice seriously? Did the wise old Japanese man know something I didn't, or had he just read it on a novelty T-shirt? There is a quote from George Mallory who said when asked why he climbed Everest (#9 on the Bucket List), 'Because it is there.' I know what he means, as I do the same if there's biscuits in the house.

If I know we have some in, I eat them. If we haven't, I go without.

The climb up Mount Fuji was easy to start, the pathway was gravelled and not very steep, but that changed two hours in and it became rougher and tougher, especially in the darkness. There are a few tuck shops on the way up where I bought a few overpriced Snickers bars to keep me going. It was the first time that my restless legs came in useful, as they were happy to carry on walking as the top half of my body snoozed.

The view was amazing, but I didn't really know where I was looking. It's more interesting when you know an area and you can look out for your house or a landmark. I couldn't really enjoy it, as, with each step I took, in the back of my mind I knew I would be doing that step again when walking back down, which is something else that makes the London Marathon easier. Once you've reached the finish line it's over. Climbing a mountain, reaching the top is the halfway point.

#9 Climb Mount Everest ✗

The main problem with mountain climbing is that once you've made it to the top, it's not over – you have to walk back down. That's got to take the edge off the enjoyment a bit, hasn't it? It's like how the Sunday dinner is ruined a little bit from the amount of washing up that needs doing after eating it. I've read that people who die whilst climbing Everest mainly die on the way down. To solve both of the above problems it would be good if they looked at fitting one of those tubes to slide down that they have at water parks.

#15 Climb Mount Kilimanjaro ✗

There's a lot of mountains on this list. I've read that people enjoy mountains as they like to go where not many people have been and they like to conquer. Man got on the moon. Today as I write this they've just said on the radio they're really close to discovering the 'God Particle'. The scientist said that humans work hard and need answers to everything and that soon there will be no unknowns, which is funny as I've just got off the phone trying to find out at what time today the curtains we've ordered will be delivered and no one can tell me. Does me head in.

I tested my invention at the summit by sitting back on a big cold rock. It worked a treat. My buttocks couldn't feel the cold at all. I came up with the name of the Pilko Pump Pant. I can now also add mountain climbers to my list of potential buyers.

Eighteen hours from leaving the bottom, an hour's break at the top, and seven Snickers bars later, I was back where I started. My feet were killing me, as my toes had been pushing against the front of my shoes and causing blood blisters under my nails that have only just cleared six months later. I felt sick with tiredness. Or maybe it was the seven Snickers bars.

When I got back to the UK I had fifteen pairs of Pilko Pump Pants made up and had a short stint on a TV shopping channel where I sold the lot. I feel that this was more of a fulfilling achievement than climbing Mount Fuji.

Conclusion

People always ask what I have taken from all my travelling and I always say health and safety. I never used to even bother reading the fire escape on the back of hotel doors but after staying in some pretty dodgy places I want to know what to do if the worst happens.

After finishing the Bucket List trips, Suzanne wanted to go on safari in Africa. We stayed in the middle of nowhere in a big tent that had no proper zipped entrance, which meant a lion could easily have walked in. The man in charge said the chances of this happening were slim, but to me that didn't mean it was impossible, so I made a plan of action just in case. It involved Suzanne having to get into the small wardrobe at the back of the tent. I made her practise several times, so she could do it as quickly as possible if a lion suddenly appeared. She wasn't happy that I used the first half-hour of our holiday making her get in and out of a wardrobe like a magician's assistant, but it meant she was prepared for the worst. I practised getting under the bed where the lion would struggle to reach me.

In the end no lion ever came in, only bluebottles from a dead hippo that lay outside the tent. A couple of nights into the holiday we could hear some growling. I went out of the tent to see a pride of eight or nine lions. Normally on holiday you worry about a mosquito in the room, here we were with the cast of *Lion King* sat outside. I called the manager on the walkie-talkie they had given us. He came down fifteen minutes later and brought some Masai men with him who then stayed by us for the rest of our holiday drinking the bottles of Coke from our small fridge. I didn't mind though as an empty fridge is another good hiding place.

When Suzanne and I got back from Africa, Ricky was already planning on sending me away again. This time he had sorted someone else to come along with me. Now, if you were to travel around the world, who would you want to take with you? A close friend who knows you well? Maybe someone who can bring some extra skills to get you through the trip? Well, Ricky had arranged Warwick Davis, the dwarf actor from *Star Wars*, to come along. That's good, innit?! Edmund Hillary had help from Tenzing Norgay, Ben Fogle had assistance from James Cracknell. I ended up with an Ewok. Still, it gave me a chance to tick off two more things from the list.

#78 Ride a gondola in Venice

I started the trip with Warwick in Venice as we took on the route that the explorer Marco Polo did. He was keen to have a go on a gondola, me not so much, but we did get in one in the end, 'cos it's the only way of getting about. Having all that water is a right pain in the arse. I do wonder if it could be sorted if they had their grids cleared. Babies need to learn to swim before they can walk in Venice. It's only a good place to live if you're a mermaid.

Down the back streets it's less busy but it stinks as the water is more stagnant. Venice has no sewer system; household waste flows into the canals and is washed out into the ocean twice a day with the tides.

#38 "Go up in a hot air balloon" ✓

I did this recently with Warwick near the Dolomites in Italy. I was a little bit on edge as the whole thing is kept in the air by a bloke blasting a flame from a gas burner. I don't have much luck when it comes to gas boilers so I was worried about being so high up and relying on a giant pilot light to keep me up there.

It's a good mode of transport as long as you want to go where the wind is going as that dictates your destination.

Warwick said he enjoyed it but I don't know how and why as he couldn't see over the edge of the basket so he may as well have been sat in a food hamper in Harrods.

Another mode of transport we used, thanks to Ricky, was a pushbike. Course, I had to do all the pedalling as Warwick couldn't reach the pedals so sat in a basket on the front. At least when ET did this, he helped by making the bike fly, whereas Warwick just sat there. I tell you, he might be small, but he's bloody heavy.

#25 Cross a country on a bike ✗

This sounds like it would be an okay thing to do but it's the locking up of a bike that's a problem these days. You're not allowed to lock them to railings or lampposts, as the local councils say they will cut the lock off. Plus, bike designers make it difficult to lock bikes as everything is quick-release so the wheels and the seat can be removed really quickly with no tools needed, which makes them easy to steal. Bikes are also really light as well so if they're not locked to anything a ten-year-old can carry them away. This is the problem with everything getting smaller and lighter: the only people it makes life easier for are thieves, removal men and bailiffs.

#42 Cycle a leg of the Tour de France

I've never watched this event, as it goes on for ages and seems to get longer every year. They ride over 2,000 miles now! I don't know why it has to be so long. I mean, 2,000 miles! They should do some courier work whilst they're at it. A lot of sport is getting longer. I put it down to the fact that channels have to pay so much to televise these events and they want value for money. Tennis goes on for ages, Formula 1 seems to go on and on. Cricket is the biggest laugh. It goes on so long they stop for lunch and bloody tea! That is taking the piss.

We had our ups and downs but in the end I had a good trip with Warwick. It was nice to have someone to moan at and share the mad experiences that we went through, even though we had different opinions on what we saw and did, now and again he gave me a new way of looking at things.

It made me wonder if I would have appreciated the Seven Wonders more if he had come along with me.

#54 Visit the Seven Wonders of the World ✓

Tick. Done this. And to be honest each one was pretty underwhelming. I remember calling Suzanne from China, the day before I was due to visit the Great Wall, and telling her that I couldn't really be doing with the Wonder part of the trips. Suzanne told me that it was supposed to be the icing on the cake, but the trouble with me is that I don't really enjoy the icing on a cake. I often pull the icing off and leave it to one side. The icing is just there to get your attention, but I wouldn't say it is the best bit. And that's how I feel about the Wonders – they were the reason I went travelling for six months in 2010, but they were never my favourite bit.

#11 Ride a camel ✓ to the Pyramids

The Great Pyramid of Giza is the biggest pyramid ever built. I think what made the job easier is the fact that when building with cement you need to mix it with sand and there's loads of that around the pyramids. I've seen the pyramids and they're in a bit of a state, with most of the render chipped off. This is what happens when you use too much sand in the mix.

The bloke who did the work didn't want to be named as he knew he hadn't done a great job so they just said some geezer had built it. Hence the name the Pyramid of Giza.

I also rode a camel. I can't be bothered going into detail, but I will never get on one again.

#63 Ride something bigger than a horse ✓

Who put this on the list?! I saw a fella riding an elephant when I was in India and I didn't see the advantage. I imagine having one of those is like having a big 4x4. They cost a lot to run and it's difficult to find a place to park it.

#57 Spend 24 hours in a jungle ✓

I spent four days in the Peruvian jungle and it was the longest week of my life. If you get bad news from your doctor, like you've only got a week left to live, I'd recommend that you go into the Peruvian jungle as it'll feel that you've lived a lot longer. I only slept about two hours a night due to the heat and the noise from the wildlife. I'm not surprised there are a lot of nocturnal animals and creatures in the jungle; they have no choice but to be awake at night due to all the bloody noise. I remember waking up around 11 p.m. with stomach cramps. I was advised earlier in the day not to get out of my tent if I needed the loo as I could end up getting bitten by something like a snake or spider, so I ended up having to shit into a carrier bag. I'd say that was an all-time low in my life. There's no such thing as a 'bag for life' when camping in the jungle.

#71 Canoe up the Nile river ✓

I wouldn't canoe anywhere. They flip really easily. Could you imagine if Noah had built a giant canoe to save all the animals? One slight ripple caused by a beaver and the whole planet's species would have been wiped out.

It always surprises me how, whenever the TV news covers a story about some flooding in a village, you always see some footage of a local bloke with shaved head and tattoos going down the local shops for a packet of fags in a canoe. I can only presume they won them on *Bullseye*.

#75 Trek the Inca Trail on Machu Picchu ✓

What do I remember about the Inca Trail? Honestly? Being hot, ill and knackered.

I remember that the hotel we stayed in was so high up it had oxygen tanks in the room that you get charged for if you use them. I normally avoid taking anything from hotel rooms/ fridges due to the mark-up on the price, but they really have you with the oxygen tank. I had to break the seal and have a go to make sure I knew how to use it just in case I woke up out of breath in the night. I know the wonder of Machu Picchu is supposed to take my breath away but not like this.

The day of the climb up the trail was hard work. I'd only been walking for thirty minutes and I felt shattered. They say there is 30% less oxygen up there. No wonder. I think it's due to all the tourists climbing this hill to the wonder: more people out of breath=more breathing=less oxygen. Simple.

It's hard to know what all the fuss is about with the Great Wall of China. The thing that surprised me the most when I visited in 2010 was how new a lot of it looks. According to the guidebooks, the wall was heavily restored in both the 1950s and 1980s. If that's the case, then surely it can't count as one of the Wonders of the World, can it? If when I went to see the Taj Mahal in India, I'd got there to find a new house with a double garage and a gravel driveway, they couldn't still sell it as the Taj Mahal, so why is the Wall getting away with it? I said at the time that 'the Alright Wall of China' is probably a fairer description.

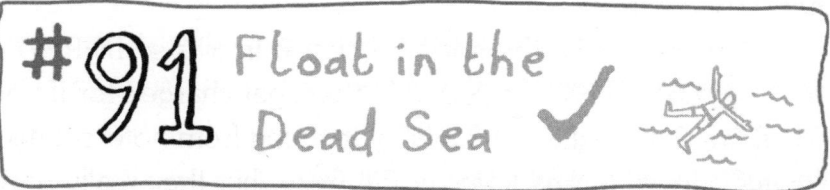

The Dead Sea was very muddy looking and not very sea-like. It was more like a lake. I was up for getting in it though as I had a little bit of eczema on my leg and the mud and salt is supposed to be good for the skin. I've seen that hippos roll about in mud all the time and you never see them with eczema so there must be some truth in it. I got in the muddy murky sea. It was hard to stand up in it as the dark green sludgy mud sucked you in. Straight away the salty water started to sting all the cuts on my wrists and knees that I'd got during my trip. I didn't realise I had so many cuts. It's like when you only find out that you have a paper cut when you start to eat a bag of salt and vinegar crisps.

I seemed to be the youngest person in the sea. Everyone else looked to be in their seventies. Maybe this is why they call it the Dead Sea – all the visitors are close to death.

#100 Hunt with a tribe ✔

I went hunting with a tribe in Peru a couple of years ago as part of the first series of *An Idiot Abroad* and, let's be honest, it wasn't a great success. I remember the tribeswomen took off my shirt, painted me with red spots like a panther and put me in a grass skirt. The tribesmen then took me to the woods and taught me how to use a bow and arrow.

That evening, I politely turned down the tribe's offer to share the chopped crocodile they'd caught on the hunt, and settled for a bit of Spotted Dick that the film crew had brought.

I'd say the problem with hunting for food is you have to do it before you're hungry, otherwise you don't have the energy, but then to hunt when you're full can't be easy as you feel bloated. I'm rubbish at shopping for food on a full stomach. If Suzanne asks me what I want for tea when I've just eaten a full breakfast I can't think and have to leave it to her to decide.

Which just leaves one more thing on the Bucket List.

#73 Write a novel

I had to double-check, but apparently this book doesn't count as a novel.

The truth is, I'm not sure I'm cut out to be a novelist. I wrote quite a few stories at school and they all ended the same way which was 'And then the alarm went off and it was all a dream!'

Who would pay to read that?

ACKNOWLEDGEMENTS

Jan Pester (main camera on all trips except for Peru); Rich Hardcastle (photographer); Freddie Claire (sound recordist and photographer); Richard Yee (Series Producer/Director on Peru); Krish Majumdar (Director on Egypt, Brazil, China); Christian Watt (DV Director); Ben Green (DV Director); Luke Campbell (Director on India and Jordan); Jamie Jay Johnson (Director on Mexico); Barnaby Lankester-Owen (DV Director); Michael Timney (Main Camera in Peru); Emma Riley (Production Manager); Claire Pocock (Production Co-ordinator); Rebecca Wadcock (Production Co-ordinator); Lynda Featherstone (Editor on India, Egypt and China); Gwyn Jones (Editor on Brazil, Jordon and Mexico); Sam Santana (Editor on Peru); James Cooper (Production Assistant); Dan Goldsack (Executive Producer); Simon Arnold (Assistant Producer); and Michael Andrews (Researcher).